LIBRARY
CONSERVATION

**PUBLICATIONS IN
THE INFORMATION SCIENCES**

Rita G. Lerner, Consulting Editor

TWO CENTURIES OF FEDERAL INFORMATION/*Burton W. Adkinson*
INDUSTRIAL INFORMATION SYSTEMS: A Manual for Higher Managements
and Their Information Officer/Librarian Associates/*Eugene B. Jackson and
Ruth L. Jackson*
LIBRARY CONSERVATION: Preservation in Perspective/*John P. Baker and
Marguerite C. Soroka*

LIBRARY CONSERVATION

Preservation in Perspective

Edited by

John P. Baker

The New York Public Library

and

Marguerite C. Soroka

Engineering Societies Library

Dowden, Hutchinson & Ross, Inc.

Stroudsburg   Pennsylvania

Copyright © 1978 by Dowden, Hutchinson & Ross, Inc.
Library of Congress Catalog Card Number: 78-16133
ISBN: 0-87933-332-4

80 79 78 1 2 3 4 5
Manufactured in the United States of America.

Main entry under title:
Library of Congress Cataloging in Publication Data

Main entry under title:
Library conservation.
  Includes bibliographical references and index.
  1. Books—Conservation and restoration. 2. Manuscripts—Preservation and
restoration. I. Baker, John P., 1933- II. Soroka, Marguerite C., 1918-
Z701.L53   025.8'4   78-16133
ISBN 0-87933-332-4

Distributed world wide by Academic Press,
a subsidiary of Harcourt Brace Jovanovich,
Publishers.

Foreword

Library enthusiasts are sometimes given to extravagant statements. Someone has said, for example, that if all man's achievements were wiped from the face of the earth and only The New York Public Library remained, civilization could be rebuilt from the collections in the Library. A staggering idea, but not quite true. The reproductions of the Pietà in the Library's books obviously could never convey the full power and beauty of Michelangelo's original work. Tragically, the statement becomes less and less true with year that passes, for because of deterioration, materials in libraries everywhere are gradually, inexorably, disappearing.

Libraries struggle to obtain funds for the acquisition of materials. Large investments are made in cataloging and binding to make them usable. But it is too often the case that these same materials are put on shelves in buildings without environmental control where they are subjected to extremes of heat and humidity and suffer abrasion from dust and particulate matter. Materials originally issued on poor paper—and much of the paper used for printing since the middle of the nineteenth century can be so described—disintegrate rapidly. "Book dandruff," as one of our more poetic librarians has called it, can be seen any day covering the floors of library stacks and reading rooms. Librarians and administrators and, yes, society have not faced up to this formidable problem.

There are a number of reasons for this. It seems to have taken about a hundred years for us to grasp the full significance of the problem. And it is not a simple matter to recognize—until perhaps it is too late—the point at which a book should be treated or to know whether it is worth preserving. Not enough has been known about book conservation as a professional discipline, and there has been a dearth of qualified book conservators. As yet there is no method of mass treatment of materials that has proved to be practicable. Microphotography as a method of preserving the intellectual content of materials has met with some resistance since its use requires the interposition of a reading machine between the reader and the matter to be read. Methods of control add significantly to the cost of library operation, already a matter of concern to trustees and administrators. And yet it could be said of most research materials that if they were worth acquiring and processing in the first place, surely they are worth preserving.

Although librarians and others have been concerned about the conservation of library materials for over a century, activity among librarians and book conservators has been particularly strong in the last decade. Conservation departments have been established in a few major research libraries. The Library of Congress has taken the lead. The Annual Report of The New York Public Library for 1976/77 is almost wholly devoted to the problem. The papers in this volume will underscore the need for action and will serve as a convenient source of information and as a guide to those already working in the field and those who are in the process of learning about it.

Obviously not every piece in every library can be saved, nor need it be. What is needed is a national plan to identify archival and library uniquities, best copies, and information sources not otherwise available and a program to preserve these national resources by restoration, microrecording, reprinting, and other means. Such a program will require imagination, cooperation, industry, and funds. Those who determine the nation's priorities must be made to realize that, without such a plan and program, the United States is in danger of losing its mind.

James W. Henderson
Andrew W. Mellon Director
The Research Libraries
The New York Public Library

Preface

Warren J. Haas of the Council of Library Resources is among the most recent to point out that scholars, librarians, and archivists do in fact have a responsibility to solve the preservation problem.* As a first step, librarians must develop a sound understanding of the meaning and the need for conservation—the *why,* the *who,* and the *what.*

The selections included in this collection were chosen because they deal primarily with the philosophical and epistomological aspects of conservation of research library materials: *why* materials must be preserved; *why* they deteriorate; *what* should be preserved; *who* should do the work and *how* they should do it; *how* workers from different disciplines must organize and collaborate if conservation objectives are to be realized. Writings dealing with the methods and techniques of preservation were purposely excluded in the selection process in an effort to avoid prescriptive aspects of conservation treatment.

The literature of conservation is voluminous, extending over more than a century and a half. Many important publications appear outside the confines of what is normally regarded as the literature of librarianship. For these reasons, the review and selection process was time-consuming. At an early stage, it was decided to include selections that emphasized principles rather than those that are important now mainly for historical reasons, or because they deal with an area of specific investigation such as the development of permanent/durable paper. It was also decided to exclude publications that deal with laboratory aspects of conservation, except insofar as they illustrate the role of the conservator and the scientist. A few articles that may be considered case studies were also included, again for illustrative, rather than prescriptive reasons.

As the review process continued and tentative selections were identified, it became apparent that organization of the collection in a coherent, logical fashion would be almost as important as the content of the individual selections themselves, if readers were to be well-served. The collection is intended for librarians and others who must grapple with the complex problems of preservation and who feel ill-prepared to do so for a variety of reasons: little, if any, formal study of conservation while attending library school; limited access to a comprehensive collection of materials on the subject; and little opportunity to attend the few courses which are now taught on a regular basis at a handful of library schools.

Special thanks and gratitude are due Dr. Arthur C. Carr, who provided encouragement and invaluable editorial assistance throughout the two years the work was

*See remarks of Warren J. Haas, as reported in "A Report on a Planning Conference for a National Preservation Program." Library of Congress *Information Bulletin* 36 (Feb. 18, 1977); pp. 129–31.

in preparation. James W. Henderson has been an inspiring leader throughout his professional career and has contributed much to furthering the goal of conserving research library materials. The editors extend special thanks to him for reading the manuscript and contributing the thoughtful foreword.

John P. Baker
Marguerite C. Soroka

Contents

VII: MANUSCRIPTS AND DOCUMENTS

VIII: PRESERVATION MICRORECORDING AND OTHER COPYING METHODS

IX: DISASTER AND SALVAGE

X: NATIONAL PLANNING

Contents by Author

LIBRARY

CONSERVATION

INTRODUCTION

Preservation is the most perplexing and unyielding problem confronting today's librarian. Ironically, this statement is true despite the fact that the need to preserve paper-based intellectual resources has been pressed with increasing urgency and mounting concern for the past 150 years.

Simply stated, the problem is this: Books, documents, and other graphic media are fragile objects, which by their very nature are easily damaged by careless or even routine handling. Composed for the most part of organic materials, they are subject to any number of hazards and vicissitudes. "Books," wrote Paul Valéry, "have the same enemies as man: fire, damp, other creatures, time, and their own content."[1] These formidable enemies have an excessively vulnerable target in paper, the universally preferred writing material.

In an essay dealing with the development of permanent/durable paper, Verner W. Clapp cites the well-known dictum of Emperor Frederick II who ordained in 1231, "that all public documents should be written on parchment 'so that they may be a testimony to future times and not risk destruction through age'."[2] Despite Frederick's concern for the permanence of records in his own time, paper prevailed, and its use became universal.

Today, we know that even under the best circumstances deterioration occurs, slowly but inevitably. In the nation's libraries there are now several millions of volumes that cannot be circulated to readers even one more time. Many of these are extremely scarce titles, and many have already suffered loss of text.

WHAT IS CONSERVATION?

Preservation of research library materials is part of a larger concern sometimes referred to as the conservation of cultural property. As it has evolved in professional usage, conservation is a broad concept and can be thought of as a term that embraces at least three closely related ideas: *preservation, protection,* and *maintenance.*[3] Since art conservation became an established discipline years before the library profession gave much thought to the problem of collections preservation, it is natural that most definitions of the concept have come from the museum world. Today there are large areas of overlapping interest between library and museum administrators and conservators, but for practical reasons the two fields are usually considered separate areas of endeavor. Moreover, for libraries it is often sufficient to retain the *intellectual content* of publications that are rapidly deteriorating rather than retain every work as an original artifact. Reprographic technology (e.g., facsimile reproduction and microrecording), which reduces the need to handle, and in certain instances to retain, fragile materials, constitutes a significant method of preservation that libraries have been quick to exploit in recent decades, but which is simply not viable as a means of preserving museum objects.

1

This collection of readings was selected purposely to emphasize the philosophical basis of conservation, its broad principles, and the interdisciplinary nature of the conservation enterprise. It is not inappropriate, therefore, to introduce the following definition provided by Richard Buck, dean of art conservation in the United States until his death in 1977:

> Administrative conservation includes at least the following elements: 1) a knowledge of the condition of objects in the collection and the surveillance of their condition; 2) an understanding of the effects of the . . . environment on the condition of objects in the collections and a surveillance of the environment; 3) the initiation of action to correct defects in the condition of objects; 4) the initiation of action to correct environmental deficiencies; 5) the consideration of the condition of objects in scheduling exhibitions and loans, and in controlling storage, handling, and transport; 6) the budgeting of funds to carry out any necessary action.[4]

A more serviceable definition, applying specifically to the conservation of library materials as opposed to museum artifacts, has yet to appear in the literature of librarianship, although Barr's statement on the "Scope of Conservation" comes close to filling the need.

HISTORY OF CONSERVATION

Conservation efforts have been traced to remote antiquity, to "whenever and wherever the peculiarly human penchant of saving and learning from what has gone before arose."[5] With the development of the various media that have been used through the ages for recording graphic information—clay tablets, scrolls of leather or papyrus, the codex—protective containers and coverings simultaneously appeared. Indeed, as suggested by Carl Wessel, if libraries themselves exist for any reason, it is to preserve mankind's historic records and his intellectual and creative expressions.

The conservation of cultural property in the modern era can be traced to the eighteenth century and the discovery of Pompeii and Herculaneum. Between 1800 and 1860, several French scientists devoted research to the problems of preserving antiquarian treasures; later in the century, Pasteur presented a series of courses on geology, physics, and chemistry, developed especially for students at the Ecole des Beaux Arts. In 1919, the mycologist Pierre Sée selected for the subject of his thesis a study of the fungi that attack paper. By the early 1930s, basic and applied research in the preservation of library materials was in progress at the Lenin State Library in the USSR, and in 1938, the Istituto di Patologia del Libro was established at Rome.[6]

In the United States, Harry Miller Lyndenberg, Director of the New York Public Library, gave much thought to the problem of preserving library materials and wrote extensively on the subject during the 1920s and 1930s. About the same time, William J. Barrow became interested in the causes of paper deterioration, and in 1932 established a document repair facility at the Virginia State Library in Richmond. The disastrous fire at the Jewish Theological Seminary in New York City in April of 1966 and the flood in Florence, Italy, which occurred in November of that year, provided important impetus to research in the salvage, repair, and restoration of paper, books, and bindings on a colossal scale.

Today, laboratories for basic and applied research in conservation and restoration are still extremely small in number. The field of investigation remains large.

NOTES AND REFERENCES

1. Valéry, Paul, *Littérature* (Paris: Gallimard, 1930):9.
2. Clapp, Verner W., "The Story of Permanent/Durable Book Paper," *Restaurator* (1972), Supplement No. 3, p. 1.
3. Buck, Richard D., "On Conservation," *Museum News* 52 (September 1973): 15–16.
4. Ibid.
5. Ogden, Lynn, et al., "Introducing Conservation," *CCI, The Journal of the Canadian Conservation Institute* 1 (1976).
6. Some of the information in this paragraph is based on a descriptive brochure by Francoise Flieder, "La Centre de Recherches sur la Conservation des Documents Graphiques," *Hors Série du Courrier du CNRS* 12 (April 1974).

I: WHY PRESERVATION?

Paper 1: Commentary

In our work as librarians, as in daily life, it is easier to describe what we are doing than to explain why we are doing it. This collection of papers begins with the philosophical question "Why preservation?" because the editors believe it is essential that librarians have a clear understanding of the philosophical base on which preservation efforts rest.

If it is agreed that libraries are the storehouse of mankind's collective memory and that libraries should be able to provide access to any item in their collections to any qualified user within a reasonable length of time, it must follow that individual libraries have a responsibility to maintain, protect, and preserve their collections. Which materials should be preserved and for how long depend on the nature of the material and the type of library.

That preservation is the indispensable means of assuring the availability of knowledge and access to it, both now and in the future, has been a basic tenet of scholarship since time immemorial. This tenet was reaffirmed recently by the American Council of Learned Societies. A proposal framed by that organization in 1975 called for a national inquiry into the production and dissemination of knowledge. As viewed by those who wrote the proposal, preservation is a key element in the broad spectrum of scholarly communication—that is, a spectrum that commences with the creation of text, extends onward to publication, thence to acquisition, organization, and storage in libraries, and finally, through bibliographic structures, to access and use.[1]

Nowhere in the literature of librarianship is the question "Why preservation?" more cogently dealt with than by Edwin E. Williams in "Deterioration of Library Collections Today." As Associate University Librarian of the Harvard University Libraries, Williams has been directly involved with preservation planning and administration for a number of years. In addition, he served as secretary to the Preservation Committee of the Association of Research Libraries for several years and is current chairman of the Preservation Committee of the Research Libraries Group. His article was prepared originally as the opening presentation of a two-day conference on the deterioration and preservation of library materials, held at the Graduate Library School of the University of Chicago in 1969.

REFERENCE

1. *ACLS (American Council of Learned Societies) Newsletter* 26 (Spring–Summer 1975): 1–8.

ADDITIONAL READINGS

Alden, John E., "Why Preserve Books?" *Catholic Library World* 30 (February 1959): 267–72.

The following general works on conservation of library materials are recommended.

Cunha, George M., *Conservation of Library Materials,* 2nd ed., 2 vols. (Metuchen, N.J.: Scarecrow Press, 1971–72).

Langwell, W. H., *The Conservation of Books and Documents* (London: Pitman, 1957), 114 pp.

Winger, Howard W., and Smith, Richard Daniel, eds., *Deterioration and Preservation of Library Materials* (Chicago: University of Chicago Press, 1970), 200 pp. Originally published in *Library Quarterly* 40 (January 1970).

1: DETERIORATION OF LIBRARY COLLECTIONS TODAY

Edwin E. Williams

In discussing the deterioration of library collections today, it would be possible to deal with the topic very briefly—not quite as briefly as with the subject of snakes in Ireland, but in a single sentence. This would read, *Everything in library collections is deteriorating today, was deteriorating yesterday, and will continue to deteriorate tomorrow although we ought to retard the process.*

Enough is known to justify this statement; it is when details are examined and countermeasures are considered that complications arise and the limitations of our knowledge become evident. It is hardly easier to generalize about the deterioration of books than about the aging of human beings. Beginning as identical twins, two copies of the same book may deteriorate at very different rates as the result of use and of storage conditions, which vary, even within the stacks of a single library, from one shelf to another. Life expectancies of different kinds of paper range from a very few years to centuries, and paper, of course, is not the only substance with which we are concerned. The conference will also deal with bindings and with photographic films; perhaps the conference program should also have provided for consideration of magnetic tapes and other things on which increasing stores of information will be recorded as the computer extends its empire. There are those who wonder why we worry about the deterioration of something as obsolete as the book.

This line of thought, however, would get us into tomorrow before we have dealt with today, much less with yesterday. It seems to me that we must begin with a glance at least toward the past; if some familiarity with history were not essential to an understanding of the present, perhaps we would be foolish to deplore or resist the deterioration of our library collections. Our problem has a long history. It occurs to me that the most serious mistake in that long history may have been made at an early date when knowledge began to be recorded on substances more pliable and more perishable than the baked clay tablet, which will not tear, will not burn, and will not turn into a pulpy mess when it is soaked in water. Have not library collections been highly perishable ever since? Have we not repeatedly sacrificed permanence for convenience and economy?

Vellum, to be sure, was more durable in many respects than papyrus, but vellum, after a few centuries, was superseded by a Chinese invention, paper. We were warned as early as the twelfth century, when the emperor of the Occident, Frederick I, Barbarossa, prohibited the use of paper in deeds and charters because he feared it was too perishable [1]. The account of "Paper Deterioration—An Old Story" by Lee E. Grove [2], which was published five years ago, begins with a fifteenth-century Benedictine abbot, Johann Tritheim, who believed that vellum would last for a millennium but had his doubts about paper.

I wish only to give a few names,

dates, and quotations in order to suggest how frequently the problem of paper deterioration has been considered during the past century and a half. In July 1823 two different British periodicals called attention to it. An item in the *Annals of Philosophy* entitled "Frauds and Imperfections in Papermaking" protested the practice of mixing sulphate of lime or gypsum with the rags and gave directions on how to detect this fraud; it also referred to "the slovenly mode in which the bleaching by means of chlorine or oxymuriatic acid is effected [3, p. 68]. In *The Gentleman's Magazine* for the same month, John Murray wrote:

Allow me to call the attention of your readers to the present state of that wretched compound called *Paper*. Every printer will corroborate my testimony; and I am only astonished that the interesting question has been so long neglected and forgotten. It is a duty, however, of the most imperative description;—our beautiful Religion, our Literature, our Science, all are threatened.

. . . I have in my possession a large copy of the Bible printed at Oxford, 1816 (never used), and issued by the British and Foreign Bible Society, *crumbling literally into dust.* I transmitted specimens of this volume to the Lord Bishop of Gloucester, and to Mr. Wilberforce. No doubt it must be difficult to legislate on such a subject, but something must be done and that early. I have watched for some years the progress of the evil, and have no hesitation in saying, that if the same ratio of progression is maintained, a century more will not witness the volumes printed within the last twenty years. *MS. Records* are in the same fatal condition. [4, pp. 21–22]

Murray concluded that "the chief causes of destruction consist in the employment of sulphate of lime, &c. in the pulp, and bleaching the rags previously, or the paper subsequently, with oxymuriatic acid gas *(chlorine)*." A footnote by the editor added: "It is notorious that the great mass of printing papers are now made of *cotton* rags; and that to produce a better colour, the pulp undergoes a chemical process, which materially injures its durability" [4, p. 21].

Leaving it to the experts to judge the validity of Murray's chemical diagnosis, I should like to observe only that his remarks have a very modern sound and that it is not encouraging to reflect that he seems to have enlisted no support, although he followed up his article with two monographic publications [5, 6, 7].

Within the literature of paper deterioration there is a whole subliterature on newspapers. Here the chronology appears to begin with Justin Winsor; at least it was reported in 1891 that "fifteen or twenty years ago" (that is, before he became the first president of the American Library Association or the librarian of Harvard College) Winsor had tried to persuade Boston newspapers to use more durable paper [8, note at end, signed "Eds. L. J."]. Long afterward, from 1910 to 1913 and again from 1918 to 1920, the ALA had a Committee on Deterioration of Newsprint Paper; there were distinguished chairmen—Frank P. Hill and Harry Miller Lydenberg—but the committee was no more successful than Winsor had been.

As we all know, the problem of newspapers has been solved, at least in one sense. The reservation is added because it could be argued that the preservation of newspapers in their original form has been abandoned as a lost cause; we rely upon microfilm to preserve the text, and a subsequent paper of this conference will inform us regarding deterioration of the film copies on which we depend.

Certainly microfilm is much more durable than newsprint; yet the history of our success in this field may not be entirely reassuring. My point is that our present solution to the newspaper problem seems to have been technically feasible long before Hill and Lydenberg tried to find a solution, and even before Winsor made the first attempt. I say this because in 1870, during the siege of Paris, microfilm had been successfully used to reproduce documents. The pigeons who flew film copies over the German lines were never entirely forgotten, and there was a European article in 1907 on "a new form of book—the microphotographic book" [9]; but it was not until the 1930s that American libraries began to use microphotography to any significant extent. If its possibilities were almost entirely overlooked for more than sixty years, one naturally wonders what possibilities we may now be neglecting.

During the sixty years that followed the publication of John Murray's book in 1829 there appears to have been relatively little interest in deterioration of paper, but the closing decade of the nineteenth century produced a number of contributions to the subject. In 1891, for example, Rossiter Johnson wrote on "Inferior Paper a Menace to the Permanency of Literature" [8], and in 1897 J. Y. W. MacAlister told the Library Association that, "as librarian of the Leeds library, I made certain simple experiments and observations which convinced me that many of the books on our shelves there, even if left untouched, would not outlast the present generation of readers" [10, p. 295]. Specifications for book papers were formulated in a report made during the following year to the Society of Arts by its Committee on the Deterioration of Paper [11]. In 1898, also, the librarian of Congress discussed the subject in his annual report, [12, pp. 45–6, 58–62], and the Italian government was petitioned by a conference of librarians to establish paper standards [13, p. 147].

The first year of our own century brought the publication (on paper that is now extremely brittle) of the *Procès-verbaux et mémoires* of the International Library Congress at Paris, including a paper by Pierre Dauze, who observed (I translate) that "Relatively recent works have completely disappeared from circulation or become more rare than incunabula. . . . Librarians, on whom rests the responsibility for leaving in perfect condition to their successors the precious stores in their care, show themselves gravely disturbed [*se montrent sérieusement inquiets*]" [14, p. 228–29]. He recommended that governments buy only books on paper meeting standards approved by official laboratories, and that good paper be required in copies supplied to libraries under the provisions of legal deposit.

In 1907 Cyril Davenport wrote that "there is no doubt that the large majority of our modern books will not be in readable condition in about a hundred years' time from the date of their publishing" [15, p. 82]. During this period the Bureau of Chemistry of the United States Department of Agriculture published results of research on the durability of paper [16], and some twenty years later, as reported in early volumes of the *Library Quarterly* [17, 18], a series of studies by the Bureau of Standards included in its findings a number of recommendations on optimum storage conditions for the preservation of records.

Our present efforts may be regarded as belonging, in the long history of deterioration and preservation, to a chapter that began about a dozen years ago. Thus far there have been two major figures in this chapter, and they are important, regardless of how their technical contributions may be appraised, because of the attention they have drawn to the problem. I refer to the Barrow Laboratory and Association of Research Libraries (ARL) committee that I serve as secretary; the two have been related, and both have been greatly indebted for assistance and counsel to Verner Clapp and the Council on Library Resources, Inc., which he served as president from 1956 to 1967.

On June 1, 1957, "the Virginia State Library, under a grant from the Council on Library Resources, Inc., and with the technical supervision of W. J. Barrow, began . . . a study of the deterioration of modern book papers" [19, p. 7]. The findings were published in a seventy-page booklet. Subsequent grants and studies produced two more booklets which, like the first, appeared as publications of the Virginia State Library [20, 21], and these have been followed by a series of W. J. Barrow Research Laboratory publications [22].

In 1959 the report of the first study gave "actual findings of the physical condition of 500 typical non-fiction books printed in the United States in the first five decades of this century [19, p. 7]. Its most striking and widely quoted conclusion was that "if material which should be preserved indefinitely is going to pieces as rapidly as these figures indicate, it seems probable that most library books printed in the first half of the 20th century will be in an unusable condition in the next century [19, p. 16].

If one recalls the closely similar statements that have been quoted from Murray (1823), MacAlister (1897), Dauze (1900), and Davenport (1908) —to say nothing of others that could have been cited—one might suppose that this would not have been regarded as news. On the other hand, it was based on a far larger sample than any of the previous statements, and this sample had been subjected to careful testing. There was also an encouraging prospect that financial assistance for further work on deterioration and preservation could be obtained from the Council on Library Resources. The result, in any case, has been a more systematic and persistent effort than had been prompted by any previous cry of alarm. This conference is both an evidence that the effort is continuing and an opportunity for review of what has been done thus far. Leaving technical questions to those who are qualified to deal with them, I propose to consider problems of organization and strategy that librarians face; hence I shall have much more to say about the ARL committee than about the Barrow Laboratory.

Interest aroused by the report of 1959 led the ARL to discuss paper deterioration at its meeting in Montreal on June 18, 1960, and it was decided at this meeting to establish a committee "to develop a national program for the preservation of research library materials with its primary concern directed toward the preservation of retrospective materials" [23, pp. 6–7]. Closely related efforts were already under way. The Subcommittee on Micropublishing Projects of the American Library Association Committee on Resources, under the chairmanship of Raynard Swank, had recently drafted a proposal for a cooperative national microfilm deposit, with objectives that included preservation, bibliographical control, and physical accessibility [24]. Wesley Simonton was at work on bibliographical control of microforms [25], and in

Washington on September 16, 1960—a week before the first meeting of the new ARL Committee—there had been a discussion of permanent/durable book paper at which Robert Kingery of the New York Public Library had presented a working paper on "The Extent of the Paper Problem in Large Research Collections and the Comparative Costs of Available Solutions [21, pp. 36–41].

These were all questions that must be considered by the ARL committee. At the outset it assumed that the solution to its problem would probably be found in microreproduction; at the first meeting it agreed "that the study should not neglect chemical treatment of books as a possible alternative to filming for preservation, though such treatment would not offer the desirable by-products of economy in space and increased accessibility of resources [26, p. 3]. It should be added that the committee has never seriously considered what might be called the "rare-book aspects" of preservation. It has assumed that it ought to deal with the great bulk of research collections, which will have to be rescued by relatively inexpensive mass-production techniques; and consequently it has not investigated conservation and restoration methods that are too costly to consider except for very valuable books, manuscripts, and bindings.

An essential first step, in the opinion of the ARL committee, was to determine the quantitative extent of the problem. Consequently its first special project, a study made for it by the Research Triangle Institute and financed by the Council on Library Resources, was a statistical sampling of the National Union Catalog. This indicated that, in 1961, the National Union Catalog listed 14,376,000 different volumes containing 2,999,998,000 pages; slightly more than 57 percent of these pages were in volumes published since 1869, and 56 percent of them were printed abroad. These figures take no account of serials. Though the findings were published over my signature [27], I have never been convinced that they make a great contribution toward solution of the problem.

The second project, at any rate, was far more significant. Late in 1962 a grant from the Council on Library Resources enabled the ARL committee to engage one of its members, Gordon Williams, director of the Center for Research Libraries, to make a comprehensive study [28].[1]

Two points regarding this study should be emphasized. First, the questions with which it dealt were discussed repeatedly and at length by the ARL committee; during many of these discussions it appeared that agreement might never be possible, but the final report won the support of all members. Second, it was unanimously adopted in principle by the Association of Research Libraries at its meeting of January 24, 1965; it stands therefore —until changes are approved—as a statement of the association's position, a plan of action that has been approved by librarians of the institutions most vitally concerned with the problem of deteriorating library materials. Hence it can be described as the most significant single document on the subject, and it seems to me that its major recommendations ought to be kept in mind as we consider the papers that are to be presented here. It is five years old, and we should try to judge how much it may have deteriorated. Are modifications indicated by what has been learned since it was prepared?

[1] This study also appears in *Library Journal* [29].

Do we need further research to test the validity of some of its recommendations?

Evidently I must attempt to summarize it, though it is not a verbose document and condensation is difficult. It begins by citing evidence of deterioration; here its source is the Barrow report of 1959, which dealt only with American publications printed between 1900 and 1939. This section might now be strengthened by reference to findings of the Barrow report of 1967, which analyzed the results of testing fifty books from each decade of the nineteenth century [30]; but this further data would not seem to call for any modification of the conclusions.

The objectives of an effective and efficient preservation program are stated as follows:

It must preserve all books of significant value ("books" is here used in the general sense to include all forms of written records); it must preserve the maximum amount of information carried by the original books; it must provide for the longest period of preservation practicable with present technology and compatible with the other requirements; it must provide for the continuous and ready availability of the preserved materials to anyone who needs them; and it must avoid unnecessary duplication of effort and expense. [28, p. 12]

The report then deals with the question of preserving original books as opposed to photographic copies only:

the primary importance of most books lies in their text, . . . but books can also be important in other ways. . . . There are those in which the primary interest is in some other intrinsic part of the book—the paper or binding, for example, or the decorative illustrations. . . .

. . . A copy can indicate, but cannot reproduce precisely, most of those qualities that make a book significant as an artifact . . . [but] most copies, which are made primarily to reproduce the text, do not even indicate some of these characteristics. Microform copies, for example, do not usually show the binding, end papers, . . . watermarks . . . ; neither do they identify cancels or show gatherings. Characteristics such as these are sometimes of critical importance in evaluating the authenticity or priority of the text, and sometimes are important . . for the evidence they supply about the taste and technology of the society that produced the book.

. . . [Moreover] even photocopies are not infallibly accurate, . . . they can copy illegibly; . . . and operator carelessness can omit whole pages or sections. . . .

. . . We must therefore conclude that in order to preserve all the information that may be significant in a book it is essential to preserve the original itself, and that even though copies of books are adequate for many uses, the availability of the original is also necessary to verify the accuracy of the copy. Further argument for preservation of the original for as long as possible is the recent evidence . . . that negative microfilm may have a shorter life expectancy than the original book. [28, pp. 12–14]

Originals cannot be preserved as long as possible, however, unless they are used as little as possible—used only when a copy will not serve the purpose. It follows, if photocopies must normally be supplied to the user, that "physical preservation of the original book is not simply a prudent alternative to the preservation of the text in microfilm, but is another operation which must be judged on its own merits" [28, p. 16]. However,

this cost need not be purely an additional cost. . . . Many books are infrequently used and, if physically preserved, copies of them would not have to be made until someone wanted to consult the text, or until the preserved original was no longer usable, and in either case this would not be for a great many years for many books. If, however, . . . the original were not preserved, a microform copy of every deteriorating book would have to be made as soon as possible. Data is presented [in this report] . . . showing that to microfilm a book is more expensive than physically to preserve it. . . .

Still further, the possibility of future improvements in methods of microcopying urges deferring this operation for as long as possible. [28, p. 17]

The decisive consideration clearly is economic, which means that cost estimates supporting the choice are constantly subject to change. Moreover, technological changes can alter the processes and products of filming, while specifications for optimum storage conditions may be altered from time to time as our knowledge increases.

If needless filming is to be avoided, there clearly must be a central record, if not a central collection, of master negatives. Likewise, any plan for the preservation of original books will be wasteful unless it provides for preservation of a single copy only of each ordinary book, and this obviously entails a national system supported by research libraries—the single preservation copy must be "nationalized" in some way, though this need not mean that all such copies would be physically assembled in a single national center.

Preservation of originals was a question on which opinions changed as the study proceeded, and there was another major point on which economic considerations proved to be decisive in changing the views of the ARL committee or some, at least, of its members. This was the question of selecting materials to be preserved. At the outset it had been supposed that selection would be a difficult problem; yet the report recommends simply that we preserve what has been selected and added to research libraries, since it would cost too much to review that selection—that is, it would cost more to identify volumes that could be discarded than to preserve these volumes.

To be specific, the cost estimates indicated that one would have to eliminate approximately 4 percent of books examined to justify the reappraisal project economically. Would it in fact prove impracticable to eliminate this much from our research library holdings? From the Harvard University Library, for example, this would mean weeding more than 300,000 volumes. There are certainly more than this that need not remain forever in the Harvard stacks. Yet the weeding in question here is an elimination of books from the world's collection, a decision that each book discarded is no longer to survive anywhere. Undoubtedly juries could be found who would be ready to condemn books by the millions, but books presumably should be judged by those who know them. Indeed, should not each book be judged by the scholar most likely to be interested in it, and, if he judges it to be useful—or even potentially useful—will it not have to be reprieved? Anyone who has observed the reactions of scholars when books are transferred to storage would be reluctant indeed to suggest that thousands of volumes be completely eliminated.

The report recommended, therefore, that we seek to preserve one copy of everything that is in research libraries, and that we preserve an original example of each work as long as we can, depending on film copies for ordinary use. In order to do this it recommended that a federally supported central agency be created to

1) undertake the centralized preservation of deteriorating records deposited by libraries; 2) coordinate its own preservation program with local programs of individual libraries to assure that all significant records are preserved while avoiding unwitting duplication; 3) assure the ready availability of microform or full size photocopies of deteriorating materials to all libraries; and 4) itself preserve, in the interest of textual preservation, economy, and

the the ready availability of copies, all microform masters made at its expense or deposited
by others, and coordinate the preservation of
microform masters made by other agencies.
[28, p. 21]

In one sense, consideration of the
problems of a central agency that has
not yet been created may seem to take
us a long way beyond the scope of a
paper on "Deterioration of Library
Collections Today"; but we are not
here to discuss deterioration purely as
an interesting natural phenomenon; we
are concerned with what can be done,
which means that we ought to examine
the machinery proposed by Gordon Williams and approved by the ARL.

The agency would operate a central
library that would "accept from other
libraries and physically preserve, by
deacidification and storage at the lowest practical temperature (or by improved techniques . . .), any example
of an original written record," provided
that another "example in equally good
or better condition is not already adequately preserved," that it is cata-
logued or "part of an organized and
coherent collection deposited in its entirety," and that it is complete or "as
complete as any example known to
exist" [28, p. 21]. Further:

> In order to provide for the maximum
> availability to the nation of the text of the
> preserved books, the central library will, sub-
> ject to copyright restrictions, make or cause
> to be made at its expense, a microform nega-
> tive of any book in its collection whenever a
> library wants to buy or to borrow a copy of
> that book. It will lend to a library without
> charge a microform positive . . . and it will
> sell a microform positive or full size copy
> from its negative for the cost of the positive
> or copy alone. . . .
> All negatives of preserved originals in the
> center will be retained by the center as master
> negatives, stored under optimum conditions
> for their longest possible retention (and physi-

cally separate from the preserved original),
and used only to make positive prints for
use. [28, p. 23]

It was easier to decide what such a
central library ought to do than to
agree on how libraries can be induced
to deposit books in it. Their participation is essential, as the report explains:

> the nation must depend upon libraries to
> provide the original books for preservation by
> depositing those from their own collections.
> Not only is it uneconomic to think of the
> central preservation library buying its own
> copies for this purpose, but many items that
> must be preserved are no longer available for
> purchase, and in any event it is a part of
> the responsibility of research libraries to help
> assure the continued availability of their books
> to their present and future patrons. The re-
> search libraries must therefore accept the
> positive responsibility to cooperate fully with
> the central agency. . . .
> They must do this, first, by obligating them-
> selves not to dispose of any catalogued book,
> or organized group of books, from their col-
> lections without first ascertaining whether or
> not an example as good as their own, or
> better, is already preserved. If . . . [not], then
> the library must deposit its example for pres-
> ervation rather than dispose of it otherwise.
> This imposes no obligation on any library
> to deposit examples from its collection until
> it wishes, and in many cases libraries will
> naturally prefer to retain the original examples
> . . . for as long as possible. . . . But in order
> to assure the longest possible physical preser-
> vation it is desirable that the books be in as
> good condition as possible when preserved,
> rather than already deteriorated to the point
> of near unusability. . . . Any library may
> buy from the central agency a copy (micro or
> full size) of any preserved record for the cost
> of the print. . . . But in order to provide an
> inducement to libraries to deposit as early in
> the book's life as possible, the library first
> depositing a "usable" or "good" example of
> a record will be allowed to buy a positive
> microform copy of that book for half the
> cost of the print . . . immediately upon deposit
> . . . or at any time in the future. [28, pp. 24–25]

The report provides for the grading
of copies deposited in order that pub-

lished lists can indicate the condition of each item; thus, when considering a deposit, a library will be able to estimate whether the copy already being preserved is better than its own. The center will also encourage libraries to develop their own "preservation collections"

by making microform copies of such locally preserved materials available for use under the same terms as if the material had been deposited for central preservation. In other words, the central agency will make when requested, or authorize to be made locally at its expense, a microform negative . . . and allow the library first preserving its usable or good example to buy a positive print for half the cost of the print. The central library agency will own and control this negative, insure that it is permanently retained as a master copy, and make prints from it readily available to any library. . . .

Books preserved locally in this way, with the same chemical treatment, cold storage, and protection, as if in the central library, will be regarded as adequately preserved. They will be given the same bibliographic control as books preserved centrally, and except in unusual cases will not be duplicated in the central collection. [28, pp. 25–26]

The report also recommends the immediate acquisition and preservation of a copy of each new book published in the United States or acquired under the Farmington Plan or the provisions of Public Law 480. The center would build up a file of master negatives of works not yet deposited for preservation, and would make positive film copies available to libraries on a cooperative basis. Bibliographical control would be provided through the National Union Catalog by means of compact lists of preserved books which would simply refer to serial numbers in that catalog.

Alternative patterns of support by the federal government are considered in the final section of the report. Re-

sponsibility might be assigned to an existing agency such as the Library of Congress, to an independent bureau or commission, or, by contractual arrangement, to a nongovernmental agency. While I plan to make a suggestion on general strategy, this specific question of agencies is one on which the ARL committee did not make a firm recommendation, and neither shall I.

Indeed, while this is one of the questions that you might wish to debate as you review the comprehensive plan that I have tried to summarize, it may not be one on which members of this conference will have much that is new to contribute. Another such question is raised by the policy of accepting the selection of research materials that has already been made—that is, on the one hand, to preserve what is in research libraries without reappraisal but, on the other, to make no effort to gather in and preserve materials that these libraries have overlooked. No doubt there will always be some scholars and some librarians who question this policy, and it might be an interesting topic for debate; but, unless someone demonstrates that we now have relevant information that was not available five years ago, I suggest that we shall do better to concentrate on other matters.

In its recommendation that we preserve original books instead of depending entirely on film copies, as we do for newspapers, the report would seem to be on firmer ground now than it was when adopted in 1965. By this I mean that photographic reproduction has not grown any cheaper, while the prospects for inexpensive deacidification of books seem to be brighter than they were.

There are other questions that have troubled the ARL committee during its discussions of the past five years, and one of them seems to be especially appropriate for consideration at this conference. Do we know enough about the process of paper deterioration to prescribe conditions of optimum storage and to build storage facilities—either centrally on on our own campuses—that will fit the prescription? The Barrow findings emphasized temperature and concluded that we ought to keep our books very cool. Humidity, however, is a complicating factor to which somewhat less study has been devoted than to temperature, and there has been no thorough investigation of the effect of changes in environment such as those that will take place if books are kept in a very cold place from which they must be removed in order to be consulted.

In preservation, as in many other projects, we shall never do anything if we wait until we have all the information that might be desirable, but it does not follow that immediate action is always wise. The real question is whether it is likely that our planning of storage facilities would be modified substantially by the answers to specific questions that probably could be answered in a relatively short time—two or three years—if research were now begun. There are differences of opinion regarding this on the ARL committee, but the Council on Library Resources, by its continued support of work at the Barrow Laboratory, as well as by its recent grant to the Imperial College of Science and Technology in London [31], appears to support the view that investigation of optimum storage conditions is needed.

Since subsequent papers will deal with this, as well as with deacidification and other treatments designed to extend the life of books, with the preservation of film, and with binding practices, I should like to turn from these questions; when they are discussed, I hope we shall keep in mind the relation they have to the ARL proposal. Meanwhile, there is another family of problems that ought be be mentioned; these relate to organization and library cooperation.

Some work on these problems has been done since Gordon Williams completed his report. A grant from the Council on Library Resources enabled the ARL committee to sponsor a Pilot Preservation Project conducted at the Library of Congress in 1967 and 1968. This was an experiment in comparing copies of volumes in the Library of Congress brittle-book collection with copies of the same volumes in other libraries; costs of identifying such copies and of obtaining reports on their condition were investigated. As a base for the experiment, 1,085 titles—most of them extremely brittle and some of them lacking portions of text—were selected from a collection of 35,000 volumes that have been withdrawn from the general collection at the Library of Congress because of their brittle condition. Reports were received on 795 titles, and it was found that from one to three reports were usually sufficient to locate a copy that, while usually brittle, was complete and otherwise in excellent condition. Moreover, 15 percent were in a rare-book collection or were specially protected in some other way.

On the basis of the study, it was concluded that it is administratively feasible to establish a national preservation collection of materials now deteriorating in the nation's research libraries. This assessment, however, extends only to the identification of brittle or deteriorating materials in other libraries and to a determination of the physical condition of such materials. Although no special attempt

was made to do so, the establishment of a central register of best copies appears to offer no particular problems. . . .
[The study did not investigate] the willingness of these libraries to contribute volumes to a national preservation collection; . . . their willingness to accept responsibility for preserving books in their own collections that have been designated as national preservation copies; . . . [or] the need for development of indemnification procedures. [32]

It has been seen that the plan of the ARL committee proposed certain inducements and indemnifications, but I think it is true that neither Gordon Williams nor those who approved his report would be willing to guarantee that these will be effective; experience, it has been assumed, may dictate modifications. It should also be noted that two persons who support the recommendations in every detail may still make distinctly different predictions. The plan provides for a central national preservation collection, but it also provides that each library may store on its own premises, under approved conditions, some of the books that have been "nationalized" as preservation copies. One of us, therefore, might envisage a future in which a single enormous preservation collection will contain one copy of nearly every book that has been acquired by any research library, the exceptions being a relatively few volumes of the kind that we shelter in our rare-book collections. Yet another advocate of the plan might envisage a future in which the central national collection will contain only the marginal and very infrequently used books that libraries gladly discarded, and the great bulk of the "national preservation collection" would be dispersed, housed in special "preservation stacks" of major research libraries.
Presumably the outcome will depend

in part on the inducements that are offered and the organization that is created; moreover, regardless of which future one prefers, either is acceptable. When it comes to sources of financial support, however, there has appeared to be no alternative and there has been no difference of opinion—the problem of deterioration is too large, it is agreed, to be solved unless substantial federal funds are provided.

It will surprise me if anyone wishes to debate this conclusion of the ARL committee, but I should like to suggest that its implications have not been fully explored. If federal funds are to be obtained, presumably members of Congress will have be be convinced that deterioration is a serious and urgent problem. Scholars, of course, are the real victims of deterioration, and it seems unlikely that congressmen will be persuaded to appropriate funds unless scholars help to persuade them. Librarians generally—not just a few librarians in a few of the largest research libraries—must also be enlisted in the campaign.

As it is, few librarians have been particularly active, and not many scholars have volunteered. Librarians of the relatively new and small institutions are busy acquiring new books and reprints of old ones; their shelves are not filled with brittle books and, while they recognize that the old and enormous research libraries are national resources on which they must depend, they naturally regard deterioration as primarily a problem for those who are fortunate enough to have inherited great collections. With regard to the scholars, I think we should realize that the great majority are not directly and vitally concerned. Those scholars whose research is focused on contemporary materials—and they include most scientists—rarely encounter a book that is falling apart. It is historians, after all, who are menaced by deteriorating books. To be sure, every subject has its historians, but the percentage of scholars who are studying the past has clearly been decreasing during recent decades.

Yet the historians, if they had not been relatively apathetic, could have made themselves heard and could have convinced many of their colleagues on the faculty that something must be done. There seems to be a disparity between the alarming statements that have been published and the alarm that has been generated in individuals, even historians.

Perhaps this can be explained by a visit to the shelves. When one goes through the stacks of one of our venerable and enormous research libraries with a visitor—congressman, professor, or librarian—one does not find large numbers of volumes that have crumbled "literally into dust," as John Murray said his Bible was doing 146 years ago. If the library still has newspaper stacks, with bound volumes in them instead of microfilms, fairly dramatic instances of crumbling can be found, but it is hard to find genuinely shocking examples in our book stacks, even when one goes to the shelves on which some of the most brittle volumes have been segregated. (The number that have been segregated for this reason may seem surprisingly small—only 35,000, it has been seen, at the Library of Congress, representing a small fraction of 1 percent of its total holdings.)

As it is, when one tries to demonstrate the problem to a visitor, most of the volumes that are pulled from the shelves will appear at first glance to be in satisfactory condition, though the paper in many of them will be too brittle to bend very often or even very far without breaking. A few, in which leaves have broken loose, evidently ought to be rebound but cannot be. Even so—particularly if he observes that many of the books have not circulated for a decade or more—this is not likely to look like a crisis to the visitor.

Has the literature of deterioration exaggerated? We have never scientifically sampled and tested the holdings of a research library, but we have the Barrow findings, indicating that most of our books will soon be "in an unusable condition." Perhaps we must consider what *unusable* means.

The best of books are not strong enough to survive much rough and careless use. On the other hand, very few books—even among those in which the paper has deteriorated below the "one-fold" level—cannot survive very careful and gentle use. Glass, after all, is one of the most lasting substances; even the most fragile glass ornament will survive for centuries if it is not dropped or crushed, but it cannot be folded even a little way, even once. Like glass, much of our brittle paper may last a long while if it is not bent. If this were not so, we could hardly advocate the large-scale preservation of original books; we should have to film at once.

My point is that the distinction between *permanence* and *fragility* may sometimes have confused us, and is likely to complicate matters when we try to explain the problem of deterioration to congressmen and even to scholars. We know that some damage is inevitable, even in a rare-book reading room, to very fragile books. We know that books in our general stacks will not always be used carefully, that leaves will break loose from bindings, that some of these will be lost or bent again, and that portions of the text will be lost. It should be possible to explain this, but it may not be easy: essentially we are saying that millions of books in research libraries are unusable; yet thousands of them are in fact being used every day.

Such difficulties may help to explain the long history of unsuccessful efforts to spread the alarm from 1823 to 1957, as well as the fact that our current campaign has not been victorious thus far. It is not my conclusion that we are entitled to be sorry for ourselves or to give up. We have met to re-examine what we know and to decide what further investigation is needed. In addition I propose that our strategy be reconsidered.

Librarians, like members of many other groups, talk to one another so much that they often forget, when talking to "outsiders," that the library ideology and dialect may not be understood. No librarian needs to be reminded that we preserve books—just as we acquire them in the first place—in order that they can be used. We have to preserve if we are going to disseminate; but this may not be entirely self-evident to others. If we are honored by an attack from the anti-establishment forces, their epithet is not likely to be "pig"; more likely it will be "squirrel." Unfortunately there are those—conservative and moderate as well as radical—who regard us as misers, gloating over wealth that has been accumulated for its own sake.

The ARL committee is the Committee on the *Preservation* of Research Library Materials. Reviewing its history now, I fear I, as its secretary, have been culpable in not more vigorously

and persuasively suggesting that *Dissemination* ought to be substituted for *Preservation*. Perhaps I was so busy preserving a record of its deliberations for the minutes that I failed to disseminate my opinion.

It would have been possible, without changing any feature of the plan formulated for the committee by Gordon Williams, to have presented it as a plan for dissemination—for making research library holdings of the nation increasingly accessible to scholars. In a document entitled "The Preservation of Deteriorating Books," however, access inevitably appears to be something of a by-product. It was not neglected, but a title role is a title role and top billing is top billing; preservation was the star in this show.

Would we not do better, at least whenever nonlibrarians may be listening, to speak of preservation as a by-product of accessibility and continued dissemination? A successful heart transplantation is not acclaimed because it keeps alive a heart that would otherwise have died with its original proprietor; our national plan will be acclaimed not because it keeps books from crumbling but because it contributes to the health of American scholarship. One approach is to ask the Congress for appropriations to protect property that has been amassed by major research libraries; the other is to demand that Congress meet the cost of opening up this national resource to all the country's scholars and of making sure that it will be kept open.

This should not be put down as merely a cynical public-relations ploy. It is not deceptive packaging. If we conclude that books need to be kept cold in order to preserve them, we are not going to call the whole plan a book-

refrigeration project. Since preservation is no more our real objective than refrigeration is, I insist that it is a misleading label and the dissemination is the honest one.

As has been suggested, the ARL proposal could, without alteration, be given a better title. However, if it were rewritten to emphasize the objectives of dissemination and accessibility, it is possible that the reworking would suggest some modifications in the machinery that is recommended. Such modifications would not be desirable if they made the plan any less effective

in insuring preservation. In theory it would be possible, though Gordon Williams made it clear that this would make no sense, to preserve merely in order to preserve—one could bury collections under a Greenland glacier. But clearly it is not possible to disseminate a text of which no copy remains in existence.

We have difficult and therefore very interesting problems to consider here, but let us not become so deeply engrossed in them that we fail to keep in mind and to state as clearly as possible why they must be solved.

REFERENCES

1. Walton, Robert P. "Paper Permanence." *Publishers' Weekly* 116 (September 7, 1929):979.
2. Grove, Lee E. "Paper Deterioration—An Old Story." *College and Research Libraries* 25 (September 1964):365–74.
3. "Frauds and Imperfections in Paper-making." *Annals of Philosophy* 6 (July 1823): 68.
4. Murray, J. Untitled letter. *Gentleman's Magazine* 93 (July 1823): 21–22.
5. Murray, John. *Observations and Experiments on the Bad Composition of Modern Paper.* London: Whittaker, 1824.
6. Murray, John. *Practical Remarks on Modern Paper.* Edinburgh: Blackwood; London: Cadell, 1829.
7. Grove, Lee E. "John Murray and Paper Deterioration." *Libri* 16 (1966):194–204.
8. Johnson, Rossiter. "Inferior Paper a Menace to the Permanency of Literature." *Library Journal* 16 (August 1891):241–42. Reprinted from the New York *World*.
9. Goldschmidt, Robert, and Otlet, Paul. "Sur une forme nouvelle du livre: le livre microphotographique." *Bulletin de l'Institut International de Bibliographie* 12 (1907):61–69.
10. MacAlister, J. Y. W. "The Durability of Modern Book Papers." *Library* 10 (September 1898):295–304.
11. "Report of the Committee on the Deterioration of Paper." *Journal of the Royal Society of Arts* 46 (May 20, 1898): 597–601.
12. "The Durability of Paper." *Report of the Librarian of Congress* [John Russell Young] *for the Fiscal Year Ended June 30, 1898.* Washington, D.C.: Government Printing Office, 1898.
13. Società Bibliografica Italiana, "Processi verbali delle adunanze pubbliche." *Revista delle Biblioteche e degli Archivi* 9 (October 1898):145–51.
14. Dauze, Pierre. "La question de la conservation du papier dans les bibliothèques publiques et privées et un moyen de la résoudre." In *Procès-verbaux et mémoires* of the Congrès international des bibliothécaires, Paris, August 20–23, 1900. Paris: Welter, 1901.
15. Davenport, Cyril. *The Book: Its History and Development.* London: Constable, 1907.
16. Wiley, Harvey Washington, and Merriam, C. Hart. *Durability and Economy in Papers for Permanent Records.* U.S. Department of Agriculture, Report no. 89. Washington, D.C.: Government Printing Office, 1909.
17. Scribner, B. W. "Report on Bureau of Standards Research on Preservation of Records." *Library Quarterly* 1 (October 1931):409–20.
18. Scribner, B. W. "The Preservation of Records in Libraries." *Library Quarterly* 4 (July 1934):371–83.
19. *Deterioration of Book Stock: Causes and Remedies: Two Studies on the Permanence of Book Paper.* Virginia State Li-

brary Publications, no. 10. Conducted by W. J. Barrow and edited by Randolph W. Church. Richmond: Virginia State Library, 1959.

20. Church, Randolph W., ed. *The Manufacture and Testing of Durable Book Papers*. Virginia State Library Publications, no. 13. Based on the investigations of W. J. Barrow. Richmond: Virginia State Library, 1960.

21. *Permanent/Durable Book Paper, Summary of a Conference Held in Washington, D.C., September 16, 1960*. Virginia State Library Publications, no. 16. Richmond: Virginia State Library, 1960.

22. W. J. Barrow Research Laboratory. *Permanence/Durability of the Book*. 5 vols. Richmond: Virginia State Library, 1963–67.

23. Minutes of the Fifty-fifth Meeting of the Association of Research Libraries, Montreal, June 18, 1960.

24. American Library Association, Committee on Resources, Subcommittee on Micropublishing Projects. "A Preliminary Report on a Proposal that There Be Established a Cooperative National Microfilm Deposit." Manuscript, May 20, 1959.

25. Simonton, Wesley. "The Bibliographical Control of Microforms." *Library Resources and Technical Services* 6 (Winter 1962):29–40.

26. Minutes of the Association of Research Libraries, Committee on the Preservation of Research Library Materials, Cambridge, Mass., September 21, 1960.

27. Williams, Edwin E. "Magnitude of the Paper-Deterioration Problem as Measured by a National Union Catalog Sample." *College and Research Libraries* 23 (November 1962):499, 543.

28. "The Preservation of Deteriorating Books: An Examination of the Problem with Recommendations for a Solution." Report of the ARL Committee on the Preservation of Research Library Materials. In Minutes of the Sixty-fifth Meeting of the Association of Research Libraries, Washington, D.C., January 24, 1965.

29. "The Preservation of Deteriorating Books." *Library Journal* 91 (January 1 and January 15, 1966):51–6, 189–94.

30. W. J. Barrow Research Laboratory. *Permanence/Durability of the Book*. Vol. 5. *Strength and Other Characteristics of Book Papers 1800–1899*. Richmond: Virginia State Library, 1967.

31. Council on Library Resources. "Recent Developments." News Release no. 271, February 22, 1969.

32. Shaffer, Norman J. "Library of Congress Pilot Preservation Project." *College and Research Libraries* 30 (January 1969): 5–11.

II: THE NATURE OF
LIBRARY MATERIALS

Papers 2 Through 7: Commentary

A basic knowledge of materials is an important element in the constellation of skills and expertise of the librarian who specializes in the field of conservation. Edward C. Lathem, in a paper included in this volume, stresses that the conservation officer should know as much as possible about as much as possible. Conservators need to have the theoretical knowledge necessary for a basic understanding of preservation problems and their solutions, but there is a question of how much the librarian needs to know about such matters. Certainly the conservation librarian needs at least a general knowledge of the nature of library and archival materials.

There are few library schools that prepare the beginning librarian to cope with conservation and preservation problems. Writing in 1968, Paul N. Banks stated, "Librarians, and particularly library schools, would appear to assume that books take care of themselves."[1] A survey completed in 1976 by Gay Walker showed that only twelve courses were being offered for academic credit in the nation's schools of library science.[2] If the number of theses and dissertations on conservation-related subjects can be taken as measure, the scene is equally discouraging: Of 214 titles in the most recent comprehensive listing, only one can be described as having a bearing on conservation of library materials.[3]

Librarians tend to view books and other library materials as media of communication or as artifacts that are important for their informational content and graphic features. A special habit of thought, usually inculcated only through reading and special training, is required to view books as physical objects, subject to the same physical laws as other organic substances. Furthermore, at least a general understanding of the nature of materials is essential for the librarian since the administration of conservation programs frequently involves interprofessional cooperation and communication with bookbinders, conservators, scientists, and others having a technical and scientific background.

The selections that have been chosen for inclusion in this section describe in general, nontechnical terms the physical and chemical characteristics of the materials most commonly found in books, documents, microforms, and other objects collected by libraries—that is, paper, inks, adhesives, film, leather, and parchment. It is hoped that these readings will focus the reader's attention on the need to develop awareness in this area, at least to the extent necessary for general understanding and purposes of communication.

NOTES AND REFERENCES

1. Banks, Paul N., "Some Problems in Book Conservation," *Library Resources and Technical Services* 12 (Summer 1968): 337.
2. Walker, Gay, *Preservation Training and Information: Report of a 1976 Survey* (Chicago: American Library Association, Resources and Technical Services Division, Preservation of Library Materials Committee, n.d. 2 leaves.
3. Tryon, Jonathan S., "Theses and Dissertations Accepted by Graduate Library Schools: 1974 Through December, 1975," *Library Quarterly* 46 (October 1976): 424-36.

ADDITIONAL READINGS

In addition to the works listed under Additional Readings in Part I of this volume, all of which contain chapters or articles on materials, the following are recommended.

Paper:

Sutermeister, E., *The Story of Papermaking* (New York: Bowker, 1954), 209 pp.

Ink:

Casey, Robert S., "Ink," *Encyclopaedia Britannica* 12 (1973): 257-59.

De Pas, Monique, and Flieder, Francoise, *Historique et Perspectives d'Analyse des Encres Noires Manuscrites* (Paris: Centre de Recherches sur la Conservation des Documents Graphiques, 1972), 31 pp. A paper presented at the 1972 Plenary Meeting of the International Council of Museums Committee for Conservation.

Adhesives:

Blomquist, Richard F., *Adhesives-Past, Present and Future* (Philadelphia: American Society for Testing and Materials, 1963). Edgar Marburg Lecture, 1963, 34 pp.

Permanence/Durability of the Book, vol. 4, "Polyvinyl Acetate (PVA) Adhesives for Use in Bookbinding" (Richmond, Va.: W.J. Barrow Research Laboratory, 1965), 66 pp.

Film:

"Film," Chapter 9 in Nelson, Carl E., *Microfilm Technology* (New York: McGraw-Hill, 1965).

Leather and Parchment:

Stambolov, T., *Manufacture, Deterioration and Preservation of Leather* (Amsterdam: Central Research Laboratory for Art and Science, 1969), 89 pp. A paper presented at the 1969 Plenary Meeting of the International Council of Museums Committee for Conservation.

Reed, R. *Ancient Skins, Parchments and Leathers* (New York: Seminar Press, 1972), 331 pp.

Saxl, H., "A Note on Parchment," in Charles Singer, et al., eds., *A History of Technology,* vol. 2 (Oxford: Clarendon Press, 1956), pp. 187-90.

2: PAPER

W. J. Barrow

FROM the earliest times to the present, the cellulose fiber has been a most important material for recording the writings of mankind. This fiber gives physical strength to papyrus, cloth, wood, palm leaves, paper, and many other materials that have been used for writing and printing. Paper has replaced all of the other materials for this purpose, and also the much-used parchment and vellum of the medieval period.

Basically, paper consists of fabricated cellulose fibers and a sizing material such as animal glue or starch. Its physical strength is derived from the individual fibers as well as fiber-to-fiber bonding. The size controls the rate of absorption of ink and aids in the bonding of the fibers. The principal sources of this fiber are linen, cotton, hemp, jute, straw, and wood. The type of fiber used at different times depended upon its availability in at least a partially purified state. In the raw state, these fibers contain fats, waxes, and in some cases lignin, etc., which must be removed before a fiber of high purity is obtained.

When the art of papermaking was first introduced in Europe, linen was the fiber generally available. Cotton was used also, but it was a costly fiber and did not become common until after the invention of the cotton gin by Eli Whitney in 1793. Rags or clippings of linen and cotton cloth were the principal source of the cellulose fiber used in the manufacture of writing and printing papers during the period of this study. Hemp, jute, and straw also appear in the papermaking literature during the eighteenth and nineteenth centuries, but these fibers were most often used for making wrapping paper and similar products. It was not until several years after the discovery of chlorine by Karl Wilhelm Scheele in 1774 that it was possible to bleach these fibers sufficiently to use them in low-grade writing and printing papers. Evidence substantiating these statements may be found in the early and recent studies on papermaking, and particularly in the late studies of both Dard Hunter and R. H. Clapperton.

Cotton is the purest cellulose fiber occurring in nature, and requires but little chemical treatment before it can be made into paper. Linen must first go through a retting process (the removal of noncellulostic materials by microorganisms) before it is suitable even for weaving.

Both of these fibers must be bleached to make them white enough for writing and printing papers. When properly processed and stored, these two fibers have a high degree of permanency. Hunter states that the earliest dated paper is from A.D. 264, and there are undated specimens which are thought to have been made about a hundred years earlier. The generally accepted date for the invention of paper is A.D. 105. Lucas has examined pieces of linen cloth estimated to be seven thousand years old. Some of the earliest papyri, which also depend upon the cellulose fiber for physical strength, have been estimated by Lucas to be about five thousand years old. The studies of Leggett show that recently excavated linen fibers are estimated to be ten thousand or more years old. It may be said that this fiber is very stable and will last almost indefinitely if unaffected by certain agents which are destructive.

Custodians do not always fully appreciate the efforts made by the early papermakers to produce a lasting and durable paper. Many of them have concluded that the procedures and materials used by these craftsmen came about by accident and not by intelligent planning. There is much evidence in the literature indicating that considerable thought was given to producing a paper of high quality. A great deal of their knowledge was gained by trial and error, but observations of their predecessors' products were likewise a factor.

An unsigned German manuscript of the late sixteenth century, translated by Blanchet in 1900, stressed many points which enter into good papermaking procedures. This was true of other writers, and particularly true of Father Imberdis, who lived in France during the seventeenth century. His treatise on papermaking was also translated by Blanchet. Imberdis was the first to recommend certain specifications for paper to be used in writing fine books which should be expected to last for centuries. He advised "That it be white, that sad wrinkles do not streak it, and that bold roughness does not stand out on its surface." To test paper for sufficient sizing, he recommends that "Shaken in the hand the paper will not fall like a rag, but like parchment it will ring . . ." and, "Cover it with saliva; if on any point moisture deposited on its surface does not come out on the reverse side, do not question it."

Rags for Papermaking

When a comparison is made of papers made during the fifteenth century with those of the following century, little or no difference in their structure is apparent. Therefore, if technical treatises of the fifteenth century on the art of papermaking were available, most likely the procedures used would be the same as described in the literature of the sixteenth and seventeenth centuries. During these two latter centuries, the writers on this subject stressed the importance of using new, strong rags for the best grades of writing and printing papers. The worn and discolored rags were generally used for making wrapping paper, cartridge paper, blotting paper, pasteboard, and so forth. This practice accounts for the fact that many of the records of these centuries are in an excellent state of preservation. Toward the end of the seventeenth century, the demand for paper became great, and soon the supply of new white rags was insufficient to fill the needs. The buyers of paper, and especially those in the colonies which were in the soft currency areas, were often forced to purchase any quality available. They were soon buying inferior papers made of a large percentage of worn and deteriorated rags. This practice of using low-grade rags for making paper was condemned often by the writers of the eighteenth century.

The addition of bluing to paper made of yellowed and deteriorated rags gave the yellowed paper a relatively white appearance. This optical illusion, or gentle art of faking, may have fooled many purchasers of paper, as for centuries whiteness had been looked upon as a sign of purity. This addition made possible the use of low-grade rags in making writing and printing papers. Further camouflaging of low-grade and certain dyed rags was accomplished by dyeing the paper blue. Some of these colored rags, which could be redyed blue, were new and could be made into a strong and lasting paper. The art of bluing was well understood by the cloth bleachers, as the *Cyclopaedia* of 1728, by Ephraim Chambers, mentions smalt, Dutch lapis, and indigo for bluing.

During the eighteenth century, sulfur dioxide and oil of vitriol (sulfuric acid) were mentioned in connection with the bleaching of cloth, but nothing appears in the literature to indicate that it was used in the bleaching of rags for papermaking. The use of sulfur dioxide for whitening linen cloth was mentioned by Pliny in the first century. About the end of the eighteenth century, chlorine became the agent for whitening the yellowed, deteriorated, and colored rags. A description of the procedures used in this process appears in volume XIII of Dobson's *Encyclopaedia* (Philadelphia, 1798). The indiscriminate use of this compound caused much deterioration within the cellulose fibers, and in many instances produced a paper of high acidity. The lack of controlled methods in its application accounts for much of the deterioration found in papers of the nineteenth century. For technical data on the effects of chlorine on paper, it is suggested that the following bibliography be consulted: *Permanence and Durability of Paper*, by Morris S. Kantrowitz, Ernest W. Spencer, and Robert H. Simmons.

From about 1700 onward, the demand for paper became greater, and the quality progressively worse. Rags of all sorts and conditions were treated in various and sundry ways to produce fairly white stuff for the making of paper. According to Hunter, even the linen wrappings of the ancient mummies of Egypt were robbed and sold for this purpose during the nineteenth century. Besides the low physical strength of many of these rags and wrappings, quite a few contained almost every conceivable type of foreign matter. Fortunately, some of it was washed out during the papermaking processes. Even under modern methods of purification, old, used rags do not make a strong paper. This statement is well substantiated by the findings of Merle B. Shaw, George W. Bicking, and Martin. J. O'Leary of the National Bureau of Standards in *A Study of the Relation of Some Properties of Cotton Rags to the Strength and Stability of Experimental Papers Made from Them*. These investigators also found that papers made of low-grade rags lacked good stability. The use of low-grade rags accounts for some of the papers made after 1700 being in a weakened condition today. The indiscriminate use of chlorine after its discovery in 1774 is also a factor in the deterioration of many documents.

Manuscripts that were written before 1700 with ink of low acidity and which have been properly stored are, as a rule, in a good state of preservation. Until this date, no method was employed to bleach or camouflage discolored rags as the supply of clean, new white rags or clippings from garment making was sufficient to meet the demand for writing and printing papers. At that time, the method of bleaching or whitening the cloth was relatively noninjurious to the fibers. Basically, this process consisted of first washing the cloth with soap and water, and then soaking for several hours in lye water. This lye was an extract of wood ashes, and contained the carbonates and phosphates of sodium, potassium, magnesium, and calcium. This operation in bleaching was followed by rinsing in water and spreading on the grass in a meadow with intermittent wetting. The action of sunlight, moisture, residual lye, and oxygen from the grass were all factors in this bleaching. The cloth was afterwards soaked in milk or sour bran. All of these operations were repeated until the desired whiteness was obtained, which usually took from four to six weeks. After the bleaching, the cloth was starched and whitened by the addition of chalk (calcium carbonate) and bluing. Data will be presented later which indicate that the calcium carbonate from the lye and chalk has had a beneficial effect on the permanency of many of these early papers. It is not known when this method was discovered, but R. S. Hatch, one of the contributing authors of *Cellulose and Cellulose Derivatives*, edited by Emil Ott, states that a similar method was used by the ancients.

Preparation of Stuff

After the rags were sorted for color and quality, they were washed in a container called a puncheon which had holes at various intervals to allow water to drain from the rags. When well washed, they were then placed in small piles and allowed to ferment for four to five days. They were watched carefully for any tendency "to mildew, discolour, and take fire." When "fermented sufficiently," the rags were cut into one-half inch pieces and beat in slowly circulating water with large stamping hammers for about twelve hours. After this operation, the half stuff thus formed was placed in large wooden boxes while wet and "mellowed a week, more or less, according to the weather." After this mellowing period, they were beaten a second time and again allowed another period of "mellowing." This was known as the second stuff, which was beaten a third time in "the pit mortar." This macerated material, called stuff, was used to form the sheets of paper.

Today, many do not look upon fermentation as a method of purification, but as one of contamination. This procedure of fermentation by the early papermakers did remove the insoluble starches and other materials used in sizing cloth. The action of various enzymes produced by the different microorganisms converted the starches to soluble compounds and liquefied any animal glue present. This greatly simplified the beating operation as these undesired products could then be washed from the rags. Imberdis describes this fermentation process as "either the rag loses here a needless liquid or it softens and becomes less difficult to triturate or finally like manure, it acquires there an unknown virtue." In many instances, there was likely some loss in cellulose when this process was allowed to continue too long. The workers were continually warned to watch this process and "not let it ferment needlessly." The "Hollander," a type of beater invented just before 1682, eventually eliminated this procedure. Regardless of possible criticism of the fermentation process, the early papermakers did produce artistic and very stable papers by this method.

Water was a most necessary item for washing rags and forming the sheet of paper. Several of the early treatises stress the importance of using the purest water available. Imberdis recommended that a mill be placed above the city or village in order that no rubbish or trash contaminate the stream. He states, "In my eyes a stream is excellent for paper when, across its crystalline waves, shine numerous pebbles and the trout, abundantly speckled on the sides, leap about and frolic in close schools." This type of stream reminds one of those in a somewhat mountainous area. Frequently, the bicarbonate of calcium is found in such waters.

Washing and drying the rags in this type of hard water would precipi-
tate small amounts of calcium carbonate in the cellulose fibers. This is
another possible source of this compound found in many papers, and, as
previously stated, data relative to its beneficial effect on paper will be
presented later. For many years, calcium carbonate has been considered
an essential ingredient in the soil which produces the grapes for the fine
wines of France, Germany, Spain, Portugal, and Italy. In America, it is
needed in the water used in making good sour mash whiskey and in
raising the best jumping horses.

Judging from the literature, the workmen were constantly reminded
of fire hazards and were encouraged to keep the mill and equipment
clean and in good working order. The unsigned German manuscript
translated by Blanchet recommends the following: "Be careful not to go
upon the piles (rags) with dirty shoes, so that the mud does not fall in
the stuff and does not soil the paper which is being made." The ferrous
metals were generally prohibited in certain parts of the equipment as
they would rust and damage the paper.

Forming the Sheet

After the fibers had been properly prepared by beating, they were trans-
fered to a vat in preparation for forming the sheet of paper. It was
desirable to have the right proportions of stuff or pulp to the amount of
water in order to form paper of a given thickness. The frame used in
making the sheet of paper consisted of small brass wires either woven or
laid parallel across a rectangular wooden frame. This frame was plunged
into the vat containing the fibers suspended in water, and shaken when
removed from the liquid. During the shaking motion the fibers became
interlaced and interlocked as the water drained from the stuff through
the wires. The wet sheet was transferred to felts, and pressed to remove
the surplus water. After the pressing operation, it was hung up on hair
ropes to dry.

Forming the sheet required a craftsman of good physical strength
and considerable skill. The even distribution of fibers over a sheet, so
often found in many old books, is a remarkable accomplishment of these
early papermakers. A highly skilled craftsman can produce a sheet with
about an equal number of fibers lying in each direction. This is better
than can be accomplished on a machine, yet, on the other hand, a machine makes paper more uniform in thickness. There are a few admirers
of handmade paper who claim that forming a sheet by hand gives greater
permanence to the paper. To concur with this opinion would be the
same as agreeing with one who claims that handpumped water tastes

better than that pumped by a motor. The chemical purity of new strong fibers is the factor of primary importance in this respect.

Sizing of Paper

After the newly fabricated sheet was thoroughly dry, a "cool temperate" day was selected for the sizing operation. The object of this process was to render the paper less absorbent, thus preventing ink from feathering. Imberdis stated that size was made by boiling the ears of mutton and cattle in water, and that sometimes the intestines were used. Writers of the eighteenth century recommended the parings from tanners, curriers, and parchment-makers. These later writers specified the addition of alum and, occasionally, white vitriol. The previously mentioned bluing was sometimes added to give the eighteenth- and nineteenth-century papers made of old and yellowed rags the appearance of being white. The new sheets of paper were lowered into this gelatinous solution long enough for them to become saturated, then removed and air dried.

Printing papers require much less size than writing papers due to the nature of the two inks. For good writing properties, a certain amount of size is needed, but when there is an excess of this amount there is an increase in stiffness and a decrease of flexibility within the sheet. On the other hand, a small amount of size increases the physical strength of an unsized sheet. This increase in physical strength may have caused a few archivists and librarians to conclude that resizing old paper is a worthwhile procedure as they are of the opinion that this size perishes over a period of time. With the exception of moldy documents or some other unusual condition, this size does not necessarily deteriorate. About twelve years ago, ten writing papers of the seventeenth and eighteenth centuries were submitted to the Bureau of Standards for testing. They had from 2.6 to 5.8 percent glue, which was no indication that the sizing had perished. No starch or resin was found in these papers. As a rule, these early writing papers do not exhibit feathering when written on with modern ink, which proves that they have retained at least a large portion of the original sizing. This does not apply to early printing papers as relatively little sizing was needed. It would be of interest if those who advocate this practice of resizing old papers offered data showing approximately how much physical strength was added by this procedure.

It is not known when alum was first used in the sizing of paper, but it was mentioned in the *Diary* of John Evelyn in 1678. It does not appear again in papermaking literature until about mid-eighteenth century. It was used to harden the size, which, in turn, lowered the rate of absorption in paper and further prevented feathering of ink. This alum was potassium aluminium sulfate in a somewhat unpurified state. It increased the acidity of the paper, which is an undesirable condition for documents of permanent value. White vitriol (zinc sulfate) occasionally appears in the same literature with alum, but whether it was used to any extent is not known. As a rule, sulfates are considered somewhat harmful to paper, but more information is needed relative to this particular compound.

Polishing

The object of polishing paper is to give it a smooth surface for writing. A wolf's tooth or a polished pebble was recommended by Imberdis for this purpose, while others suggested various types of smooth stones or flints. In order to make playing cards smooth and more easily manipulated, these stones were rubbed over sheep's tallow before polishing. This practice was forbidden on writing paper as any deposit of tallow would hinder the proper penetration of ink.

Another method of imparting smoothness to the surface was by pressing a group of papers in a screw press. Later, they were removed and restacked to allow each sheet to be pressed again in contact with a new surface. Repeating this procedure several times gave additional smoothness to a sheet. Another method of applying pressure and polishing, but less commonly used, was by beating a group of papers with a mallet or hammer. All of these methods eventually gave way to the calender rolls which polished paper much more efficiently. According to the recent investigation of Julius Grant, calendering was introduced in England in 1830.

The Finished Paper

We are indebted to the early and highly skilled craftsman for producing such beautiful, and, in many cases, permanent papers. When first made, in all probability these papers were a very light cream color. This was due to the limitations of the bleaching methods then available. The previously mentioned Ruscelli of the sixteenth century stated that an ink made of powdered white egg shells which had been bleached in the sun would produce writing easily read on the whitest of papers. From this statement, it can be concluded that these early papers were never as white as we know paper today.

In addition to the good efforts of the papermaker, the inkmaker endeavored to make an ink that produced writing of great blackness and "splendor." The skill of the scribe also contributed to making many manuscripts real works of art. The occasional use of shining sand, which appeared to be fine particles of mica, gave some of the writings a unique sparkle. The creation of many early manuscripts required the best efforts of many skilled and artistic craftsmen.

Data Obtained by the National Bureau of Standards from Tests on Early Papers

In 1939, ten record papers of the seventeenth and eighteenth centuries were given to the National Bureau of Standards for testing. A summary of the results obtained are as follows: The fiber analyses revealed that "most of these [papers] appear to be all linen fibers but [samples] 9 and 10 obviously contain some cotton and the others may. The fibers are in such poor condition that definite differentiation between linen and cotton was not possible." The acidity of the eight papers low in physical strength varied from pH 4.0 to 4.3 by cold extraction, while those two papers in relatively good condition had pH 5.8 and 6.5. Eight of these papers had an ash content of from 0.8 to 4.2 percent, and six of these papers contained calcium carbonate or "any rare earth carbonates" in varying amounts. Since the acidity was high in the eight papers of low physical strength, it was natural to conclude that this was one of the principal causes of deterioration. This acidity and a high ash content caused some speculation as to the source of these compounds.

Other Test Data Obtained with the Assistance of Robb and Moody

About five years ago, the firm of Robb and Moody, chemists of Richmond, Virginia, were employed to analyze the ash of eight other papers of the seventeenth and eighteenth centuries. The ash varied from .99 to 4.18 percent, and was composed primarily of silicia, aluminum, calcium, magnesium, potassium, sulfates, phosphates, and small amounts of iron and sodium. The hypothetical combinations of these elements would indicate the presence of potassium aluminum sulfate or alum which was used in the sizing operation. The calcium and magnesium salts could have been carbonates, phosphates, and sulfates which likely came from first, the lye made of wood ashes used in bleaching the cloth; second, the water containing the bicarbonates of these metals used in the papermaking process; and third, the calcium could also be from chalk used in whitening the cloth after bleaching. The silica may have come from the above-mentioned lye, bleaching meadows, water, and many other sources. The iron also had many possible sources, but much of it may have been an impurity in the alum. In two papers, nickel was found which was possibly from pulverized greenish blue glass or a type of smalt used as bluing to camouflage the yellowed rags used in making the paper. In these two papers, relatively large amounts of silica were found which further indicated the presence of ground glass.

The tests for acidity and folding endurance of these eight papers were made in my laboratory. Two of these papers were in excellent condition, and had a high folding endurance. The acidity of the one made circa 1675 was quite low (pH 6.6) and the other, made circa 1722, was slightly alkaline (pH 7.6). In both papers, the amount of calcium and magnesium was much in excess of the aluminum and potassium. Originally, the calcium and magnesium salts were likely alkaline carbonates and phosphates, while the potassium and aluminum salts were the probable acid alum.

Three of these papers had a relatively low folding endurance, and the acidity was somewhat high, with a pH 4.5 to 4.7. The amounts of calcium and magnesium were only slightly more than the aluminum and potassium. The other three papers were very weak with almost no folds recorded on the testing machine. The acidity was much higher, with a range from pH 4.1 to 4.5. This was likely due to the acid alum, as the aluminum and potassium were in excess of the calcium and magnesium.

Findings of Other Investigators

It may be concluded from the preceding investigation that the predominating alkaline salts of calcium and magnesium have been a factor in the preservation of two of these papers. On the other hand, the acid alum ($AlK (SO_4)_2$) has had a deteriorative effect on the paper when occurring in sufficient quantities. Similar findings were made by Merle B. Shaw and Martin O'Leary of the National Bureau of Standards, when they added calcium carbonate as a filler to modern book papers and subjected them to artificial aging. The stability of these papers made with low-grade fibers was increased considerably by the addition of this carbonate.

The investigation of W. V. Torrey and E. Sutermeister of the S. D. Warren Company on three early Chinese and two European papers of the fifteenth and sixteenth centuries indicated that calcium compounds were in the two latter papers. They reported these two papers were alkaline and in good condition. Harry F. Lewis, of the Institute of Paper

Chemistry, also found calcium compounds in certain leaves of a book printed in 1576. These leaves were likewise alkaline and in good condition, while others in the same book were acid, discolored, and physically weak.

Conclusions

It may be concluded from these various tests on early papers that the investigators found that high acidity was associated with deterioration. On the other hand, when mildly alkaline calcium compounds, and in some instances, magnesium compounds, occurred in sufficient quantities, the papers were in good condition. These papers were either slightly alkaline or contained relatively little acid. Some of these investigators further concluded that these alkaline compounds had prevented the papers from becoming acidic due to various agents during storage. The historical and test data that I have presented indicate that one of the principal sources of this high acidity was alum in the sizing, and the alkaline compounds were from lye made of wood ashes for bleaching cloth, from hard water in the papermaking process, and from chalk for whitening the cloth.

3: INKS

W. J. Barrow

[*Editors' Note:* Table 1 has been omitted.]

THE writing inks of primary interest in this study are the blacks and the occasionally used reds and blues. The two common black writing fluids were composed of either carbon or iron and galls. The carbon ink was known to the Romans as *atramentum scriptorum*, and sometimes was called simply *atramentum*. It is the earliest known writing fluid. The iron ink was known as *encaustum* during the Middle Ages, later as iron gall ink, and today as gallotannate of iron. Recent investigations have indicated that it was used as early as the time of Christ, but did not come into general use until several centuries later. An examination of the ink formulae and manuscripts of the period 1400 to 1850 indicated that the iron gall ink, or *encaustum*, was used almost exclusively in the Occident.

Carbon Inks

The carbon inks were composed generally of either soot, lampblack, or some type of charcoal to which were added gum arabic and a solvent such as water, wine, or vinegar. The carbon blacks gave color to the ink and the gum arabic performed the following functions: it emulsified the oils in the blacks, gave vicosity to the fluid, helped to hold the carbon particles in suspension, and formed a binder to hold these particles to the document. This ink was usually kept in a powdered form, and water was added "when there was an occasion to write."

The carbon particles of this ink do not fade over a period of time and are unaffected by light rays and bleaching agents. As a rule, these particles and gum arabic contain no compounds which are considered injurious to paper. These properties are very much valued in inks. However, this ink has two capital imperfections which no doubt account for its limited use. It may smudge during damp weather, and it can be easily washed from the document. These characteristics must have alarmed the ancient and medieval scholars who realized that their manuscripts might, in time, suffer the same fate of earlier ones which were being de-inked to recover material for writing.

This factor may have prompted Pedanius Dioscorides (fl. A.D. 60), a Greek physician, scientist, and writer, or one of his predecessors, to add a little ferrous sulfate to his carbon ink. After a few days, the ferrous sulfate will convert gradually to a basic ferric sulfate and various oxides of iron to form a hard encrustation. This makes the characters more difficult to wash off. The addition of this chemical may account for many of the palimpsests in existence. It is a very soluble compound and would penetrate the fibers of the document to form, in due time, the brown, insoluble compounds mentioned above. When a document written in this type of ink was de-inked by washing, the brown compounds of iron remained on or below the surface of the sheet. Even a scraper, also used to remove writings, was not always fully effective without damaging the writing surface of the sheet.

It is also entirely possible that the ancients may have reasoned that if a little ferrous sulfate made their carbon ink less easily washed from a document, then more would do a better job. With much larger additions of this chemical, brown writing with black particles would result. This undesirable appearance could be corrected easily by the addition of galls, which would produce a mixture of both carbon and iron gall inks. They well understood that a black compound was produced when the extracts of galls, sumac, and so forth were added to either iron or copper sulfates. This principle was used in making hair dyes, blacking for shoes, and other items. More research is needed to substantiate this possible development of iron gall inks. Aurelius Cornelius Celsus (b. circa 25 B.C.), a Roman physician, and other contemporaries of Dioscorides used the *atramenti* to heal cuts and burns in the human body as well as for writing inks. In some of these formulae are found not only carbon and gum arabic, but also ferrous sulfate and galls. The addition of the latter two compounds could have been either to improve the aforementioned ink properties or for purely medicinal reasons.

Iron Gall Inks

The basic ingredients of *encaustum*, or iron gall inks, are copperas, galls, gum arabic, and a solvent such as water, wine, or vinegar. If compounded with the proper amount of gum arabic, this ink will flow easily from a quill pen and penetrate the fibers of the paper to form a black, insoluble compound. Writings made of these inks are difficult to bleach or remove from the paper without leaving some evidence of alteration. These were qualities highly valued in ink, and were often mentioned in the formulae as the principal reason for their use. The characteristics of this ink along with the nature of paper fibers make the de-inking of manuscripts, as practiced on vellum in the ancient era and the Middle Ages a highly impractical operation. Scholars should be grateful for both the introduction of paper and iron inks, for otherwise many early manuscripts would today be indecipherable palimpsests.

For many centuries, the ingredients of this highly valued ink have been essential in the development of pharmacy, tanning, dyeing, and many other processes. The production of many of these ingredients has changed but little basically during the past several hundred years.

Copperas

Today, copperas is technically known as ferrous sulfate, but during the period of this study (1400–1850) it was known by many other names, such as green vitriol, sal martis, sulfate of iron, copperas, and often as just vitriol. The ancients usually spoke of it as *chalkanthon*, but it was known also by other names, which no doubt accounts for some of the translators confusing it with copper sulfate. Gaius Plinius Secundus (A.D. 23–79), the famous Roman writer and scientist, recommended a streak test on papyrus which had been dipped previously in gall extract to distinguish these two compounds. The wide variations in the quantities prescribed in medicines also indicated that they well understood the difference.

Dioscorides and Pliny describe two methods of making copperas. One was by exposing certain yellow earths to the action of frost and rain water which was carried off and gradually evaporated. The other was the natural evaporation of water from certain wells in Spain which were known to contain ferrous sulfate. Each of these writers had a high regard for the crystals which were "azure" in color, and formed like a "bunch of grapes." A description of a process used in 1678, and similar to the first process described above, may be found in *Philosophical Transactions of the Royal Society* (XII, 1056). This consisted of oxidation of pyrites on exposure to air, and rain water was allowed to dissolve and carry off into a lead chamber the copperas and sulfuric acid formed in the process. Heating the solution with scrap iron produced a greater yield due to interaction of the iron and sulfuric acid.

Arthur and Charles R. Aikin of London stated in 1807 that the same process was followed in France, but in Germany no scrap iron was used. Since the use of this scrap iron varied from place to place, the amount of residual sulfuric acid in the copperas crystal would also vary. This may account, in some instances, for the high acidity found in some early writings. This, in turn, would cause deterioration in the cellulose fibers of paper.

The Aikins further state that this process had changed little since the reign of Queen Elizabeth. They and others recommended for ink making the use of the clear green crystals of copperas in preference to those containing ochre (basic ferric sulfate), which produces sediment in the ink.

Galls

Gall is an excrescence produced when the commonly called gall wasp punctures the bark of an oak tree and deposits an egg. When the larva develops, the tree produces the gall, which serves not only as a home but also as food for this insect. If the larva dies or leaves the gall at a certain stage, the tree discontinues the production of tannic and gallic acids within the gall. The highest content of these acids is attained just before the insect leaves its home by boring a hole through the wall of the gall. The extract of these galls contains tannic and gallic acids which combine with the iron in copperas to form the black pigment of iron gall inks.

The unperforated blue or Aleppo gall was the type usually recommended as it has the highest content of gallic and tannic acids. The brown English gall, "vulgarly called oak apples," and those of southern Europe were generally considered inferior to the Aleppo. According to the Aikins, Davy extracted 12.5 percent soluble matter from ordinary galls, and 46 percent from Aleppo, the latter extract containing about 90 percent gallic and tannic acids. Modern methods of extraction by Charles A. Mitchell and Thomas C. Hepworth have shown that the Aleppo contains 52.9 percent to 79.5 percent tannic and 3.2 percent to 11.2 percent gallic acids, while the British gall contains only 3.8 percent to 36.7 percent tannic and 0.0 percent to 1.5 percent gallic acids.

There were various methods used to properly extract the "virtue of the gall." Pietrus Maria Caneparius, a Venetian physician of the sixteenth and seventeenth centuries, recommended that galls be boiled as long as it takes to repeat the Pater Noster three times. In many instances, the formulae called for soaking the galls for four to twelve days in the sun in the summer, or by the fire in winter. Fermentation as well as heat was a factor in this extraction process. William Lewis, mid-eighteenth-century scientist of England, found through experimentation that a greater yield was obtained by reducing the galls to a powder than by the general practice of breaking them into several pieces. He, as well as some of the ancients, was aware that oak bark, sloe bark, sumac, pomegranate peels, and other plants contained these acids, but he was unable to extract them in sufficient concentration for making ink. One of the earliest mentions of galls was by Theophrastus (circa 370–285 B.C.), Greek scientist and author, who describes the different types and mentions their use in tanning and dyeing.

Gum Arabic

The acacia tree is the source of gum arabic, which according to the Aikins was imported from Egypt and the Levant. In describing this gum, they state that it "oozes" from the tree into round, yellowish-white drops about the size of a partridge egg. In the formulae, it is frequently referred to as gum. Caneparius called it the "tears of Arabia," and states that it gives body to the ink and keeps it from flowing too freely. Lewis attributes the following properties to gum arabic: it gives viscosity or body to make the ink flow well; it prevents the ink from spreading; and it suspends the coloring matter and does not sour easily.

The ancient ink formulae also contained gum arabic which was no doubt used not only to give proper viscosity to the writing fluid, but also in some cases as an adhesive to hold the ink particles to the manuscript. I have experimented with various inks and found that gum arabic is needed in ink when a reed or quill pen is used, but this is not true with the modern steel or fountain pen. Many of the modern ink chemists have not realized that the early chemist had a good understanding of the need of proper viscosity in a writing fluid, and they have in some cases incorrectly concluded that the only use of this gum in iron gall ink was for an adhesive.

Solvents

Rain water was the solvent most frequently recommended in the formulae for making iron gall ink as it was the purest water generally available. In a few instances, river or spring water was mentioned, but in areas of hard water, additional sedimentation would form in the ink if this water were used. Vinegar was suggested in a few formulae, but its acrid and unpleasant odor probably limited its use. White wine was second in popularity among the solvents. Lewis states that white wine gave a better color to ink when first made, and that this effect was more pronounced with vinegar. A slight increase in solubility of the gallic acid and a somewhat inhibiting effect on mold and bacteria might result due to the alcoholic content of wine. These relatively small virtues seem to lend themselves to forensic disputation. I have tried making ink with French white wine and, in my opinion, the delightful ethereal odor given off by this solvent is probably the principal reason for its frequent use. Since odors affect the brain, it may be appropriate to suggest using vinegar for the solvent when writing to an enemy, and wine when writing to a friend.

Ink Making

The aforementioned copperas, galls, gum arabic, and solvent were all needed to make an ink suitable for writing on paper with a quill pen. In compounding this ink, generally the galls were first placed in the solvent to extract the tannic and gallic acids, then the copperas and gum were added. The iron of the copperas combined with these two inorganic acids to form the black pigment, which today is called gallotannate of iron. The gum arabic gives viscosity to the fluid to produce an even flow from a quill pen, and also helps to prevent feathering of the writing should the paper be insufficiently sized. Besides the formation of the black pigment, gallotannate of iron, sulfuric acid was also formed during this chemical reaction. This acid is nonvolatile, and is injurious to paper fibers. Evidence of its detrimental effect on manuscripts will be presented later.

A copy of an interesting procedure for compounding this ink, circa 1483, was sent to me by Mr. L. C. Hector of the British Public Records Office, London. It may be found in that institution's Miscellanea of the Chancery 34/1/3, and is as follows:

To make hynke, take galle and coporos or vitrial (quod idem est) and gumme, of everyche a quartryn other half quartryn, and a half quartryn of galle more, and breke the galle a ij. or a iij., and put ham togedere everyche on in a pot, and stere it ofte. Wythinne ij. wykys after ʒe mowe wryte therwyth. Yf ʒe have a quartryn of everyche, take a quarte of watre; yf halfe a quartryn of everyche, than take half a quarte of watyr.

When first made, the above formula produces very pale writings, but if the ink is aged for two or more weeks, it has sufficient blackness to distinguish the characters as they are written. These characters continue to darken, and maximum blackness is reached within thirty days. On exposure to air, the gallotannate of iron oxidizes from the ferrous to the ferric state. In the ferrous state, it is relatively colorless, and in the ferric state, it is jet black. It was this factor that prompted the inkmakers to specify in most of the formulae that the ink be stirred intermittently for about two weeks.

It was during mid-eighteenth century that Lewis found a method of overcoming this problem of giving color to freshly made iron gall inks. He experimented with the addition of various berry juices, but found them detrimental to the color of the writing when exposed to sunlight. Logwood extract was the dye he found most satisfactory for this purpose, but it was gradually replaced by other dyes. If this ink were kept corked from the air, it had far fewer solid particles, and this made its use possible in a fountain pen.

None of the earlier formulae in table 1 specify the addition of indigo. However, a blue coloring material which appears to be indigo is occasionally found in writings previous to the study of Lewis. The most probable reason for its use was to give the needed color to freshly made iron gall ink. According to the recent work of Mitchell and Hepworth, indigo was used for this purpose by Eisler in 1770, and it was later used by other workers in this field.

The addition of aqua vitae, brandy, or spirits was frequently recommended to keep ink from freezing and breaking its container. Some of the eighteenth-century inkmakers condemned this addition due to the facts that the ink faded more quickly in an inkwell and had a tendency to feather on paper when writing. However, according to the literature, freezing was a serious problem in cold climates. It is of interest to note that Campbell E. Waters, of the National Bureau of Standards, did not encounter this difficulty when he froze ink in a refrigerator.

Ink Powders

The factors most likely responsible for the development of powdered or portable ink were the possibility of freezing and the difficulty of carrying a liquid ink on a journey. Gerolamo Ruscelli (d. 1566), Venetian scientist, and Caneparius both recommended powdering the ingredients of *encaustum* and adding as much soot "as you wish, or what may seem sufficient." When traveling, wine was added "when there was an urgent need to write." With so little time allowed to extract the gallic and tannic acids of the powered galls, this formula would basically produce a carbon ink similar to that of Dioscorides. Some gallotannate of iron would be produced by this procedure, but the amount would be small.

Another type of ink powder was made by evaporating the liquid iron gall ink in a *balneo mariae* (water bath) and powdering in residue. When a solvent was added, this ink would write as black as or blacker than it did before evaporation. A powder of this nature was compact, which made shipment much simpler, and molding and freezing were no problems under ordinary storage conditions. It was often advertised for sale in the newspapers of Virginia and other colonies during the eighteenth century, which indicates its use had become general.

It is not known when this procedure of making an ink powder was developed. Mitchell and Hepworth state that Holman was granted a patent in 1668 for its manufacture, but no description of the process was given. I have found small quantities of this powder in the inner margins of record books as early as 1680. The earliest description of the process found is in Robert Dossie's *The Handmaid to the Arts*, printed in 1764.

Ink Containers

Many different types of containers for storing ink were suggested by the early writers. Ink powders could be stored in almost any type of container, but paper offered a simple and inexpensive method of packaging. A communication in the Executive Papers deposited at the Virginia State Library, dated 19 December 1782, from L[eighton] Wood to James Simmons requesting "half dozen papers of Ink Powders" seems to substantiate this idea.

The containers for liquid ink were not so simple as those for ink powders, and were generally made of glass, metal, horn, or wood. Lewis warned against the use of copper or lead containers, and he recommended the use of an oaken cask as it has the same astringent materials (gallic and tannic acids) as found in galls. About one hundred and fifty-five years earlier, the recommendations of Caneparius were quite different, and were as follows: "Keep the ink in a lead vase, for lead increases the blackness. The ink can be kept, however, in a glass vase, if the vase is thoroughly cleaned. You can also keep it in a vitreous potter's vase, or in a gourd which has hardened with age. Container should be kept closed or at least covered, so as to keep out the dust which will mess up the ink in a marvelous manner."

Writings Made with Iron Gall Inks

The iron gall inks used during the period of this study have produced, in nearly all instances, writings which have retained good legibility. Those writings that have faded can, in most cases, be traced to adverse storage conditions. Light rays, mold, and bacteria are the principal agents in

this respect. Originally, such writings were black, but the majority of
them have gradually turned a rusty brown. It is difficult to say exactly
how long it takes for this change in color, but, in my opinion, the usual
time varies from about twenty-five to one hundred years. The factors
effecting this change are the proportions of the ink ingredients, the
amount deposited on the paper, and the composition of the paper. The
action of each of these factors may be accelerated by poor storage
conditions.

This color change takes place in writings produced from inks which
have been compounded with insufficient gallic and tannic acid in proportion to the amount of copperas. This improper ratio exists in many
of the formulae of table 1, which accounts for there being more brown
than black writing in early manuscripts. A good example of these in-
correct proportions may be found in the formula of Caneparius,[1] and it
is as follows:

Vini albi lib. iiii, aceti acerrimi cyathus unus, gallae fractae unc. ii. admis-
ceantur per quatuor dies, mox decoquantur vulcano usque ad evaporationem
ipsius quartae partis, tunc colentur, & colaturae addere licet gummae Arabicae
tritae unc. ii. & optime admiscendo exponatur igni, & bulliat tempore quo
dicerentur tres pater noster, hinc tollatur ab igne, & addatur Vitrioli Romani
triti unc. iii. assidue ligno agitando donec sit fere frigefactum, deinde re-
ponatur in cucurbita vitrea, quae optime clausa teneatur soli caeloq; sereno
per tres dies naturales, his expletis coletur atque servetur.

Lewis found that on exposure to sunlight, writings made of formulae
of this type soon turned brown, and that a ratio of one of copperas to
three of galls by weight gave the best results. This is in line with modern
methods of calculating the proper proportions of these compounds.

When documents are written with ink composed of insufficient gallic
and tannic acids, the excess ferrous sulfate slowly converts to a basic
ferric sulfate and complex oxides of iron. These rusty brown compounds
seem gradually to have an adverse effect on the black gallotannate of
iron and convert it to a similarly colored compound. I have found that
when exposed to sunlight, early specimens containing brown writing did
not fade any faster than the black, and both had better stability than new
writing of a similar formulae. It was also found that the old writings required stronger solutions of oxalic acid to eradicate them. This investigation indicates that these iron compounds are like many other chemicals
which become more inert over a long period of time.

For several centuries, there have been some custodians of manuscripts
and some scientists who have assumed that when writings become yel-

1. The ingredients and their proportions may be found in table 1.

lowed, this change of color was an intermediate step between the original black and complete obliteration. If this were true, the majority of the manuscripts written during the early period of this study would now be indecipherable. As previously stated, nearly all of these early manuscripts are today highly legible. This fact, along with the aforementioned inertness of rusty brown writings certainly does not justify thinking that there will be further fading if such manuscripts are properly stored.

This change in color of writings from black to brown prompted Caneparius and later scientists to attempt to revive the so-called faded ink to its original blackness. The use of gallic acid, tannic acid, ammonium sulfide, and other compounds has been tried, and in all cases the revival either was unsuccessful, badly stained the paper, or left residual compounds which may be injurious to the premanency of the manuscript. Other interesting attempts to revive faded writings are described in *Patologia e terapia del libro* by Dr. Alfonso Gallo of the Instituto di Patologia del Libro. These various treatments are to be avoided, with a few exceptions, and then they should be carried out by one who has a good understanding of the many factors involved.

The Effects of Iron Gall Ink on the Permanency of Paper

Since Latin was the scientific language of the medieval period, it was only natural that the appropriate name of *encaustum* was given to the inks made of copperas and galls. *Encaustum* means "to burn in," which is characteristic of these inks. In fact, the sulfuric acid produced by the interaction of ferrous sulfate and the organic acids of the galls does burn into the paper, and in some cases where there are heavy deposits of ink, it burns a hole through the paper. The oxidation of paper by sulfuric acid, found in concentrated iron gall inks, is much slower but similar to that produced by fire. If this acid is present in sufficient quantities, it will migrate to surrounding areas of writing, and in time produce a dark brown, and in some instances, almost black discoloration in the paper. The latter condition is found only occasionally, but it is accompanied by extreme embrittlement of the paper, poor visibility of the writing, and difficulty in photographing. Even when the concentration of this acid is not quite so great, it still migrates to adjacent sheets, discoloring the fibers and producing reversed brown writing. In some instances, this causes confusion when reading a photographic reproduction.

It is entirely possible that observation of this migration prompted the development of letter-press copies. Occasionally, examples are found in which the acid has migrated to the opposite side of a sheet and produced brown writing not reversed. The principle of making these copies consisted of effecting rapid migration of the soluble gallotannate of iron in the ferrous state from the document to the thin copy sheet. This was accomplished by moistening the thin sheet and pressing it in contact with the original until both were somewhat dry. In due time, this migrated ink would oxidize to the black ferric state. Sometimes sugar was added to slow the drying in writings. This sugar and also gum arabic frequently caused adhesion of some of the black ink particles to the copy sheet. This was an aid in producing blackness to the letter-press copy, but the best copies were those in which migration had taken place.

Lewis was the first to write about high acidity in iron inks, and also the first to conclude that this was the cause of deterioration in many manuscripts. He tried using lime to neutralize this acid, but it adversely affected other needed properties in the inks. Placing pieces of iron in the ink was recommended for this purpose, and this did decrease the amount of acid present in the ink, but it also increased the content of copperas.

A nonacid iron ink was first discovered in 1908 by Silberman and Ozorovitz of Rumania, but a practical method of manufacture was made possible only recently by the work of the Organic Section of the National Bureau of Standards and the laboratory of the United States Government Printing Office. This new ink is composed of iron, ammonia, and gallic acid, and is technically known as diammonium hydroxyferrigallate. I have used this ink in my fountain pen for the past six years, and have found it unnecessary to clean this pen during that time. On the other hand, difficulties may be encountered if other types of iron inks are used in the pen without a thorough cleaning. While this is the greatest improvement made in iron gall inks during the past two hundred years, unfortunately it has not been placed on the market by manufacturers. The future custodian would benefit considerably from this development if its adoption should become general in creating records.

In a recent study of inks, Elmer W. Zimmerman, Charles G. Weber, and Arthur E. Kimberly of the National Bureau of Standards found that the mineral acid of iron inks was detrimental to the permanency of paper. Their experiments indicated that copperas was also injurious to paper, but that the other ingredients, such as gum arabic and tannic and gallic acids, had no adverse effect.

The studies and data previously presented might make one think that all manuscripts are suffering ill effects from iron gall inks. This is not true, but it does raise the question as to why some iron inks have caused deterioration while others have not produced any adverse effects. This prompted me to undertake a study of early ink formulae, and the data collected, as well as the results of experimentation, were published in 1948 (see Ink Bibliography).

A survey was made of early manuscripts to determine whether the brown or black writing was the most injurious to paper. Among several hundred manuscripts examined, fifty were found in which the ink had eaten holes through the paper. Three contained brown writing, and forty-seven contained black writing, which was a strong indication that the black writing was the most injurious. Tests were made on fifteen samples of seventeenth- and eighteenth-century manuscript fragments, and, as a rule, the black writings were much more acid than the brown writings. With one exception, the uninked margins were less acid than the inked areas, and in this exception, the pH was the same.

This finding was then further confirmed by preparing two inks, one with sufficient tannic and gallic acid to give permanent black writing, and another with only one-fourth as much of these acids, which will produce brown writing in a matter of time. After artificial aging of 72 hours at 100° C., papers containing lines drawn with the permanent black ink exhibited much greater decrease in the folding test and were more acid than those containing the ink which in time produces the brown writing. Each of these inks contained six grams of copperas per 100 cc. of distilled water, which is considered quite concentrated for present-day ink, although many formulae in table 1 specify much greater concentration.

When the amount of copperas is the same in two given inks, then more sulfuric acid is produced in the one containing sufficient tannic and gallic acids to react with all of the iron in the copperas than in the other ink with insufficient tannic and gallic acids which react with only part of the iron present. In other words, the amount of sulfuric acid produced is in relation to the amount of tannic and gallic acid present to react with the quantity of iron in the copperas. This, in turn, accounts for black writing being usually more acid and injurious to paper than brown writing.

It was concluded from this study that most concentrated inks which produced the black writing were the most damaging to the permanency of the paper. These inks were naturally the most acid, and there are several formulae in table 1 which would make inks of this type. Two other factors sometimes causing increased acidity were residual sulfuric acid in the copperas and evaporation of a portion of the solvent in an inkwell. Large amounts of this concentrated ink deposited in relatively small areas are also a large factor in manuscript deterioration. This can be caused by the use of a broad penpoint, close writing, and the utilization of both sides of a sheet for writing.

Many early manuscripts written with iron gall ink are in a good state of preservation. These manuscripts have relatively little or no acidity in them. Some of the factors which contribute to this condition are a narrow pen point, formation of large letters, writing on only one side of the paper, a low concentration of ink ingredients, no residual sulfuric acid in the copperas, and alkaline salts present in the paper. It will be shown later that many early papers contain alkaline salts which sometimes existed in sufficient quantities to neutralize a portion or most of the acidity in moderately acid inks.

Among those manuscripts needing restoration, many show some evidence of discoloration and deterioration from acid inks. In a few cases, the acidity of iron gall inks had been the entire reason for the need of restoration, as the inked areas are in a crumbling condition while the uninked margins are in an excellent state of preservation. With the exception of deterioration by microorganisms, fire, and light rays, acid inks have been a contributing factor in the embrittlement of a large majority of manuscripts. Unless some method of eliminating or neutralizing this nonvolatile acid is effected, it will continue its activity until the paper fibers are reduced to dust. Procedures for deacidification will be presented later.

Red Ink

Extract of brazilwood was the coloring material most frequently used in making red ink. The raspings of this wood were allowed to soak for several days in either vinegar or urine. Gum arabic was then added to give proper viscosity for writing. Most of the formulae recommended the addition of alum, which has an adverse effect on the permanency of paper.

In John Barrow's *Dictionarium Polygraphium* of 1735, there may be found a typical example of making red ink from brazilwood, and it is as follows: "To make Red writing INK. Take rasping of Brazil one ounce, white lead and alum of each 2 drams; grind and mingle them, infuse them in urine one pound, with 2 scruples of gum arabick, or a dram at most."

This dye is highly soluble when first extracted, but after about two hundred years, writings made of this ink become relatively insoluble. This is another example of the decreased solubility of a compound as time passes. After a few decades, these writings lose their brightness, becoming a dull reddish brown, but only a few have become undecipherable due to fading.

According to the recent studies of William F. Leggett, brazilwood was known in the medieval period, and was imported from India. When the Portuguese discovered the east central part of South America, they named this country "Terra de Brazil" due to the abundance of these trees growing along the shores.

In addition to the extract of brazilwood, vermilion was another source for producing red ink. Vermilion is mercury sulfide, and is insoluble in water. It was first powdered and "sufficient to give a good color" was added to water or vinegar. The glair of eggs or gum water was also added to give viscosity and to act as an adhesive for the insoluble particles. The egg glair softens more slowly than gum arabic under high humidity, which made some of the writings less likely to smudge than others. According to Mitchell, this red ink was frequently used by the Romans to make their capital letters.

Blue Inks

Indigo was known to the Romans as *indicum*, and was classified by several of their early writers as one of the *atramenti*. It has been used not only in inks, but also in paints, medicines, cosmetics, dyeing, bluing cloth and paper, etc. A. Lucas questions the general use of indigo by the ancients for dyeing, but thinks it was used as an ink. Dr. P. K. Gode, of Poona, India, is now trying to establish the earliest possible date of its manufacture and export to the West. Indigo was first made in India and comes from the leaf of *Indigofera tinctoria*, a member of the order Leguminosae. It was known to the Incas, and, like cochineal and brazilwood, was one of the early dyes exported from the Americas.

There are relatively few formulae to be found for making blue ink from indigo. These formulae recommended that powdered indigo be added to water containing gum arabic. Its color holds up well over a period of time, but writings made of this ink smudge during damp weather, and can be washed from the paper.

These indigo writings are unaffected by certain microorganisms that are very damaging to some inks. Recently, I had the opportunity to inspect several moldy manuscripts from tropical Guatemala and Honduras. In some areas of these manuscripts, the iron inks were obliterated, but the indigo ink was unaffected. Some dyes inhibit the growth of microorganisms, and this may account for the use of indigo by the early

Roman physicians in treating cuts and burns. Another unusual property of this type of writing is that it turns a bright blue when first laminated with cellulose acetate film, but gradually reverts to its original color within a few weeks or months. For detailed information, consult *The Library of Congress Quarterly Journal*, vol. X, no. 1 (November, 1952). The cause of this change is not definitely known, but it is thought that under heat, a very minute amount of the residual acetic acid of this film reduces a small amount of the indigo blue to indigo white. There are others who think that this could be caused by the slight solvent action of the plasticizer or a trace of sulfurous acid in the film. Applying the plasticizers to prepared specimens did not produce this change, however, and the manufacturer of the film used doubted that there was any sulfurous acid present. Regardless of the cause of this change, in time this indigo white oxidizes back to its original color.

Prussian blue (ferric ferrocyanide) was not discovered until the latter part of the seventeenth century, and it did not replace indigo as a blue ink until about the mid-eighteenth century. It gained considerable popularity as a writing ink after 1800. The formulae specified the addition of powdered Prussian blue to gum water to make a suitable writing fluid. This iron ink is unlike the iron ink made with galls as it has exhibited no evidence of injury to paper. While writings of this ink are relatively unaffected by light rays and bleaching agents, it does smudge when damp and is affected by moderately strong alkali. Many of the writings made with this ink a hundred or more years ago still retain a high degree of luster.

Printing Ink

The ink used for early printing was composed of a pigment and a vehicle such as boiled linseed oil. Soot or some other carbon black was used in making the black inks, and the colored ones contained the pigments usually used by artists. The linseed oil served as the binder for these inks, and it oxidized and polymerized into an insoluble compound after its application to paper. These printing inks resemble the paints used by the artist more than the writing inks used by the scribe.

The black printing inks made of carbon and boiled linseed oil are the most permanent of all inks. They are not affected by light rays and bleaching agents, they are insoluble in water, and they are difficult to remove from a document without leaving evidence of alteration. If the linseed oil is properly prepared, it is not considered injurious to the permanency of the paper. Occasionally, a book is found in which there has been migration and discoloration of the oils, but this has been attributed by several to the use of fish oil or some other substitute. As a rule, these early black printing inks have held up well, and only occasionally is one found in which the binder has been injurious to the paper.

According to Caneparius, printers of his time made their ink with a varnish containing Arabian sandarac and flaxseed or nut oil which was boiled with the soot of pitch. He states that this was an improvement over a formula of soot of pitch and flaxseed oil recommended by Antonius Musa Brasarola (1500–1555), an Italian physician, botanist, and author. Caneparius further states that another ink, which he describes as almost a perpetual crust (*fere perpetuum Stuchum*), was used to fill the engraved letters on marble tablets, etc., and was composed of flaxseed oil and pitch. It is entirely possible that the early printing inks evolved from this so-called almost perpeutal crust, or ink, as they are similar in composition, and the latter was used for several centuries before the invention of printing from movable type. Caneparius thought that Brasarola was of a similar opinion, as the latter states that the ink of the chalcographer became the ink of the typographer.

Joseph Moxon recommended in his *Mechanick Exercises* (1683) that the oil be boiled, but that setting fire to it was unnecessary. He also recommended that one-half to one pound of rosin be added to each gallon of oil. He and his successors of the eighteenth century advocated the addition of bread and onions to the oil when it was boiled. Hard soap makes its appearance in the literature in the earlier part of the following century. A thorough search for early printing ink formulae and a study as to the effects of their components on paper have never been made. Information resulting from such an investigation is greatly needed by those interested in the restoration and preservation of documents.

Other Inks

There were other writing fluids described in the literature as inks, but there is very little evidence that they were used for writing purposes. In most cases, they should be classified as water colors for illuminating manuscripts and other decorative purposes. The data on the commonly used black, red, and blue inks have been presented to give the archivist and librarian a better understanding of the various characteristics of the writings which are in their custody. A broader knowledge of ink properties will assist the custodian in evaluating good storage conditions and restoration procedures for books and manuscripts.

Summary

Among the inks discussed in this chapter, the iron gall ink has proved to be far more damaging to papers than any of the other inks. It is impossible to make this ink by the old formulae without creating sulfuric acid, which is the principal, or at least a contributing agent to the deterioration of many manuscripts needing restoration. Writings made with iron gall ink have turned a rusty brown in many instances, but these complex oxides of iron are very stable compounds under normal storage conditions. As a whole, iron gall ink may be considered the best record ink developed.

The carbon, indigo, Prussian blue, and vermilion inks have good color stability, but they smudge easily during very damp weather, and can be washed from the paper. The water-soluble red extract of brazilwood is not light-fast, but as time passes it becomes less soluble and has retained its color reasonably well under favorable storage conditions. As a whole, printing inks have exhibited relatively little injury to paper, but more research is needed regarding their effects on paper. Also, additional research is needed on the other inks mentioned above.

4: ADHESIVES

W. H. Langwell

UNTIL comparatively recently the whole question of adhesion was treated in an empirical manner. During the last few decades, however, a much more systematic development has been evident, probably because the new synthetic adhesives have been developed by firms with well-equipped research laboratories. The development has not yet gone far enough to place the subject on a scientific basis, but it has progressed far beyond the rule-of-thumb empiricism of a generation ago.

In the past, the bookbinder was content with two adhesives—starch paste and glue. Today, he can still prepare both these materials in a form good enough for permanent archive work, but if he wishes to use one of the multitude of ready-prepared pastes he is likely to be very much embarrassed by the enormous variety to choose from. The newer synthetics are, in most cases, so very different from the old-fashioned pastes and glues that, in the absence of guidance, he may be excused for avoiding them for permanent records.

Since the question of adhesives for archives is so important, and since the development of new adhesives is likely to be accelerated in the future, the following short general account of the principles of adhesion, as applied to adhesives, should give the archivist and bookbinder a sound background against which to judge present and future developments in this field.

The use of adhesives in bookbinding should be regarded as a necessary evil, on the principle that joints are potential sources of weakness. It is not so much that the adhesive itself may be weak but that the contact between it and the materials to be joined may be so. Furthermore, most adhesives dry to a hard, horny layer which, in the case of paper, will usually have an abrupt edge, thus, if the paper is bent it will, in all probability, bend sharply about this edge, concentrating most of the stress along it and causing it eventually to crack. This, perhaps, is the strongest argument against single-page binding, no matter how good the adhesive or how strong the paper.

Adhesives hold two paper surfaces together, either by mechanical or chemical binding or both. In mechanical binding, the adhesive is forced into minute undercut hollows in the surface of the paper to which it is applied and, on drying, these form hard dumb-bell-like anchors in the substance of the paper. This action can be rendered visible by suitable magnification of a cross-section of a glued paper or wood joint.

The chemical binding is rather more difficult to explain in simple terms, but it can be illustrated quite simply by applying thin paste to clean paper and to paper thoroughly impregnated with wax. The clean paper will be "wetted" by the paste while the waxed paper, with its chemically-different surface, actually repels the paste. If the adhesive fulfils the requirements of both actions in a high degree it is likely to give a comparatively strong joint. This is seen in the case of two layers of paper properly pasted together when, after drying, the joint will be found to be stronger than the paper and, when torn apart, the break will be in the paper and not in the paste.

The first essential, therefore, of a good adhesive is that it shall wet the surfaces to be joined; otherwise the joint will be weak, as in the case of the joint between paste and wax. In order that the adhesive shall have a good chance of wetting the surfaces, assuming that it is capable of so doing, it must be fluid or plastic at some stage of making the joint. For example, if the glue in a joint is allowed to cool and set before the joint is made it will lose most of its adhesiveness and a weak joint will result.

However, once the two parts of the joint have been brought together, the quicker the glue sets the sooner the joint can be handled without damaging it, and the sooner the glue dries, the sooner the joint will reach its final strength. There should therefore be three stages in the setting of an adhesive: a fluid stage for free manipulation, a quick initial set after the joint has been brought into position, and a final set to reach maximum strength.

Practical adhesives vary greatly in their "sets," as regards both the time and the conditions under which they take place. Sometimes the initial set takes place by cooling, as with glue, sometimes by evaporation, as with paste. The final set, so far as adhesives used by the archivist are concerned, usually takes place by evaporation. This type of setting almost always results in shrinkage which, if severe, may cause the adhesive to shrink away from the surfaces of the joint and leave it weak or defective.

A further essential, though it is perhaps rather an academic point, is that the adhesive should itself be about as strong as the materials to be joined. For instance, wax will make a joint between two steel surfaces if applied hot and allowed to cool, but such a joint would be too weak to have much practical value owing to the comparative weakness of the wax.

Finally, if an adhesive makes the paper to which it is applied too wet, it can cause severe cockling, due to uneven or excessive expansion, and may give trouble on drying. If these considerations are borne in mind it should be easier to understand the properties of practical adhesives than it would otherwise have been.

STARCH PASTES

Starch paste may have been used by the Egyptians to join sheets of papyrus into long rolls; it is still one of the most commonly-used adhesives for paper. The obvious reason for this long vogue is that it satisfactorily fulfils the many practical requirements for an adhesive and does so cheaply.

Starch paste, especially in some of its modern modifications, has a wide range of useful properties as an adhesive for paper and leather and, though it may not allow of the speed of working possible with animal glues, it has the compensating advantage of greater convenience. If one part of almost any flour or, better still, starch is mixed with ten parts of water and heated to boiling point an excellent paste can be obtained. Provided it is used before gelling and reversion sets in and before active mould growth spoils it, it would be difficult to improve on this simple and inexpensive paste.

Most modern modifications are aimed at improving its flow qualities, by preventing or retarding the onset of gelling by preserving it against mouldiness and putrefaction or by increasing the resistance of the finished joint to moisture. It is useful, when departing from the simple paste, to keep these factors in mind and not accept extra trouble or cost which cannot be offset by some compensating advantage.

Industrial Paste Manufacture

Ready-made pastes are very attractive to the archivist. They can be made with an amazing variety of properties to cover a wide range of individual requirements and they save the trouble and mess involved in the home-made product. Against these advantages must be placed the disadvantages of extra cost, uncertainty of composition and possible unsuitability for permanent archive work. The following notes should give some idea of the range of commercial pastes available, with their good and bad points.

In industrial practice, the best pastes are made from starches and only the cheaper grades from the less pure flours. The flours contain much of the gluten of the grain or tuber from which they were made and, consequently, pastes made from them are much more liable to putrefaction than those made from the highly purified starches. Furthermore, the flours sometimes impart an undesirable colour to the paste. The starches most commonly used are tapioca, sago, corn (maize), white potato and, more recently, waxy maize and sweet potato. There is a strong family resemblance between them all, though they differ to a small extent and each has a field in which it best fulfils requirements.

If ten per cent pastes are made from any of these starches they will not differ much while still warm. On cooling, however, only the paste from rice starch and waxy maize will remain fluid for any length of time; the rest will set to gels at varying rates. If the paste is to be applied with a brush, the fluid condition is much more desirable and, consequently, with the gelling pastes it is usual to stir or beat them on cooling to break down the gel structure and render them more brushable. After gelling, most pastes shrink and exude a certain amount of clear liquid—the so-called reversion.

Natural starches are often modified to give pastes with special properties, usually an increase in the starch to water ratio. For example, if the starch is treated with either alkali, acid or oxidizing agents, it can be made much more soluble in water and the normal 1 to 10 ratio can be increased to as much as 1 to 1 without making the paste too stiff to work. Another very common method of achieving the same result is to roast the starch, either with a small amount of acid at moderate temperatures or without acid at higher temperatures, to produce the range of white and yellow dextrins and British gums. The latter, at the end of the range, are completely soluble in cold water and give clear solutions which are still fluid at a 1 to 1 ratio.

As a result of these treatments, a wide range of properties, apart from the starch to water ratio, can be made available. The tackiness, initial set, water sensitivity and spreading power can all be varied to suit the requirements of different spreading mechanisms and of the different materials to be joined. Any archivist, whose consumption of paste is sufficiently high to make it worth while, can have his special requirements catered f. often at moderate cost.

The small user who cannot expect to command this special treatment will usually have to make his own paste and there is no reason why he should not fare as well as the larger user. If he buys ready-made pastes he will have to take them without knowing whether they may contain excess acid, alkali, oxidizing agent or any of the many antiseptics and fungicides available to the paste-maker. In the section dealing with the practical aspect of small-scale paste-making, the preparation of a few representative pastes is described (*see* p. 78).

Home-Made Pastes

These home-made pastes can be given properties which are especially suitable for permanent archive work and can be used without the risk attending the use of commercial pastes. A few general remarks on home-made pastes might be of interest here. It is doubtful if anything can surpass well made starch paste for simplicity in preparation, cheapness and effectiveness for paper and leather. There is a fairly close chemical similarity between the cellulose of paper and the starch of the paste, while the water is an excellent medium for preparing the paper to receive the starch.

Acid is the arch-enemy of paper, affecting its durability perhaps more than any other single factor, while starch, owing to its less highly organized structure, seems to suffer less severely. For this reason, paste should not be made with alum or any other acid antiseptic or preservative. The effect of the alum is to break down the starch molecule sufficiently to enable a higher starch to water ratio to be reached. A much better way of doing this is to add white dextrine to a straight starch paste. A ratio of 1 to 1 can be reached in this way.

When paste is prepared every few days there should not be much need for an antiseptic. But for paste that is to last for a week or longer, pure phenol (carbolic acid) should be used. (It has a much more effective antiseptic action than alum.) This substance, even in its pure form (ice crystals), tends to turn pink; if this is objectionable it can be avoided by using an equal amount of salicylanilide in place of the phenol. One commercial form of salicylanilide is known as "Shirlan."

Practical bookbinders often use mixtures of paste and glue for certain purposes, chiefly because the paste slows down the initial set of the glue while the glue imparts tack and quicker initial set to the paste. If pastes are prepared with a small proportion of glue they revert much more slowly than unmixed pastes. Some of the synthetics, such as methylcellulose and carboxymethycellulose (C.M.C.), are superior to glue in this respect. Formulæ embodying these suggestions are given on page 79.

Cold Water Starches

These are starches so modified as to give acceptable pastes on merely mixing with cold water. They are used largely by paper-hangers and decorators and are suitable for rough work generally. They frequently consist of modified starches or starches gelatinized by heating with a minimum amount of water: if the added water is kept low enough the final product will remain in the form of a loose powder while the bulk of the individual grains will be burst and gelatinized. They give rather coarse-grained pastes and, besides starch, may contain dextrins, other modified starches and various antiseptics and modifying agents. They are un-desirable for permanent archive work because of the uncertainty of their composition, but for convenience they could hardly be beaten.

GLUES AND GELATINES

Glues and gelatines are made from animal skins and bones. The essential difference between the two lies in the greater purity of the gelatine. Most glues and gelatines could be accommodated in the range bounded by the very pure photographic gelatines at the one end of the scale and by scotch glue at the other.

The skins used are generally the trimmings cut from the hides and skins to be used for tanning. They are soaked in lime to remove hair and then further soaked in strong limes until well swollen, whereupon they are thoroughly washed in successive lots of water, at increasing temperatures, until most of the lime has been removed and systematically extracted. The liquors are concentrated to the required strength and allowed to cool and set to a jelly which is cut into sheets or slabs and dried in the air. The best products come from the lowest temperature extraction. When bones are used they are treated in dilute acids to remove the mineral matter from them, after which they are treated in the same way as the skins.

ALBUMEN

Albumen is usually made from slaughterhouse tankage (blood); it is in fact dried blood serum. It is not heated during its preparation so that it remains soluble in water.

CASEIN

Casein is the albumen extracted from milk. Milk is curdled by natural or artificial means and the curds, consisting largely of casein, are collected, dried at low temperature and ground to powder.

Only the glues are of much interest to the bookbinder and the archivist. The casein adhesives, so useful for wood, can only be made workable by adding fairly strong alkalis and this rules them out for use with paper and vellum. When these adhesives have dried and set they have the advantage of being rather less affected by moisture than glues. Albumen, too, is not used by the binder as an adhesive because it requires heat to set it. When set it also is less moisture-sensitive than the glues. Gelatine could be used in place of glue but, besides being more expensive, its initial set takes place too rapidly for convenience. Thus, in practice, glue is the only one of this class of animal adhesives which finds a use in archive work.

GENERAL PROPERTIES OF GLUES

The most useful properties of glues, from the bookbinder's point of view, are their moderately rapid initial set and high "solids to water" ratio. In practice, this means that the binder can work much faster using glue than he can when using paste, since he can handle glued joints very soon after making them. The high solids ratio means that cockling is reduced to a minimum.

Although paste can usually replace glue when time is not important, glue has a special value for rounding and backing because it passes through a plastic range just before becoming air dry. This gives the glued spine of a book a very convenient malleability, facilitates the rounding and reduces the liability to "starts."

Thin hot glue has a greater power of penetration into paper than paste, a property which gives it a better mechanical hold by the "dumb-bell" effect. The high solids ratio enables glue to fill the gap between poorly fitting surfaces, a distinct advantage when carefully surfaced joints are not possible.

All glues consist of gelatine more or less modified by heating and more or less contaminated by non-gelatine from the skin, bones, etc., used in their manufacture. Good glue can be made from either skin or bones and it would be a very poor glue indeed that would not be strong enough for joining paper, boards, leather and other bookbinding materials. Generally speaking glue, if used correctly, has mechanically much greater strength than the binder can possibly need, but it saves time.

Gelatine is the constituent responsible for the malleability of glue and, usually, the higher the proportion of gelatine in a glue the shorter is the time of initial set and the sooner the joint can be handled. At the same time, a high gelatine glue can set too rapidly and require great skill in handling if weak joints are to be avoided. Repeated heating of glue, as often happens to the glue in a gluepot which is not being frequently replenished and cleaned out, will degrade the gelatine and lengthen the time of initial set and may ultimately give an adhesive with little more set than paste.

Small amounts of acid and alkali are used in glue manufacture but are generally removed before the glue comes on the market. Modern glues are often sold in pearls, cubes or powder. The use of these forms, provided that the glue itself is of good quality, is to be strongly recommended because they soften and swell rapidly in cold water and melt smoothly without prolonged heating.

A very satisfactory glue for bookbinders is a light coloured cabinet maker's glue. This is rather high in gelatine and may set too rapidly for some purposes; this is easily remedied by adding a little phenol (carbolic acid) which has the added advantage of preserving the glue and rendering it somewhat less palatable to insect and other pests.

FLEXIBLE GLUES

Flexible glues are often used by the binder, especially for the less important books where the glue remains as the "backing." They are usually ordinary glues containing glycerine or, according to more modern usage, sorbitol. The softening effect of the latter substance, which is prepared from sugar, is supposed to last longer than that of glycerine but it is doubtful whether flexible glues are really required for the most durable bindings. It should be borne in mind that these softening agents, "humectants," owe their efficacy to the fact that they absorb moisture from the air and, in extreme cases, they may absorb so much that there will be a risk of mould growth on the glue, even under such abnormal conditions, unless sufficient antiseptic has been added to prevent this happening.

LIQUID GLUES

There are a number of ways of lowering the setting temperature of glues and it is possible to carry the lowering to the stage where the glues remain liquid at room temperature. Where large surfaces have to be glued and sound joints are essential, as, for example, in building up the laminated wood airplane propellers, the time of initial set must be lengthened for practical reasons. A special glue containing cresol has proved itself to be very satisfactory for this purpose for, though it is not liquid at room temperatures, it has a very low melting point and correspondingly long setting time.

In addition, the use of cresol, or other phenol of this type, acts as an effective antiseptic and enables the glue to be marketed with the correct amount of water and ready for use after gentle warming. Such glues would be satisfactory for the binder though they might not be as good as the acetic acid glues for rounding since they seem to have a rather short range of malleability.

Acetic acid glues can be made to remain liquid at room

temperatures but since this involves the use of rather an excessive amount of acetic acid a convenient compromise is to use sufficient to give a glue which sets at about 60°F.

Acetic acid is not sufficiently strong to damage paper and it disappears during the drying, leaving a more or less normal glue behind. This glue gives satisfactory results for rounding and backing and is well worth a trial; it is liquid at the usual workshop temperatures and avoids the necessity for the conventional gluepot which is hardly a practical proposition for the small binder who only occasionally needs glue.

The acetic acid content will slowly corrode the tin-plate and copper of brushes so care should be taken to wash these after use. It might also affect the colour of some papers and linens; these materials should, therefore, be tested before the glue is used. The gluepot is a "messy" piece of apparatus, except where it is in constant use by a careful worker, and, with a little ingenuity, it should be possible to dispense with the need for glue, except for rounding and backing and for some rather open-textured linens.

VEGETABLE GLUES AND GLUE SUBSTITUTES

Some starch adhesives, such as yellow dextrins and British gums, can be dissolved in water to give a high enough "solids to water" ratio to justify their use as a substitute for glue in certain cases. They lack the rapid and clear-cut initial set of glue but, with some practice, they can be made to give fairly satisfactory results and they offer the great advantage of always being ready for instant use, thus avoiding the need for the gluepot. As the making of these special pastes will be rather beyond the capacity of the ordinary binder's workshop, the commercial products will normally have to be used and this raises the difficulty of deciding whether they contain anything likely to be detrimental to permanent archives.

MISCELLANEOUS ADHESIVES

The adhesives listed here are, generally, of rather more limited value to the bookbinder than glue or paste.

Gum Arabic

Solutions of gum arabic in water have long been used as adhesives for paper. They are not of much interest to the bookbinder, though the archivist may occasionally come across them. Their chief use is for postage stamps and general office purposes. They produce clear, easy brushing solutions which have no marked initial set but pass through a tacky stage on drying. The properties for which they are most prized are ready solution in water after drying, so that stamps and envelope flaps only need moistening to give good and rapid adhesion, and their agreeable flavour. They will normally be too "moisture sensitive" for permanent work, though their readiness for immediate use, cleanliness and ease of application with a brush make them convenient for less important documents. They have an advantage over the cheaper British gums of not becoming sticky on exposure to a moist atmosphere.

Gum Strip

These modern string substitutes have recently become popular for sealing packages and similar rough jobs for which they are very suitable. They are not likely to be used for archives though there are many unimportant uses to which they may be put. Like all "re-moistening" adhesives they are necessarily moisture sensitive and joints made with them can readily be unmade by moistening them with water, though not with non-aqueous solvents.

Rubber Adhesives

Rubber solutions in naphtha or carbon tetrachloride are sometimes used as temporary adhesives for paper and cardboard. On drying, the film of rubber which remains has a small holding power, often good enough for certain purposes. Their chief advantage is that the film of rubber can readily be rubbed or pulled off, when it has served the temporary need, without damaging the surface of the paper or cardboard. Their chief interest to the bookbinder is a historical one. About 1880, rubber "solution" was used as the adhesive for single-sheet bindings, which showed signs of becoming popular about this time, because of its cheapness and the very agreeable flexibility of the bound book.

Unfortunately, the rubber gradually perished and, after a few years, the books became piles of loose sheets again. Most libraries still have some examples of these epitaphs to the bookbinder's optimism. This single-sheet binding—the so-called "perfect" binding—is being revived at the present time using the modern synthetic adhesive polyvinyl acetate in place of rubber. These bindings are less likely to fail through the perishing of the adhesive but are just as likely to do so through other inherent weaknesses. They will be mentioned again when synthetic adhesives are being considered.

Synthetic Adhesives

Modern synthetic adhesives are a somewhat numerous class and, although they have mostly been advocated for joints where waterproofness is important, they are in general less convenient to use and more expensive than glues and pastes.

The occasions on which the adhesive used in bookbinding is likely to be called upon to withstand actual wetting are extremely rare and may in normal practice be disregarded, although there are cases of stores of valuable books being under water due to fire or the bursting of water mains, when the use of a more water- and rot-proof adhesive than glue might possibly have saved them. However, as paper itself is neither waterproof nor water-resistant, the binder will probably find glue and paste more satisfactory for his purpose, unless the more expensive adhesive has something other than mere waterproofness to offer.

In this connexion, it is important not to lose sight of the fact that great strength in an adhesive cannot in most cases be used to advantage since the materials to be joined have a low tensile strength and a joint will break at its weakest point. So long as the adhesive is a little stronger than the material to be joined, there is nothing to be gained from strengthening it further. With these facts in mind the newer adhesives can be separated fairly definitely into the satisfactory and the unsatisfactory.

Most of the modern plastics and polymers fall conveniently into one of two categories: they are either thermo-plastic or thermo-setting. The differences are deep-seated and each category has its own field of usefulness. The thermo-setting plastics, in their final state, are generally infusible at temperatures up to the charring point and are insoluble in solvents. The great majority of these materials are made either from phenol and formaldehyde or from urea and formaldehyde. The urea is nowadays sometimes replaced by melamine.

They are much used for mouldings where heat and pressure can be used for setting them. Once set, they can only be shaped by cutting, they no longer become plastic on heating and they are, for all practical purposes, insoluble in solvents. Before reaching the final stage, however, they can be used as adhesives for ply-wood, for which purpose they have largely supplanted the older glue, casein or albumen adhesives. The phenolic resin bonded plywood can withstand some years of exposure in the open air in England without exfoliation, while samples buried in soil have rotted away leaving the adhesive behind. The urea and melamine resins are used for similar purposes.

The objection to both these types of resin for archive work is that they require a dangerously high acidity to set them at low temperatures in a reasonable time. Unless considerable changes are made in their properties these plastics should not be used for archive work.

Polyester and epoxy resins are a more recent development in this field and may have more to offer the archivist when they have had longer to settle down into their different fields of application. For the present, therefore, all the thermo-setting resins should be regarded as essentially "heavy duty" adhesives, more suitable for use with wood and metals than with paper and leather.

The thermo-plastics are a much more varied class and have some interest for the archivist. These, like the thermo-setting

7—(G.465)

resins, are ploymers but they can be softened at moderate temperatures to become plastic and mouldable and are usually soluble
in various solvents. Most of these plastics are horny or rubbery
solids and, when mixed with a suitable solvent or plasticizer,
become sticky and develop adhesive properties. It would hardly
be possible to give even a summary of this numerous class of
materials. There are a few of them, however, which have shown
themselves to have a real interest for the archivist.

The most interesting of these is polyvinyl acetate, especially
in the emulsion form. Of all the modern synthetics, this, so far,
seems to hold out the most hope of competing with the more
conventional starch and glue adhesives for paper and leather. It
can be given a wide variety of attractive properties and, so far
as can be judged at present, should be as permanent as the archivist
could reasonably demand. It is a clear, water-white, horny solid
which softens when heated to rather less than the boiling point of
water. By the addition of a small amount of plasticizer, such as
dibutyl phthalate, it becomes first rubbery and then tacky. It
could be used in solution in a non-aqueous solvent but in this
form it is much too viscous for most purposes and, if thinned
down sufficiently, would have a very low solids content.

The emulsion form is the most interesting; it may have a
solid to liquid ratio as high as glue and still be fluid enough to
work easily under the brush. Modern P.V.A. emulsions are
becoming deservedly popular for bookbinding; the more
rubbery ones make excellent flexible adhesives for the spine of a
book. One of the advantages of P.V.A. in emulsion form is that
it can be diluted with water and is always ready for immediate
use. When dry, the film of P.V.A. remaining in the joint is
fairly waterproof and rotproof. The rubbery form seems likely
to preserve its flexibility indefinitely at ordinary temperatures.

Before drying, adhesion can be effected without pressure and,
even after drying, P.V.A.-treated surfaces can be made to adhere
by warmth or pressure. One great advantage of P.V.A. is that
it is a good adhesive for silk, nylon and Terylene fibres and fabrics,
for which glue and paste are not very satisfactory. Since it is less

affected than paper by water, some care should be taken to deal with curling if it is used on one side of the paper only.

An important practical difficulty in using the emulsion is that it quickly gums up the fibres of any brush on which it is allowed to dry. The only remedy for this is to dissolve out the P.V.A. with methylated spirits or one of the lacquer solvents, such as acetone or ethyl acetate which should always be kept handy in case of accidents. The gumming up of brushes can be avoided by keeping a jar of water handy and by putting the brushes into it after use. Once this habit has been acquired it becomes second nature and enables brushes used for P.V.A. emulsion to have a more normal life.

Pressure-Sensitive Tapes

These are usually thin, transparent viscose (cellophane) ribbons with a permanently tacky adhesive on one side. They stick with great tenacity to almost anything solid immediately they make contact with it. So far as archives are concerned, they are usually a nuisance and the archivist's chief concern is to remove them without removing the surface of the paper at the same time. This can be done by applying a small amount of a solvent, such as methylated spirit or carbon tetrachloride, to one edge of the tape, raising this edge as soon as it is free and allowing more solvent to flow into the opening thus made. Gradually the tape should yield and then, with more solvent on a plug of cotton-wool, the paper should be sponged until free from sticky adhesive.

[*Editors' Note:* Material has been omitted at this point.]

5: TYPES OF FILM TYPICALLY EMPLOYED IN MICROPUBLICATION

A. B. Veaner

[*Editors' Note:* In the original, material precedes this excerpt.]

Three major types of film are currently in use for micropublication: (1) vesicular, (2) diazo, and (3) silver halide.* All three of these films consist essentially of a flexible, transparent base with chemical coatings or layers in which light-sensitive materials are suspended. For silver halide films, the base material is commonly cellulose triacetate; vesicular and diazo films are usually manufactured on a plastic, polyester base. It is important to note that the only film regularly used in production work at the camera is silver halide film. The other two major types of films are used only as working intermediates or as distribution copies for certain restricted applications such as current information systems. Neither diazo nor vesicular film at this time possesses enough sensitivity to be useful in cameras for production work, although much experi-

*Three other types of film have recently been introduced: 3M's heat-developing "Drysilver" film, Itek's RS film, and Photohorizons' "free radical" duplicating film. "Drysilver" film is used mainly for COM and data processing applications. RS and "free radical" films are new products whose utility for archival micropublication applications has yet to be evaluated. For these reasons, these three new types of film are not considered in this Handbook.

mentation is underway in this connection. Eventually, it is hoped that a less expensive and more plentiful photosensitive material than silver halide for camera films will be found, but such a substitute would have to be reasonably equal in sensitivity and durability.

Vesicular Films. Vesicular film is sold commercially under the trade names *Kalvar* or *Xidex*. Unlike silver or diazo films, which rely upon the *absorption* of light to create images, vesicular film creates an image by *scattering* light. The image consists of miniscule bubbles—or "vesicules"—which deflect incident light away from themselves. Hence, a vesicular film appears somewhat whitish or milky when not in a microviewer. Because of its optical properties, a vesicular film may appear to the naked eye as either a positive or a negative, depending upon the source and angle of illumination. The image seen on the microviewer, however, is not particularly distinguishable from conventional film images, and its polarity is readily apparent.

Vesicular films are exposed by ultraviolet light and dry-processed by the application of heat. Therefore, no problem of chemical contamination arises. However, the permanence of the vesicular image is affected by the "fixing" or "clearing" step in reproduction, which consists of re-exposing the film to high intensity ultraviolet light. This renders the remaining unexposed sensitized material in the film insensitive to further exposure. If this step has not been properly carried out, it is possible that the film image could be degraded by continued exposure and development to random (unstructured, nonimage) light in a microviewer. There is enough ultraviolet light and heat content in a viewer lamp to expose and develop vesicular film which has not been completely desensitized. Thus, a long period of projection of a single frame* might easily damage the image on an uncleared or unfixed vesicular film. Unfortunately, there is no simple test to determine in advance whether a vesicular film has been properly cleared.

Films and equipment are available to create either positive or negative vesicular images, and a single reproducing machine is available which can process both positive and negative vesicular films.

The stability and archival permanence of vesicular film has not yet been established. Tests on properly processed films have been encouraging, but not conclusive. Vesicular film is now used mainly for working intermediates, or for distribution copies in current information dissemination systems where data are updated by total file replacement at fairly frequent intervals. It has also been found useful wherever it is incon-

*A frame is the area occupied by a single image or exposure.

venient or impossible to provide conventional wet processing for film duplication.

Diazo Films. The term "diazo" indicates the presence of two nitrogen atoms. Certain organic compounds containing two nitrogen atoms have the property of turning dark in the presence of alkaline substances such as ammonia, but this property can be destroyed by ultraviolet light. Here is how a diazo system works: A transparent or translucent original is brought into contact with a diazo material and ultraviolet light is applied through the original. Wherever the original is clear or translucent, ultraviolet light will strike through it, penetrating the diazo material and destroying its ability to become darkened in the presence of alkaline substances. Wherever the original is dark, the ultraviolet light cannot penetrate, and the diazo material will retain its ability to darken. Thus, when diazo film is developed (usually by exposure to ammonia vapors), an image of the same polarity as the original is formed in the diazo material. This technique is an easy and convenient imaging method, but is suitable only for materials imprinted upon a base substance which is transparent to ultraviolet light. Its use is therefore restricted to making copies of master or intermediate films by the "contact printing" method, in which the unexposed stock is brought into direct contact with the transparency bearing the image to be copied.

A diazo image is a dye image and this provides two properties:

1. The image is grainless and homogeneous because each particle is at the molecular level. The dye image in diazo film completely permeates the film coating. Hence, diazo images are somewhat less susceptible to the effects of film scratches than are silver film images.
2. The dye may be subject to fading or decomposition under certain circumstances—such as exposure to strong ultraviolet light sources.

Diazo film is also used as an intermediate or working copy from which to make distribution copies, or occasionally, in certain applications, as the distribution copy itself. (If a diazo intermediate is used repeatedly to make further diazo films, the powerful ultraviolet lamp in the duplicating machine may progressively weaken the sharpness of its images. Therefore, a diazo intermediate is usually used to produce silver halide distribution copies, since the lamps in silver halide microfilm duplicators have much less ultraviolet content than the mercury vapor lamps used in diazo film duplicators.)

Diazo films have been greatly improved in recent years: a variety of colors is now available, a denser black can be printed, and under proper conditions of storage and use (including protection from sunlight and excessive ultraviolet radiation), the images are of sufficient durability for applications in which archival permanence is not important. The use of high contrast diazo film may be accompanied by a significant loss of detail in halftones. Lower-contrast films should therefore be used as intermediates for further duplication wherever halftones are numerous, such as in newspaper files.

Like vesicular film, diazo film is used mostly to disseminate copies of files having a high frequency of content turnover and file replacement, such as manufacturers' catalogs, repair manuals, and technical data sheets, all of which require frequent updating. Its use for the preservation and dissemination of archival research materials is not yet recommended.

Silver Halide Films. Silver halide film is the oldest commercial microimaging material and, given proper care, appears to be the most durable. Also, silver emulsions can be manufactured with a much wider variety of speeds and sensitivity to colors and light intensity than any other material available at this time.

Within the past decade, certain blemishes have been noted on silver halide microfilms. Most of the defects have turned up on camera negatives or on the fogged (fully darkened) leaders of positive prints. These blemishes, known as "redox" blemishes, have for some reason rarely affected the image area, but they do appear fairly frequently on the rest of the film. The origin of these blemishes has been much studied, and the mechanism of their formation is just now being understood. Peroxides originating from poor quality paper and cardboard containers, as well as certain other gaseous pollutants, have been identified as the main contributors to the formation of redox blemishes. Conservative processing techniques, such as the consistent use of the conventional solution temperature (68 degrees Fahrenheit), the avoidance of ammonium thiosulfate in the fixer, the avoidance of hypo eliminators, the use of plenty of wash water, and gentle drying, are also believed to minimize these blemishes. If the film develops blemishes at any time after purchase, inspectors are advised to determine where that film was processed in order that they may be reported to the United States National Bureau of Standards as recommended in [46]. Film inspectors are encouraged to check their retrospective holdings of microfilms periodically, since the blemishes do not show up immediately after processing.

Several preventive measures have been devised. One of them involves gold toning and another a minor change in processing—namely, the addition of potassium iodide to the fixer.

For some time following the discovery of the blemishes, the Eastman Kodak Company promoted the use of gold toning to suppress the formation of these defects. Although gold toning has proved to be practical and useful under certain circumstances, there is no long-term evidence that it is an absolute preventive. The treatment is available from Kodak's Recordak subsidiary, either in connection with original processing or as an after-treatment.

Recently it has been discovered that the addition of 0.2 gram of potassium iodide per liter of fixer makes it practically impossible to generate microfilm blemishes under laboratory conditions. It is reported in [49] that no blemishes have been found on films coming from laboratories which have added potassium iodide to the fixer. The iodide treatment is also more convenient and less expensive than gold toning.

Other methods for dealing with microfilm blemishes have been reported in the *Proceedings of the National Microfilm Association,* and in the *Journal of Micrographics.* Details on the detection and reporting of these blemishes are contained in [46], which also has colored plates illustrating their appearance. Dr. Carl E. Nelson has published a complete survey of present knowledge of microfilm blemishes; his paper [49] contains an exhaustive bibliography on the subject. McCamy and Pope [47] have more recently published a definitive study on the cause and prevention of redox blemishes, concluding their work with the following ten specific recommendations:

1. Use safety base permanent record film as specified in the American National Standards Institute Specifications for Photographic Films for Archival Records. [28]
2. Use no higher densities than are required for the intended purposes, and use dark characters on a light background if this is feasible.
3. The residual thiosulfate concentration should not exceed 1 microgram per square centimeter, but one should not attempt to reduce it to zero. The optimum concentration appears to be about 0.5 microgram per square centimeter in a clear area.
4. Keep processing machinery and film clean.
5. Avoid scratching film.
6. Store films in containers made of inert materials, such as metals or plastics of proven quality. With good ventilation and clean air, the containers need not be sealed.
7. Do not permit storage temperature to exceed 70 degrees Fahrenheit nor the relative humidity to exceed 40 percent.

8. Avoid wide-range cycling of temperature and humidity, since these accelerate the imbibition of gaseous contaminants.
9. Inspect films on a regular schedule, using proper sampling and microscopic inspection techniques.
10. Maintain records of processing and storage conditions so that the next generation of archivists will be able to understand our successes or failures and act on the basis of facts.

Care in use and proper storage conditions are as important as preventive treatment. "Cinch marks" (see page 34), for example, have been found to create ideal nuclei for redox blemishes.

The silver imaging process is highly dependent upon gelatin for its light sensitivity. This material may be subject to biological attack if the relative humidity in the storage environment regularly exceeds 60 percent. To minimize attacks from airborne bacteria and microbes, silver halide microfilms should therefore be stored in accordance with the recommendations of ANSI Standard PH5.4-1970 [34].

Film Stock

Until about twenty years ago, two kinds of film stock were manufactured in the United States: a triacetate or "safety base" film, and nitrate film. The latter is chemically similar to guncotton and is considered extremely dangerous and unstable. It is capable of self-decomposition and spontaneous combustion, even if stored in sealed containers. No nitrate base film has been manufactured in the United States since approximately 1951, nor is nitrate base film currently being manufactured in France or Great Britain.

Only silver halide film manufactured in conformity with ANSI Standard PH1.28-1969, *Specifications for Photographic Film for Archival Records, Silver-Gelatin Type, on Cellulose Ester Base* [28] should be used for archival micropublications. Films conforming to this standard are edge-marked at frequent, regular intervals with the words "safety film," or their equivalent in other languages. (For example, French and German films conforming to the standard are marked "film de sécurité" and "Sicherheitsfilm," respectively.) Safety film is sometimes also edge-marked with a solid triangle. It is very important to note, however, that even the presence of the words "safety film" or the triangle can be misleading, for a safety base master film might have been reproduced upon a nitrate base distribution film.

Note that the standard cited above applies only to silver film. Neither vesicular nor diazo film is now manufactured with a nitrate base, though it is possible that a few diazo films might have been produced on a nitrate base at some time in the past. Therefore, for all practical purposes it is safe to assume that vesicular and diazo films have a safety base.

To summarize, all unmarked silver halide films are suspect, except those known to have currently originated within the United States, England, or France. Silver halide films originating elsewhere, or whose age cannot be determined, should be checked carefully, whether marked or not.

If the presence of nitrate film is suspected, a simple, positive test can be applied: a ¼-inch circle of film should be removed from a nonimage area with a paper punch and dropped into a flask of trichloroethylene (obtainable from any chemical supply house). Nitrate film will sink, whereas safety film will float. Caution: fumes of trichloroethylene are hazardous to human health and the material should never be used except in a well ventilated area—preferably next to an open window. If trichloroethylene is not available, another positive test is burning. Because nitrate film is an extremely dangerous nitrocellulose, this test should only be conducted in the open air with a small quantity of film and away from any flammable materials. Nitrate film burns explosively with great speed, whereas safety film burns very slowly when a match is applied, smolders when the match is removed, and the flame quickly goes out. To obtain a sample for burning, a paper punch can be used in the same way as for the trichloroethylene test.

Other tests for safety film stock are cited in ANSI Standard PH1.25-1965, *Specifications for Safety Photographic Film* [27].

Film Coatings

Coatings or proprietary treatments which are claimed to protect microfilm from scratches and abrasions have been marketed for some time. However, testing performed for the Library Technology Program in 1963 indicated that "none of these coatings is an effective means of preventing damage to library microfilm by abrasion in use" [21]. None of the available coatings can be applied by a local library; all require that films be sent to a service bureau for application of treatment. Perhaps the best evidence of the ineffectiveness of these coatings is that they are not used by the nation's largest micropublishers catering to the library market. In fact, one of the oldest and most experienced of the micropublishers, which marketed its own proprietary coating process for a while, has ceased to treat its own film with this service.

Until otherwise established, therefore, the usefulness of presently available protective film coatings is, at least, dubious.

Archival Permanence

Since one of the reasons why libraries are acquiring microform publications is to replace those parts of their collections of conventional printed materials which are deteriorating, the question of the archival permanence of micropublications is of some importance.

"Archival permanence" refers to the ability of both the images and the base materials of microforms to retain their original characteristics and to resist deterioration over an indefinite period of time.

There are three main factors which affect the archival permanence of microform products: the kind of materials used in their production, the manner in which the materials are processed by the laboratory, and the conditions under which the products are stored and used.

At the present time, cellulose-ester safety-base silver halide film is the only type of film that can be recommended for archivally permanent master films; this is also true of distribution copies in the case of roll film and microfiches. As we pointed out earlier, distribution copies of micro-opaques are printed on opaque materials, including photosensitive paper. The archival permanence of these materials is also a function of materials, production methodology, and storage conditions. Photostatically produced micro-opaques (e.g., *Microcards**) must be protected from excess humidity and must be free from residual processing chemicals. Micro-opaques produced by miniaturized printing (e.g., *Microprint*** cards) must be protected from abrasion, but are not generally subject to fungal attack and do not contain photographic chemicals.

The effect of a laboratory's processing procedures on the archival permanence of microform products cannot be overemphasized. The use of chemical solutions of the proper strength and temperature, careful controls, and constant testing are absolutely necessary. A fuller discussion of laboratory procedures is contained on pages 46–48 of this Handbook under the heading "Laboratory Inspection." It should be noted here, however, that perhaps the most important single factor in ensuring archival permanence is that the finished product be completely free of certain harmful residual chemicals.

*Microcard Corporation
**Readex Microprint Corporation

Two chemical tests are currently employed to check for harmful residual chemicals which might impair the archival permanence of silver halide films.

The Crabtree-Ross test is the procedure described in ANSI Standard PH4.8-1958 [31]. Technically, the Crabtree-Ross test should be performed within 24 hours after the film has been processed. The reason for this is that residual thiosulfate—the harmful material detected by the test—is itself an unstable compound which breaks down into secondary compounds known as trithionates and tetrathionates. These compounds, if sufficiently concentrated, also contribute to the destruction of the silver image. Unfortunately, the Crabtree-Ross test is not useful for the detection of these breakdown products. However, since it takes some time for this breaking down to be completed, it is generally conceded that the Crabtree-Ross test is useful for up to two weeks after processing.

The methylene blue test [50] is a new procedure which is superior to the Crabtree-Ross test in several ways. First, it gives a positive indication of the presence of harmful chemicals by a change of color if these chemicals are present beyond a prespecified concentration. Second, the methylene blue test reveals the presence of all three chemicals: thiosulfates, trithionates, and tetrathionates. Third, the test can be performed any time after processing. It is expected that the methylene blue test will be adopted as an ANSI Standard in the very near future.

These tests require a laboratory setup and considerable skill, patience, and knowledge. This Handbook is not designed to train librarians or others to perform them. Few libraries will have the facilities and personnel for accurate, repeatable testing; they will either have to depend on their assessment of the competence and efficiency of the publisher's production laboratories, or turn to outside laboratories which do have the proper facilities and personnel to make the tests. Further details on the tests may be found in ANSI Standard PH4.8-1958 [31], and also in [50].

Proper storage conditions for microforms were discussed briefly on pages 10–11 in relation to the preservation of master films. A full discussion of optimum conditions for the storage and use of microforms is, however, beyond the scope of this Handbook. It can only be said that improper storage conditions will definitely have an adverse effect on the useful life of microforms, as will heavy use, particularly by careless users, or with poorly designed or maintained viewing equipment.

"Permanence" is, of course, a relative term. For some uses, particularly for current information systems with frequent file replacement, "permanence" over a long period of time is not important. For others, such as the addition of a micropublication to the standing collections of a research library, it can be quite important—especially if it is anticipated that a publication will be used only infrequently, since there will be limited opportunity to review and check such an item among tens or hundreds of thousands of units which might be contained in a large collection. Numerous studies have shown that properly processed microforms made of high grade, chemically stable materials will, under proper conditions of storage and use, last as long as material printed on acid-free paper, i.e., for hundreds of years.

[*Editors' Note:* Material has been omitted at this point.]

6: THE NATURE OF LEATHER

J. W. Waterer

[*Editors' Note:* In the original, material precedes this excerpt.]

Leather is a manufactured product that can be made from the skin of any living creature by a great variety of methods, the aim of which is to preserve from putrefaction the unique collagen fibre tissue which forms the middle layer (*corium* or *derma*) of the three of which skin is formed, whilst discarding the outer layer that forms the epidermal system and the bottom layer of adipose tissue. During the last half century there has been a ferment of development in leather manufacture and it is impossible, for reasons of space, to describe here all the kinds of leather that are now available. It is, however, approximately correct to say that the three basic processes that have been used from time immemorial are still employed: these, in ancient terminology, have been known as *tanning, tawing* and *chamoising* but today the three main groups which have arisen from the basic processes are usually called *vegetable tanning, mineral tanning* and *oil tanning*, the term 'tanning' being used loosely of the latter two. There are a few modern processes which fall outside these groups. Beyond these processes which in general terms convert raw hides and skins into 'leather', there is a great variety of methods of 'dressing' and 'finishing' which impart particular characteristics to both the qualities and the appearance of leather. The principal methods will be described briefly.

For ages before the making of leather settled down into the three quite different processes enumerated above, raw hides and skins were converted, by a large variety of primitive methods some of which still survive here and there, into kinds of 'leather', which, however crude, served many essential purposes.[1] In prehistoric times scraping was employed to remove adherent flesh and hair after partial putrefaction had been artificially induced to facilitate its separation. This was a preliminary to beating and pounding to work oil and grease into the raw skin, and was followed by a 'slicking' process to stretch and flatten the pelt. When brain substance was added to grease and oil a notable advance was made. Brain substance contains phosphorus compounds which induce a very elementary kind of 'tanning' known as phosphatide: for centuries it was a much prized commodity and many a skull of slaughtered man and beast was cracked open to obtain it. Even in the second half of the nineteenth century, ox brains were used (with several other substances) in the manufacture of the so-called 'Helvetia' leather (a supple, water-resistant leather that would, for long periods, withstand exposure to all kinds of weather). Eskimo women chewed hides to soften them, which probably promoted enzymic action, and used fish or seal oil (which is prone to oxidation), to induce a kind of 'tannage'. Smoking was employed from Paleolithic times, and sometimes still is in remote places, but usually in combination with some other process. The term 'smoke tanning' is sometimes used but is misleading. The effect of smoke (usually from a wood fire) upon raw animal skin or flesh is primarily preservative: it had been used from time immemorial to keep food from putrefaction for a period, as it still is for fish and meat. Very little work appears to have been done on this subject: some think that the tarry products and aldehydes found in most kinds of smoke as a result of imperfect combustion may provide some protection against decomposition for collagen fibres, but the present writer has yet to be convinced that pelts merely cured by smoking, are in any real sense comparable to leather made by a genuine tanning process.

The preparation of hides and skins for conversion into leather

The preparatory processes are, in principle, the same whatever method is to be employed to convert the raw material into 'leather', whether *skins* (of small or young animals including calf, pig, goat, sheep and also birds and reptiles) or *hides* (of the larger animals including adult cattle, horse and buffalo): their purpose is, in effect, to isolate the *corium* and prepare it for the treatment that follows, which is intended to render the final product imputrescible. Some pelts arrive at the tanyard direct from the slaughter-house,

---

[1] See, for example, Gansser, A., 'The Early History of Tanning', *CIBA Review*, **81**, 1950; same author, 'Prähistorisches Gerben', *Der Gerber*, **60**, *No. 1437/8*, 1934; Schwerz, F., 'Leather Dressing in the Stone Age', *CIBA Review* **8**, 1938, and Stambolov, T., *Manufacture, Deterioration and Preservation of Leather*, ICOM Central Research Laboratory for Objects of Art and Science, Amsterdam, 1969.

in which case they have first to be thoroughly cleansed; others come 'cured', that is sun-dried, dry-salted or wet-salted, or 'pickled', and have to be appropriately cleansed and otherwise treated, before the removal of hair and wool by scraping after immersion in a succession of lime-liquors. This may be achieved by commencing with old, weak liquors and finishing with new, strong ones, or alternatively they may be tumbled in revolving drums with certain chemicals such as sodium sulphide. In the case of sheepskins, the wool of which it is desired to preserve in perfect condition, the skins may be subjected to the ancient process of 'sweating'—that is, hanging them in a warm place until the wool is loosened by bacterial action; or the flesh may be coated with a paste of lime and sodium sulphide which penetrates to the roots within a few hours. The purpose of these processes is to loosen hair or wool and the epidermis so that both can readily be removed (by scraping off, either by hand or by machine), and to bring the pelts into a suitable con-dition to respond to the succeeding processes. The bottom layer (the adipose tissue) is then cut away (with a special 'fleshing' knife) and the isolated *corium* is ready for con-version into leather by a method which may fall under one of the following broad headings, or sometimes by a combination of two of them.

Vegetable process (tanning)

This process utilises the 'tannin' which is present, in varying degree, in barks, woods, leaves or fruits of certain kinds. In olden times the pelts were laid in pits interspersed with layers of bark, the pit being then filled up with water. From time to time the pelts were lifted out, piled up and then returned with fresh bark to strengthen the liquor, and this was continued for up to eighteen months. Today most tanning is performed in revolving drums using liquor prepared from tannin extracts, which cuts the time down to a matter of days or, with skins, even to hours. Familiar examples of vegetable tanned leather include full substance (the natural thickness, about 4·5mm) cattle-hide leather used for harness, strapping, footwear soles and certain items of military equipment, and the thinner kinds of cattle-hide leather used for upholstery, travelling bags and cases, brief-cases and the like, which in olden times were produced by the skilled operation of shaving the hides on the flesh side to the required thickness, but today by the use of a band-knife machine that splits hides horizontally into two or more layers, all of which have their uses but of which the outer or 'grain' layer is the most important. Some skins also are vegetable tanned, such as sheepskin intended for 'basil', pigskin, calfskin for certain purposes and goatskin especially when intended for 'morocco' leather. The natural colour of vegetable tanned leather in the 'crust' stage—that is, after tanning but before finishing—ranged from pale brown, through biscuit, to a nut or reddish brown, according to the particular tanning agents employed.

Mineral process (originally tawing)

The original and very ancient process was performed with a solution of alum and salt (typically three parts of salt to twelve of alum) and was called 'tawing': sheep and goat skins were steeped in this liquor for 10–15 minutes and then dried. Tawed leather is pure white but very amenable to dyeing: when freshly made it is stiff and harsh but is readily softened by 'staking'—that is, pulling backward and forward, in various directions, over a blunt blade set in a stake of convenient height. It is, however, a material of open texture and therefore for many purposes was consolidated by 'stuffing' (see *Dressing*). Its character is completely different from that of any other kind of leather: in fact it is not a true leather at all because the process is reversible—that is, by immersion in warm water the material can be reconverted into the original raw skin. Therefore it cannot be washed with soap and water as can true leathers. In later times it was 'dry cleaned', for example when used for gloves, but as tawed gloving leather was nearly always 'stuffed' its quality was thereby impaired because the solvents used would remove the oil and grease which were key ingredients of the 'stuffing'.

A new form of mineral tannage was introduced in 1884 when chromium salts were used for the first time; other metallic salts have been introduced since but chrome 'tanning', as it developed, revolutionised the mineral process, resulting in such leathers as box calf and glazed kid which are supple and highly resistant to water and therefore are largely used for footwear uppers, gloves and beautifully soft 'persian' (hair-sheep) leather for clothing. Chromed leathers are hard-wearing, stable, not subject to 'red rot' and will withstand hot, even boiling, water; but their resilient, open texture and their antipathy to the normal adhesives make them unsuitable for some kinds of work, including bookbinding. They are generally pale duck-egg blue (prior to staining or dyeing) and cannot be made pure white. Therefore alum tawing continued to be used to make white leather until the introduction, in this century, of zirconium salts and the 'synthetic' tannage based on aldehydes, which produce pure white leather that is washable.

Oil process (originally chamoising)

This process, known since medieval times as 'chamoising' because it was used to make very soft leather from chamois skins, probably developed from man's first attempts to make use of raw skins, waste products from slaughter for food, which when dry were hard and horny. Efforts would be made to restore the original suppleness by treating them with oils, fats or fatty materials such as brains. Whereas certain oils (e.g. seal oil) would undergo oxidation and other changes producing compounds with tanning action, brains contain 'phosphatides' which also produce a primitive type of tannage. The chamoising process consists in first 'frizing' the grain surface—that is, scraping it to facilitate entry of oils from both sides (this is not necessary when making modern 'chamois' or 'shammy' leathers from sheepskin splits from which the grain layer has already been removed). The wet pelts are then liberally sprinkled with cod-liver oil (or other marine animal or fish oil) and subjected to a severe pummelling in the 'stocks'. This is repeated several times and the skins are then either hung in a warm 'stove' or piled up and allowed to generate heat; this promotes oxidation of the oil, and the resultant products combine with the fibres. The skins are then washed (certain types are shrunk in a warm soda solution) and dried.

Today oil 'tanned' leather is exemplified chiefly by 'shammy' or 'wash' leather which is now made from sheepskin splits but in early times was made from antelope skins; it was then used for clothing, linings, bags, purses and pouches, in some cases being also subjected to some of the processes employed in dressing tawed leather: it is distinguishable by its pale yellow colour. Its principal use today, apart from 'wash' leather, is for gloves.

An analogous process was also employed in the making of 'buff' leather, so called because originally made from the hide of the European buffalo, and 'doeskin' (deer) which was used for doublets, gloves, saddle-seats and other things, including, in the nineteenth century, military equipment. Buff leather is little used today but will be found in the museum in the form of military coats and items of equipment, particularly of the seventeenth and eighteenth centuries. Chamoised leather is tough, washable, extremely durable and not subject to 'red rot'.

Combination tannages

The use of two different processes to produce leather of a specific character is not modern. For example, at least five hundred years ago a durable and lasting leather was made by a combination of tawing and chamoising, and many other examples could be given, but the principle has become more general since the development of the chrome process—for example, vegetable tanning followed by chrome or *vice versa*. These so-called 'semi-chrome' leathers possess important characteristics of both methods; for instance, they can partake of the firmness of structure provided by the vegetable process combined with the suppleness and chemical stability derived from the chromium method.

It must be emphasised that the foregoing section covers merely the basic methods described in outline, and that although up to the end of the nineteenth century most leathers fell within the three main categories, many changes have taken place since and the pace of development is constantly accelerating. Whilst the age of an object, if accurately determinable as prior to about 1800, is a fairly safe guide to the mode of tannage of its leather—vegetable, alum or oil—it is becoming more and more difficult to judge the nature of later leathers without scientific aid.

Dressing

This term indicates processes that follow the actual conversion of raw hides and skins into leather and are intended to modify its character to meet specific needs. For example, sole leather is rolled (in olden times hammered) and lightly oiled to render it solid and firm, yet possessing a degree of pliability; harness and strap leather is 'curried', a process that consists in working into wet leather a mixture of cod-oil and tallow ('dubbin') to make it strong, water-resistant and pliant and to ensure long life; tawed leather may be 'stuffed' with flour, egg-yolk, oil and grease to give it more 'body' and render it strong but soft; chromed leathers such as box calf, are fat-liquored to make them pliable and water-resistant, and may be further softened by 'boarding', which involves folding the skin grain-to-grain and rubbing it backward and forward, in two directions, with a cork-covered board; this process produces the characteristic surface pattern of minute creases at a right angle to each other producing the tiny 'boxes' from which the term derives.

Finishing

This term implies processes that affect not so much the properties of the leather as its outward appearance, although there are some, like the 'boarding' mentioned above, that do both. Traditional finishing processes include:

1. Staining—that is, the colouring of the grain surface with clear dye, stain that may contain pigment, or pigmented nitro-cellulose, applied by brush or spray.
2. Dyeing, the colouring of leather to a varying depth below the surfaces, by immersion.
3. Graining or embossing of a surface pattern that may be of artificial character, or the simulation of a genuine leather grain pattern, originally done with small engraved rollers, but now with heated, engraved metal plates in a press.
4. Plating, producing a smooth, glossy surface, originally with a heated metal hand tool, but now by means of a heated, highly polished metal plate in a press.
5. Boarding (see also above), in the case of 'morocco' leather (goat skin) the 'bringing up' of the natural grain pattern into the characteristic granular surface, or the minute creasing of upholstery hide or 'willow' hide, by folding the leather, grain to grain, and rolling it backward and forward with a cork-covered board.
6. Enamelling to produce 'patent' leather.
7. The abrading of the flesh side to produce a 'suede' finish or on the grain side to make a 'velvet' finish.

There are also many other devices, including the questionable one of printing patterns in colour on the surface by which the material loses its natural character and charm.

Untanned hide or skin

Under this heading come parchment and vellum, principally used for writing upon but also, at times, for covering boxes, caskets and other objects; forel, a type of parchment used for the binding of books intended for hard wear; and rawhide, used as a covering for luggage and the like and also for a number of industrial purposes where long life and maximum resistance to hard wear are essential. None of these is 'leather' because no 'tanning' process has been employed. The material is prepared for its purpose by liming, de-greasing, scraping and smoothing with powdered pumice, repeated a number of times, and finally drying under tension. It has little in common with leather and cannot be subjected to the same treatment: it is adversely affected by water or damp, in certain circumstances will putrefy, and can be dissolved in hot water, making size or glue.

[*Editors' Note:* Material has been omitted at this point.]

7: PARCHMENT–ITS HISTORY, MANUFACTURE AND COMPOSITION

Michael L. Ryder

Hamlet: Is not parchment made of sheep-skins?
Horatio: Ay, my lord, and of calf-skins, too.

In making parchment, the skin is not tanned as it is in the manufacture of leather, but is merely stretched and dried. Parchment is therefore akin to raw-hide which is used to make such articles as whips and ropes, but is not given such a fine finish as parchment.

Although parchment is principally known as a writing material this is not its only use. In fact, possibly as early as the Middle Kingdom of ancient Egypt (about 2000 B.C.) it was used to cover drums, and in the sounding boxes of other musical instruments such as tambourins. A mandolin of the 18th Dynasty (about 1400 B.C.) was said to have been covered with parchment made from gazelle skin.[1] It was used for drums in Asia Minor possibly as early as 1000 B.C.[2] The parchment used for this purpose today is a thicker and cruder product than that used for documents. In the Middle Ages parchment was used to cover windows, being "cleared" in linseed oil in order to make it translucent. Also in the Middle Ages old parchments were often oil tanned to make chamois leather for clothing.[3] There is a shield made of Oryx hide by the Taureg tribe of the Sahara in the University Museum of Archaeology and Ethnology, Cambridge, which is pale and stiff like parchment and apparently un-tanned.

History

From remote times, skins, first raw, and according to Latour,[4] later tanned, were used as writing material by the people of the Near East. Although writing on skin is usually associated with the Old World, certain New World peoples, notably the Maya and Aztecs of Central America, apparently developed this practice independently. I am indebted to Dr. G. H. S. Bushnell for the information that deer skin was used. This was preserved (i.e. tanned) by smoking and made smooth with a permanent coating of lime plaster. Driver[5] states that the first mention of documents written on skins occurs in the time of the Egyptian 4th Dynasty (about 2700 B.C.). He states that the oldest extant documents on leather are a roll of the Egyptian 12th Dynasty (about 2000 B.C.) in Berlin, another of the 17th century B.C. in the British Museum, and a parchment of the fifth year of Rameses II (about 1292–1225 B.C.). It is not clear, however, whether or not the original identification of such documents as being leather or parchment would be borne out by modern scientific investigation. Although Saxl[2] stated that the Hebrews used leather as a writing material, Reed and Poole[6] found no evidence of this in the Dead Sea Scrolls. Mongait[7] listing some documents of the 8th century A.D. found in a Sogdian castle in Tajikstan, mentions paper and leather, but not parchment. (An erroneous translation here is unlikely because the English and Russian words for parchment have the same root.

Other than in ancient Egypt skin remains of great age are rarely found. But the "writer on skin" is depicted on Assyrian monuments from about 800 B.C.,[5] and from the days of Nebuchadrezzar II

---

[1] A. Lucas, Ancient Egyptian Materials and Industries. London, 1948.
[2] H. Saxl, "Parchment" in C. Singer, et al. (eds.), A History of Technology, II. Oxford, 1956.
[3] H. Saxl, An Investigation of the Qualities, the Methods of Manufacture, and the Preservation of Historic Parchment and Vellum with a view to Identifying the Species of Animal used. M.Sc. Thesis, Leeds University, 1954.
[4] A. Latour, Paper, a Historical Outline. CIBA Review, VI, (72) 2630.
[5] G. R. Driver, Aramaic Documents of the 5th Century B.C. Oxford, 1957.
[6] R. Reed and J. B. Poole, A study of some Dead Sea Scroll and leather fragments from Cave 4 at Qumran. Proc. Leeds Philos. and Lit. Soc., IX, 1962, 1–13.
[7] A. L. Mongait, Archaeology in the U.S.S.R., Harmondsworth (Middx), 1959.

(605–561 B.C.) onwards not only is papyrus often mentioned in cuneiform texts,[8] but the "writer on skin" is clearly distinguished from the "writer on clay tablets". According to Forbes,[8] the adoption in Mesopotamia of Aramaic script which was not suitable for use on clay tablets stimulated the use of parchment there before the 8th century B.C.

Ctesias (c. 400 B.C.) quoted by Diodorus Siculus (1st century B.C.) stated that skins (cows' hides) were used by the Persians for historical records,[5] and Herodotus (5th century B.C.) said that skins of sheep and goats were once used for writing upon by the Ionians and added that barbarians still use them. Here Herodotus may have been under the impression that the parchment, which was in fact widely used as a writing material by the Greeks, was papyrus, and it is possible to confuse papyrus with parchment unless a close examination is made.

It seems to have been Pliny (1st century A.D.) quoting Varro (1st century B.C.) who perpetuated the story of the "invention" of parchment by king Eumenes II (197–159 B.C.) of Pergamum near Smyrna in Asia Minor. He is said to have invented parchment as a substitute for papyrus in the famous library at Pergamum when the Egyptian pharaoh (Ptolemy Epiphanes, 205–182 B.C.) forbade the export of papyrus in the hope of preventing the growth of the library. The word parchment (Latin: pergamena) is of course derived from Pergamum, although this term was not in common use before the 4th century A.D. Before that date the term "diphthera" was used in Greek, and "membrana" in Latin. The edict of Diocletian (about A.D. 300) mentions pergamena, and also parchment makers (membranarii and diphtheropoii). So strong is the fame of Pergamum, however, that Forbes [8]considers it may in fact have been the home of the invention of a treatment to make parchment more suitable for writing upon. Although more difficult to prepare, and therefore most costly, parchment had the advantage over papyrus of being more durable, particularly in the relatively damp Mediterranean climate. Parchment gradually became the normal writing material probably reaching Rome in the second century B.C. when the librarian Crates of Mallus visited that city, but Forbes states that its use was long restricted to de luxe items.

In Greek and Roman times parchment used for writing was cut into rectangles which were sewn together to form rolls similar to the rolls of "leather" and papyrus used by the Egyptians.[2] The script was written in vertical columns, and in order to read the scroll one or two columns were exposed at a time by unrolling it with the right hand, the scroll being re-rolled with the left hand. The office of the Master of the Rolls in Britain acts as a reminder of the persistence of this system for important documents. The book, first known as the codex, came into use in the second century A.D. In this, the rectangular sheets that had previously been sewn into a roll were folded once to form a folio, twice into a quarto, or thrice to form an octavo. The sheets were then bound into a *Volumen*, a word reminiscent of volvulus (a scroll).

Parchment arrived in north west Europe along with Christianity, and became the most important writing material of the Middle Ages in Europe. But from the 12th century onwards it was slowly displaced by paper from the East which was brought into Europe by the Arabs in Spain.

Terminology

According to Forbes[8] in the early Middle Ages in Europe the best (virgin) parchment was made from the skins of unborn lambs or calves. This was called "pergamena virginea" or "pergamena vitulina". From the French word "vel" for calf comes the word *vellum* now used for finer qualities to distinguish them from thicker and harsher *parchment*.

Ustick[9] discussed the possibility of an historical distinction between the terms parchment and vellum. He said that parchment was the earliest word in English occurring as early as about 1300 in the Cursor Mundi, whereas the term vellum was not used until about 1440. Although the term vellum should strictly be reserved for the product made from calf skin, he considered it hard to establish such a distinction. On the other hand the term parchment seems in fact originally to have referred to the product from sheep and goat skins. In England by the 16th century, however, the terms parchment

[8] R. J. Forbes, "Parchment" in *Studies in Ancient Technology*, IV, Leyden, 1956.
[9] W. L. Ustick, "Parchment" and "Vellum", *Trans. Bibliog. Soc.*, XVI 1935, 439–443.

and vellum seem to have been interchangeable. But in the same century one author referred to "vellum parchment", which Ustick regarded as meaning a fine quality.

At that time, too, when paper began to be used for printing, and fine parchment was reserved for documents, the coarser varieties were used for book covers. But fine parchments were still being used for paintings, particularly miniatures, and one painter of miniatures writing about 1600 said that virgin parchment "such as never bore hair" should be used, i.e. skin from a foetus so young that the hair or wool had not yet risen above the skin surface. The hair remains in such a parchment will not be sufficiently well developed to allow identification, and in fact where I have identified parchment as coming from calf it has been thicker than sheep and goat parchment, i.e. from an infant, and not a foetal animal. In keeping with the above statement that the coarser varieties were used for bookbinding, the cover I examined from a book from Fountains Abbey dated about 1450 was in fact a coarse calf parchment. Plenderleith[10] said that calf parchment (vellum) is usually harder than sheep parchment and was used for binding rather than writing.

According to Ustick,[9] by the early 17th century the modern distinction of a vellum being a fine parchment seems to have been firmly established in common usage, vellum being often called virgin, abortive or uterine parchment regardless of the animal source. But certain dictionaries since that time have maintained that vellum is parchment made from calf skin. By the following reasoning it will be seen that, originally at any rate, a fine parchment would in fact also be a foetal calf parchment. If a thin foetal skin lacking pores is required then the only animal providing a sufficiently large skin at foetal age is the calf. By this argument then calf skins would originally be used to make fine parchments, so that the term vellum would become the accepted term for a fine parchment, although later, fine parchments may have been made from sheep and goat skins.

Interesting support for this reconciliation of fineness with source comes from the Birrell papers.[11] These belonged to the Birrell parchment-manufacturing family of Kinross, and one document of the early 19th century states quite conclusively that "vellum is parchment made from abortives or at least sucking calves". There is a letter among the papers dated 1740 complaining to the excise office that (presumably higher) vellum duty is being charged whereas only parchment is made. And the quarterly excise return forms of the late 18th and early 19th centuries had separate printed columns for parchment and vellum.

Manufacture

The skin of mammals consists of two main layers: a thin, outer, epidermis, and a thicker, inner layer known as the dermis or corium, from which leather and parchment are made. The dermis is composed mainly of fibres of the protein collagen, that is quite distinct from the keratin proteins which are soft in the epidermis and hard in hairs, nails and horn. Hairs and wool fibres (which are biologically virtually the same) grow in epidermal depressions in the skin known as follicles. There are sweat glands and sebaceous (grease) glands associated with the follicles. The layer of the dermis enclosing the follicles is known as the papillary layer, and this gives leather a grain that is characteristic of different animals. Beneath the papillary layer the collagen fibres of the dermis are coarser, forming a more open network, and this layer is called the reticular layer. At the base of the dermis many animals have a layer of fat. During the manufacture of leather and parchment the hairs are removed, and most of the epidermis, too. In order to obtain a thinner product, the skin is often split (today by machine) in a region roughly corresponding to the boundary between the papillary and reticular layers.

According to Forbes[8] in ancient times skin from hogs, asses and even wolves was used in the manufacture of parchment, and Thompson[12] suggests the use of rabbit skin, although sheep, goat and calf skins seem to have been preferred for finer qualities. Recent studies by Saxl,[3] Reed and Poole,[6]

---

[10] H. J. Plenderleith, *The Conservation of Antiquities and Works of Art.* Oxford, 1956.
[11] The Birrell Papers. National Library of Scotland, MS. 2207 (5).
[12] D. V. Thompson and G. H. Hamilton (eds.), "De Arte Illuminandi", Yale, 1933.

and myself,[13, 14] showed that virtually all parchments were made of calf, sheep or goat skin, no certain identification of any other animal having been made. Saxl[3] considers that skin from wild animals is unsuitable owing to pigmentation. Plenderleith[10] stated that the most common source of parchment is sheepskin, and my studies confirm this. Saxl,[3] on the other hand, claims that among medieval parchments, whereas those from sheep predominated in Britain, those from goats predominated in continental Europe. I have, as yet, been able to examine only two parchments from the continent (see below) and these were from either hairy sheep or goats.

Good parchment must be fine (*i.e.* thin), strong yet flexible and have a smooth surface, and it is extremely durable. Before discussing the ways in which the manufacture of parchment has varied through history it is necessary to outline the main processes and describe what might be regarded as a basic (medieval) method. The first process common to leather manufacture is the removal of hair, which is commonly loosened with lime (alkali) before being scraped off with a blunt knife. The second and essential process in parchment manufacture is drying under tension. In this the skin is usually stretched on a wooden frame, while the third process is carried out, which is the application of more lime to remove moisture and grease. The effect of the stretching is to cause the collagen fibres of the skin to lie in sheets parallel to the skin surface.[3] This is a major difference from leather in which the original three-dimensional net-like weave of the fibres is retained. This explains why parchment (but not leather) can be torn with the hand into a number of thinner sheets.[6] In the fourth and final process the parchment is finished while still in a taut condition; the surface is made smooth by shaving it with a sharp, semi-circular (or often semi-lunar) knife, and rubbing it with pumice. Despite this, the flesh side can usually be distinguished from the grain side by its rougher texture and often darker colour, and in books, the pages are usually mounted grain to grain-side and flesh to flesh-side in order to give a uniform appearance.

Parchment was originally made from the full thickness of the skin, and in the Middle Ages the product was made thinner by shaving. The modern practice is to use only the flesh-side of a split skin to make parchment, the grain side containing the hair roots, and exhibiting the grain pattern, being used for book-binding leather. But according to Jewish law[6] the ancient Hebrews used split as well as entire skins. A unsplit skin was known as a *gewil*, the grain-split as a *kelaf* and the flesh-split as a *duxustus*. How the skins were split is not clear, but in view of the ease with which parchment (but not skin) can be split it may have been carried out towards the end of manufacture, possibly immediately before the finishing process.

The Jewish law[6] seems to be our most detailed source of information on parchment manufacture in Antiquity, although the Jewish method was in part unique, as authors such as Forbes[8] have found only scanty evidence before the Middle Ages. The Jews were allowed to use the skins of clean animals only. As these were cloven-hoofed, cud-chewing animals, the identification of calf, sheep and goat amongst the Dead Sea Scrolls makes sense. They apparently used salt to preserve skins until manufacture commenced. various methods of dehairing seem to have been used by the Jews, possibly at different times. These include treading in a thoroughfare, soaking in water to allow bacterial action, treatment with dung (bacteria) and fermentation with vegetable juices and flour. There seems to be no mention of alkali. According to Forbes[8] the first source of alkali for depilation was stale urine (ammonia) which was superceeded by lye of wood ashes before the use of lime became established by the Middle Ages. The use of lime seems to have come from the Arabs.[3] Illustrations show that the curved knife dates back to antiquity, and this probably stems from the similar tool (often of bone) that primitive peoples still use to scrape flesh and fat from a skin during leather dressing. Thompson[15] considers that the curved blade owes its shape to the original practice of scraping wet skins. This would require a blade curved to a smaller arc than that into which its pressure forces the pliable skin.

The Palestinian Jews seem to have been unique in finishing the parchment with a light dressing of vegetable tannin, and a dressing of oil, but neither were used in sufficient quantity actually to cause

---

[13] M. L. Ryder, Follicle Arrangement in Skin from Wild Sheep, Primitive Domestic Sheep and Parchment. *Nature*, 182, 1958, 781–783.
[14] M. L. Ryder, Follicle Remains in some British Parchments. *Nature* 187 1960, 130–132.
[15] D. V. Thompson, Medieval Parchment-Making. *Trans. Bibliog. Soc.*, XVI 1935, 113–117.

tannage.[6] Although parchment must be free from grease, Saxl[3] considers that the high content of grease in some sheep skins causes partial oil tannage (and a yellow coloration) of parchments made from them. Whereas Poole and Reed state (from the Law) that animal sinews were used to sew parchments together, some stitching I examined was flax, like the cloth used to wrap the scrolls. Worn-out scrolls were not destroyed, but stored in jars to allow decay. Instead, the dry climate preserved many of them for us.

One of the first proper descriptions of parchment manufacture, quoted by Forbes,[8] is given in a Wattenbach manuscript of the 8th century A.D. The skin was placed three days in lime water to loosen the hairs, which were then scraped off with a knife. Powdered chalk was rubbed into the skin during drying. The hides used were calf in the north of Europe and sheep and goat in the south.

Saxl[3] traced the continuity of parchment manufacturing methods from ancient times through the Middle Ages to the present day. During her research Saxl actually made parchment by *medieval methods* she discovered in original manuscripts, and together with those given by such authors as Thompson[15] these are summarised by Saxl.[2] She describes a method for a week-old calf skin as follows. The skin was washed well and then soaked in clean water for 24 hrs. It was then put into a lime paste containing 30% of freshly-slaked lime and left there for periods varying from 8 days in hot weather to 16 days in cold weather. The hair was then scraped (or rather pushed) from the skin with a blunt knife, while the skin was lying over a rounded wooden support known as a beam.

So far the process is similar to the first stages of leather manufacture, but a skin to be made into parchment would be washed and stretched on a frame before being limed again. In the Middle Ages the frame was a hoop,[15] but by the 18th century the modern rectangular frame was in use. The skin is tied to the frame with cords, one end of which is wound round a peg in the frame, and the other around a fold in the edge of the skin supported by a round object known as a pippin.

According to Saxl the quality of the parchment depended on careful control of the drying on the frame, and it was several times partly dried then wetted again with cold water. During drying, the surface was shaved smooth with the curved knife and it was finally "pounced" smooth with pumice. The Wattenbach manuscript (above) indicates how chalk was used to assist the drying particularly in colder climes of northern Europe. This whitened the parchment and had the effect of removing excess grease; some medieval methods included a sprinkling (with the mouth) of "good ale", which would act as a degreasing agent.[15] It was usual for medieval scribes to pounce the skin again before writing on it,[15] and it was given a coat of size (glue) particularly before illumination. Pouncing is not carried out during manufacture today because about the 18th century a new form of sizing was evolved in which the size was in fact formed in the surface of the parchment by dissolving it with hot water. The Birrell family of Scotland who described their method about 1860[16] may have been referring to this when they criticised the contemporary English habit of applying chemicals to the skin so that it becomes soft and clogged the pen. On the other hand they may have been referring to the tanning process of alum tawing that was sometimes carried out. They polished with a pumice stone but regarded the essential operation as the "sheaving" with the curved knife, and indicated more than any other source how very skilled this part of the craft was. The knife had to be razor sharp and ground to a particular angle. A dehairing knife belonging to William More a successor of the Birrell family and the last parchment manufacturer at Kinross was presented to the National Museum for Antiquities of Scotland in 1926; this still has an encrustation of lime containing wool fibres.

Today, the shaving knife is still used, but the skin is dehaired rapidly with sodium sulphide, split by machine and dried in an oven while being stretched. Some 19th century parchments I have examined had regularly-spaced pin-holes along the edge suggesting that they had been held like a textile fabric for drying in a tenter. I am indebted to Messrs. G. W. Russell & Son, Ltd., Leather Manufacturers, of Hitchin (established 1783) for the information that they believe themselves to be one of only three firms making parchment in Great Britain today, although some parchment is made in France and Italy. They use only sheepskins, preferably from animals between one and two years

---

[16] R. Annan, *Proc. Soc. Antiq. Scot.*, III (III), 385.

old, from which the wool has already been removed (by fellmongers). The parchment made is used for diplomas and is mainly exported to America.

If skin is stretched less strongly the parchment formed is likely to be transparent. Transparency was useful in illumination when the painting was allowed to show through from the reverse side, and a patent for making parchment transparent by treating the flesh-side with potash was taken out by Edwards of Halifax in 1790.[10] Plenderleith[10, 17] discusses some chemical aspects of parchment and points out that it is in fact alkaline owing to remaining traces of lime. This may explain why it is not attacked by acid atmospheres as much as is leather. Parchment will absorb moisture, and if water absorption continues to the extreme the parchment will hydrolyse (into glue). For this reason parchment should not be washed, in the way that leather can be washed, but if cleaning is necessary this should be carried out with a damp sponge, and the parchment should be dried quickly in a good draught. Parchment is best kept in a Relative Humidity of 60% at a temperature between 60 and 70° F.; if a parchment becomes too dry and brittle it can be relaxed between sheets of damp blotting paper.

[*Editors' Note:* Material has been omitted at this point.]

---

[17] H. J. Plenderleith, *The Preservation of Leather Bookbindings*, London: British Museum, 1946.

III: CAUSES OF DETERIORATION

Paper 8: Commentary

As a summary of the principal factors known to contribute to the deterioration of library materials, the article by Carl J. Wessel, a scientist currently employed in private industry, is among the most authoritative in the literature. The presentation is comprehensive and is characterized by admirable simplicity of language and lucidity of expression that are not frequently encountered in literature on scientific subjects written for the nonscientist. Included in the article are a number of definitions and brief explanations of such physical phenomena as durability, permanence, deterioration, environment, relative and absolute humidity, temperature, heat, and object humidity, a general acquaintance with which is essential for those engaged in the theory and practice of conservation.

Wessel's bibliography of ninety references to literature published through 1970 is among the most extensive yet published on the environmental factors that contribute to the deterioration of objects commonly collected by libraries. The accompanying tables and illustrations are of considerable interest in their own right, adding weight to the view that Wessel's article is a significant and lasting contribution to the literature on conservation of library materials.

ADDITIONAL READINGS

Banks, Paul N., "Environmental Standards for Storage of Books and Journals" *Library Journal* 99 (February 1, 1974): 339–43.

Feller, Robert L., "Thermochemically Activated Oxidation: Mother Nature's Book-burning," *PLA (Pennsylvania Library Association) Bulletin* 28 (November 1973): 232–42.

National Research Council, Prevention of Deterioration Center, *Deterioration of Materials: Causes and Prevention,* Greathouse, G. A., and Wessel, Carl J., eds. (New York: Reinhold, 1954), 835 pp.

Smith, Richard D., "Paper Impermanence as a Consequence of pH and Storage Conditions," *Library Quarterly* 39 (April 1969): 153–95.

Thomson, Garry, ed., *Museum Climatology,* International Institute for Conservation, Conference on Museum Climatology (London: Butterworths, 1968), 296 pp.

Weiss, Harry B., and Carruthers, Ralph H., *Insect Enemies of Books* (New York: New York Public Library, 1945), 63 pp.

8: DETERIORATION OF LIBRARY MATERIALS

C. Wessel

Man has been concerned, in one way or another, with environmental deterioration of materials for a long time, perhaps since he first appeared. Certainly by biblical times. St. Matthew records, "Do not store up for yourselves treasure on earth, where it grows rusty and moth-eaten, and thieves break in to steal it" (*1*).

Undoubtedly he did not refer to the treasures of the library for this would have contradicted preservation of his message for following ages.

The reasons we have libraries may be quite different in the minds of different people. One of the reasons, which most people will probably agree on, is to preserve for those who follow us our thoughts, intellectual and artistic creations, and man's historical records. Some of what is recorded and gets into libraries is not very important, and it does not make much difference if it lasts any longer than the people or events about which it is written. But some of the recorded material is very important and should be preserved for as long as there are men to read it. Sometimes we do not know one from the other. Thus, in the past it has been policy usually to nod in the direction of preservation by trying to utilize the most stable materials known to the art and science of the times, gambling that what is important will be recognized in time to take precautions to extend the useful life of the material on which it is recorded.

The deterioration of library materials is a complex subject because there are so many different kinds of materials used in the making of the documents, books, manuscripts, illustrations, charts, maps, bindings, magnetic tapes, photographic films, and the great many other forms which library items take, and there are so many different factors in the environment which cause the deterioration. Furthermore, there are many uses to which these library items are put, and many ways in which they are handled and stored. Finally there is much variation in knowledge regarding deterioration on the part of librarians and the clients who use them. The subject is often discharged with the same aplomb that goes with death and taxes.

As is the case with many things which men have manufactured, the design of books and documents, and the many other items in library collections, have not taken account of, and the materials used in their manufacture have often not been chosen, with a view to permanence. Admittedly there are exceptions, such as in certain paper and bindings for extra heavy handling and use (see Figure 1). Furthermore, even when permanence is one of the guiding principles, the materials available are often not resistant to the elements of the environment which tend to degrade them (see Figures 2, 3, and 4).

How few times, for example, have we custom-designed and manufactured, with carefully chosen climate-resistant materials, books to be used and stored in the tropics (hot-wet), as compared to those for use in temperate climates! The same may be said for books to be used in desert regions (hot-dry) or cold regions of the world (cold-wet or cold-dry)! Usually we manufacture things with materials which have come into common use where we happen to be, or in our country, and can compete in price. Little thought is given as to how well those things will resist time and the environment. There are some specialized exceptions such as particularly historic documents. Yet there are too many striking cases of vastly important historic documents in which the material is utterly unsuited to its important mission. Although in this discussion of the library materials deterioration problem we shall, of course, give examples of deteriorated items and we shall

FIGURE 1. *A fifteenth-century vegetable-tanned leather binding in which the leather is in excellent condition with the exception of breaking at the hinges from mechanical wear and tear over five centuries. (Photograph courtesy Paul N. Banks, Newberry Library, Chicago.)*

attempt to assess the problem realistically, truly this is hard to accomplish because we simply do not know the worst cases—they are long gone because they disappeared due to a deterioration.

The disregard of, or the inability to solve, the deterioration/permanence problem is not something peculiar to modern times. And most of the present-day library deterioration problems have been inherited from the past—immediate or remote. But modern times have tended to magnify the problem because of the great proliferation of library items and the highly competitive economic system modern man lives under. Not surprisingly, some of the early library materials utilized very permanent materials—baked clay tablets and stone, for instance. But as man moved ahead and had to produce greater and greater quantities of materials for documentary purposes, and had to do it on a competitive basis, the materials

FIGURE 2. *Water and mud damage from the Florence, Italy, flood of November 4, 1966. (Photograph courtesy Paul N. Banks, Newberry Library, Chicago.)*

FIGURE 3. *Extreme moisture damage. Staining of paper, fungal attack, and cracking and destruction of binding materials. (Photograph courtesy James Gear, National Archives, Washington, D.C.)*

FIGURE 4. *Deterioration of natural adhesive. (Photograph courtesy Paul N. Banks, Newberry Library, Chicago.)*

tended to become more and more fugitive. Little thought was given to permanence. Today, let it be hoped, we at least recognize a deterioration/permanence problem and attempt to determine just how lasting are the materials on which we impress our messages.

In this exposition of the library materials deterioration problem we shall not try to examine in minute detail the great variety of materials involved; that would simply be too big a job and not necessary. For example, some authorities state that there are some 7,000 different kinds of paper! Certainly there are untold varieties of leather from hundreds of kinds of animals; there are numerous inks; the different kinds of glues, adhesives, coatings, we leave to your imagination; now that synthetic plastics are so widely used, they too are appearing in libraries in numerous forms—bindings, threads, microfilms and microfiche, magnetic tapes, photographic negatives and positives, and so on and on. It will be our intent to treat "classes" of materials—paper in general, leather, glues, plastics, etc.

Then there is the matter of environment—that all-pervasive complex of energy forms and chemical substances which we must have in order to exist, but which in the deterioration sense comprises a miasma waiting to bring degradation and

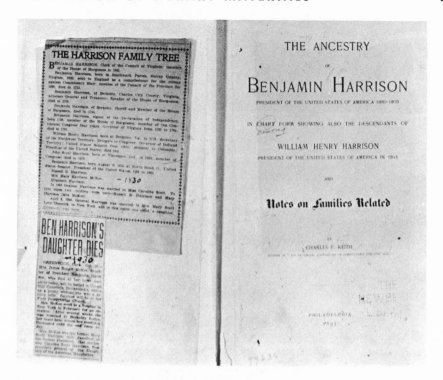

FIGURE 5. *Damage from migration of injurious substances from deteriorating groundwood paper. (Photograph courtesy Paul N. Banks, Newberry Library, Chicago.)*

destruction to the library collection. Again, we cannot examine this in detail. But we shall attempt to analyze and appreciate the more significant factors so that we can understand how environment causes our deterioration problem.

Regarding use and handling of library collections, it is not our mission to discuss these very much under deterioration. Not that these do not have a great part in destroying library collections. Misuse (see Figure 5) and bad handling practices cause rapid and enormous damage to books and other library items. But then, too, so do fire, flood, earthquake, windstorms, and war (see Figure 2). But these are not what we generally mean when we talk about "deterioration." Storage is a different matter. The general discussion of the entire exposition will have bad storage conditions in mind. Good storage will be emphasized in another section of this Encyclopedia.

Finally, there will be a companion section in this Encyclopedia on *Preservation*. There, hopefully, one will find a discussion about how to slow down or even almost stop deterioration. There will be discussion of how it is possible to overcome many forms of deterioration and bring permanence to many of the items in most libraries by treatments, restoration techniques, environmental controls, use of improved and carefully selected materials, careful handling, and a variety of other techniques.

Various authorities have been calling attention to the library materials deterioration problem for many hundreds of years. The book and newsprint paper deterioration history is threaded through with efforts of farsighted people. These dedicated souls tried hard to get the message around that support was needed to underwrite investigation of this problem. Further, they tried to show that unless materials of sufficiently high quality and permanence were used for new books, and restorative treatments applied to books already deteriorated, truly our library collections would not be available in a usable condition to posterity.

We know, for example, about an Egyptian scribe who reported some 3,000 years ago that papyrus scrolls in his charge had been wetted by rain and had to be dried and unrolled to see if the ink writing had been washed off (2). Further, the Chinese in about A.D. 500 felt they knew enough to preserve paper for several hundreds of years. Evidently the subject was common enough in the mind of Shakespeare so that he included it in one of his works.

Williams (3), in his review of deterioration of library collections, recalls the concern of Frederick I, Barbarossa, emperor of the Occident who, in the twelfth century, banned the use of paper in deeds and charters because he feared it to be too perishable. Grove (4) in 1964 traced concern over the matter of paper deterioration to the fifteenth-century Benedictine abbot Johann Tritheim who, worried about paper, placed more faith in vellum. William (3) also brings to our attention that newsprint paper deterioration supports a whole literature of its own and was recognized as a problem sometime around Civil War days. Grove (4) traces from the early 1860s the story of the introduction of papers with inferior permanence properties into the newspaper business, and the many and varied efforts, some quite well founded and thoughtful, some rather naive, either to employ better papers or to try and restore strength and permanence to newspaper collections already on inferior papers.

Although we all know that there are many kinds of materials used in books (the term "books" is meant to include all forms of written records), and we know further that all materials tend to deteriorate to a greater or lesser extent, the one general class of materials that seems to have attracted the most attention in the history of the library materials deterioration problem is paper.* This is not difficult to understand in view of the central role played by paper in the history of libraries. This is not to denigrate the role of other important materials such as the various forms of leather, cloth, threads, and adhesives. It does not overlook the ancients' use of baked clay tablets or messages scratched on stone, or the use of animal skins, papyrus, parchments, and vellum. Nor does it overlook modern efforts to record messages on photographic films or magnetic tapes. "Hard copy" of the written word has involved paper for a very long time, and it still does. Paper is still the "workhorse" in recording the messages we need in all walks of life and which end up in libraries.

*The term "paper" as used in this discussion refers only to the paper used in printing and publishing. It does not refer to the many hundreds or thousands of varieties of so-called "industrial papers."

The written record resides, for the most part, on paper. In spite of the many excellent properties of paper, some of the papers made in the past, and some of the papers being made today, do not enjoy long life. Long life here is intended to mean hundreds of years. Under the proper conditions of composition and environment, this perishable commodity can be remarkably stable and *will* persist for those hundreds of years. Unfortunately, there are too many cases of undesirable composition and bad environment.

The litany that could be recited illuminating the periodic complaints of men about the deteriorative ills of paper and other library materials is a long one. Borrowing some of the highlights from Williams (3) and Grove (4) and alluding to others (5), we recite only the following small part. About a century and a half ago, two British publications called attention to paper problems. In July 1823 one dealt with problems presumably caused by the chemicals used in making rag papers and John Murray in *The Gentlemen's Magazine* alluded to paper as "that wretched compound called paper." He went on to say that his copy of the "Bible printed at Oxford, 1816 (never used)" was "crumbling literally into dust," concluding that the cause of his misfortune was the chemicals employed in the making of the paper. We suspect that he did a disservice in his remarks, as do some disciples of deterioration prevention today, by overstating the matter.

Williams makes reference to Justin Winsor, the first president of the American Library Association, who spoke about deterioration problems of newspaper, probably about 1875, and attempted (largely unsuccessfully) to convince some Boston newspaper publishers to use more durable paper. The American Library Association recognized the deterioration problem by supporting a Committee on Deterioration of Newsprint Paper from 1910 to 1913 and from 1918 to 1920. In 1891, Rossiter Johnson called attention to inferior paper as a menace to permanence of literature, and in 1897 J. Y. W. MacAlister, Librarian of the Leeds Library, predicted that many of that library's books would not outlast the generation of readers he served. In 1898 the British had a Committee on the Deterioration of Paper; the Librarian of Congress discussed the subject of paper deterioration in his annual report; and the Italian government was petitioned by a group of librarians to set paper standards. In 1900 Pierre Dauze in France wrote that librarians were deeply disturbed by the library deterioration problem; in 1907 Cyril Davenport thought that in 100 years from the date of their publication a large majority of modern books would not be in a readable condition. In 1909 the U.S. Department of Agriculture, Bureau of Chemistry, published results of research on the durability of paper; in 1931 and 1934 Scribner of the National Bureau of Standards published studies on the preservation of records in libraries. In 1954 the present author tried to summarize many of the deterioration problems faced by paper makers and users (6).

Many of the efforts to resolve the deterioration problems associated with paper and other library materials have been met with apathy, ideas of misplaced thrift, charges that preventive or remedial actions would involve unjustifiable costs, ridicule, and sometimes downright antagonism.

There is another side of the story of course. There is a great deal of material printed that *is not* intended to be permanent, and to insist that all things that might end up in a library be printed on media that will endure forever is overdoing it. There *is* much in the paper and printing industries that has been built around paper as we have known it for the past hundred years or so, and to expect that this technology will be changed overnight is asking too much. Shatzkin (7) has reviewed the factors involved in publishing on permanent papers, and Thomas (8) has reviewed alkaline printing papers. Permanence is not the only quality to be considered. Other important properties must not easily be sacrificed to gain small improvements in permanence. A wholesale shift to neutral or alkaline papers, presumably to gain permanence, would tend to cause disruptions in the paper and publishing industries that would be difficult to handle. There appears to be willingness on the part of many in the industries, however, to make such a shift, if it is shown to be necessary and justifiable, but on the basis of a slower and more orderly transition.

Recently much has been done to bring the library materials deterioration problem to the attention of large numbers of people and to the levels of governmental, educational, industrial, and institutional administrations necessary to get effective programs of deterioration prevention underway. This applies both to introduction of permanent materials and to the commencement of programs of remedial treatment for important collections which are in various stages of deterioration already.

Notable has been the work of W. J. Barrow, reported in a group of publications (9–16) initially from the Virginia State Library, Richmond, Virginia, and later from the W. J. Barrow Research Laboratory, also in Richmond. Although Sutermeister (8), among others, had reported the deteriorative influence of high acid content in paper which results in rather rapid embrittlement and loss of strength, it took the work of Barrow to start a program in motion. Much credit is due to the Council on Library Resources, which provided the financial support for a considerable part of Barrow's work, and to Verner Clapp, who served as president of the council at the time.

What started the most influential of Barrow's work was a project to test the physical strength of nonfiction book papers as used in publications appearing from 1900 to 1949. The sample was statistically significant—a total of 500 books, 100 for each of the five decades represented. These books were chosen from a large number of publishers and various university presses. The tests were standard tear resistance and folding endurance. The results were sufficiently depressing as to cause Barrow to state, "If material which should be preserved indefinitely is going to pieces as rapidly as these figures indicate, it seems probable that most library books printed in the first half of the 20th century will be in an unusable condition in the next century." The measurement of the paper sample pH values indicated that most were definitely on the acid side. Subsequent work by Barrow on books from earlier decades provided much additional valuable data.

The Association of Research Libraries (3), aroused by Barrow's 1959 report, decided in 1960 to establish a committee "to develop a national program for the preservation of research library materials with its primary concern directed toward the preservation of retrospective materials." At almost the same time a conference, sponsored by the American Library Association and the Virginia State Library, was held in Washington, D.C., to discuss "Permanent/Durable Book Paper" (*17*). At this conference Robert Kingery of the New York Public Library described the extent of the paper problem in large research collections and estimated costs to combat the deterioration. Among other things of a grave nature, he stated that about 10% of the collection of about 2,000,000 volumes in the Reference Department of the New York Public Library needed immediate attention because of deterioration problems. He estimated that as much as 50% of the collection needed some conservation attention.

The ARL Committee decided that as a first step it would be desirable to determine the quantitative dimensions of the paper deterioration problem. A study by the Research Triangle Institute and financed by the Council on Library Resources undertook to make a statistical sampling of the National Union Catalog. The findings indicated that in 1961 the catalog listed 14,376,000 different volumes containing 2,999,998,000 pages. Slightly more than 57% of the pages were in volumes published since 1869, and 56% of them were published abroad. No serials were included in the study (*3*).

The next important study, sponsored by the ARL Committee and funded by the Council on Library Resources, came in 1962 in which Gordon Williams made a comprehensive survey of the problems associated with the preservation of deteriorating books and gave recommendations for a solution. As E. E. Williams (*3*) points out, the findings of this study were debated at great length by the ARL but finally the results were adopted unanimously by the association. This is significant in that it thus represents the official attitudes of librarians of the institutions most vitally concerned with the problems of deteriorating books.

The Gordon Williams report (*18*) offered a flexible comprehensive plan whereby, with the proper support including that of the federal government, it will be possible to undertake actions which would insure the preservation of all books of significant value. It encompasses the use of approaches to the problem including preservation of books themselves whenever this is possible, as well as copying books on microforms. Furthermore it provides for the continuous and ready availability of the preserved materials to anyone who needs them. Finally it recommends that a federally supported central agency be created to play a major role in the program. Yet, one need not conclude from this that a mammoth federal center will be created for doing all the work and keeping all the books. Several alternative systems are discussed.

A National Commission on Libraries and Information Science was created in July 1970. Among many facets of the library and information science field that this commission will find itself responsible for will be that of providing the leadership and support for a national effort in library materials deterioration prevention as well as preserving the immense national resources now in libraries.

In our discussion of environment as the cause of deterioration, other terms like permanence, stability, and durability will come into use. People in the paper industry make a definite distinction between permanence and durability. "Durability" connotes how well the paper will stand up under conditions of use and rough handling. "Permanence" connotes how well the paper resists aging, retains chemical stability of its components, and thus retains its original properties. Permanence is basically a chemical phenomenon; durability is a function of the physical properties of the fibers in papers and the way they are compounded to form a sheet. There is obviously a relationship between permanence and durability, and the proper balance must be achieved.

Deterioration as used here is a loss in the quality or value of a material or a decrease in its ability to fulfill a function for which it was intended. Generally, it is limited to impairment due to natural causes, as for example moisture, dryness, acids, alkalies, dust, moderate heat or cold, ultraviolet radiations, slow electro-chemical reactions, or biological creatures including rodents, insects, bacteria, and fungi. We are all familiar with such common examples as iron rust, insect holes in paper, brittle paper, rotten wood, cracked paints, and crumbled leather bookbindings (see Figure 6). Usually these changes, caused by physical, chemical, and biological environmental factors, proceed at a fairly slow rate.

On a somewhat more analytic basis deterioration is a process of transition from a higher to a lower energy level. Most chemical substances like to rest in a lazy, comfortable, stable state. The more noble elements like gold remain in their stable elemental state and do not readily combine with other elements to form molecules of compounds. Less noble elements tend to form combinations with other elements where they find relative stability. Often when man makes chemicals into forms that he finds useful, he makes them unstable. And they respond to this by trying to revert to the stable states. For example, iron is made by converting stable ores, such as iron oxides, to elemental iron, perhaps in an alloy like steel. But iron does not want to be a free element. So it reacts with things like oxygen or the sulfides to be stable again, and that stable state is called rust. As things made of rust do not have the strength or other properties of iron or steel, the iron is said to have deteriorated.

Similarly, cotton and other plants make the sugar glucose and out of that biosynthesize cellulose from which various papers are made. Cellulose is a rather complex molecule made up of atoms of carbon, hydrogen, and oxygen. Carbon in this form is very useful in libraries as paper. But, when the conditions are right, the cellulose tends to break down into simpler molecules than cellulose and eventually to the stable carbon dioxide which can not serve as paper. Some of the conditions which affect paper cellulose in this way are acidity, heat, and light. These, together with biological agents, are agents of deterioration.

There are always forces that tend to cause reversion to stability whether it is rusting of metals, rotting of paper, deterioration of threads used in binding, or the destruction of glues or adhesives by ozone or whatnot. The total of the so-called forces that tend to cause changes in energy level may be termed the "environment." Environment determines which of the agents present in a given

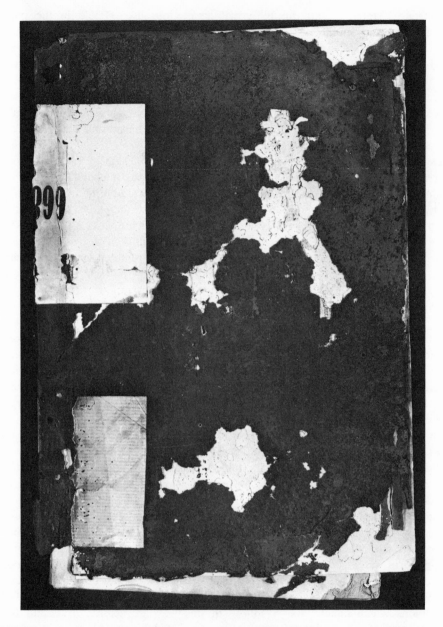

FIGURE 6. *Leather binding and paper showing extreme damage presumably due to acid, dampness, mildew, and insects. Approximately late eighteenth century. (Sample courtesy James Gear, National Archives, Washington, D.C.)*

spot will shorten the useful life of materials. The intensity or amount of physical deteriorative agents—heat, sunlight, dust, sand, and grit—vary according to geographical location and the climate of the region. Chemical agents, i.e., moisture, salts, alkalies, acids, and all the polluting substances we now find in our atmosphere, are also functions of climate and, of course, of industrial effluents for the amount and intensity of their action. On the other hand, the biological agents we are here interested in—the fungi (molds), bacteria, insects, and animals such as rodents—depend upon the existence of optimum conditions of humidity, temperature, and nutrients to thrive in an active destructive way and so might be regarded as corollaries to the physical and chemical agents.

Of these various environmental factors, the major ones we must pay particular attention to as far as deterioration of library materials is concerned appear to be those shown in Table 1. But it should be noted that although acid gases are listed as environmental, a great deal of the acid is introduced into the paper not by the so-called natural environment but rather by the chemicals used in the manufacture of the paper. The important fact is that deterioration is caused by acid regardless of whether the paper encounters it in manufacture or in the environment. Therefore, the discussion of acid deterioration of paper will not emphasize where the acid came from so much as what the acid does to the cellulose fibers of the paper (see Figures 7 and 8).

The atmosphere is commonly thought of as the gaseous envelope, or air, that surrounds the earth. A representative composite analysis of dry air is shown in

TABLE 1

Environmental Factors Important
in Library Deterioration Problems

    I. Atmospheric factors
        Pollutants
           Particulate matter
             Dust, dirt, etc.
        Gases
           Acidic components
           Oxidants
        Normal constituents
           Water
   II. Radiant energy
        Light
        Heat
        Other radiation effects
  III. Biological factors
        Microbiological agents
           Fungi, bacterial, actinomycetes
        Macrobiological agents
           Insects, rodents

FIGURE 7. *Muster rolls from the Civil War. Deterioration due to acid paper, acid ink, and carelessness. (Photograph courtesy James Gear, National Archives, Washington, D.C.)*

Table 2. The analysis of air is usually made after it has been freed of solids, such as dust, spores, and bacteria, and from water vapor. Water vapor, or humidity, represents a very important constituent of atmosphere. It will be discussed here as a separate topic because of its great independent influence on library materials. The composition of air varies with altitude, and certain constituents such as ozone may vary considerably. The figures in Table 2 may, however, be regarded as representative of the common components.

TABLE 2

Composition of Dry Air [a]

Substance	% By weight	% By volume
Nitrogen	75.53	78.00
Oxygen	23.16	20.95
Argon	1.27	0.93
Carbon dioxide	0.033	0.03
Neon		0.0018
Helium		0.0005
Methane		0.0002
Krypton		0.0001
Nitrous oxide		0.00005
Hydrogen		0.00005
Xenon		0.000008
Ozone		0.000001

[a] Ref. *19*, p. 25.

FIGURE 8. *This damage is thought to be due to acid paper but was accentuated by acidtype ink which caused the embrittled paper to break away approximately along the lines of lettering. Date on sample is 1844. (Sample courtesy James Gear, National Archives, Washington, D.C.)*

The atmosphere contains a host of other substances called pollutants, especially in industrialized urban areas. As the major and largest library collections tend to be concentrated in urban areas to serve the greatest concentrations of people, the problem is clearly aggravated.

Most of the pollutants occur in very small concentrations in comparison with the normal atmospheric constituents, yet some occur in high enough concentrations to have adverse affects. To provide an idea of the dimensions of air pollution, the emissions of the principal pollutants into the atmosphere in the United States have been estimated by the National Research Council of the National Academy of Sciences to be about 125 million tons per year at the present time (20). The

TABLE 3

Principal Atmospheric Pollutants in the United States [a]

	Millions of tons/year	%
By Type		
Carbon monoxide	65	52
Oxides of sulfur	23	18
Hydrocarbons	15	12
Particulate matter	12	10
Oxides of nitrogen	8	6
Other gases and vapors	2	2
TOTAL	125	100
By Source		
Transportation	74.8	59.9
Manufacturing	23.4	18.7
Generation of electricity	15.7	12.5
Space heating	7.8	6.3
Refuse disposal	3.3	2.6
TOTAL	125.0	100.0

[a] Ref. *21*, p. 11.

amounts by types and sources are shown in Table 3. Other estimates go as high as 300 million tons per year (*22*).

A complete listing of all substances found as contaminants or pollutants in the atmosphere would require several pages. Table 4 presents a partial listing. Those representing the greatest known hazard to library materials for the most part will be those that are either acidic or oxidizing. Notable deleterious substances in the library and museum fields are sulfur dioxide, the oxides of nitrogen, and ozone. These substances play roles in a rather complicated system of photochemical atmospheric pollutants which are seriously damaging to man, animals, vegetation, and materials.

Sulfur dioxide, or at least the SO_2-containing pollutants from coal burning, has been recognized since the thirteenth century as a damaging pollutant in the atmosphere. But photochemical air pollution is a fairly recently recognized phenomenon, first noticed about 25 years ago because of its effect in causing cracking of rubber products and damage to plant species.

One of the symptoms of photochemical air pollution is the presence of high concentrations of oxidizing substances. Photochemical smog consists of mixtures of gaseous and particulate (aerosol) products resulting from atmospheric photochemical reactions of gases evolved primarily from the combustion of organic fuels. Ultraviolet radiation from sunlight is responsible for the initiation of atmospheric reactions between the oxides of nitrogen and such photochemically reactive substances as olefins, aromatic hydrocarbons, aldehydes, and to a limited extent some

TABLE 4

Atmospheric Substances Considered as Pollutants

Particulate matter (aerosols)	Gases
Dust, dirt, smoke	Carbon monoxide
Coal and coke dust	Nitric oxide
Fly ash	Nitrous oxide
Salt particles	Sulfur dioxide
Calcium and ammonium sulfates	Ozone
Nitrates	Olefins
Chlorides	Aromatic hydrocarbons
Solid oxides	Aldehydes
Soot	Paraffins
Tars	Hydrogen sulfide
Spores	Halogen compounds
Bacteria	Ammonia

paraffins, producing a dynamic complex of oxidizing substances not yet completely defined chemically. A number of products are formed in this photochemical smog-forming process through the initiating photodissociation of nitrogen dioxide with the concomitant formation of atomic oxygen. This permits ozone formation, already present normally to some extent in the atmosphere and known to be a principal oxidizer. In addition, there is formation of the strong oxidants, the organic peroxides, of which the peroxyacyl nitrates have been identified. These comprise an homologous series of organic peroxide nitrogen compounds which have been designated as PaNs compounds. In addition to the foregoing, there are formed other unidentified oxidants, oxygenated compounds such as carbonyl compounds (aldehydes and ketones) and certain degradation products such as carbon monoxide and carbon dioxide. Thus the principal identifiable photochemical atmospheric pollutants are thought to be ozone, the PaNs, and the oxides of nitrogen, chiefly nitrogen dioxide. The latter, comprising usually about 10% of total oxidants, are relatively weak oxidants.

A seemingly anomalous phenomenon in the air pollution field should be noted. It is especially interesting to the librarian because of the importance of the acidic sulfur dioxide to the degradation of paper. Sulfur dioxide is a reducing substance whereas the photochemical air pollutants we have been discussing are oxidizing substances. Ordinarily one would expect that such oxidants as ozone and sulfur dioxide should react with each other until there is an excess of one or the other. The extreme dilution of these pollutants in the atmosphere, however, permits them to coexist, and one may note oxidizing and reducing degradation phenomena simultaneously (23).

Water occurs in all the normal states of matter—solid, liquid, and gas. It also takes many forms—ice, snow, glaze, sleet or hail, ice fog, liquid water, rain, water in the aerosol form of fog or mist, and finally water vapor. Water vapor is water

TABLE 5

Relationship between Temperature, Absolute Humidity, and Relative Humidity (24)

Temperature		Absolute humidity (g/kg)		
°C	°F	20% relative humidity	60% relative humidity	100% relative humidity
0	32	0.38	2.28	3.82
20	68	1.43	8.69	14.61
40	104	4.55	28.30	48.64
60	140	12.50	83.55	152.45

in the gaseous phase and is usually referred to in terms of humidity. For the consideration of the librarian, water vapor is the most important form of water. The materials of the librarian—his buildings, his collections, and practically all that he works with—are protected for the most part against all forms of water except water vapor. This discussion will cover water only in the vapor form and will not consider the less usual, albeit devastating, damage which may come about from such phenomena as floods or liquid water damage as might be caused by sprinkler systems and the like.

Humidity measurements include absolute and relative humidity. Absolute humidity is measured in terms of the mass of water vapor per unit volume of natural air. Relative humidity expresses the ratio of the actual water vapor content of the air to its total capacity at the given temperature. The warmer the air, the greater the amount of water vapor it is capable of holding. When air holds as much water vapor as it is capable of holding at that temperature, it is said to be saturated, and is at its dew point.

An enlightening way of showing the relations between temperature, relative humidity, and absolute humidity is that of Table 5 taken from Plenderleith and Philippot (24). This shows how the actual amount of water in the atmosphere increases, for a given relative humidity, as the temperature rises.

We are here concerned more with the effect of humidity on library materials than on library workers or patrons. Nonetheless, because temperature and humidity conditions in libraries are usually chosen with both materials and people in mind, a few remarks should be made about factors of human comfort. Cold air with high humidity feels colder than dry air of the same temperature. On the other hand, hot air with high relative humidity feels warmer than it actually is. These effects are due to a combination of heat conduction from the body at the temperatures and humidities involved as well as to the cooling effect on the body brought about by evaporation of water from body surfaces. The feeling of comfort or discomfort experienced by man is then a result of both temperature and humidity. The U.S. Weather Bureau has developed a temperature–humidity or comfort index which gives values in the 70 to 80 range, reflecting outdoor atmospheric conditions of temperature and humidity as a measure of comfort or discomfort in warm weather. This index, I_{th}, is measured as follows:

$$I_{th} = 0.4 \text{ [dry bulb temperature (F°)} + \text{wet bulb temperature (F°)]} + 15$$

When this index is 70 most people feel comfortable; at 75 about half the population is satisfied; at 80 most people are uncomfortable. Without unnecessarily over-simplifying a subject that is complex at best, man is an aqueous creature. In order to exist in his most healthy state he must maintain a proper water balance with his surroundings. This may sometimes call for humidity conditions that would be considered a bit on the uncomfortable side. He cannot suffer dehydration of any magnitude for more than short time periods without serious physiological effects.

The various materials the librarian is dealing with daily also must remain in equilibrium with the proper humidity in order to retain their most desirable properties and endure for long periods of time. These conditions are not necessarily the same for all library materials. It stands to reason that some sort of happy medium must be chosen so that most materials involved are in or near some reasonably favorable range of humidity.

When considering the matter of humidity and temperature with reference to the possible damaging effects of the heat and water on objects (books, manuscripts, museum items, etc.), it is very important to remember that it is the temperature and humidity conditions of the object that control deterioration reactions. These conditions are not always the same as the measured ambient or atmospheric conditions except when they are under constant control. For example, in a library, if an object such as a book is at a temperature higher or lower than that of the air in the library, the relative humidity of the layer of air close to the book will differ considerably from that of the ambient room air. This has given rise to the term "object humidity" (25), which, of course, refers to the relative humidity of the thin film of air in closest contact with the surface of the book. If the temperature conditions in a library vary greatly over the period of a day, relative humidities thought to be in the safe range, perhaps 45 to 55%, can rise to much higher humidities conducive to mildew or other damage to books, paper, leather, and other objects.

The nature of water is such that it is important both as a chemical agent and as a physical agent. Often it acts in both roles simultaneously. For example, when water dissolves carbon dioxide, a small amount of the water reacts chemically to form the compound H_2CO_3. Most of the water, however, plays the physical role of acting as a solvent medium for ionization and the production of hydrogen ions, responsible for the acidic properties of the solution. Water may be regarded as extremely active in promoting reactions between other substances, entering into chemical reactions itself, and serving as the medium for the interaction of numerous otherwise inert substances.

Among its most important roles, water is required for the hydration of many substances in our everyday life. Some of these roles are not completely understood, and often not sufficiently appreciated. The role of water as a plasticizer for certain materials such as nylon is important in preserving the properties of the substance over long periods. The maintenance of proper water levels in paper, wood, and leather, to mention a few materials, is absolutely required to prevent drying out with consequent brittleness and eventual disintegration. The discovery of ancient records or historical and art objects usually poses severe restoration problems of at least partial rehydration before the objects can be handled to any great extent or studied and exhibited. The objects have endured because they were dry and undisturbed, but to be of practical value they must if possible be restored to a water content consonant with usable properties.

On the other hand, the presence of excessive water in materials can bring about destruction. Certain constitutents of materials such as dyes and adhesives may be dissolved out. Other components may become hydrated to the point of becoming pulp as in the case of cellulosic materials in paper. Or excess water may cause certain materials to become adhesives and cause pages of paper to stick together almost beyond separation.

Excessive water may also bring about the completely different problem of biological attack. This is usually manifested as the growth of fungi or mildew and is accompanied by the characteristic musty odor but more importantly by staining of paper, leather, and other materials and weakening or even destruction of the materials if permitted to progress too far.

To obtain an idea of the humidity conditions in his particular city, the librarian has access to the records of the U.S. Weather Bureau. Certain of this information in relation to the materials deterioration problem also has been consolidated in texts (6,26). To obtain a balanced and meaningful idea of the conditions of humidity, one should look at values for relative humidity, precipitation, and temperature. A more complete set of data would also include values for the saturated vapor pressure, for vapor pressure, for depression of wet bulb, and for dew points. The relationship between absolute and relative humidity must also be kept in mind.

There are many other factors that play a part in determining the real significance of the climatic environment of a given location. Some of the elements that are important include local variations in conditions. For example, we all know that rainfall is measured at relatively few spots for a given city. In large cities it may simultaneously be raining in some but not other sections. Humidity and temperature conditions may vary from spot to spot depending upon such factors as existence of local bodies of water, vegetation, and protection from sun. Daily ranges vary from spot to spot. In extreme climates, as in the desert, precipitation values may not have much significance. For example, there may be long periods of no rainfall at all. Suddenly the area may receive a 2-inch rain. This could give an average value of perhaps 0.17 inch per year—a meaningless figure. Wind conditions also can influence conditions significantly and vary greatly from spot to spot and time to time.

Of all the chemical and physical agents of deterioration, sunlight probably accounts for the most widespread destruction of materials *outdoors*. Materials used mainly indoors for the most part are protected from the powerful effects of solar radiation. Nonetheless, they are subject to damage by the radiant energy of natural light entering the building via windows, skylights, and doors, and by artificial sources of illumination. Thus, although light is not regarded as being as damaging to library collections as some other deteriorative factors, it is certainly worthy of attention. The effectiveness of radiant energy as an agent of deterioration is explained by the fact that some portions of the electromagnetic radiation spectrum are able to bring about photochemical reactions with the materials being irradiated either alone or in the presence of other agents like moisture or oxygen.

Sunlight, or solar radiation, and certain sources of artificial light are important in photochemical and photosensitized reactions because they are the sources of the radiant energy that make the reactions possible. In nonphotochemical reactions, the energy is provided by heat. Solar radiations comprise wavelengths from about 1,500 to 1,200,000 Ångström* units in the electromagnetic spectrum. Radiation is classified according to wavelengths of which the shortest are as low as 10^{-14} centimeter and the longest are measured in kilometers. The shortest are known as cosmic rays, followed by gamma radiation, X-rays, ultraviolet rays, visible light, infrared rays, radio waves, and radiations from power lines, the last having wavelengths measured in kilometers. Of solar radiations, about 99% of the energy lies between wavelengths of 1,500 and 40,000 Ångströms. About half the energy is in the visible region between 3,800 and 7,700 Ångströms, and the other half in the invisible ultraviolet and infrared.

Two fundamental laws of photochemistry are at work in photochemical reactions. The first states that light must be absorbed by the reacting atoms or molecules; the second law states that one molecule of a reacting substance may be activated by the absorption of one light quantum. A light quantum is the smallest amount of energy that can be removed from a beam of light by any material system. Whereas a molecule can absorb multiples of quanta, it cannot absorb less than one. The power or energy of this quantum unit is expressed by the term $h\nu$, where h is Planck's constant or approximately 6.6×10^{-27} erg sec. The frequency of the particular light is expressed by ν. The energy of quanta in long wavelength radiation ranges (low frequency radiation) such as infrared is much lower than that in the short wavelength (high frequency) radiation such as ultraviolet.

We can now relate to the energy required for chemical reactions to proceed. Most chemical reactions that proceed with reasonably slow rates at room temperature require something like 25 kilocalories (kcal) per gram-molecule for activation. Those which go on only at very high temperatures may require 100 kcal per gram-molecule or even more. For the breaking of bonds between atoms such as carbon-carbon and carbon-hydrogen bonds, 84 and 100 kcal, respectively, are required (27). By reference to Table 6, we can see why radiation in the short wavelength

---

*An Ångström unit $= 1 \times 10^{-8}$ centimeter.

TABLE 6

Energy in Various Types of Radiation (28)

Description	Wavelength (Ångströms)	Frequency	Calories/ einstein
X-Rays	1	3×10^{18}	2.84×10^8
Ultraviolet	1,000	3×10^{15}	284,500
Ultraviolet	2,000	1.5×10^{15}	142,300
Ultraviolet	3,000	1×10^{15}	94,840
Visible (violet)	4,000	7.5×10^{14}	71,120
Visible (blue-green)	5,000	6×10^{14}	57,000
Visible (orange)	6,000	5×10^{14}	47,400
Visible (red)	7,000	4.3×10^{14}	40,600
Visible (red)	8,000	3.7×10^{14}	35,500
Near infrared	10,000	3×10^{14}	28,450
Infrared	100,000	3×10^{13}	2,845
Far infrared	1,000,000	3×10^{12}	284

regions such as blue-green to ultraviolet are required to activate the majority of photochemical reactions and why these wavelengths are so important to the materials deterioration problem. In the longer wavelength (low frequency) ranges of the solar spectrum, as with infrared, the energy of quanta is relatively small. Quanta can influence vibrations and rotation and thus heat molecules in this range, but they cannot provide enough energy to overcome the forces which hold their atoms together. In the visible and especially the ultraviolet ranges of the spectrum, chemical bonds can be broken. The only limit of these reactions in the atmosphere is due to the presence of the ozone layer in the upper atmosphere which does not permit radiation of wavelengths below 2,900 Ångström units to reach the earth's surface (27).

An informative example of the comparative damaging effect and the luminosity of radiant energy is provided in Table 7. This is taken from a report by the National Bureau of Standards describing work done in connection with preservation of the Declaration of Independence and Constitution of the United States (animal parchments). The particular sample was of a low grade paper and is used only for illustration. Animal parchment deterioration under light is not as rapid as is the case with this sample of paper. The influence of wavelength of the radiation on ability to destroy the paper is clearly demonstrated.

In brief summary then, in photochemical reactions the energy supplied by radiation must first be absorbed and may result in displacement of electrons in the reactants. If the energy of electronic excitation displaces atoms within a molecule, chemical reaction may take place. If the atomic displacement is large enough, the molecule may dissociate. If atoms are displaced, but not enough to be expelled, molecular reactions may occur. The energy of the particular radiation must be at least as great as or greater than the energy of activation of the reaction. Whether

TABLE 7

Comparison of Damage and Usefulness Factors of Radiant Energy (*29*)

Wavelength (millimicrons)	Relative damage factors	Relative luminosity factors (usefulness)
360	145	0.0000
380	107	0.0000
400	66	0.0004
420	37	0.0040
440	20	0.023
460	12	0.060
480	6.5	0.139
500	3.7	0.323
520	2.1	0.710
540	1.2	0.954
560	.7	0.995
580	.4	0.870
600	.2	0.631
620	.1	0.381
640	.05	0.175
660	.0	0.061
680	.0	0.017
700	.0	0.004
720	.0	0.001

or not activation and reaction occur depends not upon the total amount of energy in a beam of radiation but upon the intensity of the radiation, i.e., the amount of energy per quantum.

It is difficult to visualize any phenomena in the material world in which heat or cold is not involved in some way, for the complete absence of heat would be that point at which there is no molecular motion—absolute zero or zero degree Kelvin. Heat is, then, the energy a body possesses by virtue of the fact that its molecules are in motion. There is always some heat in a body except at absolute zero, and for our purposes we should think in terms of how much heat is available rather than whether or not there is heat in a body. Heat, and its correlative cold, or the absence of heat, act as powerful agents of chemical and physical deterioration for two very simple basic reasons. The physical properties of almost all materials are greatly influenced by changes in temperature, and second, the rate of almost all chemical reactions is greatly affected by the temperature of the reactants.

The concepts of heat and temperature are often confused. Temperature, or the degree of heat content of a body, is a function of the speed of motion of the molecules in the body. Heat depends upon both the speed of motion and the number of molecules. Thermodynamically, heat is defined as energy in transmission because of a temperature gradient. Heat, then, may be viewed as the energy that passes from one body to another because of differences in temperature. These bodies may be gases, liquids, or solids, or any combinations of these states of matter.

There are three modes of transmission of heat—convection, conduction, and radiation. All three are important in the library materials permanence problem. Convection is the process of transmitting heat by means of the movement of heated matter from one place to another, and takes place in liquids and gases. The heating of a building with a hot-air furnace is a good example of convection at work. The air heated by the furnace expands, becomes less dense than the cold air above it, rises, and thus causes movement of heat throughout the building by currents of heated air.

Conduction is the process of transferring heat from one molecule to another. An example is that of a bar of metal in a flame. As the molecules nearest the heat of the flame are heated and move more rapidly from the heat, they strike adjacent molecules. These in turn strike more molecules and the heat is transmitted throughout the bar of metal.

We have already discussed radiant energy briefly in the section on light. Heat is also transmitted by radiation. Whereas in the cases of convection and conduction, heat is transmitted via material media, radiant energy may be transmitted through space in waveforms. This radiant energy, falling upon a body, causes molecular motion with the resultant heating of the body.

As in the case of most other environmental factors, heat rarely has the opportunity to act alone. Deleterious effects are usually caused in combination with other factors such as humidity, sunlight, pollutants, and biological agents. Changes in temperature are often very damaging because of expansion or contraction of materials with consequent cracking. The action of heat in driving off water or other solvents and plasticizers and the consequent brittleness often can cause destruction of paper, leather, some plastics, and other materials. Heat plays a very important part in affecting the speed of chemical reactions. A rise of $10°F$ roughly doubles the rate of many chemical reactions. Included in these may be reactions with air pollutants. Holding materials at low temperatures is often an acceptable method of prolonging useful life.

The influence of heat on the water content of materials and of the atmosphere is important in the library materials permanence problem. With a given water content of the atmosphere, a sudden drop in temperature will bring about a rise in relative humidity. If the rise is sufficient, condensation of the water, leading to the formation of liquid water, can occur on the surfaces whose temperature has dropped. If this occurs often enough or for a sufficient time, water damage to susceptible materials can result. Condensation due to temperature changes in air-cooled buildings is discussed in considerable detail by Verrall (30). This is recommended for study by those responsible for such libraries, especially those in older buildings, in small wooden buildings, or in buildings with crawl space.

Finally, the influence of heat in combination with biological agents cannot be overlooked. Although humidity is a much more important environmental factor as far as occurrence and damage by microbiological agents, heat does play a part even with these organisms. Heat plays a much more important part with the macro-biological agents—insects and rodents.

The biological agents of deterioration do not cause great damage in the majority of urban libraries in the United States. However, this should not be misunderstood to mean that the biological deterioration problem no longer exists in any urban libraries or is not a serious source of trouble in some libraries throughout the world. The problem of deterioration of books and archival materials caused by bio-logical agents often becomes of great importance in some countries. Certainly if one includes museums along with libraries, biological agents assume tremendous importance in damaging historic and artistic cultural works. Museums, of course, commonly include in their collections many materials rarely if ever found in libraries and many of these are particularly susceptible to damage by biological agents. It is of the greatest importance to be aware of infestations of certain microbiological and biological agents when newly discovered materials are brought into museums and/or libraries. It is essential that such materials be treated to destroy the organisms before they enter the collections. Although rare book col-lections do not constitute large parts of the over-all collections in many of our modern urban libraries, it is nonetheless essential that such newly introduced materials of often uncertain history and composition be examined and treated adequately before acceptance.

Fungi (molds), bacteria, and actinomycetes constitute organisms referred to usually as microbiological agents (see Figure 9). Taken alone they are usually too small to be studied by the naked eye. In sufficiently large numbers their colonies are, of course, visible. Theoretically, the bacteria could be of importance to libraries. However, few if any cases have been recorded. There are bacteria which do attack cellulosic materials, such as those found in paper, and do considerable damage. But library environmental conditions are not conducive to such attack, and only a few cases of actinomycete damage to library materials have been recorded.

The fungi constitute the most important of the microbiological agents to the librarian for the most part because they thrive best at relatively dry conditions in comparison with bacteria. That is to say, although fungi require high relative humidities, they do not thrive well in the presence of liquid water. Bacteria, on the other hand, require comparatively aqueous conditions for growth and multiplication.

The fungi are extremely numerous in genera and species and are ubiquitous. Spores of fungi are to be found just about anywhere under, on, and above the earth, and await only the proper conditions of moisture, temperature, and some-times light to vegetate, grow, and reproduce. It is perfectly safe to state that every library in the world is liberally seeded with perhaps hundreds of genera and species of fungi. Thus, the important idea in control of fungi is to maintain temperature and humidity conditions at levels not conducive to growth of the microorganism. This does not mean that cleanliness and removal of dust and dirt do not assist in reduction of the fungal problem, but it does mean that cleanliness is only part of the story.

The growth and reproduction of fungi are influenced by a number of environ-

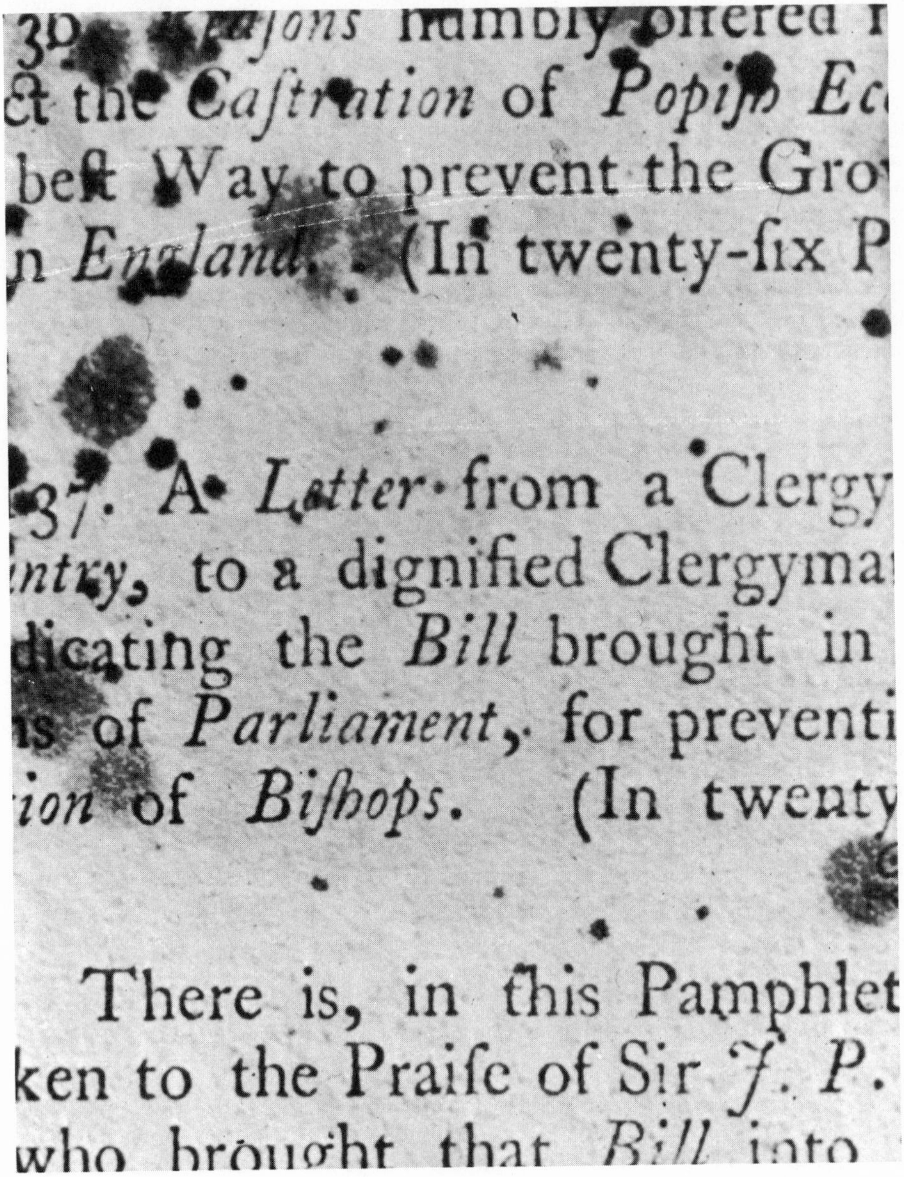
39. ...ons humbly offered
& the *Caſtration* of *Popiſh Ec*
beſt Way to prevent the Gro
n *England*. (In twenty-ſix P

37. A *Letter* from a Clergy
ntry, to a dignified Clergyma
dicating the *Bill* brought in
is of *Parliament*, for preventi
ion of *Biſhops*. (In twenty

There is, in this Pamphlet
ken to the Praiſe of Sir *J. P.*
who brought that *Bill* into

FIGURE 9. *Fungal spotting damage. (Photograph courtesy Paul N. Banks, Newberry Library, Chicago.)*

mental factors—temperature, relative humidity, light, oxygen, and nutrients. Fungi are much more tolerant of relatively large temperature ranges than they are of other environmental factors. That is, they may be expected to be viable at unexpectedly low and unexpectedly high temperatures. Three temperatures are important to growth and reproduction—the temperature below which no growth and reproduction occur, the temperature range at which most rapid growth takes place, and the temperature above which no growth occurs. Fungi of one sort or another have been found to grow at temperatures approximating freezing and as high as 50–55°C. Low-temperature growth of fungi is common as witness events that often occur in your refrigerator. The temperature range for optimal growth and reproduction is variable depending upon genera and species of fungi but may be said to approximate 15 to 35°C or about 59 to 95°F. The average optimum is about 86°F when the relative humidity is 95 to 100%. The absence of growth and reproduction at low temperature does not signify death of fungal spores. Many will withstand prolonged periods of freezing or subfreezing temperatures and, upon restoration to favorable temperatures, will again grow and reproduce. However, alternation of below-freezing with above-freezing temperatures is not tolerated well by most species. High temperatures and especially high temperatures combined with moist conditions will kill most fungi and fungal spores. In order consistently to kill fungal spores, steam pressure at 15 pounds per square inch, corresponding to a temperature of 250°F, for 15 minutes is required. (This is not a recommended way of sterilizing library materials!)

Relative humidity is very important to growth of fungi. Generally it is believed that below 70% relative humidity there is little opportunity for growth. At 80 to 95% relative humidity most forms grow well. Above 95% relative humidity growth is luxurious. We must not forget, however, that the combination of temperature and relative humidity is important. Optimum humidity at 86°F is between 95 and 100% relative humidity. Optimum temperature at close to 100% relative humidity is about 100°F. Optimum temperature at lower humidities, e.g., 70% relative humidity, is considerably lower.

Light does not appear to be an essential requirement for most fungi. Generally, fungi will grow either in the light or dark. The characteristics of light in libraries does not appear, therefore, to be of any consequence to the fungal problem either pro or con.

Although there are many bacteria which can thrive under anaerobic conditions, most fungi require oxygen for growth. This requirement has no influence on the library problem. Fungi require several nutrients, some of which do have an influence on growth in libraries. Required are carbon, hydrogen, nitrogen, sulfur, potassium, magnesium, and phosphorus. Certain trace elements may also be required such as iron, zinc, copper, manganese, and in some cases calcium. Certain of the vitamins are also needed. These nutrients may be provided in many forms; e.g., carbon may be provided in the form of carbohydrate. The inorganic requirements may be in the form of salts of metallic elements. Nitrogen is essential, in the reduced form of ammonium ion, as oxidized nitrate, or in the organic form of amino acids or proteins.

The fungal nutrient problem is interesting to the librarian for several reasons. Certain fungi will consume cellulose and can therefore do irreparable damage to

FIGURE 10. *This paper, late eighteenth century, several sheets thick, shows severe damage by insects as well as by mildew. The right edge suffered too much moisture and adheres badly where mildew stain shows. (Sample courtesy James Gear, National Archives, Washington, D.C.)*

paper. Others thrive on the nutrients in leather, in glues, pastes, and other adhesives, or on binding threads. Some, though not consuming constituents of books or other library materials, stain surfaces because of certain highly colored metabolic products.

As was brought out above, many of the constituents of polluted atmospheres,

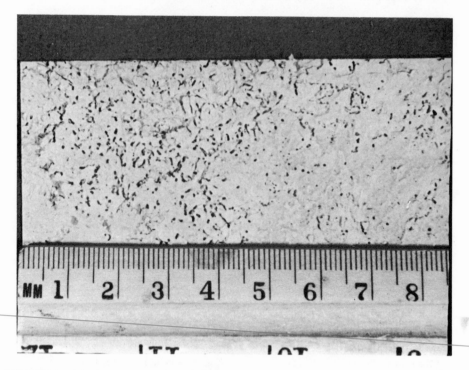

FIGURE 11. *The board removed from a binding which has been riddled with insects. (Photograph courtesy Paul N. Banks, Newberry Library, Chicago.)*

especially the particulate matter, are the salts and organic matter needed by fungi. It becomes important then in the air pollution problem to control the situation not only to prevent soiling or even chemical reaction with library materials but also to reduce provision of microbiological nutrients.

Numerous orders, families, genera, and species of insects are of importance to libraries (see Figures 10 and 11). Like the microbiological agents, insects are not considered to be a major problem in most urban American libraries. Again, cleanliness, awareness, and periodic inspections rather easily control insects. They can be eradicated by fumigation or the application of insecticides, but they should not be scorned as potential problems. They can be brought in by careless patrons; there are numerous cases where thoughtless users have left such insect attractants as food particles, candy wrappers, and similar matter in books. The introduction of insect infestations in acquisitions of old collections from poorly kept quarters makes it practically mandatory to sterilize such materials before adding them to shelves or storage areas. Table 8 provides some ideas of the varieties of insects which from time to time have been encountered in libraries around the world. Types of materials which may be attacked are also shown.

No effort will be made to discuss the environmental, respiratory, or nutritional requirements of these many insects. These factors vary widely. Suffice it to say that

TABLE 8

Insect Agents of Deterioration

Insects	Materials attacked
Thysanurans	Starchy material, glue, book-
Silverfish	bindings, photographs, labels,
Bristletails	paper sizings, onionskin paper,
Fishmoths	cellophane, wax paper, slick
Firebrats	magazine paper
Termites	Books, paper, pasteboard,
Reticulotermes	blueprints, documents, labels,
Calotermes	cardboard boxes. Termite damage
Heterotermes	is often accidental
Cockroaches	Bindings, leaves of books,
German, small tan	magazines, paper boxes,
American, large brown	parchment, leather, fabrics
Oriental, large black	
Australian cockroach	
Smoky-brown cockroach	
Brown banded cockroach	
Surinam cockroach	
Wood cockroach	
"Bookworms"	Consume or damage all types
Sitodrepo panicea	of materials in books, paper,
Anobiidae of genera:	paste, bindings, cover, etc.
Catorama	
Dorcatoma	
Stegobium	
Gastrallus	
Stegobium paniceum	
(bread beetle)	
Death-watch beetle	
Furniture beetle	
Booklice	Starch, glue, bindings
Psocids	
Cerambycidae	Various library materials
Longhorned beetle	
Dermestidae	Books: leather or
Longhorned beetle	silk bindings
Clothes moths	Many book materials

insects are found under numerous combinations of climatic conditions (from extremely dry to hot and humid) and occurrence of nutritional factors. Low temperatures, however, discourage most insects.

Atmospheric pollutants are important to the librarian not only because of their physiological effects on himself and his clients but because of their deleterious effects on his collections. Thomson (31) summarized air pollution as it pertains to conservation chemists, and librarians interested in protecting their collections will find much of interest in his review.

There is no question but that the public, as well as the government officials in the United States, are now quite aware that the air pollution problem is of vast importance to all aspects of American life. Far reaching programs have already commenced to alleviate conditions. But the problem is still with us and we must be aware of the damage that has already been done and continues to occur.

Even if we are successful in reducing or even eliminating the introduction of particulate matter into the air by industrial emitters such as chimneys and stacks, it is unlikely that it will be possible to eliminate all problems of common dust, dirt, sand, and the conglomerate of finely divided particulates which are caught up from streets, buildings, fields, and other sources and blown about by winds. Thus, it will probably always be necessary to clean up such materials from library collections by dusting or use of vacuum cleaners or preventing the particulates from entering the buildings by using high efficiency filters.

A glance at Table 4 reminds us of the types of particulate matter. Although much of the dust and dirt is quite dry—which is why it is so easily picked up by the wind—it nonetheless soils book pages and bindings. If conditions are moist, such dirt can stain the materials and be difficult to remove. If it contains nutrients for fungi and conditions are moist, mildew can occur and cause spotting, staining, and discoloration. The abrasive action of dust and dirt on paper and other library materials such as leather is also a serious deterioration problem. If the dust or dirt carries acidic or alkaline substances and conditions are moist, it can alter the pH of the paper or other materials and cause deterioration. Dust and dirt on photographic films can cause scratches (*32*). Users also warned against the dangers of dust and dirt with magnetic tapes (*33,34*).

One of the most important deterioration problems librarians have faced for years is that of book paper as a consequence of low pH, i.e., high acid content (see Figures 12 and 13). As mentioned earlier, this problem is not solely from the environment. Much of the acid has come from methods of manufacture of the papers which have gone into books all over the world for a very considerable time. Yet, part of the problem is caused by acidic components, especially sulfur dioxide, in the atmosphere. Nitrogen oxides in the polluted atmosphere of many of our cities give rise to some nitric acid. This too adds to the hydrolytic degradation problem with paper.

The subject of permanence, or its opposite—impermanence ("aging")—of paper, as well as of many other library materials, has a very large literature (*5,6,35-46*), and includes, in addition to the effects of acid, those of heat, light, biological agents, paper composition, and miscellaneous causes of deterioration.

The subject of acid deterioration of paper was reviewed recently by Smith (*47*). There does not appear to be any question that acidity causes paper impermanence. Numerous investigations of the subject have produced overwhelming evidence. The deterioration is characterized as hydrolytic and is chiefly an attack catalyzed by hydronium ions on cellulose, the chief fibrous ingredient of paper. The rate of

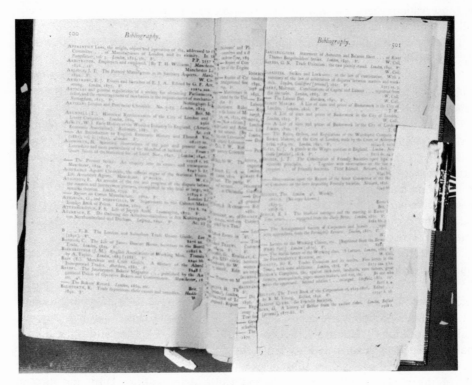

FIGURE 12. *Extreme embrittlement of paper, presumably from excessive acidity. (Photograph courtesy Paul N. Banks, Newberry Library, Chicago.)*

the deterioration increases with hydronium ion concentration, i.e., with a lowering of the pH values of the paper as measured on a water extract. The deterioration is manifested by a decrease in strength (tear resistance) and a loss of flexibility (folding endurance).

A very considerable portion of the acid in papers can come from the materials used in manufacturing, chiefly alum-rosin sizing. Barrow was one of the first modern research workers to call attention in an effective way to the fact that the acidity causing impermanence in paper is a consequence of the constituents used in the manufacturing process. This acid source appears to be more important than that of polluted atmospheres. Some earlier workers had, of course, discussed the matter. At the turn of the twentieth century expert opinion thought that a minimum pH of 4.0 for a hot-water extract from first-class, permanent book paper was acceptable (47). We now know that this is much too acid and that paper with this acid content will embrittle too quickly with time.

The opinions about the pH required for stable permanent papers altered as time passed. By 1928 workers were claiming that the pH of hot-water extracts should be at least 4.5 and preferably above 4.7. By 1936 it was recognized that

FIGURE 13. *Acid deterioration of paper only about 20-years old. (Photograph courtesy Edward E. White and Hannah B. Friedman, New York Public Library.)*

a hot-water extract pH of less than 5.0 is a major cause of deterioration in even the best classes of paper. By 1937 claims were being made that a minimum hot-water pH of 6.0 is necessary for permanent printing papers (*47*). Recent recommendations leave the impression that hot-water pH extract values should approximate neutrality, i.e., pH 7.0, or even be on the alkaline side of neutrality (*47*).

Although acidic components of paper play the major role in paper deterioration, the acidic components of polluted atmospheres cannot be dismissed. There is excellent evidence that atmospheres containing SO_2 can lower paper folding endurance as much as 15% in 10 days when the SO_2 concentrations approximate what might be expected in badly polluted cities. Slow oxidation of carbohydrates of paper with the production of carboxylic acids and an accompanying production of hydronium ions or decrease in pH occurs in accelerated aging of papers and presumably also in natural aging.

Discussions of the acidity due to sulfur emissions are usually in terms of sulfur dioxide which, in contact with water, forms sulfurous acid. To get sulfuric acid, a much stronger acid and oxidizing agent than sulfurous acid, sulfur dioxide, must be oxidized to sulfur trioxide. When sulfur dioxide is emitted from stacks or chimneys it is almost immediately oxidized to the trioxide, probably catalyzed by ash constituents. The sulfuric acid formed in the presence of water is largely responsible for the bluish smokes typical of what is called "sulfur dioxide" emissions. In areas where strongly oxidizing materials such as nitrogen dioxide, ozone, peroxides, and the peroxy-free radicals are present, more rapid sulfur dioxide oxidation to trioxide may be expected. Automobile exhaust and also olefins in the presence of nitrogen oxides also appear to cause more rapid sulfur dioxide oxidation by the photochemically produced oxidants. The presence of iron and manganese salts also materially increases SO_2 oxidation to SO_3 (48).

For some time there was a question of whether sulfur dioxide pollution of the atmosphere could cause paper deterioration in books. Numerous kinds of paper in books, however, have been demonstrated to pick up enough acidity by SO_2 penetration throughout an exposed book to have devastating effects on permanence. Although the position of the paper in the book and the distance from the edge of the paper has an influence, no parts of the paper appear to escape deteriorating effects (47). Hudson (49) was able to measure the pH of a sample of twenty-five books varying from 150 to 350 years of age. His results confirmed that atmospheric pollution is one of the causes of low pH values, particularly at the edges of pages.

Hudson (42,50) also developed a method for measuring affinity of sulfur dioxide for paper and for examining the effects of such variables as temperature and humidity on this affinity. He found that even good quality papers easily pick up sulfur dioxide at concentrations that can be expected in the atmosphere of any normal city. The moisture content of the paper is closely related to the rate of sulfur dioxide pickup. Pickup rate is increased by storage under damp conditions. High pickup is also favored by high ambient temperatures. The conditions in books would be different, of course, than the test conditions because most of the paper in books is protected by the edges. Other studies have shown, however, that there is diffusion of acid into the body of the book. Still other investigations have shown that chemicals can migrate from page to page or document to document (51).

Langwell (41,43) found that SO_2 itself is not damaging to paper. But he too found it combines readily in the presence of metallic impurities to form sulfuric acid which is seriously detrimental. These metallic impurities occur in most modern papers and in many papers made after the middle of the eighteenth century. Parchments, vellums, and papers made before about 1750 are regarded as immune to this attack.

The role of the nitrogen oxides in the deterioration of paper and other library materials has not been investigated as extensively as that of the sulfur oxides. In addition to the role of helping oxidize sulfur dioxide to sulfur trioxide, the nitrogen oxides can themselves play an important part in deterioration. This extends beyond the role with paper and into the realm of other polymeric materials in library usage such as rubber adhesives and synthetic elastomers used as fabrics, threads, and adhesives. The nitrogen oxides are being investigated extensively as modern air pollution problems, and it is hoped they will be investigated at greater length as library problems.

Sulfur acids also play an important part in the deterioration of leather (6,52,53).

FIGURE 14. *Corner of a book bound within the past 15 years. The joints have started cracking and powdering despite the fact that the boards have probably not been opened more than a dozen times. The leather seems to be held together by its pigment finish. (Photography courtesy Paul N. Banks, Newberry Library, Chicago.)*

Many old leathers are more acidic than fresh leathers. What has been referred to as "red rot" is actually an acidic deterioration. Sulfur dioxide from polluted atmospheres, catalyzed at the leather surface to trioxide and subsequently converted to sulfuric acid, is thought to be the degrading agent. This form of deterioration is very damaging to the leather and can cause its complete destruction. The leather becomes dry, reddish-brown and porous, and tends to peel or powder. The leather is easily scratched, corners wear easily, and cracks appear (see Figure 14).

Smith reviewed the subject of preservation of leather bookbindings from sulfuric acid deterioration (52). This review summarizes the salient points:

1. Sulfuric acid is a prime cause of leather bookbinding deterioration.
2. Sulfuric acid is introduced into leather directly during certain steps of the tanning process and indirectly by adsorption and oxidation of sulfur dioxide from the atmosphere.
3. The chemical mechanism of deterioration by sulfuric acid on leather is hydrolysis.

4. The critical point of leather deterioration by sulfuric acid is approximately a pH of 3.

5. The addition of grease does not protect leather from deterioration by sulfuric acid.

6. Leather bookbindings can be protected to a limited degree by addition of certain salts.

7. Ideal protection for leather bookbindings would consist of isolating leather bookbindings from contamination by sulfuric acid and requiring storage in air-conditioned areas.

Certain deterioration problems faced by photographic materials should be included in the discussion of deterioration by atmospheric pollution, inasmuch as we are discussing acidic components and other agents of chemical deterioration such as sulfur dioxide, nitrogen oxides, peroxides, and hydrogen sulfide. Library acquisitions can include motion picture films, sheet films, roll film negatives, microfilm records in a variety of formats, photographic prints on film or paper, and possibly color films and prints. The deterioration problems encountered by photographic materials have been summarized by Eaton (54).

It has been known for many years that cellulose nitrate films are not stable and constitute a fire hazard. This material is not acceptable for archival use (32). Because nitrate films are chemically unstable, they give off nitrogen oxides which can form nitric acid in humid atmospheres. This will attack the photographic emulsion and make it sticky in appearance (55). The film then rapidly deteriorates. The nitrate film decomposition products can also attack acetate or "safety" type films which may be nearby and damage them.

The acetate "safety" films are made of cellulose diacetate, the triacetate, and mixed esters, such as cellulose acetate propionate or cellulose acetate butyrate. The acetate films have a high degree of chemical stability. The newer polyester films are equal to or better than the acetates in permanence and have good resistance to high temperatures. Cellulose acetate films are considered to be as stable as the best grade of paper.

Some of the deterioration problems of photographic materials are due to the processing steps, some to the backing used such as paper, and some to the environment. Needless to say, paper used as backing must be of high purity and quality and have good permanence itself.

Inadequate fixation or washing can produce later fading of the image. Residues of silver-hypo complexes can decompose to give an over-all yellow-brown stain of silver sulfide in the nonimage areas, residues of hypo complexes can decompose to give an over-all yellow-brown stain of silver sulfide in the nonimage areas, and residues of hypo (thiosulfates) can attack the silver image (54).

Photographic films and print images are not necessarily permanent even after complete fixation and washing. Although they contain very little or no hypo and silver salts, the images are still susceptible to environmental conditions such as the presence of hydrogen sulfide, sulfur dioxide, hydrogen peroxide, and certain organic vapors (paint fumes), and high humidity and temperature (54).

It is usually recommended that photo prints be dry mounted for archival purposes to avoid pastes, adhesives, and cements. These are often hygroscopic and may contain sulfur compounds which can cause fading in local areas. One should also avoid the use of rubber bands around film rolls because of residual sulfur from vulcanization. Adhesive tapes, tape splices, bleached papers, and printing inks also should be avoided as deteriorative to films and prints (54).

About 1961 it was noted that many microfilms were evidencing spots and other blemishes. These were referred to as "aging blemishes." McCamy and his associates investigated the phenomena, identified six types of blemishes, and decided they were caused by oxidation-reduction reactions initiated by gaseous reactants (56–58). The gaseous reactants were traced to the cardboard cartons the films were stored in. It was found that the spots can be caused by peroxides formed in the natural aging of the paper. The peroxide formation increases with humidity. These cartons were also found to release measurable amounts of formaldehyde and formic acid which can cause spots. They also found that certain types of plastics used as dividers with the microfilm can provide an acid environment which, combined with the peroxides, also can contribute to spot formation. In all of the experiments on the aging blemish phenomena they found that humidity was an important factor—high humidities contributing to the problem. Temperature was also involved but not as importantly as humidity. Recommendations were for storage at conditions not to exceed 40% relative humidity and 70°F (56–58).

Wilson (59) investigated the degradation of cellulose acetate films of the type used by archival agencies for the repair and reinforcement of weak or damaged documents. This information is chiefly of interest in connection with degradation of the films during hot application to the documents.

There appears to be a close relationship between the environmental factors of light, heat, and moisture and the deteriorative processes they trigger in paper. It is indeed difficult to separate the effects caused by the three factors. For this reason it has been common to discuss their combined effects as a general process of "aging." Certainly all three factors exert their influence simultaneously most of the time in library stacks, storage areas, and reading rooms.

It is appropriate to recall that the phenomena of stability, permanence, and durability of paper are also usually considered as a function of "aging." As pointed out earlier, permanence is usually considered to be a function of the chemical stability of paper whereas durability is considered as a function of the physical properties of the fibers and the way they are compounded to form a sheet. A paper intended for rough handling for a short lifetime must be durable but not necessarily permanent.

It is necessary to keep in mind, therefore, that the individual as well as the collective effects of light, heat, and moisture are mainly on the chemical stability of paper. One of the ways to determine the effects of these environmental factors on paper is by a time exposure. Some of the tests performed and the properties tested are reflectance (color and brightness); pH (acidity); folding endurance (brittleness);

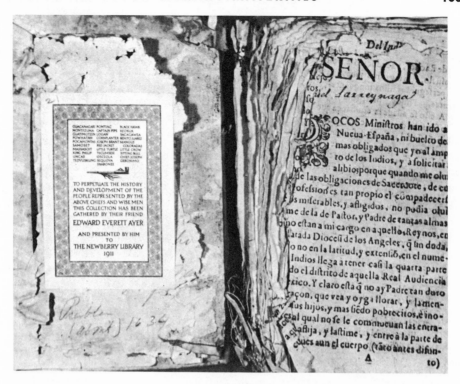

FIGURE 15. *Severe microbiological damage from prolonged dampness along the spine area. (Photograph courtesy Paul N. Banks, Newberry Library, Chicago.)*

and tear, burst, and tensile (strength) measurements. The commonest are folding endurance and pH.

High temperature exposures of paper, even for short periods, cause yellowing and brittleness. Moderate heat over long periods has a slow aging effect on paper. Low temperatures are regarded as preservative to paper. A combination of moderate high temperature and low humidity will cause paper to dry out and become brittle. A moisture content in equilibrium with 30% relative humidity represents about as low a value as is safe for paper. If humidity is held above 75% relative humidity for long periods, mildewing will occur (Figure 15). It is recommended generally that the temperature be about 70 to 80°F and the relative humidity be 45 to 55% for effective preservation of paper (*6,60*). James Gear (personal communication, May 1969) at the National Archives states that they maintain a temperature of 74 ± 4°F and a relative humidity of 50 ± 4%. The new National Agricultural Library at Beltsville, Maryland was built to specifications equivalent to 50 to 60% relative humidity in the temperature range 74–78°F (*61*).

Werner (*62*) recommends for archival materials—chiefly paper and parchment—that the atmospheric moisture should be controlled between 50–60% relative humidity at a temperature of 60 to 75°F. At the same time, Werner gives 68%

relative humidity as the critical value above which mildew and mold growth will occur. Plenderleith (36) also states that 68% relative humidity is the absolute danger limit in the temperature range 60–75°F. In actual practice, he states that 65% relative humidity is preferable as the permissible upper limit to guard against mildew.

Launer and Wilson (63) found that 100°C (212°F) for 3 days will cause extensive damage to paper. Mild heating will cause yellowing of paper made from new-rag, refined sulfite, old-rag soda-sulfite, and newsprint pulps, especially those bleached by light. They found that the yellow color caused by heating could be bleached out by light, and that the bleaching caused by light could be nullified by heating.

The effects of heat on paper vary greatly depending upon the quality of the paper and the nature of the various constituents used as fillers. Shaw and O'Leary (64) found that rag papers characterized as good book paper were not appreciably affected in heat tests. Purified wood pulp also produced a fairly stable paper. Paper made from a mixture of sulfite and soda pulp was less stable than those made from the purer fibers. There was a close relationship between the purity of the cellulosic fibers used and the stability of unsized papers made from them, but only when a small amount of alum and no rosin size was used. In other tests the acidity of the paper has had a great bearing on its ability to withstand heat.

Barrow (12, Vol. 1) measured folding endurance of new book paper after heat-aging at 120, 100, 80, and 60°C and plotted the data as regression lines for each temperature. This showed that it takes 7.5 times longer to reduce this paper's folding endurance to a given value for each drop of 20°C in temperature. The times required to reduce the paper from 219 to 65 folds by heating at temperatures from 120 to 60°C and, by extrapolation, the times required to produce the same result at temperatures below 60°C, are shown in Table 9.

Smith (47) utilized Browning's and Wink's (65) Arrhenius equation approach and calculated the effect of storage temperature on paper permanence. Permanence was expressed in terms of paper "half-life," similar to the concept usually employed

TABLE 9

Effect of Temperature on Paper Deterioration [a]

Temperature (°C)	Time (days) [b]	Temperature (°C)	Time (years), est.
120	0.4	40	3.5
100	3.0	20	26
80	22.5	0	195
60	169	−20	1,463
		−40	10,973

[a] Ref. 12, Vol. 1.
[b] Time required to reduce folding endurance from 219 to 65 folds.

TABLE 10

Effect of Storage Temperature on Paper Impermanence (47)

Average storage temperature		Paper half-life (years) [a]
°F	°C	
140	60	1
122	50	4.1
104	40	18
95	35	40
86	30	88
77	25	204
72.5	22.5	320
68	20	490
63.5	17.5	760
59	15	1,200
50	10	3,100
41	5	7,900
32	0	21,000

[a] One folding endurance half-life is defined as 1 year at 60°C (140°F) for purposes of estimating half-life at lower temperatures.

in expressing the decay of radioactive elements. For example, a paper with an original fold endurance of 100 folds would, after an expenditure of its half-life, have a value of 50 folds, after a second half-life, 25, and so. Although an over-simplification of the matter, some of the results obtained at various temperatures for an ideal, high quality paper, defined as having a folding endurance half-life of 1 year when stored at 60°C (140°F), are shown in Table 10. The accuracy of the prediction increases at higher temperatures or as the temperature of the experiment is approached.

Luner (44) also discusses the Browning and Wink application of the Arrhenius equation for developing values by which to predict paper aging. He points out that there are a number of difficulties inherent in the use of the Arrhenius equation which are not readily apparent. Further, the characteristics of the various papers have a strong influence on the results. More information is needed on the chemical and physical reactions that contribute to loss of paper permanence over a tempera-ture range before the Arrhenius relationship can be used with confidence to predict paper permanence. Nonetheless, the equation appears to be a very useful tool in studies of paper permanence properties in libraries.

Smith (47) joins the effects of temperature and acidity on paper permanence, using considerations similar to those used with reference to storage temperature. For this purpose he defined a paper as having a half-life of 100 years at a pH of 6.0 and a temperature of 68°F (20°C). He then varied the pH and temperature to

TABLE 11

Action of pH and Temperature on Paper Half-Life (in Years) (*47*)

Temperature (°F)	pH		
	6.0	5.0	4.0
	Hot Water pH		
68	100	53	28
72.5	65	35	18
77	42	22	12
86	18	10	5.1
95	8.2	4.6	2.4
104	3.7	1.9	1.0
	Cold Water pH		
68	100	10	365 [a]
72.5	65	6.5	240
77	42	4.2	150
86	18	1.8	66
95	8.2	0.82	30
104	3.7	0.37	17

[a] Figures in this portion of the pH = 4.0 column are given in days and were computed by extrapolating the cold water pH line.

obtain half-life values. The effect of pH change on half-life was estimated as 53% and 10% half-life retention for an increase in acidity* of one hot and one cold water extraction pH unit, respectively. The effect of temperature change on half-life was estimated as in the previous example. Table 11 provides his results. The method of prediction indicates that both pH and storage temperature have strong influences in producing the deteriorated condition of books in many libraries.

Humidity, or rather the water contained in paper, might be considered as the third most important factor, after pH and storage temperature, relating to paper deterioration in libraries. Although we have seen that excessive dryness is thought by some to cause paper to become brittle, and certainly too much moisture is conducive to mildew or fungal growth, apparently the role of moisture is not that easily dismissed. Some water in paper, as in many materials, is in a bound form; it cannot enter into or catalyze chemical reactions as easily as free water. The water in paper in equilibrium with 50% relative humidity has been reported by Browning and Wink (*65*) to hasten the rate of deterioration during accelerated aging by ten times that of a bonedry paper.

Recommendations of a relative humidity of 50% for storage and for library stack and reading room values may emphasize current physical properties of a paper at the expense of its future properties (*47*). It is very difficult, however, to recom-

*Represented by a decrease in pH value.

mend the optimum value, for there is not sufficient information available today, particularly with reference to values below 50% relative humidity.

The effect of relative humidity and temperature on paper is discussed at some length by Wink (66) who brings out that properties such as folding endurance are extremely dependent upon humidity control. Mason (67), in discussing the effects of low humidity climates on brittleness in paper, suggests that water should be added to the atmosphere since, for every 10% rise in relative humidity, the folding strength of paper doubles. Obviously, this curve levels off fairly rapidly. In making recommendations for rare book collections, Mason (67) suggests a separate air conditioning machine—a system capable of maintaining a *constant* temperature of 70°F (or lower if personnel can stand it) and 50% relative humidity. This would introduce costs, however, that many libraries might not be able to afford. Storm (68), in making recommendations for preserving rare book collections, stipulates 68–75°F and 45–50% relative humidity. Storm states, however, that 65°F would be better for books of all ages and kinds but is a little chilly for people.

Noblecourt (69) suggests the following relative humidities for storage of library materials at 60–75°F: 45 to 63% for newspapers, leather, buckram, printed books, maps, music, manuscripts, parchment, engravings, prints, and drawings; and 50 to 63% for postage stamps, adhesive labels, and acetate and celluloid base photographic films. These conditions, though mentioned in connection with reducing the occurrence of or the attack by mildew, were also made with the thought in mind of preserving other characteristics of the paper and library materials.

Raistrick (70) calls attention to the effects of heat and moisture on leather, stating that a common cause of deterioration is the combined action of the two factors. Such damage shows itself in loss of strength and hardening of the leather. Storage in the region of 40°C (104°F) and 100% relative humidity causes considerable loss of strength of most types of leather. Increased stiffness and crackiness, loss in area, and fall in shrinkage temperature are also reported. In the tests Raistrick performed, all leathers lost about 50% strength after 5 weeks at 60°C (140°F) and 100% relative humidity.

Temperature and humidity are also important factors in the stability and permanence of photographic materials in storage. Eaton (54) warns against storage of photographic materials in moist air and above 50% relative humidity to avoid fungus growth. However, he points out that very low relative humidities can cause film brittleness, curl, and static charge. Generally, he recommends, the temperature should be 70°F and relative humidity 40–50%. We might recall that in connection with the aging blemish problem with microfilm McCamy (56) recommended that humidity not be permitted to exceed 40% nor temperature to rise above 21°C (69.8°F). Eastman Kodak (32) warns against high humidity as potentially causing films to buckle or flute. They also point out that metal film reels can corrode at high humidities, and rust particles can damage the image. But, they say, prolonged storage under 25% relative humidity can cause the film to become dry and brittle so that it may crack or break if handled carelessly.

Temperature and humidity are factors that must be given attention when storing magnetic tapes. Here, however, the permissible ranges appear to be much broader. The ranges of 40 to 90°F and 20 to 80% relative humidity appear to be acceptable (*34*). It is suspected that these ranges will be tightened considerably after more years of experience with this medium. A helpful bibliography on magnetic tape aging knowledge is provided by Davison and his colleagues (*33*).

As for light, recalling the admonitions of many people who have written on the subject of materials deterioration by light, Stolow (*71*) summed up the matter succinctly for museum curators as follows:

> The deteriorating effects of light on museum collections depend on the intensity of the radiation; the time of exposure; the spectral characteristics of the radiation; and the intrinsic capacity of individual materials to absorb and be affected by the radiant energy. External factors also influence the rate of deterioration—humidity, temperature, and active gases in the atmosphere. We know we cannot consider light as a single danger; high temperature, high humidity, and the presence of oxygen usually speed up the process of deterioration. Essentially, we must take into consideration: the characteristics of the radiation, the materials exposed, and the condition of their exposure. Until laboratory tests prove to the contrary, any museum curator must assume that the extent of photochemical damage will be reduced in direct proportion to the reduction of the intensity of illumination or the time of exposure—no matter what the light source. He must also remember the important factor of temperature: for with a ten-degree rise in temperature the rate of chemical change can double. Depriving an object of oxygen . . . can also serve to minimize photochemical change in that oxygen is often necessary to propagate intermediate steps in photochemical reactions.

Stolow's remarks apply to library collections also. Practically speaking, librarians usually cannot provide the special environments for their collections that curators can for unusual objects. But for rare library items, the situations are much the same for the two types of institutions. The deteriorating effects of light are not considered as serious for library materials as are those caused by acidity, heat, and humidity, but light warrants attention.

The effect of light, and the need for adequate lighting in libraries, archival depositories, and museum collections, have been reported on and reviewed many times (*5,6,37,39,60,63,71–85*). Of the various materials found in libraries in large quantities, paper represents the materials most affected by light. Other library materials subject to deterioration by light (*6*) include textile (cotton) binding materials, binding cords and thread, parchment, and various types of plastics, rubbers and adhesives, inks (*86*), and many dyes (*76,78*).

The effect of sunlight on inks was investigated by Barrow (*86*). He found, for example, that some of the iron-gall inks of the colonial period in America turned from black to rusty-brown, or faded out completely. His tests indicated that sunlight decomposes the tannic acid in the ink, causing the browning or fading.

The high polymer cellulose is the basic material in paper which undergoes degradation.* Cellulose itself does not absorb visible radiation and one might expect

*For a discussion of the nature of paper as it pertains to the library deterioration problem, see Browning (*87*).

that it would not be degraded by wavelengths longer than about 400 millimicrons. But several investigators have shown it to be affected by wavelengths as high as 460 millimicrons. Feller (*80*) suggests that perhaps some components of paper other than cellulose—glue, rosin, or other constituents—absorb the visible violet and blue and sensitize the paper to deterioration. The exact mode of action of sunlight on cellulose is not completely known. But there appear to be roles played in addition to that of light, by oxygen or ozone, by moisture, and possibly by other reactants.

The action of ultraviolet light upon cellulose leads to the formation of oxycellulose. Photochemical degradation of cellulose is apparently due to oxidation of cellulose by atmospheric oxygen, ozone, or some of the other atmospheric oxidants discussed earlier. The reaction is accelerated by water vapor, and is preceded by absorption of ultraviolet light (*88,89*).

It is fairly well agreed that the sunlight resistance of paper in general depends to a large extent on the composition of the paper and on the kind of cellulosic material present. Yet, all papers are susceptible to damage by sunlight. Launer and Wilson (*63*) found that photochemical stability of papers is related to the kind and source of materials used in manufacture, and they rated different papers in the following decreasing order of resistance: new rag, refined sulfite, old rag, soda-sulfite, and newsprint. The presence of rosin, glue, alum, iron, lignin, or other substances, whether included accidentally or purposely, has a strong bearing on degradation of paper by light.

Although there is no question whatever that unfiltered sunlight is a strong degrader of almost all organic materials, and all kinds of paper are certainly included, the problem of light deterioration of paper of most concern to librarians, archivists, and museum curators is not that caused by unfiltered sunlight. Rather, it is that caused by the light which enters the building through windows or skylights and the artificial light used for illuminating the premises.

Studies of the degradation of cellulose products by radiation have shown that the greatest damage is caused by ultraviolet energy of wavelengths shorter than 360 millimicrons. However, damage is still appreciable for wavelengths up to 500 millimicrons. This includes all the violet and blue part of the visible spectrum (*6,90*). Launer and Wilson (*63*) demonstrated that the light usually affecting papers is in the range of 330 to 440 millimicrons. They pointed out that direct sunlight, light from the quartz-mercury arc, and from the unfiltered carbon-arc all fail to represent the kind of light to which record papers are normally subjected in libraries and archives. They noted that exposure in these places is limited to indirect sunlight transmitted by window glass or to that from the tungsten incandescent lamp.

Launer and Wilson (*63*) used a light source filtered to eliminate all infrared as well as the ultraviolet shorter than 330 millimicrons for a series of tests. Thus they had a light source with wavelengths of approximately 330 to 750 millimicrons with a strong band at 389 millimicrons. In these tests they showed that discoloration of paper is a combined effect of light and heat. The yellowing of delignified paper, commonly ascribed to light, is due to heat or age. When heat effects were eliminated during irradiation by control of temperature, the papers actually bleached, and even lignified paper bleached when irradiated in an oxygen-free nitrogen atmosphere. The two apparently opposite effects—bleaching and yellowing—may occur simultaneously. If a white paper turns yellow when irradiated, reactions other than photochemical may be involved. Papers containing lignin will, however, yellow in air or oxygen even in the absence of heat effects. Paper scorched brown at high temperatures, or yellowed at 100°C, as well as a 250-year-old yellowed paper, were all bleached by light.

Launer and Wilson (63) also showed that water vapor accelerates the effect of light on paper made of cotton cellulose but has the reverse effect on paper made from wood pulp. Free rosin and sulfuric acid increases the effect of light on cotton, rag, and purified woodpulp papers much more than on inferior papers.

Work done by the National Bureau of Standards, in connection with the preservation of the Declaration of Independence and the United States Constitution, shows the relationship of the wavelengths of light and the damage done to paper and parchment exposed to this light. Reference is made to Table 7.

Judd (75) did studies to extend the range shown in Table 7 to 300 millimicrons. Some of these adapted values are shown in Table 12, and illustrate how rapidly

TABLE 12

Probable Relative Damage [a]

Wavelength (millimicrons)	Probable relative damage
300	775
320	450
340	263
360	145
380	107
540	1.2

[a] Adapted from Judd (75); i.e., Judd's values × 100.

relative damage increases as we get deeper into the shorter wavelengths.

Judd (75) makes the statement:

> The probable rate of damage from radiation continues to rise with decreasing wavelengths below 300 millimicrons; but this is of no interest in museum lighting because none of the light sources available emits appreciably at wavelengths below the band, 290 to 310 millimicrons, characterized by the value of probable rate of damage at 300 millimicrons. Similarly, the probable rate of damage from radiation continues to fall with increasing wavelength above 640 millimicrons and is known not to reach zero short of 1100 millimicrons (note that the infrared can be photographed to about this wavelength), but these small probable rates of damage to the average museum object are negligible compared to those associated with the shorter-wave energy emitted by all light sources suitable for museums.

TABLE 13

Recommended Minimum Illumination Values in Foot-Candles (77)

	1931	1932	1937	1938	1941	1947	1949	1952	1956
Reading rooms	10	7½–10	20	30	30	25	20	30–50	30–50
Workrooms	—	7½–10	30	20	30	25	20	30	30
Periodical room	—	7½–10	20	—	—	25	20	—	—
Card catalog	8	—	—	10	25	25	—	30	30
Stacks	1½	—	10	5	10–15	25	—	10–30	10–30
Corridors	3	3–4	5	5	5	5	—	—	5–10
Lavatories	5	—	—	—	10	10	—	—	10

What Judd says about museum light sources and damage can generally be considered to hold true for libraries. It should be recognized, of course, that the museum curator's lighting problem is somewhat different from that of the librarian. Museum objects of historical or artistic value vary greatly in their material nature. There is also always a problem of exhibiting these objects to the best artistic advantage to permit the viewer to see them as the original artist intended. Many of these objects already have suffered considerable deterioration. Many more of the objects in museums and art galleries must be displayed to the best color advantages, e.g., paintings.

Judd brings out clearly the dilemma of the museum curator (75):

> From the estimate of probable relative rate of damage of museum objects from radiation* it may be seen that every light source giving good color rendition (radiant emittance well distributed throughout the visible range, 380 to 760 millimicrons) is necessarily associated with appreciable radiation hazard. . . . The directors of museums have therefore to make a difficult choice for each museum object. Either they can display the treasure by a light source yielding a good approximation to the color rendition of natural daylight, thereby eventually destroying it by photochemical decomposition; or they can seal the treasure in a vault screened from all radiation and filled with an inert gas, thereby preserving it indefinitely but also preventing anybody from ever seeing it; or they can adopt some compromise between these two.

The librarian's problems of illumination are simpler. He wishes chiefly to provide suitable light by which clients may read or study, albeit often for extended time periods, without doing damage either to his client's eyes or to the items in his collections.

Studies of damage by radiation to museum collections are quite applicable to library problems. For example, White (77), in discussing library lighting standards, brings out the fact that recommendations for illumination in libraries have increased considerably over the period of 1931 to 1956. Table 13 shows the recom-

*Radiation values provided in Judd's tables.

mended values. White also points out that some libraries (Kent State Library and Davenport Public Library) have already gone to levels of 70 to 100 footcandles in reading rooms. Blackwell (82) reports on the lighting requirements for sample library tasks. His data ranges from 0.9 footcandle required for very easily read print to 141.0 footcandles for reading difficult spirit-duplicated samples. Some of his recommended lighting standards for libraries range considerably higher than those reported on by White.

Judd's report on museum lighting (75) provides interesting data both from the standpoint of relative damaging effects per footcandle for a large number of different light sources and for consideration against the increasing levels of illumination being recommended for libraries. Judd's data are shown in Table 14. Here he reports on six light sources—an incandescent lamp of color temperature 2,854°K; a daylight fluorescent lamp of 8,000°K; a warm-white deluxe fluorescent of 2,900°K; a cool-white deluxe fluorescent of 4,300°K; natural sunlight at 30° altitude and an air-mass of 2 with 5,300°K; and the zenith sky equivalent to 11,000°K.* He makes combinations of these sources with no filter and with four different filters, including window glass, to give a total of 30 combinations. His figures are calculated and expressed as the probable rate of damage per footcandle. Judd (75) states:

> It is believed that these computed results indicate reliably the relative rates of photo-chemical decomposition of cellulose by these light sources. Furthermore, these computed results are the best estimates of radiation hazard for museum objects generally that we can make from presently available information. These estimates are submitted as guides in the selection of light sources for museums.

It is not intended that any quantitative conclusions be drawn by combining White's and Judd's reports, only to draw attention to the manner in which increasing values of illumination bring increasing probabilities of deterioration.

This article has presented some evidence of the deterioration problems faced by modern libraries. As the rate of library growth has increased, the problem has accelerated. Furthermore, as the materials on which library items are recorded have tended to proliferate and to become more complicated, the extent of deterioration and need for preservation have increased. Society is faced today with a set of difficulties, the solution to which will require the united effort of librarians, physical scientists, administrators, funding sources, and a host of technically trained, highly skilled conservation and preservation experts.

It is encouraging to note that considerable attention is being given to the questions. Those concerned are beginning to understand what kinds of materials should be used in our books and other library media so that there will be fewer problems in the future. Some good techniques to slow down deterioration in the media already in libraries and to preserve the collections for many years to come are being developed. Librarians are coming to a realization of the environmental conditions required in libraries if collections are to enjoy long life.

*Feller (73) points out that zenith sky has the greatest proportion of ultraviolet and blue light per lumen of any source of illumination under consideration in museum lighting.

TABLE 14

Probable Rate of Damage per Foot-Candle for Thirty Light Sources Expressed in
Per Cent Relative to Zenith Sky, Sources Arranged in Order of
Probable Rate of Damage (75)

Light source	Filter	Probable rate of damage per foot-candle relative to zenith sky (%)
Zenith sky	None	100.0
Zenith sky	Kingsport water white	70.4
Zenith sky	Window glass	32.9
Sun at altitude 30°	None	16.5
Sun at altitude 30°	Kingsport water white	12.9
Cool-white deluxe	None	11.5
Zenith sky	Greenish nultra	11.3
Cool-white deluxe	Kingsport water white	9.6
Warm-white deluxe	None	9.2
Sun at altitude 30°	Window glass	8.9
Daylight fluorescent	None	8.4
Daylight fluorescent	Kingsport water white	8.2
Daylight fluorescent	Window glass	7.5
Zenith sky	Noviol 0	7.0
Warm-white deluxe	Kingsport water white	6.9
Cool-white deluxe	Window glass	6.1
Daylight fluorescent	Greenish nultra	5.5
Sun at altitude 30°	Greenish nultra	4.7
Warm-white deluxe	Window glass	4.4
Daylight fluorescent	Noviol 0	4.1
Cool-white deluxe	Greenish nultra	3.4
Sun at altitude 30°	Noviol 0	3.3
Incandescent	None	2.8
Incandescent	Kingsport water white	2.7
Cool-white deluxe	Noviol 0	2.5
Incandescent	Window glass	2.2
Warm-white deluxe	Greenish nultra	2.1
Incandescent	Greenish nultra	1.4
Warm-white deluxe	Noviol 0	1.4
Incandescent	Noviol 0	1.1

If this knowledge can be exploited to the fullest it will be possible to reduce the deterioration issue to controllable dimensions and to enhance the likelihood of handing down to the generations to come the knowledge mankind has accumulated with so much hardship.

REFERENCES

1. *The New English Bible, With the Apocrypha,* Oxford Univ. Press, Cambridge Univ. Press, 1970, Matt. 6:19.
2. Richard Daniel Smith, "New Approaches to Preservation," *Lib. Quart.,* **40,** 139–171 (January 1970).
3. E. E. Williams, "Deterioration of Library Collections Today," *Lib. Quart.,* **40,** 3–17 (January 1970)
4. L. E. Grove, "Paper Deterioration—An Old Story," *College and Research Lib.,* **25,** 365–374 (September 1964).
5. Jerry Byrne and Jack Weiner, *Permanence* (Bibliographic Series No. 213), Institute of Paper Chemistry, Appleton, Wisconsin, 1964.
6. Glenn A. Greathouse and Carl J. Wessel, eds., *Deterioration of Materials, Causes and Preventive Techniques,* Reinhold, New York, 1954.
7. Leonard Shatzkin, "Publishing on Permanent Papers," *Lib. Quar.,* **40,** 113–122 (January 1970).
8. Joseph J. Thomas, "Alkaline Printing Papers: Promise and Performance," *Lib. Quar.,* **40,** 99–107 (January 1970).
9. W. J. Barrow, *Manuscripts and Documents: Their Deterioration and Restoration,* Univ. Virginia Press, Charlottesville, Virginia, 1955.
10. R. W. Church, ed., *Deterioration of Book Stock: Causes and Remedies, Two Studies on the Permanence of Book Paper Conducted by W. J. Barrow* (Virginia State Library Publication No. 10), Virginia State Library, Richmond, Virginia, 1959.
11. R. W. Church, ed., *The Manufacture and Testing of Durable Book Papers, Based on the Investigations of W. J. Barrow* (Virginia State Library Publication No. 13), Virginia State Library, Richmond, Virginia, 1960.
12. W. J. Barrow Research Laboratory, *Permanence/Durability of the Book,* 5 Vols., W. J. Barrow Research Laboratory, Richmond, Virginia, 1963–1967.
13. W. J. Barrow, *The Barrow Method of Restoring Deteriorated Documents,* Barrow, Richmond, Virginia, 1965.
14. W. J. Barrow, *Procedures and Equipment Used in the Barrow Method of Restoring Manuscripts and Documents,* Barrow, Richmond, Virginia, 1965.
15. W. J. Barrow, "Deacidification and Lamination of Deteriorated Documents, 1938–63," *Amer. Archivist,* **28,** 285–290 (April 1965).
16. W. J. Barrow and Reavis C. Sproull, "Permanence in Book Papers," *Science,* **129,** 1075–1084 (April 24, 1959).
17. *Permanent/Durable Book Paper, Summary of a Conference Held in Washington, D.C., September 16, 1960* (Virginia State Library Publication No. 16), Virginia State Library, Richmond, Virginia, 1960.
18. "The Preservation of Deteriorating Books: An Examination of the Problem with Recommendations for a Solution, Report of the ARL Committee on the Preservation of Research Library Materials, in *Minutes of the Sixty-fifth Meeting of the Association of Research Libraries, Washington, D.C., January 24, 1965.*
19. Elbert C. Weaver, "Air," in *The Encyclopedia of Chemistry* (George L. Clark and Gessner G. Hawley, eds., Reinhold, New York, 1957.
20. James J. Hanks and Harold D. Kube, "Industry Action to Combat Pollution," *Harvard Bus. Rev.,* **44,**, 49–62 (September–October 1966).
21. Committee on Pollution, *Waste Management and Control,* National Academy of Sciences Publication 1400, Washington, D.C., 1966.
22. "Pollution: Causes, Costs, Controls," *Chem. Eng. News,* **47,** 33–68 (June 9, 1969).
23. A. J. Haagen-Smit, "The Chemistry of Atmospheric Pollution," in *Museum Climatology* (G. Thomson, ed.), International Institute of Conservation, London, 1967.

24. H. J. Plenderleith and P. Philippot, "Climatology and Conservation in Museums," *Museum*, **13**, 243–289 (1960).

25. American Society of Heating, Refrigerating and Air-Conditioning Engineers, *ASHRAE Guide and Data Book, Applications*, New York, 1964.

26. C. J. Wessel, "Environmental Factors Affecting the Permanence of Library Materials," *Lib. Quart.*, **40**, 39–84 (January 1970).

27. A. J. Haagen-Smit, "Reactions in the Atmosphere," in *Air Pollution*, Vol. 1 (Arthur C. Stern, ed.), Academic, New York, 1962.

28. Benjamin M. Duggar, ed., *Biological Effects of Radiation*, Vol. 1, McGraw-Hill, New York, 1936.

29. "Protective Display Lighting of Historical Documents: A Report by the National Bureau of Standards to the Library of Congress," National Bureau of Standards Circular 538, Washington, D.C., April 1, 1953.

30. A. F. Verrall, "Condensation in Air-Cooled Buildings," *Forest Prod. J.*, **12**, 531–536 (1962).

31. Garry Thomson, "Air Pollution—A Review for Conservative Chemists," *Studies Conserv.*, **10**, 147–167 (November 1965).

32. *Storage of Microfilms, Sheet Films, and Prints*, Kodak Pamphlet No. F-11, Eastman Kodak Co., Rochester, New York, 1955.

33. P. S. Davison, P. Giles, and D. A. R. Mathews, "Aging of Magnetic Tape: A Critical Bibliography and Comparison of Literature Sources," *Computer J.*, **11**, 241–246 (November 1968).

34. "The Care and Feeding of Magnetic Tape," Interagency Records Administration Conference, April 22, 1966, Office of Records Management, National Archives and Records Service, General Services, Administration, Washington, D.C.

35. *The Conservation of Cultural Property With Special Reference to Tropical Conditions* (Museums and Monuments, No. 11. Prepared in cooperation with the International Centre for the Study of the Preservation and Restoration of Cultural Property, Rome, Italy), UNESCO, Paris, 1968.

36. H. J. Plenderleith, *The Conservation of Antiquities and Works of Art: Treatment, Repair, and Restoration*, Oxford Univ. Press, London, 1956.

37. D. M. Flyate, ed., *Preservation of Documents and Papers*, translated from Russian by J. Schmorak, available from U.S. Dept. of Commerce, Springfield, Virginia, 1968.

38. G. Thomson, ed., *Recent Advances in Conservation; Contributors to the IIC Rome Conference, 1961*, Butterworths, London, 1963.

39. Morris S. Kantrowitz, Ernst W. Spencer, and Robert H. Simmons, *Permanence and Durability of Paper: An Annotated Bibliography of the Technical Literature from 1885 AD to 1939 AD*, Govt. Printing Office, Washington, D.C., 1940.

40. Paul N. Banks, *An Annotated Reading List of the Most Important Current Material on the Chemical Deterioration and the Chemical and Physical Preservation of Paper*, Newberry Library, Chicago, 1965.

41. W. H. Langwell, *"How Does Air Pollution Affect Books and Paper?"* Address before the Library Circle Meeting, May 12, *1958; Proc. Roy. Inst. Great Britain*, **37**(Pt. 2), 210–214 (1958).

42. F. L. Hudson and W. D. Milner, "The Use of Radioactive Sulfur to Study the Pick-Up of Sulfur Dioxide by Paper," *Paper Technol.*, **2**, 155–161 (1961).

43. W. H. Langwell, "Sulfur Dioxide Pollution of the Atmosphere," *Soc. Archivists*, **1**, 291–293 (October 1959).

44. Philip Luner, "Paper Permanence," *Tappi*, **52**, 796–805 (May 1969).

45. W. K. Wilson and R. L. Hebert, "Evaluation of the Stability of Record Papers," *Tappi*, **52**, 1523–1529 (August 1969).

46. William K. Wilson, "Selection, Use, and Storage of Records for the International Geophysical Year," Report 5321, National Bureau of Standards, June 12, 1957.

47. Richard D. Smith, "Paper Impermanence as a Consequence of pH and Storage Conditions," *Lib. Quart.,* **39,** 153–195 (April 1969).

48. Arthur C. Stern, *Air Pollution,* 3 vols., Academic, New York, 1962.

49. F. L. Hudson, "Acidity of 17th and 18th Century Books in Two Libraries," *Paper Technol.,* **8,** 189–190 (June 1967).

50. F. L. Hudson, R. L. Grant, and J. A. Hockey, "The Pick-Up of Sulfur Dioxide by Paper," *J. Appl. Chem.,* **14,** 444–447 (October 1964).

51. W. J. Barrow, "Migration of Impurities in Paper," *Archivum,* **3,** 105–108 (1953).

52. Richard D. Smith, "The Preservation of Leather Bookbindings from Sulfuric Acid Deterioration," Master's paper, University of Denver, 1964.

53. J. S. Rogers and C. W. Beebe, "Leather Bookbindings, How to Preserve Them," Booklet No. 398, U.S. Dept. Agriculture, Washington, D.C., May 1956.

54. George T. Eaton, "Preservation of Photographic Images," *Lib. Quart.,* **40,** 85–98 (January 1970).

55. E. Lindgren, *The Permanent Preservation of Cinematograph Film: Proceedings of the British Society for International Bibliography,* Vol. 5, 1943.

56. C. S. McCamy and C. I. Pope, "Current Research on Preservation of Archival Records on Silver Gelatin Type Microfilm in Roll Form," *J. Res. Nat. Bur. Standards,* **69A,** 385–395 (September–October 1965).

57. C. S. McCamy, S. R. Wiley, and J. A. Speckman, "A Survey of Blemishes on Processed Microfilm," *J. Res. Nat. Bur. Stand.,* **73A,** 79–97 (January–February 1969).

58. C. S. McCamy and C. I. Pope, "Redox Blemishes—Their Cause and Prevention," *J. Micrographics,* **3,** 165–170 (June 1970).

59. W. K. Wilson and B. W. Forshee, "Degradation of Cellulose Acetate Films," *J. Soc. Plastics Eng.,* **15,** 146–156 (February 1959).

60. Adelaide E. Minogue, *The Repair and Preservation of Records,* Govt. Printing Office, Washington, D.C., 1943.

61. Warner, Burns, Tean, Lunde, Architects, *National Agricultural Library, Beltsville, Maryland, Specifications, Mechanical-Electrical,* Public Buildings Service, General Services Administration, Washington, D.C., Secs. 51 through 67.

62. Anthony E. A. Werner, "The Preservation of Archives," *Soc. Archivists,* **1,** 282–288 (October 1959).

63. Herbert F. Launer and William K. Wilson, "Photochemical Stability of Papers," *J. Nat. Bur. Stand.,* **30,** 55–74 (January 1943).

64. Merle B. Shaw and Martin J. O'Leary, "Study of the Effect of Fiber Components on the Stability of Book Papers," *J. Res. Nat. Bur. Stand.,* **17,** 859–869 (December 1936).

65. B. L. Browning and W. A. Wink, "Studies on the Permanence and Durability of Paper. I. The Prediction of Paper Permanence," *Tappi,* **51,** 156–163 (April 1968).

66. W. A. Wink, "The Effect of Relative Humidity and Temperature on Paper Properties," *Tappi,* **44,** 171A–180A (June 1961).

67. Ellsworth Mason, "A Guide to the Librarian's Responsibility in Achieving Quality in Lighting and Ventilation," *Lib. J.,* **92,** 201–206 (January 1967).

68. Colton Strom, "Care, Maintenance, and Restoration," in *Rare Book Collections: Some Theoretical and Practical Suggestions for Use by Librarians and Students* (H. Richard Archer, ed.), (ACRL Monograph, No. 27), American Library Assoc., Chicago, 1965.

69. A. Noblecourt, *Protection of Cultural Property in the Event of Armed Conflict,* UNESCO, Paris, 1956.

70. A. S. Raistrick, "The Effect of Heat and Moisture in Leather," *J. Soc. Leather Trades' Chem.,* **44,** 167–168 (April 1960).

71. Nathan Stolow, "The Action of Environment on Museum Objects. Pt. II. Light," *Curator,* **9,** 298–306 (December 1966).

72. Keyes D. Metcalf, *Planning Academic and Research Library Buildings,* McGraw-Hill, New York, 1965.
73. Robert L. Feller, "Control of Deteriorating Effects of Light Upon Museum Objects," *Museum,* **17,** 57–98 (1964).
74. N. W. Brommelle, "Museum Lighting. Pt. 3. Aspects of the Effects of Light on Deterioration," *Museums J.,* **62,** 337–346 (1962).
75. Deane B. Judd, "Radiation Hazard of Museum Light Sources," Report 2254, National Bureau of Standards, Washington, D.C., February, 1953.
76. Laurence S. Harrison, "Report on the Deteriorating Effects of Modern Light Sources," Metropolitan Museum of Art, New York, 1954.
77. Lucien W. White, "Library Lighting Standards," *Wilson Lib. Bull.,* **33,** 297–301 (December 1958).
78. Gary Thomson, "Visible and Ultraviolet Radiation," *Museums J.,* **57,** 27–32 (May 1957).
79. Herbert F. Launer and William K. Wilson, "The Photochemistry of Cellulose: Effects of Water Vapor and Oxygen in the Far and Near Ultraviolet Regions," *J. Amer. Chem. Soc.,* **71,** 958 (1949).
80. Robert L. Feller, "The Deteriorating Effect of Light on Museum Objects: Principles of Photochemistry, the Effect on Varnishes and Paint Vehicles and on Paper," *Museum News,* **43** (June 1964), *Tech. Supp. 3,* i–viii.
81. I. K. Belaia, "Effect of Shortwave Ultraviolet Radiation from Bactericidal Lamps on Paper," *Bum. Prom.,* **32,** 9–10 (September 1957).
82. Frazer G. Poole, ed., *The Library Environment, Aspects of Interior Planning: Proceedings of the Library Equipment Institute, St. Louis, Mo., June 26–27, 1964,* American Library Assoc., Chicago, 1965.
83. Robert L. Feller, "Control of Deteriorating Effects of Light on Museum Objects. Heating Effects of Illumination of Incandescent Lamps," *Museum News,* **46** (May 1968), *Tech. Supp.,* 39–47.
84. Laurence S. Harrison, "Evaluation of Spectral Radiation Hazards in Window-Lighted Galleries," Paper presented at the I.I.C. Conference, Rome, 1961.
85. Rohm & Haas Co., "Plexiglas Ultraviolet Filtering Formulations," Bulletin No. 612, Rohm & Haas Co., Philadelphia, November 1963.
86. William K. Barrow, "Black Writing Ink of the Colonial Period," *Amer. Archivist,* **11,** 291–307 (1948).
87. B. L. Browning, "The Nature of Paper," *Lib. Quart.,* **40,** 18–38 (January 1970).
88. Edward Race, "The Degradation of Cotton during Atmospheric Exposure, Particularly in Industrial Regions," *J. Soc. Dyers Colour.,* **65,** 56–63 (1949).
89. G. S. Egerton, "The Action of Light on Dyed and Undyed Cloth," *Amer. Dyestuff Rept.,* **36,** 561 (October 6, 1947).
90. "Preservation of the Declaration of Independence and the Constitution of the United States: A Report by the National Bureau of Standards to the Library of Congress," Circular 505, National Bureau of Standards, Washington, D.C., July 2, 1951.

IV: THE ROLE OF
THE LIBRARIAN

Papers 9 Through 12: Commentary

This group of selections, as well those in Part V, deal with the tripartite nature of conservation. Conservation is an interdisciplinary enterprise in which the librarian, the conservator, and the scientist each plays an important role. Interprofessional communication and cooperation among the three groups are essential in working toward solutions to the commonly perceived problems of deterioration.

Conservation planning must start within individual libraries, where the librarian, working with appropriate administrative officers, decides what the overall conservation needs are, what the objectives of the conservation program should be, how they can best be achieved, how much they will cost, and what the priorities should be.

Of the four selections included in this section, two have been frequently cited and extensively quoted in the years since their original publication: the article by Pelham Barr, published in 1946, and that of Edward Lathem, which appeared a decade later in an issue of *Library Trends* devoted in its entirety to the subject of conservation. Barr's and Lathem's observations are as timely today as when they were first recorded.

The organization and administration of binding and of conservation planning in the libraries of Harvard University, the University of California at Berkeley, and Columbia University have undergone considerable evolution since Barr's article appeared. Evidence of increased concern for conservation at these institutions is Harvard's recent survey of preservation needs and practices in forty of its departmental libraries;[1] Berkeley's recently issued planning document for preservation of its collections;[2] and Columbia's establishment in 1974 of a Preservation Department to serve its various libraries.[3]

"Curators and Conservation" by W. G. Constable, Curator of Paintings at the Boston Museum of Fine Arts from 1938 to 1957, is included in this section for several reasons. First, it is a thoughtful statement of principles that are as relevant to the administration of library conservation programs as to museum programs, yet it has probably escaped the notice of most librarians. Secondly, it is a reminder that there are considerable areas of shared concern and much common ground between museum curators and librarians. In this sense, it points up the interprofessional nature of the conservation enterprise. Finally, it should prove of particular interest to librarians who administer collections that include artifacts of any sort and who find it necessary to enlarge their perspective to include in their thinking the idea of the library as museum.

In the years since Edward Lathem's article was originally published there have been a number of changes and developments in library conservation that should be mentioned. ALA's Committee on Bookbinding has ceased to exist, its concerns having passed to the Preservation Committee of the Resources and Technical Services Division. A third edition of the *Library Binding Manual,* edited by Maurice Tauber, was published in 1972 by the Library Binding Institute. It remains a useful source of information on most aspects of library binding. Adelaide Minogue's *Care and Preservation of Records* can no longer be considered a reliable guide to the techniques of document repair. There is great need, however, for a technical manual that would provide detailed information on acceptable methods and permanent/durable materials for use in the repair and restoration of documents.

As noted in the introduction to James Henderson's "Memorandum on Conservation of the Collections," the document is an amplification of Section II of "The Librarian as Conservator," an article written by him and Robert G. Krupp. Henderson's memorandum, here published for the first time, is one of the few known efforts to formulate a comprehensive plan and specific recommendations for the conservation of a vast collection of research materials. It holds particular interest and significance as an administrative model, illustrating the kind of detailed planning that libraries, particularly research libraries, must develop and implement.

NOTES AND REFERENCES

1. The results of Harvard's study, prepared by the Preservation Committee, are reported in *HUL (Harvard University Libraries) Notes* 416 (April 7, 1977).
2. Brock, Jo Ann, *A Program for the Conservation and Preservation of Library Materials in the General Library* (Berkeley: University of California, 1975), 45 pp.
3. A recommendation for the establishment of a Preservation Department at Columbia University's Libraries was included in Boos Allen and Hamilton, Incorporated, *Organization and Staffing of the Libraries of Columbia University: A Case Study* (Westport, Conn.: Redgrave Information Resources, 1973), 210 pp.

ADDITIONAL READINGS

Adams, Randolph G., "Librarians as Enemies of Books," *Library Quarterly* 7 (July 1937): 317–31.

Henderson, James W., and Krupp, Robert G., "The Librarian as Conservator," in Winger, Howard W., and Smith, Richard Daniel, eds., *Deterioration and Preservation of Library Materials* (Chicago: University of Chicago Press, 1970), pp. 176–92.

Poole, Frazer G., "The Research Library and Book Conservation," *Bolletino dell' Istituto di Patologia del Libro* 29 (January–December 1970): 99–121.

——, "Thoughts on the Conservation of Library Materials," in Cunha, George M., and Tucker, Norman P., eds., *Library and Archive Conservation* (Boston: Library of The Boston Atheneum, 1972), pp. 13–25.

Smith, Richard D., "Guidelines for Preservation," *Special Libraries* 59 (May–June 1968): 346–52.

Tauber, Maurice F., "Conservation of Library Materials," Chapters 15–17 in *Technical Services in Libraries* (New York: Columbia University Press, 1954).

9: BOOK CONSERVATION AND UNIVERSITY LIBRARY ADMINISTRATION

Pelham Barr

S ILENCE, rarely broken, seems to surround the subject of book conservation and the administration of binding. This applies to libraries in general and to college and university libraries in particular. Discussion of book conservation (under other names) is generally concerned with the techniques of maintenance and the routines of preparing materials for binding. In the literature of library administration, binding receives little mention, and surveys of individual libraries are skilful in satisfying the amenities with the briefest of nods. On organization charts, binding supervision usually is placed in a box in some out-of-the-way corner.[1]

This polite neglect of the subject in discussion reflects its neglect in action, and conditions in many college and university libraries reveal, sometimes painfully, the results. This is not—and, because of the very nature of the problems, cannot be—a criticism of the hundreds of librarians, directly active in conserving millions of books, who are doing their work effectively. What is usually found to be hampering their work, chaining their activities, gagging their judgment, and often leading to crises and waste, is a fundamental problem of administration which should concern librarians and other institutional authorities.

What are the symptoms of book conservation and binding troubles, and what can be done about them? Without going into individual case histories, it is possible to analyze the conditions which have come to

the attention of this writer in the course of ten years of dealing with the questions and confidences of hundreds of librarians and binders. The records show these to be the most frequent conditions which break out into troublesome "situations" requiring action: (1) valuable (old, rare, irreplaceable) materials deteriorating; (2) growing backlog of unbound stock which should be bound; (3) wearing out of items in heavy or continuous demand; (4) material "in bindery" when needed; and (5) poor binding (short life, poor appearance, inconvenience in using) and consequent spoilage.

The causes and their various permutations and combinations, which are revealed most often as origins and aggravators of trouble, are, at the operating or procedural level: (1) neglect of material in library, inadequate safeguards and precautions, abuse by readers, unnecessary wear and tear, too late discovery of material needing attention; (2) poor re-selection of materials for binding, including neglect of some and unnecessary attention and expense for others; (3) faulty scheduling in library or bindery, or both; (4) absence of adequate specifications or instructions, or insufficient understanding of them in bindery; (5) inadequate preparation of materials for binding; and (6) general incompetence of binder.

The librarian who has observed any of these conditions and diligently seeks to remedy them is confronted with the question, What changes, if any, are needed at the levels of supervision? Or, is the real problem a broader one of the administration

[1] A systematic search by Arthur R. Youtz, New York Public Library, confirms the impression of the writer.

Reprinted by permission of the American Library Association from *Coll. Res. Libr.* 7:214–219 (July 1946).

of the library? Or, beyond that, are there vital factors in the situation which touch even broader problems of university administration, requiring perhaps years of patient education of university authorities? It is very difficult to answer these questions unless the diagnostician can compare what he finds with some definite picture of what book conservation should be and what place binding should have in it.

Scope of Conservation

The scope of book conservation may be outlined by following its essential tasks from the time of receipt of a piece of material (and before) to the time of discard: (1) selecting material before purchase with respect to usability and useful life; (2) examining condition and probable future condition of all material received, whether by gift or purchase, and prescribing conservation treatment, if necessary, before use; (3) providing proper housing of all material, in accordance with its conservation needs as well as its accessibility; (4) assuming responsibility for its condition at all times; (5) assuring its proper handling by staff and patrons; (6) organizing systematic inspection so that need for conservation attention is promptly recognized; (7) deciding on the proper treatment of all material needing attention; (8) supervising the treatment; and (9) deciding on storing or discarding.

The administration of book conservation, therefore, tends to touch other aspects of library administration at several points— and that may be one reason for its apparent elusiveness. Binding is only one part of real book conservation, and that is why the most efficient binding supervision may not be able to cope effectively with a library's program of book conservation.

Seeking to get closer to the possible administrative difficulties underlying book conservation and binding troubles, the librarian may find solutions, and perhaps remedies, in answers to questions like these: (1) Is the organizational position of the binding supervisor high enough and is his authority adequate? (2) Are coordination and cooperation in relations with other service departments of library effective? (3) Is coordination between central library administration and departmental libraries adequate? (4) Is the over-all program of book conservation well planned? (5) Are budgeting (for the library in general and for book conservation and binding) and allocation of binding funds carefully worked out? (6) Is the staff adequate in numbers or experience? (7) Is there effective machinery for cooperation with faculty and students? (8) Are housing of collections and facilities for care good? (9) Have there been lapses in judgment in selecting bindery, either by the librarian or binding supervisor (for reasons of "economy"), or by university or state authorities (because of ignorance, politics, or compliance with statutory requirements, especially in the case of state-supported institutions)? (10) How well organized are working relationships with the bindery?

University and Library Relationship

All these questions relate specifically to the operation, supervision, and administration of book conservation and binding functions. Obviously, the organizational relations of the library to the university would tend to affect conservation of collections as well as every other phase of library operation. Administration of binding operations would necessarily be influenced by the efficiency or inefficiency of these relations between library and university and would share the high or low status of the library in the university community.

Ultimately, therefore, some of the problems of book conservation are the same as those confronting every other phase of university library activity. Whatever may be the administrative "taking over" of departmental libraries by the central library, the book conservation and binding problems of the departmental libraries will need some sort of administrative solution. If the university library suffers from inadequate funds, it is natural that conservation and binding suffer, at least in proportion.

The lag caused by university libraries growing faster than their administrative machinery is marked in the case of conservation. Here may be found, too often, not only the "traditions" of the university and its libraries, but some additional traditions of "the way we've always done it." If there is outside domination of purchasing policies and procedures, through a state official or through a university purchasing agent, it is more likely to affect binding contracts seriously than the buying of coal or typewriter ribbons. The binding department of a university library may thus have its own lag behind the general lag. It may be on the receiving end of all kinds of unsound practices, without having the power to fight for itself.

Stepchild Psychology

The "stepchild" psychology of many binding departments, in all kinds of libraries, is probably partly responsible for its neglect. It behaves the way it does because it is neglected; it is neglected because of the way it behaves. It has to deal with books when they are least attractive and with serials when they are no longer interestingly new, and it is naturally associated with mending and discarding. The "logical" place for it is in the basement or one of the not-so-respectable corners of the building. The work of preparing material for binding or of supervising bind-

ing transactions is not as exciting as ordering new books or cataloging them or handing them to faculty and students. It is a chore and it calls for somebody who loves it for its own sake. It may, however, fall to one who does not love it and is not in a position to reject it. This, in turn, necessarily adds to administrative problems.

A key problem of binding supervision is where to put it in the administrative organization of the library. It may well be that the wide variety of solutions to this problem is a significant clue to a root cause of many binding and book conservation difficulties. That there is a general uncertainty about where to put binding supervision in the library organization chart is revealed again and again when libraries are reorganized, as they have been in increasing numbers in recent years. If the binding department (or whatever it is called) is not left where it is, as is the tendency, it seems to become the sheep which won't be counted because it jumps around. The picture of the Harvard library organization, presented by Edwin E. Williams, might well serve to describe the real conditions in many libraries: "Serial records are handled by a division of the catalog department, and the binding records division, now unattached, may be added to the department in the future." In the organization chart, there is a dotted line between "binding" and the catalog department, indicating "relationships not yet established." (This is the only functional department thus left vagrant, the few other instances of dotted lines being for special collections and rooms which are common problems in many libraries.)[2] Solid lines instead of dotted in the organization charts of other libraries do not, perhaps, always picture greater certainty as to the relation-

[2] Williams, Edwin E. "The Administrative Organization of the Harvard University Library." *College and Research Libraries* 4:218-27, June 1943.

ships between binding and other departments.

Church describes in a recent article not a university library but the Virginia State Library, and, although the report is not very detailed, the omissions are significant. The conditions are characteristic of those in other libraries.[3] His chart B shows the place of the doorkeeper and the janitress in the organization, but not the binding supervisor. The proposed plan of the new building (C) provides space for "exchanges, binding," but the reference to binding disappears in the plan (D) of the actual building. The "general library division," he reports, includes the "serials section with visible file equipment for a consolidated serials record, including binding;" also "an order section to serve all divisions and conduct exchanges" and "a catalog section, all as closely related as possible." But the personnel and function chart (E) of the new organization shows no reference to a binding supervisor; presumably the person in charge of binding is a subordinate under the serials librarian.

California and Columbia

In the case of the University of California Library (Berkeley), as described by Leupp a few years back, the organization chart shows "binding" under the assistant librarian, together with the "catalog department," the "accessions department," and "gifts and exchanges."[4] The recent reorganization of the Columbia University Libraries similarly provides for dividing the functions into two groups, each under an assistant director, *i.e.,* readers' services and technical services, the latter including binding.[5]

[3] Church, Randolph W. "A Library Reorganizes through Building." *College and Research Libraries* 5:315-21, 334, September 1944.
[4] Leupp, Harold L. "Library Service on the Berkeley Campus, University of California." *College and Research Libraries* 4:212-17, 232, June 1943.

Combination of Duties

There are several ways of combining binding supervision with other duties. In one university library, the combination is "order and binding;" in another, binding is joined with photography; in a third, it is put with serials; in a fourth, the assistant librarian supervises binding. Some combinations seem to be fortuitous: the individual librarian may happen to have an unusual combination of interests or qualifications; binding supervision does not take full time; or binding supervision just "seems to fit in there."

In regard to the binding function in departmental libraries, the report of the A.L.A. University Libraries Section meeting on "Departmental and Divisional Libraries" (Chicago, Dec. 28, 1940) presents a varied picture. The paper of Fred Folmer, supervisor of departmental libraries, State University of Iowa, is summarized thus:

There are well-formulated relationships with each department of the main library: order; cataloging; serials; documents; reference; circulation; binding; reserves; library instruction. In observing these relationships, the custodian must maintain a delicate balance in loyalties between the department he serves and his colleagues in the main library. . . .

The report of the meeting continues:

Several of the speakers touched on the departmental reactions to the main library policies of acquisition and binding. Has the departmental librarian a right to change binders because he has found one who will do the work at a third less, in spite of the fact that the head of the binding department knows that particular binder's work is poor? . . .

Summing up, Dorothy H. Litchfield, who reported the meeting, declared: "The [departmental librarian's] problems of

[5] Wilson, Louis R., and Tauber, Maurice F. *The University Library.* Chicago, University of Chicago Press, 1945, Fig. 4a, p. 113.

fifteen years ago are still unsolved: personnel; cataloging; binding, etc."[6]

Theoretical Advantages

There have, of course, been cases in which the positions of the binding department head and the departmental librarian were the reverse of those in the cases cited. The advantages of centralization may become purely theoretical if the person in charge at the central library is unfamiliar with binding, if centralization involves buying binding through a purchasing agent's office which follows policies not adapted to the task, if the binder selected is incompetent, or if the specific needs of departmental libraries are not given attention. Whatever the details, it is evident that in a departmental system the logical place for authority to select a bindery is still undetermined.

Aside from the special cases of departmental libraries, what is the logical place of binding and conservation in the organization of a university or college library? This question immediately raises two others: Does the place have to be "logical?" Logical or not, can any place provide good working arrangements unless it is picked with some regard for the actual job which the binding department is supposed to do?

The adventures of logic in the wonderland of library organization are well described by Williams:[7]

... As soon as the conditions that gave rise to the original organization have changed, and as soon as relationships are affected by traditions and personalities instead of explicit regulations alone, every feature of the organization involves a good deal more than simple logic, and many changes suggested by logic must be made slowly or postponed to a more suitable time. The danger is that if too little or too late an effort is made to keep the or-

ganization changing in the proper direction, it will become hopelessly inefficient and incapable of fulfilling present needs.

Williams thus sums up the reasons why the place of binding in library administration is so often not logical. He also points out the dangers of putting off reorganization to the point of hopeless inefficiency because "so-and-so has had the job so many years" or "we'd have to reorganize a lot of other things if we reorganized the binding department" or "we haven't an appropriation to keep up the department if it is reorganized." In such cases, even if all of these conditions were eliminated, the administrator, all too often, would still find it hard to decide just where to put the binding department.

Why is there such difficulty in locating the "logical" place of binding supervision in library administration? Perhaps an obvious answer may be found in the fact that binding is a vital part of the broader function of conservation of library stock. But the deeper answer lies in the further fact that the scope of book conservation is so extensive and touches so many different library departments.

Active Recognition of Facts

There is an urgent need for more active recognition of these two facts. There is a need for reorienting administrative thought on the whole subject of book conservation and binding; consideration of binding and book conservation as they are today is not enough. A few librarians who have passed through the stress of reorganizations have become aware of this, and, in the reorganization of the Library of Congress, this awareness became clarified into a program —or, at least, definite objectives.

Conservation, as responsible custody, is the only library function which should be continuously at work twenty-four hours a

---

[6] Litchfield, Dorothy H. "Departmental and Divisional Libraries." *College and Research Libraries* 2:237-40, June 1941.
[7] Williams, *op. cit.*, p. 227.

day. It is the only function which should be concerned with every piece of material in the library from the moment the selector becomes aware of its existence to the day it is discarded. The reason this sounds so exaggerated is that it is a forgotten platitude. It applies to any library collection, whether it be of Egyptian papyrus, of the third-grade classroom library in an Iowa village, or of a university's incunabula.

There was a time when library administration was simpler, when these platitudes were living, activating principles. But, with the increasing complexity of universities and their libraries, the custodial function of the library—the "care and custody of the collection"—has deteriorated through neglect. The difficulties of welding miscellaneous collections, the slowness of growth of central libraries, and inadequate appropriations may all have contributed to the neglect. It may seem very human and "natural" that whatever time and money could be spared should be devoted to the things which just had to be done, the salvaging of material in unusable condition. But certainly this focusing on those activities of binding supervision dealing with crises has been accompanied by declining attention to prevention of crises.

Some strange phenomena in the evolution of library administration have resulted from this neglect of conservation. It became harder and harder to develop a program and procedures for book conservation, and, therefore, it was more and more neglected. As it withered away, it left binding supervision without any fundamental place in some library organizations. This is one cause of this "stepchild" situation. Some administrators have tried to dispose of the annoying department by attaching it to all kinds of other functions, which are frequently not closely related. But few have realized that it could "logically" be attached to so many other library functions for the very reason that it is essentially a conservation function and therefore fundamental in all library administration.

There are three types of situations in which a librarian may find this analysis of direct and practical interest: (1) the discovery, sudden or gradual, of one or more of the binding troubles described at the beginning of this article; (2) the need for library reorganization, partial or complete; (3) the recognition of the fact that, imperceptibly through the years, important parts of the collection have received inadequate or no attention.

If the foregoing analysis is at all valid and if the ten years' observations on which it is based do represent general conditions, the librarian confronted with one of the three situations may find some usable answer through these procedures: (1) apply frankly to the binding department the same types of questions as those which library surveyors apply to other departments; (2) through the questions indicated earlier in this article, trace out the weaknesses in the administrative relationships of the binding department; (3) plan and provide for a truly broad program of book conservation; (4) create a place for an assistant director in charge of this program, with full responsibility and commensurate power.

This last step is, of course, one which may well involve much more than the action of one librarian in one library. It is, essentially, a broad professional problem. Where are the administrators who can become library custodians in the true and effective sense of the title, when the function has for so many years atrophied? This is a problem of professional education and training and, of necessity, the spiral of making the custodian's position progressively more attractive and of attracting more and better trained librarians.

10: CURATORS AND CONSERVATION

W. G. Constable

THE term 'curator' is here regarded as distinct from that of 'conservator' or 'restorer,' which describes the technician charged with the practical business of keeping or putting the objects in a collection in good condition. With this exception it is used to cover all those who are directly responsible for the safety and well-being of such objects, whatever may be their official title or their other duties. Invariably this responsibility is part of a much wider one, including the acquisition, the exhibiting and the cataloguing of objects. But the very title of 'curator' emphasises that the physical care of whatever is in his charge is a primary obligation. Unfortunately that obligation has often been disregarded, and even today is not always fully realised, either by curators or by governing bodies. Such failure to understand that possession or acquisition of an object *prima facie* carries with it the duty of keeping it in good order is in fact only part of a much more widespread neglect in preserving the heritage of the past; a neglect which throws upon museums and similar institutions a special responsibility for being active in conservation, and in setting high standards of practice.

Of course, the whole principle of conservation can be challenged, on the ground that to lumber up the present with ever-increasing accumulations from the past is to strangle freedom and initiative to create new things. In general, however, the world has not been seriously bothered in this way, while much has disappeared that even a confirmed iconoclast may regret. Yet, in a more specialised form, this problem is always liable to confront a museum, or even a private collector. In course of time every collection comes to include what, at some particular time, opinion classes as rubbish; and it seems foolish to waste time and money on conserving things that were best allowed quietly to decay. The difficulty here is how to separate sheep from goats. The tastes of one generation are no sure guide to those of its successors; and the history of museums is full of instances of what was at one time considered negligible being at others a prized possession. It may be argued that though opinion may vary as to the worth of a particular kind of object, it is more likely to be stable as to whether they are good of their kind, and may therefore form a reasonably sound basis for choosing what to conserve. Yet when sympathy with and understanding of a whole group are lacking, judgment on particular objects in that group is apt to be fallible. Thus, for a curator or governing body to have to decide which objects are expendable seems unwise. Fortunately, however, the burden of conserving what to contemporary eyes seems worthless can be lightened in various ways. Objects of little or no value to one institution may sometimes be useful elsewhere, and can be lent on the condition that they be kept in good repair; conservation work on such objects can often be limited to preventing active deterioration, and making them safe to handle and store, without doing all the work needed to make them fit for exhibition; and from among such objects some may be used for investigation and experiment in connexion with conservation, without their running any great risk.

From general policy turn now to its application, and what this involves for a curator. One of the most important recent advances in conservation is analagous to one made earlier in medicine—that it is more important to keep an object in good health than to restore it when it is sick. Consequently, among the first aims of a curator should be to secure a suitable physical environment for the objects with which he is concerned, not only in exhibition galleries but also in storages. In this connexion major problems (unless local conditions are very kind) include control of temperature and humidity, especially to prevent excessive and rapid variations; protection against polluted atmosphere; and, for some objects, protection against certain kinds of light. Here the curator will become involved with all kinds of experts, including professional conservators, architects, engineers and building superintendents. From the conservator, with perhaps laboratory tests behind him, he should be able to get a schedule of optimum conditions; and remembering that these are likely to be ideals unrealisable except in a rarely visited underground vault, he can then face architects and engineers, remembering in their case that, as often as not, they know much better than anybody else what he ought to want, as well as how to get it. Finally, he has to present the results of his investigations to his governing body, and get their sanction, to say nothing of the necessary funds, for what is to be done. Obviously all this business cannot be settled by head-on encounters of experts; and it is the curator who has to act as negotiator and, on occasion, as arbiter, in seeking to reconcile the ideal with the practicable. His only source of comfort is that, provided what is done does not fall too far short of the ideal, no great harm will follow. Indeed there is something to be said for not coddling objects too much. Experience suggests that if they become too used to perfect conditions, as they may if kept in a little-used storage, or in a gallery where strict control of conditions is easy, the inevitable changes and chances of museum life may upset them all the more. However, a curator is not likely to be much worried in this way.

When it is remembered that some large department stores rely on their customers to supply the heating, it is easy to realise what visitors to a popular museum may do in the way of causing changes in temperature and humidity, to say nothing of the dust and dirt they introduce.

Even when all the apparatus for controlling conditions is installed, the curator has to watch its working. In the case of air-conditioning plants, for instance, it is not unknown for ducts and screens to be so neglected that the air in the museum is less clean than that outside; while temperature can vary considerably with the vagaries of a boiler, or of its attendant. Many people may notice such things; but it lies with the curator to take effective action. It is for the curator, also, to see that a satisfactory environment for objects has its indispensable complement in their careful handling. Harm done by a jolt or jar, or by a sudden blow, may not always declare itself at once, but may develop later. Proper handling is much more a matter of intelligence and training than is generally realised; and it is the curator who by example and precept should set standards and enforce them.

Next comes the matter of safe conditions of exhibition. Here the public are directly concerned; and the main problem is to find a balance between precautions and amenities. The days of ropes and barriers, and of pouncing policemen, have happily disappeared. Still, theft and deliberate damage have to be guarded against, and it is for the curator to see that the necessary deterrents and obstacles are provided. More difficult to cope with is the accidental harm due to the investigating finger, and the occasional desire of the young to embellish an object with pencil or lipstick. This raises the whole question of the putting of objects under glass. Admittedly, this is effective protection against accidental damage and the sneak-thief; and it sometimes has the additional advantage of serving as a screen against atmospheric impurities and the more dangerous elements in light, while it may give opportunity for *ad hoc* control of humidity. On the other hand, there is always the risk of dust accumulating within a case, and of a condensation of moisture, a combination which may do considerable harm. The main objection to glass, however, is that it may make objects difficult to see, in the case of dark pictures converting them into little more than mirrors ; and unless the glass is colourless, it may affect the apparent colour of the object. The use of non-reflecting and colourless glass may in future overcome these difficulties ; but, in the meantime, the curator has to settle whether he will risk an object suffering in order to make it beautiful. In any case attendants are indispensable, and it is another curatorial responsibility to see that they are sufficiently intelligent, adequate in number and properly placed. With encouragement and a little training, also, attendants can be most useful in keeping objects under observation, and reporting any changes in condition. They can thus, in a double sense, become the curators' first line of defence.

Yet, despite all the care that may be given them, objects, like human beings, are apt to fall into disrepair, sometimes gradually, sometimes with dramatic suddenness. In any event the procedure to be followed is exactly that in the case of a sick human being—first aid, to meet any immediate dangers, followed by diagnosis and by appropriate treatment. Normally, at this point, the professional conservator takes over ; and at once the difficult problem arises of his relation to the curator in this phase of his work. One view is that the initiative in examination and treatment should lie with the conservator, and that his decisions throughout should be final ; and that the curator should no more interfere with the conservator's discretion than should friends of a human patient with that of a doctor. Against this view is that the medical analogy is not convincing. In fact a human patient, his relatives and his friends have a good deal to say as to whether he should go into hospital,

and how he should be treated. Again, even in medicine, which is far more highly developed both in theory and practice than is conservation, the certainties of one generation may well become anathema to the next. Similarly, in conservation, such once universally accepted practices as 'feeding' a painting with oil, and the use of cradles on panels, are now widely discredited ; and though we may hope and believe that present-day methods are based on deeper and wider knowledge than those of the past, it would be rash to say that they are final. There is, therefore, a case for the intervention of an external authority, based on common sense and on considerations which are likely to be outside the conservator's purview. Sometimes a conservator may be old-fashioned and wedded to aims and methods now regarded as outmoded or even dangerous, and must be brought to realise that new standards have emerged, and that other ways of doing things have developed. Sometimes, on the other hand, a conservator may be seething with ideas, and full of an enthusiasm which may corrupt judgment. The new agent for the destruction of worm, the new solvent, the new protective covering, have a fascination for him, even if their safety, their long-term efficiency and ultimate effect, have not been fully tested. This experimental approach is in many ways admirable, and is, indeed, indispensable if progress in conservation is to be made ; but it tends to make an object into a laboratory specimen rather than something to be looked at, studied and enjoyed ; and transforms conservation into an end rather than a means. So it may be with standards. Some conservators hold that all alien accretions are to be removed, all repairs clearly indicated, and so on : a puritanical approach which parallels the movement in the arts towards expression of function. This represents a laudable reaction against the faking which in the past stood for restoration and misled many generations of students. Yet it has its own dangers. Exposure of the original material does not necessarily mean that an object looks as it did when it left its maker's hands. Colours may have changed both absolutely and relatively, textures may have altered irrevocably; and it is sometimes possible that a veil of old varnish, or of patina on a metal, helps the original intention of the maker to be better understood. Lastly, an important element in deciding what treatment should be given to an object is comparison with the constitution and appearance of other objects of the same type. Here the curator's knowledge may well go beyond that of the conservator, and may therefore usefully supplement it at points where decisions have to be taken.

Thus, even in the technical processes of conservation, there may be need for the knowledge and judgment of the curator; while on other occasions they may be indispensable. For example, choice may have to be made as to whether priority be given to a minor work in danger of dissolution over a masterpiece in serious but less parlous condition; it may have to be decided how far it is justifiable to expend time and labour on unimportant objects beyond the point of arresting immediate decay; or in the case of a work being found on investigation to be a repaired wreck, to say whether it should be revealed as such, or left comparatively undisturbed. Into such decisions enter not only aesthetic and historical considerations, but political ones too. A curator has to take into account the views of his governing body, of potential benefactors and of outside opinion. These may sometimes be ill-founded; and when deference to them would in any way affect the safety of the objects concerned, the curator is bound to do what he thinks best, or surrender his responsibilities. But the need for paying heed to lay opinion is sometimes useful as inducing second thoughts on a proposed course of action; and when differences of opinion are concerned not with safety but with appearance, it is well to remember that neither curator nor conservator is a final arbiter of taste. In short, it is for the curator to settle

the general policy of conservation, to see that it is carried out and, when necessary, to adjust ideals to practical necessities. Like a cabinet minister, he must use his experts; but the final responsibility is his, and his must be the final decision, which he has to justify to his superiors and to the outside world. This may seem to relegate the conservator to a secondary position. In fact, it is a necessary protection for him, enabling him to concentrate on the technical aspects of his work.

Arising out of this primary responsibility of the curator are others. One is to keep, or see that there be kept, detailed and accurate records of whatever treatment an object receives. Today the trained conservator is expected to do this, and should do it better than anyone else; but not infrequently the curator must be prepared to do it himself. Not only are such records useful in justifying what has been done and as a protection against ignorant criticism, but they provide an invaluable record of the physical constitution of an object to serve as a basis for precautions in its handling and for any treatment it may receive in the future. With an eye to the future, too, both curator and conservator should be prepared to do all they can to stimulate and assist scientific research bearing upon conservation. Only in the present century has the potential value of such research come to be realised. Previously, scientific investigations had been chiefly directed towards the problem of artists' materials, the main impulse coming from those who either sought to recapture the methods of the old masters or to find shortcuts to attaining their results. Even today the main emphasis is on the analysis of structure, partly directed towards finding out, for the information of the art historian, methods and materials used, partly for the detection of forgeries and partly as diagnosis preliminary to remedial treatment. Moreover, much of what is being done is *ad hoc*, designed to give answers to specific problems. What is needed now is systematic research into the problems of environment and of treatment. Much of this must inevitably be long-range in character if its results are to be reliable as a basis for action. For example, too little is known of the ultimate stability of the various synthetic resins which may be used as protective coverings to justify their invariable use. Also, long-range research is more likely to yield general principles applicable over a wide field than investigation designed only to meet a particular set of circumstances. It may well be, too, that this long-range research may be directed to a far wider field than that of conservation, and any solution of conservation problems that it yields may be only a by-product or an application of much more generalised conclusions. Thus, conservator and curator have a double duty : to formulate for the scientist questions whose answers not only satisfy immediate needs, but which raise much wider issues. The curator, in particular, may not be able to formulate his questions as would a trained scientist, nor even to realise the extent and significance of what he asks, or where it may fall in the field of scientific research. But nevertheless he should be actively alive to the possibility of mobilising scientists for his own purposes. Only so is substantial progress in principles and methods of conservation likely to be made.

The programme outlined above for a curator may seem heavy enough ; but sometimes it may become heavier. Most small museums, and many large ones, have not enough money, and sometimes not enough work, to justify installation of a laboratory and of even one full-time conservator. In such cases preliminary diagnosis as to what is wrong with an object has to be the work of the curator, who may also have to administer first aid. Then comes the problem of how and where further diagnosis is to take place, and necessary treatment given. If there is near at hand another museum adequately staffed and equipped, which is prepared to take outside work, all is comparatively well, despite the possible risk in taking a delicate object from one place to

another. But if there is no such museum, recourse must be had to a conservator in private practice. Many of these are highly skilled and completely reliable, but their employment may raise difficulties. The museum may not have the necessary facilities for the work of a conservator, and the object may have to go to his own workshop. Quite apart from the risks of transport, and of conditions in the workshop not being ideal, there is the considerable probability that the conservator does not have all the apparatus needed for diagnosis, and the object may have to make yet another journey ; all this probably without the curator being able to exercise any personal supervision. It is to meet such difficulties that plans are now afoot for small museums to share the services of a qualified conservator. Simpler operations can be carried out in the museum concerned ; more elaborate ones in a properly equipped workshop in one of the co-operating museums, which would be the conservator's headquarters. Such plans are more difficult to carry out than might be expected. It is not easy so to arrange the flow of work to avoid the conservator being overwhelmed at one time, and unemployed at another ; nor to establish a fair basis for sharing the cost both of work done and of the installing and maintenance of equipment. Yet the possible advantages of such co-operation are enough to compel the attention of a curator.

Another aspect of the problem of the small or insufficiently equipped museum is faced by the curator and conservator who are asked to do outside work. Such work demands as much skill and judgment as does the museum's own ; and carries with it the extra burden of convincing a fellow-curator or private owner that such and such a course should or should not be followed, and of facing criticism if results do not come up to expectations. A natural instinct is to refuse such work ; but since the practitioners of conservation still include a good many quacks, it seems desirable a museum should do outside work whenever practicable, not only to safeguard particular objects but to set standards.

Yet another problem which is becoming increasingly urgent arises out of demands for loans, either for temporary exhibitions or for long periods. If anything goes wrong with an object, the fact that it was out of the curator's control may be an explanation ; but it is not a valid excuse, unless full precautions had been taken against damage and the desirability of lending has been held to outweigh its risks. Questions that have to be asked and answered in making a decision whether or not to lend include the following : Whether the object is in a state to stand the inevitable jolting and jarring of travel, and the changes in temperature and humidity it is certain to encounter ; how an object can best be packed, and how can satisfactory packing for the return journey be assured ; whether the object will receive skilled and careful handling from the borrower, and whether the conditions of exhibition are satisfactory as regards risks of damage and theft ; also, if the object is damaged, whether there is a competent conservator available for its treatment. To answer these and other relevant questions is a curator's duty, and involves knowledge about methods of transport, the competence and carefulness of the borrower and his staff, and about the place and the conditions of exhibition. In any case, before an object *is* lent it should be thoroughly examined, and, if necessary, put in satisfactory condition for what it has to face ; an additional burden for curator and conservator.

From the foregoing, one conclusion at least is evident : that if a curator is to perform his duties properly he must not only be scholar and showman, but have some training in the principles and practice of conservation. Reading can do something ; practice in some art or craft a great deal ; regular and frequent contact with a competent conservator most of all. But nothing can replace practical experience in the care and treatment of objects, gained by experimenting with worthless material picked up for small sums, and by constant observation of the condition of objects in relation to their environment and treatment. How a curator is to find time and opportunity for such training is another matter ; but unless he does, he is scarcely deserving of his title.

11: SOME PERSONNEL CONSIDERATIONS FOR BINDING AND CONSERVATION SERVICES

Edward Connery Lathem

THE FIRST THING that needs to be said in any treatment of this topic is, of course, that matters of binding and the conservation of materials in a library are everybody's business, the concern of each member of the staff, no matter what his or her regular capacity or functions may be. But there is also a corollary to this postulate, and that is that these matters must, in addition, be somebody's responsibility. It is not enough that everyone should constantly and vigilantly direct attention to the condition and care of all library materials; there must be, as well, someone specifically responsible for the binding and conservation program as a whole. And this responsibility, moreover, must be backed by a degree of authority adequate to assure the program's proper functioning and success.

Pelham Barr in an article published nearly a decade ago defined conservation in its broadest terms as "responsible custody," a function "concerned with every piece of material in the library from the moment the selector becomes aware of its existence to the day it is discarded." Pointing out the existence of "a need for reorienting administrative thought on the whole subject of book conservation and binding;" he urged librarians to "plan and provide for a truly broad program of book conservation." [1]

Because our libraries vary in kind and size and organization, they must, of course, vary also in the provisions that can be made for conservation services. In very small institutions it will necessarily be the librarian himself who will perform whatever duties of this nature are to be undertaken, while as the scale is ascended toward the level of institutions of huge size and complex character the question of personnel becomes a more involved and difficult problem.

There is surely no necessity of providing a profusely footnoted exposition of the obvious and widely-recognized fact that persons par-

Mr. Lathem is Director of Special Collections, Dartmouth College Library.

Copyright © 1956 by the University of Illinois; reprinted from *Libr. Trends* 4:321–334 (Jan. 1956).

ticularly well qualified to oversee and direct conservation activities, especially in their broadest context, are not by any means the profession's most embarrassingly over-abundant commodity. The reasons for the existing scarcity of personnel are several in number. Prominent among them is the inadequacy of the training currently provided by most of our library schools. Louis Shores' article of a few years ago entitled "Do Librarians and Binders Play Fair?" revealed that of the twenty-six library training agencies included in his survey, all "provide some binding instruction," but that most frequently such instruction consisted merely of one or more lectures or exercises included as a part of the elementary courses in materials.[2] It is apparent that in most instances the exposure was meager indeed, and plainly much ground must still be covered if the profession is to be provided with an adequate supply of conservation personnel.

Also writing from the standpoint of binding considerations alone, Jerrold Orne states that "it is clear to all binders and to most librarians that the [library] schools are not teaching practical binding knowledge." He further observes, "Where the unusual school offers a course in this field it is commonly not compulsory, and those who do take it learn more about historical and antiquarian binding than about today's practical library binding problems."[3]

E. W. Browning suggests a second cause for the great lack of trained personnel when he says,

. . . in the past at least, there has been little or no call from libraries for assistants specially trained for binding supervision and book conservation. Too often libraries have been content to give this work to an inexperienced assistant, whose only training had been what he could learn from good or bad methods employed by his predecessor.

Libraries have asked for and library schools have trained assistants in book selection and in cataloging and classification. But of what avail are well selected books made easily available through a well organized catalog if, when found, they are not in usable condition. Every library has thousands of dollars' worth of books and other reading materials, but only in the best organized libraries are these materials cared for by fully trained and experienced binding supervisors.[4]

In Browning's opinion, then, the absence of a sufficient demand on the part of the country's libraries has, at least in part, accounted for our library schools not turning any very vigorous attention to providing training in this field.

Still another probable reason for new librarians failing to be especially interested in conservation matters is suggested by E. A.

D'Alessandro in telling of his own feelings upon transferring from a branch library in the Cleveland Public's system into binding and book repair work: "Frankly, I did not know whether I would like it or not. I did not know if I would find the challenge that I had found while serving the public for ten years or so. For a time, I was worried by the very disturbing thought that I was consigning myself to the dull, dry, dreary occupation of handling nothing but dirty, torn, and worn-out volumes. Could it be that I had sentenced myself to rattle around among the drying bones of the library's grave-yard?"

D'Alessandro discovered, however, that his misgivings, typical perhaps of the reactions of many librarians to the area of book repair, were groundless. "The past two years," he reports, "have been a revelation and an education. Instead of finding myself in a grave-yard littered with the broken backs, crushed spines, and dead bodies of books, I found myself in what verily may be called the library's rehabilitation laboratory. Thus, the Book Repair Division has become for me a proving ground, and an experimental station, wherein new equipment, new materials, and new techniques can be tested, tried, and put into operation, not merely for the sake of change, but in the interest of library economy and better service to our public serving departments." [5]

These are but a few of the causes for the lack of personnel properly trained to handle conservation services. What remedies for the existing situation are likely to develop in the foreseeable future? If, as is hoped, we are entering upon a period in which greater and greater attention will be directed toward conservation, it seems likely that we can expect librarians to be increasingly mindful of these needs and to think in terms of adding conservation specialists to their library's staff. The emergence of this "age of enlightenment," coupled with the demand for qualified personnel, may well stimulate the library schools to give more curricular emphasis to this area and its problems and students to take a more interested view of conservation matters. Hopefully, professional library organizations will become interested and play important roles in stimulating attention to training in conservation. Browning suggests, too, that libraries not able to employ library school graduates see to it that their conservation employees make visitations to binderies at least once a year, and that they also visit other libraries and attend library association meetings for the exchange of ideas and information.[6]

As for the present time, it is for most libraries pretty largely a case of making the most of the talents of personnel available and, obviously, the services of the best qualified person should be secured. Except perhaps in the largest of institutions, it really does not greatly matter who perfoms the functions of a binding and conservation officer, nor what his title may be, so long as that individual does the job effectively and well. It is the results that are important. Despite the fact that there will be advocates of all sorts of logical and functional and otherwise professedly desirable and appropriate combinations of interest and responsibility, in situations in which such a combination is required, the decision on who should take on responsibility for conservation ought surely to rest chiefly on the basis of who is best qualified. Few libraries can have a keeper of collections to devote full time to conservation affairs, and in lieu of this a doubling up of responsibilities is required. To do this on grounds of other than ability would seem to be wasteful of talent. Such an arrangement, to be sure, molds a part of the organizational structure on the basis of the individual, which under many circumstances is perhaps undesirable, but it does permit the application of the most skilled services within command to an area of activity and concern that deserves the very best that can be provided. And if preconceived ideas of a neat and orderly design for the organization chart are frustrated thereby or certain theoretical principles of administrative organization are somewhat violated, these transgressions seem to be justified in institutions not able to afford or to find a properly trained person to concern himself solely with conservation matters.

M. F. Tauber in his *Technical Services in Libraries* has, however, sounded a pertinent warning when he declares, "Too often the responsibility for binding has been given to an individual whose time is taken up with other and seemingly more important tasks." [7] This is a genuine cause for concern, too, when it is necessary to rely on only the part-time attention of a staff member to the more general and inclusive problem of conservation, and it is a danger that should neither be lost sight of nor minimized.

It is not at all unfeasible, it may be pointed out, for conservation responsibility to be shared by a number of persons, each well-equipped to handle some one of the various specialized phases of the total problem. This is especially true in larger libraries with separate departments for the administration of special classes or kinds of library resources. In this connection it must, however, be strongly recommended that the responsibility be considered—in the finest distinction of the words—really a shared and in no sense a divided one. And in such cases, also, it may be best for one individual to be considered as having the primary responsibility and authority. Cooperation on a library-wide basis is, as was pointed out at the outset, a basic requisite of the program, but coordination is, indeed, an equally important aspect, and one that takes on even greater significance when there are two or more persons engaged in the direction of different phases or segments of the program.

This rather naturally leads to the question: What should the conservation officer be expected to know? The answer can be readily given—considerably more readily, it must be admitted, than can its accomplishment be achieved. He should, in substance, know as much as possible about as much as possible. He should have at his command as much knowledge as is available about the library he serves—especially with respect to the nature of its resources and services, as well as the character of its clientele and the kinds of demands they make upon its collections. And balanced against this should be as much knowledge as it is possible to attain of the technical considerations of conservation practices, methods, and facilities.

The chief conservation problem of a library ordinarily is, of course, one of binding. In addition to having professional library training and experience, and, ideally, foreign language competence, a person directing binding operations, whether they be carried on within a library-maintained bindery or in an outside shop, should be equipped with a basic understanding of the binding processes and operations of both hand and machine work, and should be aware of the various pieces of binding equipment and their uses. He should understand the methods employed in binding and re-binding and the practices employed in mending and repair work, as well as the standards to be applied to the finished products. He should be familiar with the differing requirements for the handling of the various kinds of items processed (as children's books, reference works, periodicals and newspapers, to name but a few of the obvious groups). He must be able to decide, based on such considerations as are suggested by G. R. Lyle in *The Administration of the College Library*,[8] whether in individual cases it is better to rebind, replace, or withdraw a particular worn-out volume. He should know, also, about work flow patterns and schedules, the keeping of adequate records, and, when appropriate, the relative advantages of commercial binding as opposed to treatment within the library's own bindery for different classes of books and other resources. If all or much of the work is done by an outside bindery, it is important that he work closely with the bindery to insure a mutual understanding on both technical aspects and service, and to establish and maintain a sympathetic and cordial intercourse. As Flora B. Ludington has observed of the association between the librarian and the commercial binder, "It is only through working together with mutual trust and respect for each other's special competence that this segment of library management will be handled with the foresight that is needed." [9] The Library Binding Institute and the Joint Committee of the American Library Association and the Library Binding Institute have, as has already been discussed by J. B. Stratton, played important parts in developing cooperative considerations and solutions to the peculiar problems of bindery-library relationships and in educating both sides to the conditions of the other's environment and requirements.

Depending upon the size of the institution, there might well be other individuals participating in various phases of the administration of binding and book repair. The binding officer might, for example, have the assistance of a bindery preparations clerk or reviser, who would perform sundry record-keeping and allied duties connected with the transfer of books to and from the bindery. The qualifications for such a position would vary from library to library. It would be, for instance, advantageous in a large research library for such a person to have some background in foreign languages, whereas this would be of only slight consequence in a smaller institution where the materials were largely in English. An acquaintance with general library procedures is in most cases required, and especially a familiarity with the rules of entry. Accuracy and aptitude for detail are essential for a bindery preparations clerk in any size library.

Another of the more common units or subdivisions that exist in some libraries and function under the binding officer is a repair station or stations, often located centrally within the stacks themselves or at the circulation desk. These are sometimes referred to as "plastic" repair stations, in that much of their work consists of making minor repairs using various plastic mending products. They also serve, however, as "feeder" channels to the bindery itself for books that need extensive repairs or re-binding. The chief and comprehensive qualification required of persons manning these stations is that they have, besides a command of the processes they are to perform, a knowledge of the limitations of the services that can profitably be undertaken at such stations—of what materials ought and ought not to be given "plastic" first aid and what items are beyond the stage where they can be treated outside of the bindery.

R. E. Kingery, elsewhere in this issue, in his treatment of "The

Bindery Within the Library," has already admirably discussed the pertinent problems relating to personnel considerations for a library's own bindery. These topics require no elaboration here except, perhaps, to underscore the fact that the services of skilled bindery workers are not at all easy to secure. There are, however, certain organizations that can perform "clearinghouse" functions for inquiries about the availability of personnel. For example, craft groups like the Guild of Book Workers, an affiliate of the American Institute of Graphic Arts with headquarters in New York City, can sometimes assist with requests for craftsmen in the field of hand bookbinding and in restoration work. Some of the trade unions, on the other hand, would be more appropriate agencies to which to apply for information on workers trained in machine binding or those having specific skills limited to individual binding operations. Publications like *Book Production* (formerly *Bookbinding and Book Production*) and some of the printing journals can be used for advertising. And the Library Bindery Institute and the A.L.A.'s Committee on Bookbinding could possibly provide some help, although the location of personnel is not one of their primary objectives. On-the-job training of workers by a competent foreman will ordinarily be the means of supplying a good part of the personnel needs of binderies within most libraries once they have been set up.

A possible solution to a part of the binding problems of some of our smaller libraries that are unable to bear the costs of maintaining a bindery or repair shop of their own, but for which these facilities are in great need, is to consider whether there exists the opportunity for some sort of cooperative enterprise program with other nearby institutions which may be operating under similar circumstances of need. The matter, nevertheless, should be weighed very carefully in all its aspects—both with regard to costs and service—before any action is taken. Under ideal conditions it might well prove to be economically feasible for two or more libraries to set up a small, jointly-maintained shop to handle their bindery services.

Before leaving the subject of binding and book repair it may be well to point out for the benefit of librarians who may find themselves faced with problems in this field, but who lack an adequate background of training or experience to cope with them readily, certain published works that might be helpful in meeting these problems. Self-education, it should be realized, is an important feature of personnel considerations in the field of conservation, where so little knowledge is or can be derived from academic instruction.

The *Library Binding Manual,* prepared by L. N. Feipel and E. W.

Browning under the direction of the Joint Committee of the A.L.A. and the Library Binding Institute is a most helpful guide, and a copy should be handily within reach.[10] A good general work on binding, such as Edith Diehl's *Bookbinding: Its Background and Techniques*,[11] is also a desideratum, and the Government Printing Office's *Theory and Practice of Bookbinding* will prove a very worth-while introductory text.[12] Mention must be made, also, of two other books that ought not under any circumstances be neglected: H. M. Lydenburg and John Archer's *The Care and Repair of Books* [13] and Douglas Cockerell's *Bookbinding, and the Care of Books*.[14]

But what of some of the other more specialized classes of materials included among a library's resources to which conservation services must also be directed, but which cannot ordinarily be provided for with the same binding and repair treatment that is given to ordinary books, periodicals, newspapers, and the like? It has already been suggested that in our larger libraries where special departments exist to administer certain kinds of materials it may be advisable for the specialists in charge of such collections to share in the responsibility for conservation activities. In most instances the librarians of such custodial units will possess as part of their professional training a comprehensive command of the factors involved in the care, preservation, and restoration of the materials with which they deal, and under such circumstances their expert competence should, obviously, be relied upon to supply the need for such services to their collections.

Materials from rare books collections are, for example, usually best handled by or under the direction of their curators or custodians, who ordinarily have a strong background of knowledge about the binding and repair of rarities. In an admirably terse fashion, a committee of the Friends of the Columbia Libraries has set forth what might be termed the minimum qualifications for those overseeing rare books conservation:

It is not suggested that the collector or the librarian himself be an expert binder or restorer. Both of them, however, should be able to recognize the nature of the problem when they see leather bindings turning into powdery dust, hinges cracking, boards severed from their backs or the text badly foxed. They should have the technical knowledge to judge the qualifications of those to whom they entrust the delicate job of preservation or restoration, and to know that the processes employed have been sound and well executed. To follow any other course is fraught with danger and may even result in serious damage to rare or irreplaceable material or its total loss.[15]

In large libraries rare books departments have often set up their own special binding stations, frequently as adjuncts of the library central bindery where such exists. These are staffed by a master binder, whose presence within the department permits work to be done under the direct and close supervision of the curator and the materials to be handled with added security. A well-illustrated article in the February 1949, issue of *Bookbinding and Book Production* gives the details of the establishment and operation of a self-contained bindery unit for rare books at the Clark Library of the University of California at Los Angeles.[16]

The same approach is recommended for special departments administering non-book materials, as where libraries possess manuscripts collections and, as is often the case with colleges and universities especially, archives. If there is a manuscripts curator or archivist, or if these resources are administered by the rare book staff, it will be best to have these specialists take responsibility for their physical care. Where the program of acquisition of such resources is extensive, it may be necessary to provide one or more persons to constitute a special unit for repair and preservation services. Some of the functions associated with this work, such as the preliminary cleaning and flattening, are not complicated and will not require highly skilled workers. Others, like the washing of manuscripts, the removal of stains, and performing reinforcing processes, call for expert treatment; and qualified restorers are not easily found. Libraries installing laminating machines will usually have their operators trained by the firm selling the equipment. In connection with laminating W. J. Barrow has suggested that, "In some institutions a good knowledge of book binding is required previous to the training in restoration work." He states that a period of apprenticeship of "at least three to four years produces the best craftsmen," and that all of his own pupils thus far have had "at least a high school education." [17]

The librarian having only minor manuscripts holdings with infrequent problems of their care and preservation may use as a handbook Adelaide E. Minogue's *The Care and Preservation of Records*,[18] published as a National Archives bulletin, to which Mrs. Minogue has appended a splendid bibliography. Mary A. Benjamin in her *Autographs: A Key to Collecting* also provides a helpful section on manuscripts preservation, written in a non-technical vein for the layman.[19]

With extensive map collections, too, the map librarian can normally be relied on to perform conservation services on his holdings. Lacking such a person, the librarian with no specialized training in the field will want to refer to the information provided in Clara E. LeGear's *Maps: Their Care, Repair and Preservation in Libraries* [20] and L. A. Brown's *Notes on the Care & Cataloging of Old Maps.* [21]

This same approach, should, in similar manner, be followed in providing conservation services for other specialized classes of library materials: their care should be placed in the hands of a well-qualified custodian if he is present, or such other available conservation personnel as may exist and who may have experience in treating such resources, or, these alternatives failing, the librarian will need to refer to the best sources of information on the preservation of the particular kind of materials in question.

Taking as the basis for our consideration the broad view of conservation espoused by Barr, as a 'cradle-to-grave' concern with all library resources, there are still other services for which personnel must be supplied.

The important function of inspection and care of materials in the library's stacks has been treated earlier in this issue by R. J. Schunk in his article "Stack Problems and Care." The question of whether stack personnel should constitute a separate administrative unit within the library organization is a subject over which there has been some controversy, but it is a problem that cannot be adequately treated here in its many and varying aspects. In this connection, it must be urged, however, that whatever organizational structure is adopted, the person responsible for stack management, if he is not directly under the supervision of the library's general conservation services officer, should at least work in close cooperation with him. All personnel working in the stacks should, of course, be fully aware of proper shelving practices and should direct their activities accordingly, and they should be on the alert at all times for items requiring repair. If the cleaning of library materials is a function carried on by the library's building maintenance staff rather than by personnel immediately under the stack officer, the latter should be allowed to prescribe in specific terms how any and all of such operations shall be performed.

It has been observed that "the lack of systematic conservation is often the result of poor layout of the library building and the lack of effective or adequate equipment." [22] This points up the necessity of the conservation officer having among his qualifications not only a knowledge of the effects upon the physical well being of library resources of temperature, light, humidity, and other climatic factors and an ability to deal with these problems within the restrictions imposed by his own building arrangements, but also an awareness of the variety of equipment that is available and its relative merits for meeting the various storage and housing requirements of materials. The conservation officer will, moreover, be required to be ready and able to cope with such unromantic concerns as insect and vermin control.

There is a growing need for investigation and experimentation in the field of conservation, and this, too, involves a personnel consideration. Referring to P. E. Clapp's article "A Technical Research Laboratory for the Library," [23] L. R. Wilson and Tauber in *The University Library* observe:

The suggestion has been made that the study of such problems as materials, fabrics, lettering, sizing, paper preservation, reproductive techniques, preservation from mildew, extermination of insects and vermin, and leather preservation, as well as other technical matters of modern-day librarianship, should be investigated by· a technical research laboratory, supported co-operatively by major university, public, and reference libraries. It has also been suggested that each large library should have an individual on its staff who would serve as a general research assistant to investigate technical problems of conservation. In those university libraries which have binderies, this arrangement exists to some extent.[24]

Finally, there is the basic matter, as mentioned at the beginning, of securing the cooperation and joint-effort of all library workers in the library's over-all program of conservation, and of assuring that this activity is intelligently and persistently carried on. Here is the point at which the conservation officer will be called upon not only to exercise the broad authority which it has been suggested he must possess to make the program efficiently workable, but, moreover, to summon up sufficient tactful persuasiveness to insure that the desired ends will be achieved without friction or acrimony. In an undertaking such as this, where the work is of such a vast scope and where so wide an area of the library's total operations and services is involved, it is essential that the spirit under which the program is carried forward be one of friendly harmony. It may prove desirable in the larger libraries to issue a staff information bulletin to give all employees an awareness of the problems of conservation, a knowledge of the nature and aims of the library's conservation activities, and some instructions on what functions each staff member is encouraged and expected to perform. Tauber in *Technical Services in Libraries* provides a section of commentary on the individual roles that should be played by certain of the library departments (acquisitions, cataloging, reference, circulation, periodicals, and photography) and by the branch libraries in coordinating their conservation activities with particular regard to binding considerations.[25] This might well be expanded to cover a broader scope of concern with conservation matters. Perhaps, also, for an appropriately large library system a manual might be produced covering in detail specific approaches to different conservation problems and the procedures to be employed in performing conservation services. The alerting of key personnel to the appearance of writings bearing upon this field is important also.

The conservation officer's duties in enlisting the informed assistance of others in the program which he directs need not and should not be limited to staff members alone but may, as means and opportunity permit, be extended to library users as well. Ira L. Brown in an article entitled "Our Book Hospital"[26] interestingly tells of the thoughtfully-contrived dramatization used by one institution in impressing upon children the necessity of using their library books properly and with care. Activities with similar aims of educating the public to the requirements of conservation ought not to be neglected in dealing with all library patrons.

Some of the varied considerations centering upon the problem of personnel in conservation services have been touched upon and discussed. The vast differences that manifestly exist between our libraries make it impossible to prescribe validly the particulars for a standard or even an ideal organizational arrangement. Such structure will, as has been pointed out, depend upon the existing conditions and circumstances within the individual institutions. Similarly, and for the same reason, it is not possible to declare categorically just what the specific qualifications required of personnel will or ought to be and precisely what services they should be expected to perform. It has been urged that in approaching the question of staffing a conservation program libraries carefully survey their needs and their resources, both present and potential, for meeting these needs. No two institutions will be found to be exactly the same, and although it is, of course, desirable to learn from the experience of others, it is an unrealistic and hazardous approach to follow rigidly and precisely patterns established elsewhere or blindly to follow theoretical precepts that do not reflect all of the variables existing as a part of the distinct character of each of our libraries. An attempt has been made to suggest some of the areas of activity and concern and some of the important considerations of background and capability in matters of personnel, and to strike some kind of balance between over-generalization and over-specification in the treatment of these problems.

Because conservation itself has been a considerably neglected topic in our professional literature and in the discussions at our library association gatherings, questions of personnel in this area have been given but slight attention. Few studies have been undertaken and little writing done bearing directly upon this subject. It is to be hoped, however, that the period ahead will witness both an expanding interest and activity in personnel matters, as in conservation generally, and that as a result of this increased attention and concern we shall better serve our public of today and not be weighed in the balances and found wanting when, as L. C. Powell has put it, we are judged by the future on the basis of "how wisely we have conserved the research treasure which we inherited, increased, and willed to our successors." [27]

References

1. Barr, Pelham: Book Conservation and University Library Administration. *College and Research Libraries*, 7:214-219, July 1946.

2. Shores, Louis: Do Librarians and Binders Play Fair? *Library Journal*, 74: 704-707, May 1, 1949.

3. Orne, Jerrold: What Binders Can Teach Us. *Library Journal*, 75:837-841, May 15, 1950.

4. Browning, E. W.: More Training Needed in Bookbinding and Book Conservation. *Library Journal*, 75:190-191, Feb. 1, 1950.

5. D'Alessandro, E. A.: I Like Book Repairing. *A.L.A. Bulletin*, 47:298-299, July-Aug. 1953.

6. Browning, *op. cit.*, p. 191.

7. Tauber, M. F., and Associates: *Technical Services in Libraries*. New York, Columbia University Press, 1954, p. 303.

8. Lyle, G. R.: *The Administration of the College Library*. 2nd ed. rev. New York, H. W. Wilson, 1949, p. 145.

9. Ludington, Flora B.: Book Preservation. *A.L.A. Bulletin*, 47:425-426, Oct. 1953.

10. Feipel, L. N., and Browning, E. W.: *Library Binding Manual*. Chicago, American Library Association, 1951.

11. Diehl, Edith: *Bookbinding; Its Background and Technique*. 2v. New York, Rinehart, 1946.

12. U. S. Government Printing Office. *Theory and Practice of Bookbinding*. (Apprentice Training Series, Orientation Period) Washington, D. C., Government Printing Office, 1950.

13. Lydenberg, H. M., and Archer, J.: *The Care and Repair of Books*. 3rd ed. rev. New York, R. R. Bowker, 1945.

14. Cockerell, Douglas: *Bookbinding, and the Care of Books*. 5th ed. London, Pitman, 1953.

15. Lada-Mocarski, Polly, and Young, Laura S.: Rare Books and Manuscripts; Their Care, Preservation and Restoration. *Columbia Library Columns*, 3:3, pp. 29-30, May 1954.

16. Organizing a Rare Book Bindery. *Bookbinding and Book Production*, 48: 46-47+, Feb. 1949.

17. Barrow, W. J.: Letter dated Aug. 3, 1955.

18. Minogue, Adelaide E.: *The Repair and Preservation of Records.* (Bulletins of the National Archives, no. 5) Washington, D. C., Government Printing Office, Sept. 1943.

19. Benjamin, Mary A.: *Autographs; A Key to Collecting.* New York, R. R. Bowker Co., 1946, pp. 241-259.

20. LeGear, Clara E.: *Maps: Their Care, Repair and Preservation in Libraries.* Washington, D. C., Library of Congress, 1950.

21. Brown, L. A.: *Notes on the Care and Cataloguing of Old Maps.* Windham, Conn., Hawthorn House, 1940.

22. Tauber, *op. cit.*, p. 320.

23. Clapp, P. E.: A Technical Research Laboratory for the Library. *College and Research Libraries*, 1:251-253, June 1940.

24. Wilson, L. R., and Tauber, M. F.: *The University Library.* Chicago, University of Chicago Press, 1945, p. 542.

25. Tauber, *op. cit.*, pp. 304-312.

26. Brown, Ira L.: Our Book Hospital. *Wilson Library Bulletin*, 29:640-642, April 1955.

27. Powell, L. C.: Rare Book Code. *College and Research Libraries*, 10:307, July 1949.

12: MEMORANDUM ON CONSERVATION OF THE COLLECTIONS

James W. Henderson

1. INTRODUCTION

This memorandum on the conservation of the collections is an amplification of section II of "The Librarian as Conservator" by James W. Henderson and Robert G. Krupp, a paper prepared for the Annual Conference of the Graduate Library School, University of Chicago, in August, 1969. The present purpose is to translate that discussion into a conservation program for The Research Libraries of The New York Public Library and to make a number of specific recommendations for such a program. No effort is made to be all inclusive, and primary attention is given here to paper and books. A conservation program for non-paper materials will have to be dealt with at some future date.

The term conservation is used here in its broadest sense to include not only the restoration of deteriorated materials but also the prevention of deterioration. It includes both the conservation of physical materials and the conservation of the intellectual content of materials. Thus microrecording and reprinting are considered to be conservation measures.

Contributions to this memorandum have come from many quarters including the Preservation Committee of The Research Libraries Advisory Council, the Council itself, the Collections Preservation Coordinator, The Photographic Service, the Library Bindery, and consultants and staff involved in Conservation Program No. 3.

Reprinted from *Memorandum on Conservation of the Collections,* New York: The Research Libraries of The New York Public Library, April 1970, 28 pp.

2.   MANAGING THE CONSERVATION PROGRAM

2.1   Selection; acquisition

The conservation program begins with the selection
for acquisition, whenever possible, of permanent/durable
materials. The librarian will need to understand the meaning
of this term. With respect to paper the Committee on Permanence
and Durability of Paper of the Technical Association of the Pulp
and Paper Industry, has defined permanence as "the degree to
which paper resists chemical action which may result from impurities in the paper itself or agents from the surrounding
air; durability is the degree to which a paper retains its
original qualities under continual usage." A parallel
definition could be used to describe a permanent/durable
·binding.

While several authorities have offered specifications
for permanent/durable paper and many domestic paper mills are
now manufacturing paper according to these specifications,
relatively few currently published volumes meet even tentative
specifications for permanence and durability of paper and
binding. The Library should make a definite effort to put
pressure on publishers to utilize permanent/durable paper
and binding techniques and cooperate with the Joint Committee
on a Permanent/Durable Paper of the American Library Association
and other groups in this effort.

2.2   Screening

It is unlikely that permanent/durable paper will ever be used universally. Examination and testing of materials, therefore, will need to become a routine part of the Library's processes. Paul N. Banks has suggested that the traditional dichotomy of books as rare or ordinary be given up and that a category designated as books of permanent research value be recognized. In most archival collections there is little that is not regarded as having permanent value, however, even libraries of record discard some materials which are superseded in one way or another, and the fact that an item is to be discarded eventually is sometimes known at the time of initial processing.

The examination process might result in a division of materials into three categories: (1) those known to have been printed on permanent/durable paper and presumably to be retained permanently, (2) those to be retained permanently and printed on paper of unknown quality, and (3) materials to be discarded. Books in the second category will need to be inspected and tested to determine what type of treatment might be needed for their preservation before they are added to the collections.

Current costs both for testing and treatment make extensive screening impractical. One type of screening which would be immediately valuable would be testing for ground wood pulp papers. Since we know that this type of paper deteriorates rapidly and the test for it is simple and fast, it would be advantageous to identify papers containing ground wood and treat them before they are added to the collections. Most of these papers will have to be microfilmed eventually, and microfilming, when appropriate, before cataloging would be a definite economy as well as a conservation measure.

Materials added to the special collections need more exhaustive examination. Because of their value, all such materials should be examined by the conservator and the curator involved to determine any necessary treatments and proper storage methods and use. It should always be remembered that immediate conservation measures are important if materials are not to be damaged or allowed to deteriorate beyond repair, and that professional advice is necessary to determine proper procedures.

2.3   Treatment

A comprehensive treatment program for the collections
at the present time would include: (1) restoration, (2) regular
binding, and (3) information preservation through microrecording
and reprinting. Until such time as effective and economical
techniques for the treatment of large amounts of material become
available (see Appendix 5.4: Conservation Program No. 4) the
Library will need to be selective in the choice of materials to
be preserved and will have to make decisions with respect to the
best and most appropriate means of preserving them. Priority should
be given to materials which are unique or believed to be not widely
held and to materials of local significance.

A discussion of the restoration of books can be divided
into two general areas: paper treatment and binding. Treatment
in both areas must attempt to produce a permanent/durable artifact and should be carried out under the supervision of a person
skilled in the specialized techniques involved. Emphasis should
be placed on the clinical and structural rather than cosmetic
aspects, although certain materials will require more aesthetic
treatment, i.e., rare materials or books valued because of illustrations, plates, or bindings.

The two most important treatments for book papers are
stabilization through deacidification and reinforcement. Most
paper in the collections needs some form of deacidification.
When appropriate because of value and/or condition, deacidification
should be achieved by immersion in an aqueous alkaline solution;
otherwise, an organic solvent method may be used for bound volumes.
When mechanized deacidification of books becomes feasible, the conservation unit will have the task of working through the collections
in some systematic way for the purpose of identifying those materials
which can be saved by such a process. Reinforcement should include
an alkaline sizing as well as mending of tears, replacement of
missing portions of pages, and, in some cases, lamination by an
appropriate method.

Restoration binding involves the selection of a book
structure appropriate to a particular volume, taking into consideration the previous structure, dimensions of the volume, type
and condition of paper, type of sizing, and the book's intended
use and storage. All materials used must be of archival quality.
Decisions for treatment should be made in consultation between
the restorer and a person who is familiar with the bibliographic
value of the volume.

2.3   <u>Treatment</u> *(Continued)*

The treatment for conservation purposes of sheet
materials, e.g., unbound manuscripts, maps, prints, drawings,
and other paper supported works of art, requires added skills,
especially if the materials have fugitive images. Matting,
mounting, and backing require the same adherence to conservation principles as do the other techniques mentioned above.
Only permanent/durable board, hinges, and cloth should be
used, and special attention should be given to adhesives.
Solander cases, folding boxes, and portfolios must also meet
rigid archival specifications. Practically no advantage is
gained if valuable materials are enclosed in materials which
are injurious to them.

The problems of regular library binding are many.
Matt Roberts and Paul Banks have warned about the evils of
the destructive oversewing process which, alarmingly, is
the only method in use in commercial library binderies in
the United States today. Roberts's essay on oversewing
and its alternatives, "perfect" binding and flexible sewing,
ought to be required reading for all librarians. Roberts
describes the shortcomings of oversewing as follows: (1)
an oversewn book does not open easily and will not lie flat;
(2) oversewing presumes the destruction of the original
sections, thus making further rebinding all but impossible;
(3) the oversewn book has a greatly diminished inner margin;
(4) a book which is tightly sewn and has little inner margin
is difficult to photocopy and is frequently damaged in the
attempt; (5) paper that is even a little brittle will break
due to the unyielding grip of oversewing. So-called perfect
binding has some of the same disadvantages as oversewing and
would not seem to be well suited to volumes to be retained
permanently.

Flexible binding, on the other hand, has only a
single disadvantage -- cost. Banks points out that even
the standards for library binding developed by the Library
Technology Program do not insure nondestructive binding, since
they do not preclude oversewing. "There is only one way," he
says, "in which nondestructive binding will become more easily
and cheaply available, and that is for librarians to assume the
responsibility for learning more about the technical aspects
of the care of books in their charge, and to put pressure--
the pressure of buying power--onto the library binding industry."

2.3   Treatment (Continued)

Clearly a "conservation standard" is needed for binding materials of permanent value. The Library will have to insist that methods and standards be developed, and be willing and able to pay for them. For the present, more care should be exercised in selecting materials for binding by the destructive oversewing process.

Information preservation consists of re-formatting materials in order to preserve their intellectual content in a more permanent/durable form as opposed to the preservation of the materials as artifacts. If microrecording is chosen as a method of information preservation, the National Register of Microform Masters should be consulted to make certain that a microform of the material does not already exist. The type of microform to be utilized--microfilm or microfiche--will also have to be decided. Preparation of material for filming and the photographic work itself should be done in accordance with accepted bibliographic, technical, and conservation stand- ards, and a master microform should be created to be used only for the purpose of generating additional service copies. In like manner, when the Library receives an order for a micro- form, a master negative should be made for its own purposes and the individual or institution placing the order should be supplied with a positive copy. Master microforms should be reported to the National Register of Microform Masters so that their existence may become known and so that they may play their part in the national preservation program.

The present system of microrecording priorities (see Appendix 5.1: Conservation Program No. 1) is not satisfactory. It is frustrating to the staff to find a book in the stacks in a state of advanced deterioration or to be shown such a book by a reader and to be unable because of established microforming priorities and lack of funds, to do anything to save it from further deterioration and perhaps from disappearance. This is especially painful when the book has been called for by a serious researcher and may be the only copy or one of the few copies of the book in the country. Such a book is "rare" in one sense of the word, but it is not the kind of publication that would be suitable for a rare book collection. An effort should be made, to be sure, to preserve such a book from further deterioration, but if it was published after 1850 the likelihood is great that the paper on which the book was originally printed was poor, and the first step in the preservation of such a book may be to repro- duce it. It is generally agreed that microform is the least ex- pensive and, generally speaking, most effective means of reproduction, especially since it is now possible to reproduce in its original

2.3   Treatment *(Continued)*

size material that has been microformed. In order to allow
material of this kind to be given a place in the scheme of
microforming priorities, a special fund is needed, the use
of which would be restricted to the rescue of materials
which have been "selected" for microforming in the manner
described above.

Reprinting of materials can also be a method of
conservation in terms of information preservation. If reprints employ permanent/durable paper and bindings, this
process offers an advantage in its preservation of information
in book form. Books which are loaned to reprinters should not
be discarded unless the reprint is, in fact, permanent/durable
and all the intellectual content is reprinted. A valuable
advantage could be had if the Library were to lend to reprinters
volumes which were in need of repair and which would be dis-
assembled and then reassembled at the reprinter's expense
according to conservation specifications. Many reprinters
are now operating in this manner. In this way, the Library's
more valuable works can be restored and reprints of them obtained
in this process at no expense to the Library.

It is important to remember that treatment, as discussed here, is a highly skilled undertaking. While the field
of scientific conservation treatment is presently in its infancy, much is now known about deterioration, preservation,
and restoration of library materials. It would be inconsonant
with the role of a great research library to treat materials in
its collections so as to damage them or hasten their deterioration.

2.4   Collections Maintenance

Library materials should be stored under conditions
which protect them from deterioration due to extremes of temperature, humidity, pollution, and light. While physical
damage to materials is usually quite obvious, chemical deterioration is more insidious and is usually not evident until most
of its damage has been done. A relatively strong, durable sheet
of paper can deteriorate with amazing rapidity by invisible
chemical reaction due to deleterious substances introduced during
the manufacturing process or as a result of storage in a harmful
environment. Most chemical reactions proceed at relatively faster
rates as temperature increases. One simplified rule of thumb holds
that reaction rates double with an increase in temperature of ten
degrees Fahrenheit.

Most studies indicate that a temperature within the
range of 50 to 70 degrees and a relative humidity of 50 percent
are optimal for book and paper storage. The dangers of the extremes of humidity are, on the one hand, brittleness (when the
atmosphere is too dry) and, on the other hand, bacterial growth
(when too wet). Good collections maintenance calls for monitoring
of bookstacks for temperature and humidity control on a twenty-
four-hour basis. Adequate air conditioning for the collections
must also include systems for the removal of air pollutants and
particulate matter. Sulfur dioxide and sulfuric acid, which are
responsible for much of the deterioration of library materials,
are found in abundance in the polluted air of urban areas. Dirt
and grime not only soil materials; large particles are very abrasive and can cause significant physical damage.

It has been shown that certain wavelengths of light,
particularly ultraviolet rays, cause considerable damage to
paper and other book materials. Common fluorescent light contains a significant proportion of these wavelengths. Discoloration is the most immediate result of exposure to higher energy
forms of light, but weakening and physical failure of cellulosic
materials follow. In storage areas, constant exposure of book
spines to fluorescent light is definitely destructive. It is
important that lights in storage areas be left off as much as
possible and that fluorescent light which must remain on be
covered with shields which filter ultraviolet components.

Physical conditions of storage must also be considered
a part of conservation. Standard volumes should be shelved upright with support on both sides. Allowing books to stand at a
slant is damaging to both the binding and paper. Ideally, shelves
should not be full, but should be provided with an adjustable end
support with no sharp edges which can injure bindings. Over-

181

2.4   Collections Maintenance   *(Continued)*

packing of shelves can be quite harmful because of damage from
abrasion and the difficulty of removal. Oversize volumes should
be shelved flat with no more than three volumes per shelf. Especially large or heavy volumes should have one shelf each.
Improper shelving alone is responsible for much of the physical
destruction of bindings and paper in the Library's collections.
Cleaning of storage areas should include proper dust and dirt
removal from books.

Collections maintenance must also include systematic
inspection of all holdings by members of the conservation staff.
When adequate treatment facilities and procedures have been established, this inspection should be on a regular basis for the
purpose of identifying materials in need of treatment. Decisions
concerning the appropriate treatment would be made in consultation
between conservation personnel and the staff member in charge of
a particular collection. Eventually, a furbishing program should
be introduced to treat leather volumes with potassium lactate and
an approved leather dressing, do simple mending of pages and
bindings, and remove any harmful materials from bound volumes.

Materials are rarely handled properly in libraries. The
conservation staff should prepare instructions and familiarize the
library staff with the aims and techniques of conservation, devo-
ting special emphasis to the handling and use of library materials.
Special care must be exercised during the copying process. Copying
should not be permitted without professional supervision. Face-
down copying from bound volumes should be avoided, since it always
involves a certain amount of pressure, resulting in injury to spines
and hinges or the breakage of brittle leaves. If face-down copying
must be used for bound volumes, personnel of the reprographic department should be trained in techniques designed to minimize the
damage. Face-up copying is mandatory for rarer items, and master
negatives should be retained so as to prevent further exposure of
valuable materials to the hazards of reproduction.

The exhibition and display of materials from the collections
require special consideration because of the value of most items
selected for display and the usually injurious conditions under
which they are exhibited. Display cases are notorious for high
temperatures, low humidity, and unshielded fluorescent lighting
in high concentrations. As discussed above, elimination of these
conditions is essential to the conservation of library materials.
Exhibition personnel should be thoroughly familiar with conservation
principles, especially these related to the transportation and display of materials. In several museums, the display staff is under
the supervision of the conservation department. The present policy

2.4   Collections Maintenance *(Continued)*

statement on loans should be reviewed with respect to conservation, and guidelines for the transportation and packing of library materials should be developed by the conservation staff.

2.5   Personnel

A serious problem in administering a conservation program arises because of the shortage of qualified personnel in the field. The conservation unit will have to be directed by a person with very specialized qualifications. He should have a comprehensive knowledge of the nature of library materials and the causes and treatments of their deterioration. A sound understanding and practical experience in paper and book restoration and binding are essential, as are knowledge and appreciation of libraries and library materials. While it is not necessary for the conservator to be a scientist, he must have a basic scientific background and be able to communicate with scientists in the discussion of conservation problems. Above all, he should be able to synthesize, bringing to the field the benefits of connoisseurship, craftsmanship, and science and technology.

It should be possible to train qualified restoration, binding, and photographic technicians through a combination of formal instruction and on-the-job experience. If qualified personnel are to be produced, however, a share of the cost of training may have to be underwritten by the Library.

The restoration laboratory at the Biblioteca Nazionale Centrale in Florence was set up by a few experienced conservators who trained unskilled personnel in various specific restoration techniques in a matter of months. Thus it would appear that most personnel problems could be solved by in-house training, once competent management personnel are obtained.

2.6   Costs

Conservation is expensive. The installation and operation of air conditioning equipment with humidity control on a twenty-four-hour basis, the maintenance of an adequate cleaning and inspection schedule, the screening of materials, the utilization of proper restoration, binding, and information preservation techniques (such as reprinting and micropublishing), and the administration of a comprehensive conservation program will necessitate large expenditures of money. However, it should be apparent by now that initial costs are not the only concern of an institution founded in perpetuity and presently over one hundred years old. Since the materials in the collections are of permanent research value, we are committed to preserving them. Constant consideration must be given to the length of service achieved by a given treatment, and, since preservation is the intent, costs must be expressed in terms of the maintenance of the collections over long periods of time.

One of the clearest examples of the cost of using materials and techniques without consideration of ultimate expense was the introduction of ground wood pulp papers in the middle of the nineteenth century. Certainly such paper was cheaper, but the cumulative costs to libraries and collectors who have attempted to preserve books printed on these papers far exceeds what the original cost would have been had a more permanent paper been used.

Another example of this type of false economy is the practice of oversewing books of permanent research value, a practice approved for Class A bindings by the Library Binding Institute. If we assume an initial cost of ten dollars for an oversewn volume and a cost of fifty dollars for one which has been deacidified and flexibly sewn, we can project future costs with respect to conservation. In approximately thirty years an oversewn volume will probably require extensive restoration because of the disadvantages and destructive properties of oversewing cited in the treatment section of this memorandum. Such restoration would probably cost a minimum of one hundred dollars at current rates. The flexibly bound and deacidified volume, on the other hand, would probably still be strong, since such a volume should last three hundred years or longer. Thus at the end of thirty years, the oversewn volume will have cost one hundred and ten dollars to preserve, while the seemingly more expensive treatment has, in reality, cost less than half that amount.

2.6 <u>Costs</u> *(Continued)*

Numerous further examples could also be cited. For present purposes, however, the foregoing should suffice. It is important that long-range considerations be made with respect to any treatment given to materials in the collections, and long-range analysis must be included in a discussion of costs. Certain costs are not readily apparent, especially when micro-recording is selected as the method of preservation, e.g., the cost of recataloging, shelf preparation, and binding (if electro-static reproductions are made). Electrostatic reproduction seems to be the costliest of conservation measures, with short-run reprinting, deacidification/lamination, and microrecording following in that order. If microrecording is only an inter-mediate step toward some form of reprinting, however, total costs for preservation will be increased. It should also be remembered that immediate conservation is less costly than delayed conservation, since most deterioration usually worsens with the passage of time.

2.7   External Involvement

The Library staff, especially the conservator, will need to keep abreast of development in the conservation field and should participate in common conservation endeavors. It is important, for example, for the Library to become active in such organizations as the Air Pollution Control Association and to make certain that local and state public officials are aware of the effects of air pollution on library materials.

To be effective, too, librarians will need to be better organized than they are at present. The Association of Research Libraries Committee on the Preservation of Library Materials is one professional group in the library field which has been seriously interested in this problem. An ad hoc committee on preservation, of the Resources and Technical Services Section, New York Library Association, was established last year. This committee has been actively surveying preservation programs and needs in New York State and is planning cooperative workshops and conferences.

At a time when restructuring is the order of the day, it may not be inappropriate to suggest that the American Library Association and other library organizations take greater official cognizance of conservation. It is in the best interests of The New York Public Library to assist in the formation of committees and organizations for conservation purposes and to participate in them actively.

The conservator and his staff will need to participate in professional organizations such as the International Institute for the Conservation of Historic and Artistic Works, IIC American Group, and the International Centre for the Study of the Preservation and Restoration of Cultural Property. While the conservation of library materials remains in its infancy, it will be important for the conservation staff to help these and similar organizations arrange for the exchange of information and ideas through meetings and publications, and to encourage and fund research.

3. ORGANIZATION OF THE CONSERVATION PROGRAM

In the history of the conservation of library materials, this is not the first time that the need for an overall conservation program within the library has been pointed out nor is it the first time that it has been argued that conservation should be given its proper place in the library's scheme of organization. Nevertheless, the number of times this concept has been promulgated is few. In 1946, Pelham Barr, then executive director of the Library Binding Institute, spoke of the need "for reorienting administrative thought on the whole subject of book conservation and binding" [42, p. 218]. Pointing out that binding is only one part of conservation, he said:

> *Some strange phenomena in the evolution of library*
> *administration have resulted from this neglect of*
> *conservation. It became harder and harder to de-*
> *velop a program and procedures for book conservation,*
> *and therefore, it was more and more neglected. As*
> *it withered away, it left binding supervision with-*
> *out any fundamental place in some library organi-*
> *zations.... Some administrators have tried to*
> *dispose of the annoying department by attaching it*
> *to all kinds of other functions, which are fre-*
> *quently not closely related. But few have realized*
> *that it could "logically" be attached to so many*
> *other library functions for the very reason that*
> *it is essentially a conservation function and*
> *therefore fundamental in all library administration.*
> [42, p. 219].

Barr called for recognition of an "overall program of book conservation" [42, p. 215] and the need to "plan and provide for a truly broad program" [42, p. 219]. "Where are the administrators" he asked, "who can become library custodians in the true and effective sense of the title, when the function has for so many years atrophied?" [42, p. 219]. In this same article Barr outlined the scope of a conservation program as follows:

> *(1) selecting material before purchase with respect*
> *to usability and useful life; (2) examining condition*
> *and probable future condition of all material received...*
> *and prescribing conservation treatment, if necessary,*
> *before use; (3) providing proper housing of all material,*
> *in accordance with its conservation needs as well as its*
> *accessibility; (4) assuming responsibility for its con-*
> *dition at all times; (5) assuring its proper handling*
> *by staff and patrons; (6) organizing systematic in-*
> *spection so that need for conservation attention is*
> *promptly recognized; (7) deciding on the proper treat-*
> *ment of all material needing attention; (8) supervising*
> *the treatment; and (9) deciding on storing or discarding.*
> [42, p. 215].

One could not draw up a better outline of conservation procedures today.

Maurice F. Tauber and his associates devoted three chapters of Technical Services in Libraries, first published in 1954, to various aspects of conservation and mentioned the necessity "to emphasize the essentials of an over-all program" [43, p. 313].

Library Trends chose "Conservation of Library Materials" as the subject of its January 1956 issue, and the introductory article, written by Tauber, was entitled "Conservation Comes of Age." Here Tauber pointed to the "many areas ... still in need of basic investigation" and said that librarians were "compelled to pay heed to the future disposition of their collections" [44, p. 221]. In this same issue of Library Trends, Edward Connery Lathem, dealing with the subject of binding and conservation personnel, wrote: "It is not enough that everyone should constantly and vigilantly direct attention to the condition and care of all library materials; there must be, as well, someone specifically responsible for the binding and conservation program as a whole. And this responsibility, moreover, must be backed by a degree of authority adequate to assure the program's proper functioning and success" [45, p. 321]. Although the articles in this conservation issue of Library Trends were concerned largely with binding, most of the ingredients of a total conservation program were, in fact, discussed. In addition to binding, the contributors wrote about the applications and potential uses of microreproductions and other photographic media, restorative practices, the treatment of special and non-book materials, discarding, storage conditions and practices, personnel, and the possibility of cooperative projects.

In spite of almost a quarter-century in which the need for administrative attention to conservation has been recognized, few libraries in the nation today have anything resembling a total conservation program or a conservation unit of significance. What emerges clearly is the need for librarians to recognize now that conservation is as important to preparation for service as acquisition and cataloging and that the conservation unit should take its place as one of the library's principal technical services. We believe that it is within this part of the library's structure that conservation will have its best chance to become a matter of continuing professional attention and concern. Librarians who do not see the urgency of facing up to such an organizational requirement at this time will be well advised to begin to lay the groundwork for a conservation program. Those who are about to consider establishing a conservation unit may wish to use the Preservation Office of the Library of Congress as a model. There the conservation function has been placed in the Administrative Department, with the principal preservation officer an assistant director of that department. The office has responsibility for five activities, each of which is represented by a subunit: binding, restoration, preservation microfilming, collections maintenance (by which is meant physical care,

including cleaning of books and stacks, monitoring environmental conditions in stack areas, and the like), and preservation research [46].
All but the last of these are appropriate activities for the conservation
unit of any research library. (Because of its cost and also because of
the shortage of research personnel in the field, book conservation research should probably be concentrated in only a relatively few centers.)
The conservation unit will almost certainly become responsible also for
other activities such as lending to reprint and microform publishers,
since their publications may result in the replacement of deteriorating
materials in the library's collections.

In The Research Libraries of The New York Public Library, the
following scheme of organization is tentatively recommended:

A Conservation Division would be established in the Preparation
Services along with the Acquisition Division and Processing Division.

As head of this Division, there should be a Chief Conservator
who would be responsible for (1) coordinating the various conservation
activities within The Research Libraries, (2) general administration of
the Division, (3) development of conservation policies and procedures,
and (4) liaison with reprinting and micropublishing projects and review
of their performance, especially as it relates to meeting bibliographical
and technical standards.

The Division would consist of three sections, as follows:

(1) A Screening and Control Section. To test incoming
     materials and materials already in the collections
     and decide on the type of conservation treatment to
     be used (e.g., microfilming restoration); to prepare
     and route all material to be conserved, regardless
     of type of treatment. This section would consist
     of four subunits: (a) a screening unit; (b) a unit
     to handle loans to reprinters and micropublishers;
     (c) a unit to handle materials sent to outside
     binderies and to the Treatment Section; and (d) a
     unit to handle materials being sent to the Library's
     own Photographic Service for preservation microforming.

(2) A Treatment Section. To provide conservation binding
     techniques and to restore the paper in books and other
     forms of material. Ultimately this section would be
     responsible also for the restoration of other types
     of material, such as photographs, etc.

(3) A Collections Maintenance Section. To have responsibility
     for the physical care of the collections, environmental
     monitoring, cleaning schedules, on-spot treatment, etc.

4.   RECOMMENDATIONS

4.1   Selection; acquisition

4.1.1   Materials selected for addition to the collections should, whenever possible, be made of permanent/ durable materials.

4.1.2   Publishers should be encouraged to utilize permanent/ durable materials in the manufacture of books and other publications.

4.2   Screening

4.2.1   Materials added to the collections should be tested for ground wood content and when the test is positive, materials should be treated or copied before being added.

4.2.2   Materials added to the Special Collections should be examined by the curator concerned and a member of the conservation staff to decide on appropriate methods of treatment, storage, etc.

4.3   Treatment

4.3.1   The Research Libraries should establish a restoration workshop using the funds available under Conservation Program No. 3 (see Appendix 5.3).   Initially, the workshop would treat the materials selected under that Program as well as materials selected from the Special Collections.

4.3.2   Detailed specifications for various aspects of the conservation program should be adopted covering materials, methods, and procedures.   These specifications should include binding, restoration of paper and books, making of cases, portfolios, boxes, mats, microrecording, and reprinting.

4.3.3   The binding together of pamphlets printed on paper of varying quality should be discontinued.

4.3.4   Flexible, non-destructive binding should be utilized to the fullest extent possible, and efforts should be made to persuade the commercial library binding industry to introduce flexible, non-destructive binding techniques.

4.3.5   The Research Libraries should accelerate their own preservation microforming activities (see Appendix 5.1:   Conservation Program No. 1).

4.3   Treatment   *(Continued)*

    4.3.6   A special fund is needed to permit the microforming of materials which do not fit into the system of microforming priorities (see Appendix 5.1: Conservation Program No. 1).

    4.3.7   The system of creating master negative microforms should be continued. Positive copies should be made of negatives for public use and the negatives themselves should be added to the master negative collection.

    4.3.8   The Research Libraries should continue to cooperate to the fullest extent possible in both cooperative and commercial reprinting and micropublication ventures since such activities help to preserve the intellectual content of the collections and are an aid in the national preservation effort (see Appendix 5.2: Conservation Program No. 2).

4.4   Collections Maintenance

    4.4.1   The "Air Conditioning Feasibility and Environmental Study" should be amended to include conservation specifications with respect to temperature, relative humidity, and filtration systems.

    4.4.2   Fluorescent lights should be equipped with filters in order to prevent degradation caused by ultraviolet radiation, and all areas in which research collections are housed should be sealed from sunlight and particulate matter and pollutants in the atmosphere. Where exposure to sunlight is necessary because of building design, filtered glass or plastic should be used.

    4.4.3   Flat storage space should be made available for oversize volumes.

    4.4.4   End supports should be provided for all shelves.

    4.4.5   Overpacking of shelves should not be permitted.

    4.4.6   A systematic and regular cleaning program should be instituted, particularly after air conditioning has been installed.

    4.4.7   There should be systematic inspection of stacks to see that maintenance standards are being observed.

4.4   <u>Collections Maintenance</u> *(Continued)*

4.4.8   A furbishing program for books should be initiated which would include proper treatment of leather volumes.

4.4.9   Instructions on proper handling and use of Library materials should be prepared for the guidance of all members of the staff. Special attention should be given to copying procedures.

4.4.10   For practical purposes, rather than burden divisional preservation representatives with the task of making decisions with respect to photocopying materials in their divisions, it would be advisable to have a specially-trained representative of the conservation staff assigned to The Photographic Service to make such determinations.

4.4.11   Copying machine manufacturers should be persuaded to develop a non-destructive face-up copying machine for library purposes.

4.4.12   Exhibition cases should be designed and built incorporating conservation principles. Exhibitions should be reviewed by conservation staff. Because of the damaging conditions in the present exhibition cases, the display of vellum materials and materials with fugitive images should be discontinued.

4.4.13   Loans of materials for exhibition purposes should be reviewed by conservation staff for recommendations with respect to condition of materials.

4.4.14   Packing of materials and artifacts and their transportation should be carried out according to conservation specifications.

4.4.15   A procedure for comparing duplicates with copies on the shelf before discarding should be instituted to make certain that the better copy is retained.

4.5   <u>Personnel</u>

4.5.1   A specialist in restoration of materials should be employed to head the conservation laboratory. The head of the laboratory should train conservation technicians and conduct familiarization programs for the Library staff.

4.6   <u>Costs</u>

4.6.1   A long-range cost analysis program should be initiated for the purpose of determining the financial requirements for an adequate conservation program.

4.7   <u>External Involvement</u>

4.7.1   The conservation staff should be alert to all external developments which will bring improvement to the conservation program.

4.8   <u>Organization</u>

4.8.1   A Conservation Division should be established; the Division should be headed by a Chief Conservator.

4.8.2   The Conservation Division should consist of three sections:

(1) Screening and Control Section
(2) Treatment Section
(3) Collections Maintenance Section

5.   APPENDICES

Appendix 5.1:   Conservation Program No. 1:   Preservation Microrecording

     The New York Public Library Research Libraries were among the pioneers in the use of microfilm for library purposes. Since 1934 approximately 40,000 reels of microfilm have been made (the equivalent of 200,000 volumes). Originally microfilm was used primarily for the preservation of newspaper files, but as time went by other types of serial files and monographs were also microfilmed. In the past few years, microfiche has been preferred to microfilm for short runs of serials and for monographs.

     As the amount of material in The Research Libraries in need of preservation microrecording has increased, it has been necessary to establish a priority system. The priorities are to some extent artificial, that is, they do not result from a systematic examination of the collections nor do they represent categories of materials most in need of preservation.

     At present, the following priorities are being observed:

Priority A --   Public Orders (a negative microfilm is normally retained by The Research Libraries).

Priority B --   NYSILL (this priority results from the need to supply a microform in lieu of an original in answer to an interlibrary loan request).

Priority C --   Special Fund Material (microrecording projects for which special funds have been established, e.g., Margaret Brown Fund for Microcopying of Early American Historical Material; New York State Council on the Arts grant for microcopying of John Quinn Collection; Billy Rose Foundation grant for preservation filming of Billy Rose material).

Priority D --   Preservation Microrecording under Preservation Funds. These funds derive from the sale of microforms (Revolving Fund) or the preservation appropriation in the general funds budget. Categories of material included in Priority D are:

        Microfilm
         1. Continuation periodicals; gazettes
         2. Continuation serials
         3. Cellar material

Appendix 5.1 . . . *(Continued)*

Priority D -- . . .

Microfiche
1. Monographs cataloged old-style
2. Current periodicals and continuations
3. Monographs for prospective catalog

Since The Photographic Service finds it difficult to accommodate categories of material other than those listed above, there is no place in the system of priorities for emergency filming of deteriorating materials. A substantial amount of money is needed to establish a Special Fund for this purpose so that emergency items could be handled under Priority C.

Appendix 5.2:   Conservation Program No. 2:   Replacement Copies; Reprints;
Microcopies

The Research Libraries have for a long time attempted to replace deteriorated materials with fresh copies, when they are available, either by purchasing them or, to a very limited extent, by comparing gift copies with copies already in the collections.

It has been possible also to replace some deteriorating materials with commercially available reprints or microeditions.

Since the mushrooming of the reprint and micropublishing industries in the 1950's, The Research Libraries have lent materials from the collections to reprint publishers and micropublishers with the preservation of the collections in mind.   The policy and procedures for granting access to the collections for these purposes are stated in Research Libraries Technical Memorandum No. 23.   In return for cooperating with reprint publishers and micropublishers, The Research Libraries have normally required publishers to deposit copies of reprints or in the case of microforms, microform negatives and positives, as replacements for the originals.   In addition, handling fees have been charged and, in cases where the Library has rights of one kind or another, royalty payments have been negotiated.   These fees and royalties are deposited in a fund earmarked for book replacement.

Appendix 5.3:   Conservation Program No. 3:   Book Restoration

        Conservation Program No. 3 is an effort to conserve books in the collections published before 1850 not now located in one of the Special Collections.* Although Conservation Program No. 3 will be concerned primarily with books printed before 1850, other materials suitable for restoration will not be excluded if they qualify for inclusion in the program on some well-justified basis.

        An explanation should be given of the significance of the date 1850 and the decision to concentrate on books published before rather than after that date.

        By 1798 a paper-making machine had been patented in France and by the middle 1800's the use of such machines was not uncommon in England, Germany, France, Italy, India, and the United States. The invention of papermaking machines and their improvement during this period led to a new problem, however--a shortage of raw materials for the manufacture of paper, particularly cotton and linen rags. As late as 1854, at least ninety per cent of the fiber used in making paper was still rag. In that year a United States patent was granted for making wood pulp by a chemical process, the soda process. This process produced a soft, short-fibered, relatively weak pulp that could be made into a good paper for printing. By 1866 the soda process had come into general use.

---

*Selection criteria for the individual special collections vary considerably and there are, wisely, exceptions to the general rules. The Rare Book Division, for example, includes books published on the continent before 1600, in the British Isles before 1640, and in the United States before 1800, but it also includes Western Americana published after 1800 and modern-day special press books. The Spencer Collection includes finely illustrated or finely bound contemporary publications, and both the Manuscript Division and the Berg Collection contain manuscripts of living authors.

Appendix 5.3 . . . *(Continued)*

As long as paper was made almost entirely from new linen or
cotton fibers, it was likely to be basically strong because of the long
fibers. Also, for a long time, little or no acid was used in the paper
manufacturing process. About 1850, however, rosin was introduced into
papermaking as a size (the material which gives paper a surface that
will accept ink). Before that time gelatin or animal sizes had been
used, and for over two hundred years papermakers had used alum to set
the size. The new combination of alum and rosin created, as a side-
product, free sulfuric acid which resulted in papers that were destined
to deteriorate rapidly even if made with rag fibers. Books published
after 1850, therefore, are very likely to be in worse condition than
books published before that date. This has been borne out by the studies
of W. J. Barrow.

The Astor Library, one of The Research Libraries' two predecessor institutions, opened in January, 1854 with a collection of some
90,000 volumes. The books in the collection were for the most part
retrospective, having been collected during the lifetime of Mr. Astor
and by Dr. Cogswell on his trip to Europe after Mr. Astor's death in 1848.
The Astor Library continued to fill in the lacunae in its collection,
and the Lenox Library (founded in 1870 and The Research Libraries'
other predecessor) also placed primary emphasis on retrospective materials.
It is probably not an overstatement to say that in the lifetime of the
Astor Library and Lenox Library, (1848-1895) and (1870-1895) respectively,
there were no other libraries in the country collecting retrospective
materials more comprehensively than those two institutions, with the
possible exception of the library of Harvard College. This point takes
on added significance when it is realized that editions of books tended
to be smaller during the period before the age of inexpensive paper.
Thus The Research Libraries' collection of publications before 1850 is a
particularly valuable segment of American library resources. Many of these
books are now housed in the Special Collections, but the general collections
still contain books published on the continent of Europe from 1600-1850,
books published in Great Britain from 1640-1850, and many books printed
in America between 1800 and 1850. It is these books that will be included
in Conservation Program No. 3.

Books published after 1850--especially those printed in the
United States--are likely to be more commonly found in other libraries,
and since most of them were printed on paper of poor quality and there
is evidence to show that books fare better in other parts of the country
than in New York City, presumably the copies to be found in other libraries
are superior to the copies held by The Research Libraries. As part of a
national preservation program, therefore, books published in the United
States after 1850 might be better preserved by some other institution.
It is believed that The New York Public Library Research Libraries'
holdings of foreign materials during the whole of this period are con-

Appendix 5.3 . . . *(Continued)*

siderably stronger than those of most other libraries in the United States;
however, most of the books published during the latter part of the 19th
century and during the 20th century up to now are in much poorer condition
than those published before 1850. Why not, concentrate, then, on restoring
books of this later period? The answer is that many of them, printed on
poor paper to begin with and, having absorbed additional acid from the
atmosphere over the years, are often beyond the point of physical salvage.
If they are no longer intact, the paper will not stand up to rebinding, and
from the point of view of saving the intellectual content of the work, they
would probably be better candidates for reprinting or microforming than for
physical restoration. Furthermore, representing as they do the publishing
output of over 100 years during a period when book production was at its
highest level in terms of quantity, they constitute the largest segment of
books in the collection. If they are to be saved as physical objects (as
opposed to reprinting or microforming them), an economical method of treating
them en masse must be utilized (see Appendix 5.4: Conservation Program. No. 4).

Appendix 5.4: Conservation Program No. 4: Mass Treatment of Materials

   Conservation Program No. 4 is not in operation because the techniques for mass conservation treatment are not yet available for practical application. The method consists essentially of placing large quantities of material into a chamber and driving a solvent containing an alkaline substance and a strengthening agent into papers and bindings under great pressure. The method would be particularly applicable to materials published since 1850 and still intact.

REFERENCES

42. Barr, Pelham. 1946. Book Conservation and University Library Administration. *Coll. Res. Libr.* 7:214–219 (July).
43. Tauber, Maurice F., et al. 1954. *Technical Services in Libraries: Acquisitions, Cataloging, Classification, Binding, Photographic Reproduction, and Circulation Operations.* New York: Columbia University Press.
44. Tauber, Maurice F. 1956. Conservation Comes of Age. *Libr. Trends* 4:215–221 (Jan.)
45. Lathem, Edward Connery. 1956. Some Personnel Considerations for Binding and Conservation Services. *Libr. Trends* 4:321–334 (Jan.)
46. U.S. Library of Congress. 1967. *Library of Congress Regulations,* nos. 212–214 (Oct. 23, 1967).

V: THE ROLES OF
THE CONSERVATOR
AND THE SCIENTIST

Papers 13 Through 17: Commentary

The American Group of the International Institute for the Conservation of Historic and Artistic Works (IIC-AG) was established in 1960 and continued until 1972 when it became an independent corporate entity, The American Institute for Conservation of Historic and Artistic Works (AIC). By December 1976, the rapidly growing organization numbered 761 Associates and Fellows and 63 institutional members. The association publishes a biennial journal, a quarterly newsletter, and an annual membership directory. Conferences are held annually at sites throughout North America.

The first two selections in this section are official publications of the AIC. Practicing conservators seeking membership in the organization are required to sign a pledge to abide by and uphold the *Standards of Practice* and the *Code of Ethics*. As statements of the basic tenets that guide the professional conservators in relation to their work, their profession, and their clients, the principles set forth in these documents should be familiar to librarians working in the conservation field, particularly those who are entrusted with overseeing the repair and restoration of rarities and artifacts.

The article by Paul N. Banks, Conservator at the Newberry Library, Chicago, is one of the few published case studies detailing restoration of rare books. In it can be seen the practical application of some of the principles enumerated in the AIC's *Code of Ethics*. An important point in Bank's article is that books must be considered in "dynamic rather than static terms" when being restored. This aspect, more than any other, distinguishes book restoration from other areas of specialization within the field.

If the development of permanent/durable paper had been William J. Barrow's only accomplishment, it would be sufficient grounds for supposing that his name will be perpetuated. The full range of Barrow's work is summarized in Frazer Poole's memoir. Closely associated with a number of Barrow's investigations, Poole enumerates the scientist's many contributions to our knowledge of the components of books and documents and the causes of their deterioration. When to the numerous subjects Barrow investigated is added the extensive list of reports and articles he published, thereby making his findings accessible to later investigators, his achievements seem monumental indeed.

Basing their work in part, at least, on Barrow's findings, John Williams and George Kelly, joint authors of the last paper in this section, describe their research on mass treatments in the conservation of books. The diethyl zinc vapor-phase process of deacidification developed by them at the Preservation Research and Testing Office of the Library of Congress was granted a patent in July 1976 (U.S. Patent No. 3,969,549). At the time of writing, the process was undergoing further testing and refinement. A simple and safe method for low-cost deacidification of books *en masse* is a high priority in the preservation of library materials. It remains to be seen whether methods now in various stages of development will provide the solution so earnestly sought.[1]

From the selections in this and the preceding section, one point should emerge clearly: Cooperation and frequent communication between librarians, conservators, and scientists is the *sine qua non* in working toward practical solutions to the monumental problems facing libraries today. Those whose professional interest or responsibility lies in the conservation of library materials should have a clear understanding of the role of each of the three major professional groups who contribute to progress in the field.

NOTE

1. For a summary of current research and development in mass deacidification and paper strengthening techniques, see Cunha, George M., "Preservation of Library Materials," *The ALA Yearbook: A Comprehensive Report . . . of Library Year 1976* (Chicago: American Library Association, 1977), pp. 245–48.

ADDITIONAL READINGS

Flieder, Francoise, *La Conservation des Documents Graphiques; Recherches Experimentales* (Paris: Editions Eyrolles, 1969), 288 pp. Centre Internationale d'Etudes pour la Conservation des Biens Culturels et Comité de l'ICOM pour les Laboratoires de Musees, *Travaux et Publications* IX.

Permanence/Durability of the Book, Parts I-VII (Richmond, Va.: W. J. Barrow Laboratory, 1963-74),

Restaurator: International Journal for the Preservation of Library and Archival Material (Copenhagen), vols. 1- (1969-).

Istituto di Patologia del Libro, *Bolletino* (Rome), vols. 1-31 (1939-72).

Guild of Bookworkers, *Journal* (New York), vols. 1- (1962-).

Kathpalia, Yash Pal, *Conservation and Restoration of Archive Materials* (Paris: United Nations Educational, Scientific, and Cultural Organization, 1973), 231 pp.

Plenderleith, J. J., and Werner, A. E., *The Conservation of Antiquities and Works of Art,* 2nd ed. (London: Oxford University Press, 1971), 394 pp.

13: THE MURRAY PEASE REPORT

Murray Pease Committee

STANDARDS OF PRACTICE AND PROFESSIONAL
RELATIONSHIPS FOR CONSERVATORS
ADOPTED BY IIC-AG JUNE 8, 1963;
APPROVED FOR LEGAL SUFFICIENCY AUGUST 7, 1963

I. PREAMBLE

The following standards and procedures are approved by IIC-AG as applying to professional practice by conservators, as defined in the Articles of Association of IIC, in the examination and treatment of works of art. Such practice is considered to comprise three categories.

A. Scientific analytical study of art objects, for such purposes as identifying materials, method of construction, modifications by age or other agencies, and comparison with comparable material, but not as a preliminary to treatment.

B. Examination and treatment of works of art, whether by private or institutional operators.

C. Supplying previously developed reference data which may bear on condition, authenticity, authorship or age of specific objects. This can be either by formal publication or private communication.

II. GENERAL CONSIDERATIONS OF POLICY

These are broadly applicable to all categories.

A. *Professional attitude.* It must be axiomatic that all professional actions of a conservator be governed by unswerving respect for the integrity of works of art. Such respect is manifest not only in policies of restoration, but in selection of courses of treatment, in safeguarding against accident, protection against loss, and strict avoidance of misinterpreting technical evidence.

B. *Contractual relationships.* A sound contractual relationship includes the need for clear understanding, written in cases of private contracts, of the exact work to be done, the basis for charges if any, the extent and substance of reports, including photographs as appropriate, responsibility for insurance coverage deemed adequate for operator, owner and object, provisions for safeguarding objects, method of delivery, and any sub-contracting or re-assignment of work. It is recommended that a lawyer be consulted.

C. *Assumption of responsibility.* It should be a conservator's responsibility to contract for investigation or treatment only to
the limits of his professional competence and facilities.
Should he not be trained or equipped for a full scientific
study by generally accepted current technical means, any specific limitations must be stated and accepted by both parties
from the beginning. Wherever further opinions seem to be required such further opinion or opinions are a necessary part
of a comprehensive report. In the same manner a conservator
should be held irresponsible if he undertakes to carry out a
course of treatment for which he is inadequately trained or
equipped.

D. *Interpretation of evidence.* It is obvious that a scientific investigator has the obligation to present *all* the evidence he
has developed about an object commissioned to him for
study, favorable or otherwise, and also to supply from his
professional knowledge a clear exposition of the significance
of each part of the evidence. It will be held improper for
him to make outright formal declarations as to age, authenticity and the like (which subsequently might form the basis
of a claim or legal action) when each declaration exceeds the
logical development of the specific evidence.

E. *Limitation of reconstruction.* In replacing losses or damage, a
conservator can be expected to accord little or much restoration according to a firm previous understanding with the
owner or custodian. It is equally clear that he cannot ethically
carry this to a point of modifying the known character of the
original, whatever the motives for so doing might be.

F. It shall be considered inconsistent with the professional integrity of conservators in any of the three categories of procedure to engage in the following outside activities:
1. Issuing paid "expertises" or authentications.
2. Acting as paid or commissioned agent in the selling or
purchasing of works of art.
3. Engaging in such selling or purchasing for personal profit.
4. Making monetary appraisals of works of art.

III. PROCEDURE FOR INITIATING, CONDUCTING, AND
REPORTING IN SCIENTIFIC ANALYTICAL STUDIES
OF WORKS OF ART

Whenever it becomes necessary for owners of works of art to
request museum or commercial analytical laboratories or private
consultants to engage in scientific study of art objects for the
purpose of developing data which may bear on condition, au-

thenticity, authorship, or age of a specific object, the following procedure shall be followed by all parties concerned.

A. *Initiating the study.* The owner of the work of art, or his qualified agent, or a qualified officer of an institution shall send to the examining agency a written request with statements covering the following points as required:

1. The purpose of the study listing any specific questions which, if possible, are in need of answer.

2. Whether (a) the whole object, or (b) samples from the object are to be made available for study. If samples only are to be sent to the laboratory, the exact location of the samples on the object and the name of the person who took the samples are to be given.

3. If the whole object is to be sent to the analyst, (a) the legal owner, (b) its value, (c) to what extent it is covered by insurance, (d) by what carrier it is to be sent to the laboratory and returned to the owner, and (e) that the object is to be sent to the investigating laboratory at the owner's risk and expense.

4. Explicit permission to take samples from the object during examination.

5. Whether the investigator (a) is merely to report facts and observations, or (b) if the investigator is expected to draw conclusion from the facts.

6. Whether the laboratory findings are (a) to be kept in strict confidence, or (b) whether the findings, regardless of their nature, can be used by the investigator in formal publications and in oral declarations.

7. Whether any of the evidence produced is intended for use in legal proceedings.

B. *Conducting the study.* The analyst or laboratory official on receiving the object shall:

1. Supply a written receipt to the owner verifying its condition and inform the owner how the object will be stored and guarded.

2. Inform the owner what fees, if any, are to be charged for the analytical services. If there is to be no charge, state that fact explicitly. State also what other charges may be made for photographs, x-rays, spectrograms, and for outside analytical services, and other.

3. Make a photographic record of the condition of the object.

4. Keep a careful and detailed written record of all observations and findings, giving dates.

C. *Preparing and submitting the report.* On completion of the investigation the investigator shall:
   1. Render to the owner a typewritten report of his findings with conclusion, if conclusions have been requested. The report shall cover methods of test, kind and type of instruments and equipment used, and analytical procedures employed in sufficient detail so that, if the owner wishes, the tests can be repeated and checked on the same object by an independent investigator in another laboratory. If it has been necessary, with the owner's permission, to take samples from the object, give location and amount of each sample.
   2. List all other persons who assisted or cooperated in the scientific investigation.
   3. List what published works or authorities he has consulted in the course of the study.
   4. State what limitations, if any, he may wish to place on the use of the findings. That is, whether or not the findings may be used voluntarily in legal proceedings; whether or not they may be quoted in formal publications or in oral declarations.

IV. PROCEDURE FOR ENGAGING IN AND REPORTING OF EXAMINATION AND TREATMENT OF WORKS OF ART BY PROFESSIONAL EMPLOYEES OF INSTITUTIONS

A. *Report of examination.* Such reports shall include, in writing the following information.
   1. Date of examination and name of examiner.
   2. Identification of object with that in report. This may be done by photographs, word descriptions, measurements, and accession numbers.
   3. Descriptions of materials, structure and method of fabrication. Physical, chemical and biological identification of materials composing the object. Statement of method of determination employed or reference to published standard method.
   4. Record of alteration and deterioration. Locations and extent of physical defects, chemical alteration and its products, previous repairs and compensation. Statement of method of determination sufficiently detailed to permit duplication by another examiner.
   5. Deductions or interpretations of observations and analyses. Comments relative to the degree of alteration.

6. Where evidence indicates forgery, every available test which can supply information on materials and structure shall be employed. After thoroughly checking his results the examiner shall recommend consultation with one or two disinterested individuals qualified by scientific or art historical training to review the evidence.

B. *Proposal for treatment.* Before any treatment is undertaken a summary or copy of the examination record shall be supplied to the responsible custodian of the object. This shall be accompanied by:

1. An outline of the proposed treatment.
2. A statement of the results to be expected.
3. An estimate of the probable time required for the treatment.

The official custodian's written approval shall be secured before treatment is begun.

C. *Report of treatment.* Such report shall include:

1. A statement of the procedures followed in the current treatment with exact descriptions of materials and methods, including:
   (a) The method by which accretion or deterioration products were removed.
   (b) Method and materials used in correcting distortion in form and shape and in reinforcing, consolidating, stabilizing and protecting structure and surface.
   (c) Kind, extent and location of compensation employed.
2. Photographs as follows:
   (a) Condition before treatment with date.
   (b) Photograph in "actual state" without compensation.
   (c) Photograph after treatment with date.
   (d) Photographs as required to supply data about structure, method of fabrication and state of object as revealed during process of treatment. Photographs or diagrams which clarify method of reconstruction or compensation.

V. PROCEDURES SPECIFICALLY APPLYING TO EXAMINATION AND TREATMENT OF WORKS OF ART BY SELF-EMPLOYED PROFESSIONAL CONSERVATORS

These do not differ from those applying to institutional employees except in the fields of contractual relations and assumption of responsibility. Procedures in these fields shall include:

A. Written proposals stating:

1. Work to be done, estimated charges, and estimated date of completion.

2. Arrangements for insurance and its specific coverage, method of delivery, and provisions for safeguarding objects.
3. Any sub-contract or re-assignment of work proposed.
B. A signed contract by the owner or his authorized agent, which may be a signed copy of the letter of proposal.
C. It is recommended that a lawyer be consulted as to the adequacy of the contract until such time as a standard form be adopted.

VI. OPERATING SAFETY PROCEDURES FOR CONSERVATORS

A. *Safety of personnel.*
  1. *Radiation.* X-ray installation and operation procedures should conform to approved specifications as described in Eastman Kodak's book, *Radiography in Industry.* Most state labor departments will supply an inspection service to determine the operating safety of radiographic installations.
  2. *Toxic vapors.* Adequate exhaust and ventilation should be a part of all laboratory installations where volatile solvents are habitually used. The National Association of Mutual Casualty Companies' *Handbook of Organic Industrial Solvents* covers these requirements in detail. Suitable respirators should be available for special requirements.
  3. *Mechanical equipment.* Power tools of all kinds should be provided with adequate light, operating space, and safety guards. Their use should be restricted to properly qualified and authorized persons. Cleanliness should be rigidly enforced. Instruments producing dust, abrasive powders and the like should be equipped with positive exhaust systems, and provided with appropriate respirators for operators.
  4. *Corrosive liquids.* Standard laboratory requirements for quantity storage and operating containers of acids, alkalis, and other reagents should be rigidly followed. Only authorized personnel should have access to them.
  5. *Fire Hazards.* The building housing the studio or laboratory should conform to Underwriters' requirements in construction. Uses to which other parts of the building may be put should not be of a hazardous nature. Working and storage areas should be of fireproof construction, and equipped with adequate extinguishing apparatus.

B. *Safety of art objects.*

1. *Vapors.* The same requirements that apply to personnel should be observed.

2. *Protection against theft.* Working and storage areas should be of adequate construction, and capable of systematic locking routine. Only authorized personnel should have access.

3. *Protection against accidental damage.* Working and storage areas should be adequate for safe handling and storage of objects. Individual storage racks for paintings and shelves for three-dimensional objects should be available. Working equipment should include sturdy, well-designed furniture such as tables, easels, horses. Objects should be moved or handled only by experienced persons.

   Scondary personnel should be of responsible character and adequate training in the handling of works of art. They should not engage in activities for which they have inadequate professional training.

   Objects should not be removed from the operating or storage building except on due notice and authorization by the owner or custodial institution.

   Transportation and packing of objects should be by approved agencies and according to established methods.

14: CODE OF ETHICS FOR ART CONSERVATORS

I. PREAMBLE

Art conservation is a pursuit requiring extensive training and special aptitudes. It places in the hands of the conservator cultural holdings which are of great value and historical significance. To be worthy of this special trust requires a high sense of moral responsibility. The conservator has obligations not only to the work of art, but to its owner or custodian, to his colleagues and his profession and to the public as a whole. The following Code seeks to express principles and practices which will guide the art conservator in the ethical practice of his profession.

II. OBLIGATIONS TO THE WORK OF ART

1. *Respect for Integrity of Object*
All professional actions of a conservator are governed by unswerving respect for the aesthetic, historical and physical integrity of works of art.

2. *Competence and Facilities*
It is a conservator's responsibility to undertake the investigation or treatment of a work of art only within the limits of his professional competence and facilities.

3. *Single Standard*
With every work of art he undertakes to conserve, regardless of his opinion of its value or quality, the conservator should adhere to the highest and most exacting standard of treatment. Although circumstances may limit the extent of treatment, the quality of the treatment is never governed by the quality or value of the object.

4. *Suitability of Treatment*
A conservator does not perform or recommend any treatment which is not appropriate to the preservation or best interests of the work of art. The necessity and quality of the treatment are more important to the professional than his remuneration.

5. *Principle of Reversibility*
The conservator is guided by and endeavors to apply the "principle of reversibility" in his treatments. He avoids the use of materials which may become so intractable that their future removal could endanger the physical safety of the object.

This material was originally published by the IIC-American Group (IIC-AG) in 1968. The IIC-AG is now the American Instutite for Conservation (AIC).

6. *Limitations on Aesthetic Reintegration*

In compensating for damage or loss in a work of art, a conservator can be expected to supply little or much restoration, according to a firm previous understanding with the owner or custodian. It is equally clear that he cannot ethically carry this to a point of deceptively covering or modifying the original—whatever the motives for so doing might be.

7. *Continued Self Education*

It is the duty of every conservator to continue to refresh and enlarge the knowledge and skill of his science and art so that he may be ever ready to give the best treatment circumstances permit.

8. *Auxiliary Personnel*

The conservator has an obligation to protect and preserve the art under his care at all times by supervising and regulating the work of all auxiliary personnel under his professional direction.

III. RESPONSIBILITIES TO THE OWNER OR CUSTODIAN

9. *Contracts*

Contract practice may permit a conservator to enter into an ·agreement with individuals, institutions, corporations, city, municipal, state and federal governments to provide conservation services, provided that the contract or agreement does not contravene the principles of ethics as laid down or implied in this code.

10. *Changes in Treatment or Fee*

Any changes on the part of the conservator in the contracted planned procedure in treating a work of art, or changes in the fee which has previously been estimated should, unless circumstances intervene, be made known to the owner or custodian and approved before the changes are effected.

11. *Abrogation of Contract*

The conservator should understand that an owner or custodian is free to select, without persuasion or admonition, the services of any conservator of his choice or of more than one conservator simultaneously, and is also at liberty to change from one conservator to another at his own discretion. However after a contract, oral or written, has been made for the treatment of a specific work of art neither the conservator nor the owner may morally withdraw from it except by mutual agreement.

12. *Proper Course of Treatment*

Inasmuch as an owner is rarely competent to judge the conservation requirements of his work of art, the conservator should honestly and sincerely advise what he considers the proper course of treatment.

13. *Report of Examination*

Before performing any treatment on a work of art, the conservator should first make an adequate examination and record of condition.° The conservator is obliged to report his findings and recommendations to the owner or custodian and await instructions from him before proceeding.

14. *Record of Treatment*

A record of treatment° must also be made by the conservator. He has the obligation to record and reveal in detail to the owner or custodian the materials and methods of procedure employed in treating the work of art.

15. *Punctuality and Expedition*

It is the obligation of the conservator to estimate the length of time it will take to complete a treatment and to abide by his contract with reasonable punctuality.

16. *Fees*

Fees for conservation service should be commensurate with the service rendered, having due regard to insure justice to the owner or custodian and to the conservator and respect for the profession.

In determining the amount of the fee, it is proper to consider (1) time and labor required, (2) cost of materials and insurance, (3) novelty and difficulty of the problem, (4) customary charges of others for like services, (5) the risk involved in treating a work of high value, (6) the certainty of compensation, (7) character of the employment—casual or constant client.

An owner's ability to pay cannot justify a charge in excess of the value of the service, although his financial position may influence a lower charge.

Conservators should avoid charges which overestimate their services as well as those which undervalue them.

Because of the variation in the treatment of similar conditions it is impossible to establish with mathematical accuracy a set fee for a particular type of service.

17. *Warrant or Guarantee*

Although the conservator at all times follows the highest standards and, to the best of his knowledge, the most acceptable procedures, to warrant or guarantee the results of a treatment is unprofessional. This is not to be construed that he will not willingly and freely correct defects or unpredicted alterations which, in his opinion, have occurred prematurely following his treatment.

° Standard procedures for engaging in and reporting of examination and treatment of works of art are described in *The Murray Pease Report* (Sections IV and V).

IV. RELATIONS WITH COLLEAGUES AND THE PROFESSION

18. *Contribution to Profession*

A conservator has the obligation to share his knowledge and experience with his colleagues and with serious students. He should show his appreciation and respect to those from whom he has learned and to those who have contributed in the past to the knowledge and art of the profession, by presenting without thought of personal gain such advancements in his techniques of examination and treatment which may be of benefit to the profession.

19. *Intermediaries*

The professional services of a conservator should not be controlled or exploited by any agency personal or corporate which intervenes between client and practitioner. The conservator's responsibilities and qualifications are individual and personal. He should avoid all relations which direct the performance of his duties by or in the interest of such intermediary. This does not preclude his working under the direction of another qualified conservator.

20. *Request for Consultation*

If, for any reason, before or during treatment the owner or custodian desires another opinion on procedure through consultation with another conservator, this should not be regarded as evidence of want of confidence and should be welcomed by the conservator.

21. *Consultation*

No person engaged in the profession of conservation can expect to be expertly informed on all phases of examination, analysis and treatment. In instances of doubt, there should be no hesitation in seeking the advice of other professionals, or in referring the owner to a conservator more experienced in the particular special problems.

22. *Misuse of Reference*

Where clients have been referred for consultation or treatment, the conservator to whom they have been referred should, unless it was obviously otherwise intended, return the client to the original conservator as soon as possible. Efforts, direct or indirect, in any way to encroach upon the professional employment of another conservator are unworthy of the profession of conservation.

23. *Fee Splitting*

The payment of a commission or fee to another conservator or any other person for the reference of a client is to be condemned as unprofessional. Division of a fee is only acceptable where it is based on a division of service or responsibility.

24. *Comment on Qualifications of another Conservator*

It is unethical for a conservator to volunteer adverse judgment on the qualifications of and procedures rendered by another conservator except as such comment shall be to the mutual benefit of all concerned. In expressing an opinion of a practitioner, either voluntarily or at the request of someone outside the profession, the conservator must always conscientiously consider the iniquity of slander and must scrupulously base his statement on facts of which he has personal knowledge. If his opinion is uncertain or dependent on hearsay, it is more constructive to withhold comment and to recommend instead someone of whom he has no doubt.

V. OBLIGATIONS TO THE PUBLIC

25. *Education of Public*

In his relations with the public, every conservator should accept such opportunity as may be presented to educate the public in the aims, desires and purposes of his profession in order that a better popular understanding of conservation may be established. Such presentations should be in accordance with accepted principles of the time.

26. *Safeguarding Public Interests*

In the interests of the public as well as their own profession, conservators should observe accepted standards and laws, uphold the dignity and honor of the profession and accept its self-imposed disciplines. They should do their part to safeguard the public against illegal or unethical conduct by referring the facts of such delinquency to the appropriate professional committee. Further, it is the right of any conservator to give proper advice when it is requested by those seeking relief against negligent or unethical practices.

27. *Expertises*

Although the results of his examination and treatment of works of art may make it possible for him to contribute knowledge to the history of art and to the verification of the authorship (authenticity) of a work of art, the issuing of paid expertises or authentications may involve conflict of interest, and is not an appropriate or ethical activity for a conservator.

28. *Appraisals*

Because of his intimate contact with and knowledge of techniques of fabrication, and the physical condition of works of art, a conservator is often asked to appraise the monetary value of a work of art. Since this activity might involve conflicts of interest inconsistent with the profession of conservation and since appraising requires other specialized knowledge of market values and techniques of attribution, appraisal for a fee is not recommended, unless the individual holds an approved license.

29. *Art Dealing*

Engagement in the business of selling or purchasing for personal profit, or acting as a paid or commissioned agent in the sale of works of art is not recommended.

30. *Advertising*

It is an accepted principle that the most worthy and effective advertising is the establishment of a well-merited reputation for professional ability and integrity. Solicitation of clients, directly or indirectly by a conservator, a group, institution or organization is unethical. All forms of notices which may be construed as advertising should be avoided except:

1. Use of such sign or signs which in size, character, wording and position reasonably may be required to indicate the entrance and location of the premises in which the practice is performed.

2. Use of professional cards indicating only the name, degree, vocation, office address and telephone number.

3. Use of professional letterhead on stationery, bill and receipt forms.

4. Use of announcements of commencement of practice, change of location or restriction of practice.

5. The judicious distribution of reprints. Indiscriminate mailing of reprints, without sufficient reason, is construed as an attempt to solicit clients or an attempt to bring undue attention to the author. At the same time an author may honor requests for copies of his article.

VI. AMENDMENTS

Amendments or changes in this Code of Ethics must be initiated by petition from at least five members of IIC-AG to the Executive Committee who will direct the Committee on Professional Relations to prepare the amendment for vote. Acceptance into the Code of an amendment will be by two thirds affirmative vote of the membership of IIC-AG.

15: THE TREATMENT OF THE FIRST EDITION OF MELVILLE'S *THE WHALE*

Paul N. Banks

To my knowledge there has been presented in English only one detailed case history of the restoration of a printed book, although there have been some accounts of work on early manuscipts.[1] There are a number of reasons for this; probably two major ones. First, book conservation is several decades behind art conservation as a profession, as exemplified particularly by the facts that there are no schools whatsoever in this country where one can even learn, on a professional level, fine binding, much less book conservation, nor are there any competently-written books whatsoever on the subject as a whole.

The second major reason for the lack of serious attention to the restoration of printed books is economic. It is an unusual library, if in fact any exist, in which the average per-volume value of the holdings is greater than one-hundred dollars. Thus when a relatively simple rebacking of a leather volume may cost fifty dollars or more, and where a library may have a million volumes or more, it is difficult to create a restoration laboratory where the sophisticated treatment which is now fairly common in museums can be given to even those books which are worth substantial sums of money. I might point out that the record for the highest price paid for a printed book is $160,000, whereas of course the record for a painting is something like thirty-six times that much. Maybe we could carry that ratio to an illogical conclusion and say that the problems of book conservation are thirty-six times as difficult as those of art conservation.

The inescapable fact remains, however, that in any case where a book has any value at all as an artifact, that is, any value beyond its intellectual content, any treatment which is not carefully thought out and carefully executed by or under the direction of a competent specialist in book conservation, reduces the integrity or the durability of the book, or both.

This is supposed to be a treatment paper rather than a philosophical one, but I'd like to make one more comment before describing the restoration of a Victorian book. The conservation of books differs from the conservation of art objects in one other basic way than their value, which we have already discussed. That is, they are used—they are handled, taken on and off the shelf, leafed through, read, propped open, photocopied, exhibited open, and so on. Except in very rare cases, to ignore this fact is to deny

[1]Carolyn Horton, "The Restoration of the Salisbury Bible," *The Guild of Book Workers Journal,* V. no. 2, pp. 24–7, 1965.

the basic function and purpose of books. While thoughtful art conservators recognize that a painting, for example, "moves" in response to changes in humidity, a book in use is, or should be, a much more dynamic object than most museum pieces. It is, in fact, a kind of machine, with parts which move as it is used, and thus must be considered in dynamic rather than static terms.

So much for philosophy. I'd like to describe the treatment for you of the first edition of Herman Melville's *The Whale, or Moby Dick,* published in three volumes in London in 1851. The publisher, Richard Bentley, issued it in an edition of 500 copies, part of which was bound in a quite handsome three-piece stamped cloth binding, which is of interest in itself. The copy in question was purchased by the Newberry Library in 1968 for $3000. Thus, the literary and scholarly value, the esthetic value of the binding, as well as the monetary value of the set clearly indicate that the books should be left in essentially their present state; that is, restored rather than rebound.

Fortunately, this copy had undergone no previous restoration, so that it was intact and there was no extraneous material to remove. However, in common with most books produced in the second half of the nineteenth century, it was in very delicate health indeed. The cloth was very weak and was chipping, and the volumes were "shaken," in book dealers' parlance; that is, the sections were separating from each other.

It was decided at the outset to check the pH of the paper, since the value of the book indicated that it should receive maximum protective treatment; most paper of the period is much too acid for permanence, and the "shaken" state of the sewing removed any reservations about taking the book completely apart to deacidify it.

The acidity was measured using a Beckman electronic pH meter with a flat-head combination electrode, which was standardized with pH 4.0 buffer. The reading of pH 3.9 confirmed our suspicion that the paper was in need of deacidification, so that our first step was to take the volumes apart.

First, the tipped-on endsheets were pulled away from the "book-block" where they had not already separated from it or split in the fold. Then, the "crash" or "super" was cut in the

joint to free the book-block from the case. The cases were put
aside for the time being.

Then the book was "pulled" or "taken down." That is, the
linings were removed from the spine, the sewing threads cut, and
the sections. also sometimes called (by bibliographers) gatherings
or (by printers and publishers) signatures, separated from each
other. Happily, with most books from the second half of the
nineteenth century, this is an easy matter, because of the facts
that the animal glue used on the spine does not penetrate into the
paper to the extent that starch paste, used earlier, or synthetic
adhesives, used later, do; that this animal glue has become extremely brittle, and that early machine-made paper tended to
be stratified and rather weakly bonded internally. The effect of
all of this is that books of this period are almost always "shaken"
but, by the same token, they can often be quite easily pulled
with little discernible damage to the folds of the sections. After
the sections are separated, the remaining fragments of glue are
easily removed by running the fingernail down the outside of
the fold.

A magnesium bicarbonate solution is prepared by bubbling
carbon dioxide through a mixture of basic magnesium carbonate
and water until the carbonate is converted to bicarbonate and
dissolves. The sheets of the book were soaked in the solution for
two hours. The leaves were dried with blotters in a press; two
changes of blotters, with at first light pressure in the press, permit the leaves to shrink back to almost their original dimensions
without setting up unusual stresses which would be caused by
drying them fully under heavy pressure. The pH was measured
again, and reading of 6.65 is probably acceptable for a book
which is going to live in sulfur-dioxide-free air.

The sections were re-gathered, folded, and carefully
checked for order. Tears, lacunae, and weakened folds were repaired with Japanese paper and plasticized rice starch paste. The
book was then given a hard pressing to help control swelling in
the spine, which would create problems in making the books fit
back into their original cases. Hinges of very strong Japanese
"vellum" paper (Shizuoka) were sewn in around the first and
last sections of each volume to provide means of reattaching the

books in their cases. The books were then resewn in their original manner, using, however, unbleached linen cords and thread.

The hinges around the outside sections were tipped to the next ones to help anchor them, and the swelling created by the layers of sewing thread knocked down, although very gently in this case because of the fairly weak paper. The spine is then glued with internally-plasticized p.v.a. emulsion adhesive, in the conventional way, and the book is rounded and lightly backed. The former operation gives the spine its convex shape, and the latter creates small shoulders which help to hold the book in its case. Both operations are, of course, usual, and were here executed in the conventional manner. Both help the book to keep its shape as the spine is flexed in use.

The spine was lined with thin fabric, for strength, and with paper, to add a degree of stiffness. The fabric is super, a heavily sized cheesecloth, and the paper Permalife bond. Both are applied with p.v.a. emulsion. The book is kept in the backing press while the moisture from the adhesive evaporates, so that it will "set up" in its desired shape. After the book is thoroughly dry, the ends of the cords on which it was sewn are cut off short, frayed out, and glued down to the Japanese vellum hinge.

Now we turn to the cases or covers. The object, of course, is to reinforce the seriously weakened cloth without significantly changing the visual character of the covers. The customary approach to this is to line the spine area with new, strong material. This material must be fairly supple, so that an unnaturally stiff and flat aspect is not created in the finished book. Binder's cloth, which is often used for repairing early cloth books, is heavily sized and filled, and is too stiff for this type of restoration.

The corners are first rebuilt and recovered. The type of binder's board usually used in edition bindings of this period is very soft and pulpy, and the corners are almost always mangled. The first step in this process is to pare the edge of a piece of tough, stiff handmade paper, to reduce the step where it stops. The board is split, approximately in the middle, with a knife, and the pared edge of the piece of paper is inserted with p.v.a. The pulpy board is then impregnated with starch paste, which dries very hard, and pressed flat with the fingers, between pieces of waxed paper or equivalent. The worn-away areas of board at the tips of the corners are rebuilt with a type of papier-maché composed of filter-paper pulp and starch paste, with the inserted piece of paper acting as an anchor to prevent the papier-maché addition from cracking off at the joint.

After the papier-maché is dry, the corners were shaped with a standing disc in a flexible-shaft tool. In addition to making the shape of the added material conform to that of the orignal board, a step-down is created in the top of the board to receive the new cloth, i.e., so that there is not a step-up where the new cloth starts.

Thin unbleached Irish linen is used for recovering the corners. It is first dyed to match the existing cloth with water-soluble aniline dyes. Pieces are then cut, applied to the outside, turned in, and the existing cloth is put back down on top, all with p.v.a. The board paper is put down with starch paste.

The next step is to lift the endlinings an inch or so in from the spine on. This is done with careful strokes of a flat-bladed leather paring knife. Then, the turn-ins of the cloth at the head and tail of the case are lifted, this can usually be done with a spatula because of the light adhesion. The turn-ins have to be slit about an inch in from the spine so that they may be opened up to insert new material.

The boards are then reattached to the book-block by gluing with p.v.a. emulsion the area where the endsheet was lifted, slipping this area over the added hinge of Shizuoka vellum on the book block, positioning the board accurately, and pressing briefly to insure adhesion. Before pressing, a sheet of silicone release paper is inserted between the boards and the book block as a partial moisture barrier and to prevent any squeeze-out of adhesive from adhering to the flyleaves.

The fabric for rebacking is now prepared as for recovering the corners. A piece of the dyed cloth is cut to the length of the spine plus enough to be attached to the boards under the lifted edge of the original cloth. A piece of bond paper is cut to the length and width of the spine and glued to the piece of cloth, to provide the requisite degree of stiffening.

When the adhesive used to attach the boards to the bookblocks is dry, the original cloth is lifted from the boards, parallel to and about 3/4" in from the spine, to enable the reinforcing cloth to be inserted between the board and the original cloth. (It is almost always desirable to add reinforcing material *between* a support and the original covering, partly for esthetic reasons, and partly because strong material adhered on top of weak, original material will hold less because of the weak substrate.)

The lifted area—that is, the newly exposed board and the underside of the lifted cloth—are now glued with p.v.a. emulsion, the new cloth spine is laid in position, and the lifted sides are gently worked down on the new cloth with a bone folder. The book is carefully pressed. (Too much working with the folder, or too much pressing, will remove the embossed pattern in the cloth.)

The head and tail of the new material are turned in underneath the original turn-in, new internal hinge and the board-paper, and also adhered with p.v.a. emulsion. The original turn-in and new hinge are put back down with p.v.a., and the boardpaper with starch paste.

The final step is re-attaching the original spine with p.v.a. emulsion, after having carefully scraped off the old, rotten lining paper with a scalpel.

Author's note—To my associate, Norvell M.M. Jones, great thanks is due for acting variously as executant, model and photographer in preparing this paper.

Ed. note: This paper, delivered at the Annual Meeting of IIC-American Group, held in Los Angeles, June, 1969, is the running commentary for 110 , slides used to show each step of the treatment.

Figure 1. Volume I, before treatment, showing detached board and crumbling cloth at head of spine.

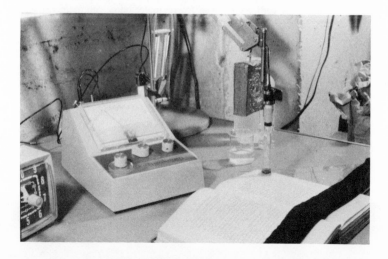

Figure 2. Determining the pH (acidity) of the paper non-destructively with the surface electrode of an electronic pH meter.

Figure 3. Heavy Japanese paper is "water-torn" for filling in. By outlining the patch with water in a ruling pen and pulling it off, a soft, fibrous edge is produced which blends with the page being mended, and which reduces the potential for breaking which would exist with a hard edge. The methylcellulose simply increases the viscosity, and thus improves the working quality, of the water.

Figure 4. The internal hinge–by which the book-block is held into
the case–is prepared from heavy Shizuoka Vellum, a Japanese
paper which is extremely tough but relatively soft. The edge
which will lie between two leaves of the text is bevelled with a
leather paring knife, and will be held just by sewing (without
adhesive), all of which reduce breaking effects.

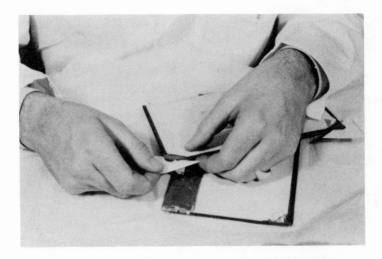

Figure 5. The corner of the board has been split edgewise, and a piece of tough handmade paper, which has had its edge pared to avoid a lump, is inserted to act as an anchor for subsequent building-up with papier maché.

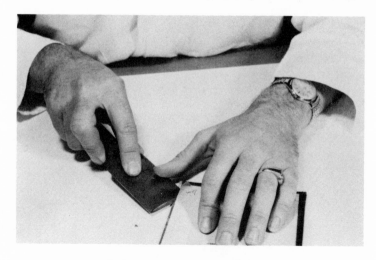

Figure 6. The endsheet is lifted from the board, using sweeping strokes with the leather paring knife.

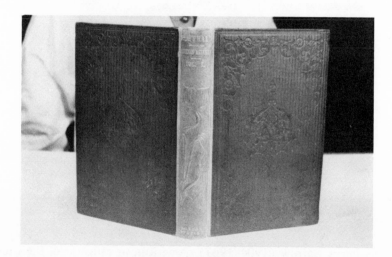

Figure 7. Volume I, finished.

16: BARROW, WILLIAM JAMES

Frazer G. Poole

William James Barrow (1904–1967), American investigator of the causes and remedies of deteriorating book paper, was born in Brunswick County, Virginia, the son of Dr. Bernard Barrow and Sallie Virginia Archer Barrow. He graduated from Randolph-Macon Academy in 1923, and later attended Randolph-Macon College. He became interested in problems of paper deterioration when, in the course of investigating the history of the Barrow family, he saw a number of old books which had been restored, and also noted the fragile and deteriorating condition of many old records. Determined to learn all he could about books and bookmaking, he went to Washington, D.C., where he studied bookbinding in the studio of Miss Marian Lane, a former student of Sangorski and Sutcliffe. During

Copyright © 1972 by Marcel Dekker, Inc.; reprinted from pages 257–270 of the *Encyclopedia of Library and Information Science,* Vol. 2, A. Kent and H. Lancour, eds., New York: Marcel Dekker, Inc., 1972, 707 pp.

this period he also made frequent visits to the Library of Congress, where he observed document restoration methods, which consisted largely of pasting transparent woven silk on both sides of deteriorating documents.

Moving to Richmond in 1932, he established a document restoration shop in the Virginia State Library building. In 1935 he moved this operation to the Mariners' Museum in Newport News, Virginia, where he remained until 1940. During this period he discovered that almost no reliable information about paper deterioration was available. The usual answer to his question of why a particular eighteenth century manuscript was brittle and unusable was that it was "old." Having examined many much older volumes which were still in excellent condition, he realized that age was not, in itself, the critical factor in paper deterioration. He also became increasingly skeptical of the usefulness of the silking process, which most restorers claimed would preserve a document indefinitely. When, in the course of his restoration work, he observed many documents which, although preserved by silking, were again deteriorating after only 20 to 25 years, he concluded that very little was actually known about the factors governing the permanence and durability of paper. In 1935, he began a research program into the causes of deteriorating paper.

The concern of others with this same general problem had prompted the U.S. National Bureau of Standards to begin a search for better materials with which to laminate documents. Eventually, the Bureau developed a procedure for applying a thin film of cellulose acetate to deteriorated documents. However, the high cost of the steam-heated hydraulic press required to apply this material led Barrow to design his own equipment. Working in his restoration shop in the Mariners' Museum, he invented the first practical roller-type laminating machine.

The original Barrow laminator was made from a ship's armor plating and the roller bearings from a tail shaft. Essentially the device consisted of two electrically heated, thermostatically controlled metal plates for preheating the materials to be laminated, and two revolving calendar rolls with a pressure range of 300 to 2,000 pounds per square inch (Figure 1). The major advantages of the Barrow design were that no artificial cooling was required, and that the pressure applied by the rollers prevented the entrapment of air between the document and the film. In addition, the Barrow process was substantially less expensive than the older silking process and required significantly less time. The first Barrow laminator was perfected early in 1938, and was thereafter used in the restoration of thousands of documents. It quickly became apparent to Barrow, however, that the procedure of laminating a thin film of cellulose acetate to each side of the document produced a laminate with very low tear resistance and relatively low folding endurance. To overcome this inherent weakness in a document laminated only with cellulose acetate, he developed a method of using a sheet of high-grade, long-fiber tissue paper on the outside of the acetate film. This produeed a laminate with considerable resistance to tearing and added greatly to the folding endurance of the document.

Despite his development of a superior process for strengthening manuscripts, he continued his investigations into the basic causes of paper deterioration. High acidity had long been believed to be a major factor in such deterioration, but it was left for Barrow to undertake the first comprehensive analysis of book papers, both old and new, and to demonstrate that, with few exceptions, deteriorated documents were highly acid, with pH values ranging from 3.0 to 5.5, while, conversely, older documents still in good condition were low in acid content or even somewhat alkaline, with pH values of 6.0 or above.

Although he continued these studies of book papers until his death, by 1940 he had become sufficiently convinced of the importance of acid as the primary cause

FIGURE 1. *The Barrow laminator.*

of paper deterioration that he began experiments with procedures for deacidifying documents before laminating them. By the mid-1940s, he had developed a method for treating deteriorating documents by soaking them first in a solution of calcium hydroxide, then in a solution of calcium bicarbonate in order to carbonate the residual hydroxide of the first solution. This process neutralized the acidity and precipitated calcium carbonate onto the paper to act as a buffer against any acid that might later attack the paper.

The Barrow claim that acidity was the basic cause of paper deterioration met with considerable skepticism in some quarters, but as the evidence accumulated it became clearly evident that his analysis was correct. Today, the deacidification of those documents that must be preserved indefinitely is accepted archival procedure in the United States and in many countries abroad.

During the course of his inquiries into the causes of acidity in paper, he found numerous instances in which the writing on old manuscripts had eaten holes through the paper. In some cases so-called "mirror writing" was observed where deterioration had occurred on the backs of adjacent sheets. Upon further investigation, Barrow discovered that the inks used on such manuscripts were of the iron-gall type. When the iron of the copperas (ferrous sulfate) combined with the gallic or tannic acids of the oak galls to form the black compound of such ink, the product was sulfuric acid. Tests of old manuscripts written in iron-gall inks revealed that the uninked margins were nearly always less acid than the inked areas.

From this study of early writing inks, Barrow's studies led to an investigation of early papermaking procedures. He had already noted that most papers produced prior to the middle of the seventeenth century were generally in excellent condition and that exceptions were usually attributable to acid inks or to adverse storage conditions. The heavy increase in the demand for paper which occurred during the latter half of the seventeenth century caused papermakers to use a mixture of old and new rags. This resulted not only in a weaker paper but in a much more absorbent paper, requiring heavier sizing to prevent inks from running. Alum, which had long been used in tanning and as a mordant in dying cloth, now came into use in papermaking as a means of hardening the commonly used gelatin size. Tests conducted by Barrow indicated that papers made after 1668 were considerably more acid than those produced before that date. After 1700, increasing numbers of old and usually discolored rags were used in paper manufacture. In turn, these required the use of bluing to make the old rags appear white. In 1774, the German chemist Scheele discovered chlorine, thus making possible the bleaching of even the dirtiest rags. Unfortunately, the properties of chlorine were not fully known, and its indiscriminate use by papermakers decreased the strength of the already weakened fibers from worn rags, and left acidic chlorides which caused further deterioration.

In about 1830 the alum rosin sizing process was introduced into the United States. Whether aluminum sulfate or potassium aluminum sulfate was used at this time is not known. In either case, a chemical reaction occurred which precipitated insoluble aluminum resinate onto the paper to size the fibers and make them less absorbent to ink. This reaction, however, also produced free sulfuric acid. Barrow's tests of some 240 writing papers made in the period between 1700 and 1900 showed that most had a pH of 5.0 to 4.0. By the middle of the nineteenth century the need for paper-making fibers had grown to the point at which rags could no longer supply the demand, and methods for using wood fibers in papermaking were developed as a result. Wood fibers, however, contain approximately 50% noncellulosic compounds which, if not removed before they are processed into paper, quickly break down into acidic compounds. Thus, unless wood fibers are well purified they provide still another source of acid to further hasten the deterioration of the sheet. Barrow's work demonstrated that the combination of inadequately purified wood fibers and alum rosin sizing produced paper which was not only weak to begin with but which, because of the residual acid and acidic compounds in the sheet, almost literally destroyed itself.

From 1940 to 1957, Barrow's research into the problems of paper deterioration were supported by his own resources. In 1957, the Council on Library Resources awarded a grant to the Virginia State Library for an investigation of the deterioration of modern bookpapers to be directed by Mr. Barrow. With the first grant, two studies were conducted, the results of which were published by the Virginia State Library in 1959, under the title *Deterioration of Book Stock, Causes and Remedies*. The initial research program led Barrow to the conclusion that the chemical wood papers, so commonly used in printing nonfiction books during the first half of the twentieth century, were much too weak and too acid to guarantee a reasonable life in either use or storage. In fact, 97% of the book papers so tested were found to have a life expectancy of fifty years or less.

The object of the second study under the 1957 grant was to determine the stability of modern stock book papers and to develop a procedure which would increase the longevity of existing printed materials. Using an adaptation of the procedures he had developed previously for deacidifying manuscripts, Barrow demonstrated that modern book papers could be adequately deacidified and the rate of deterioration significantly decreased by soaking such papers for approximately 20 hours in a saturated solution of calcium and magnesium bicarbonates.

This confirmation of his earlier conclusions, and the demonstration that it was possible to successfully treat newly manufactured book papers to neutralize acidity and materially prolong the life of such papers, led Barrow to the realization that it should also be possible to produce a new and better book paper with built-in permanence and durability. Again, financial support for his work was supplied by the Council on Library Resources in a grant effective March 1, 1959. The project came to a conclusion in March 1960, and the results were published by the Virginia State Library under the title, *The Manufacture and Testing of Durable Book Papers*.

In order to establish reasonable specifications for a strong book paper, Barrow selected seven books printed between 1534 and 1722, all of which were in excellent condition after several centuries of use. His first investigation had shown that the chemical tests usually applied to paper, such as copper number, water extractables, alkali solubles, and viscosity, gave inconsistent and meaningless results. In consequence, he elected to use only acidity as a chemical test, and folding endurance and tear resistance as physical tests. All three were methods which could be measured under standardized procedures established by The Technical Association of the Pulp and Paper Industry (TAPPI). Equally important, the two physical tests selected seemed to be those which most closely simulated the stresses to which book papers were subjected under conditions of actual use.

During this investigation six experimental and two commercial-type book papers were manufactured by incorporating strong, well-purified chemical wood fibers in the furnish, and by using a size (newly available on the market) compatible with alkalinity. The alkalinity of the finished sheet was further increased by adding calcium carbonate as a filler to serve as a buffer during storage. These were the first of what Barrow designated permanent/durable book papers. Such papers, developed in accordance with the Barrow specifications, were first produced commercially in 1960, and have had growing acceptance since that date. Commercial runs of permanent/durable book papers produced since 1960 have shown an increase in the expected permanence and durability.

The original, "Tentative Specifications for Durable, Non-coated, Chemical Wood Book Papers" are as follows:

"Based on 25″ × 38″ size at 60 lb per ream:

1. The paper must be free of ground wood and unbleached fibers.

2. On the basis of a minimum of 15 test strips, from 15 different sheets selected at random from a ream, initial folding endurance of conditioned strips shall average not less than 300 folds in the weakest direction as measured on the M.I.T. tester at ½ kilogram tension.

3. On the basis of a minimum of 12 test strips (selected as in 2) and tested by 5 tears through 4 strips initial tear resistance of conditioned strips shall average not less than 60 grams in weakest direction as measured on the Elmendorf tester.

4. After artificial aging at 100° C ± 2° the average of strips (selected and tested as in 2 and 3) shall not show less than the following fold and tear for the days of aging indicated:

Days	Fold	Tear
12	200	53 grams
24	140	48 grams
36	100	43 grams

5. The pH of the paper shall not be less than 6.5 at time of manufacture, and after heat aging (as in 4) for 3 days shall show no sharp decline.

6. Opacity of the paper shall not be less than 90.

7. Procedures for testing shall follow TAPPI unless otherwise indicated."

In the course of these efforts to produce a permanent/durable book paper, it became necessary to develop testing procedures which would measure the longevity of the new paper and thus permit valid comparisons with older book papers. As a basis for such tests, Barrow accepted a theory put forth about the turn of the century and more fully developed later by the National Bureau of Standards: that controlled heat aging of paper at 100°C ± 2° simulates natural aging, and that such artificial aging for 72 hours is equivalent to approximately 25 years of natural aging. During this study Barrow undertook a program of extended aging, using heat treatment for periods up to 48 days—the equivalent of about 400 years.

Earlier work in this field had recorded the data from heat aging in terms of the percentage retention of tear and fold at each point in time. In the course of his accelerated aging experiments, however, it became evident that paper degradation followed a logarithmic pattern, and this fact enabled Barrow and his colleagues to develop a method for plotting and analyzing data of heat-aged paper by which the position and slope of the deterioration curve (regression line) could be determined on either semilogarithmic or linear graph paper. With the use of the least-square method and a surveyor's planimeter, rather than a digital computer or desk calculator, the new graphical procedure was simpler to use and gave quicker results.

Although there was criticism of Barrow's accelerated aging techniques, it was widely accepted as: (1) a definite improvement over previous methods, (2) valuable for estimating the potential longevity of paper (although it was recognized that estimates of potential life might vary by 10 to 20%), and (3) especially helpful in measuring the comparative effects of additives, and so forth, on a particular paper, during heat aging (see Figures 2 and 3).

Barrow's contributions to the preservation of books and documents during the years 1936–1961 were of major significance in the field of document restoration.

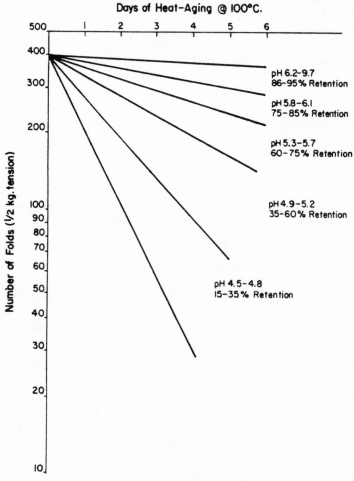

FIGURE 2. *Percent retention of folding endurance after 3 days' heat-aging calculated from values on the regression lines formed by heat-aged test data for 41 papers and listed according to their pH range (cold extraction). (Barrow, 1963)*

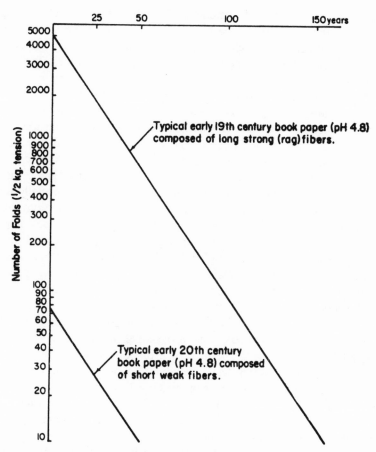

FIGURE 3. *Two types of book papers with identical pH and rates of deterioration, but because of difference in initial number of folds it requires 100 years longer for the strong paper to reach the low strength of 10 folds. (Barrow, 1963)*

His convincing demonstrations of the fundamental causes of paper deterioration, and the proof that it was economically feasible to produce permanent/durable book paper from wood fibers, "changed the face of an industry," and provided librarians and archivists with the procedures necessary to preserve their deteriorating collections.

In his investigation of writing inks and their effects upon paper deterioration, he found numerous examples in which the acid in the writing ink had not only eaten holes in the sheet upon which the writing appeared, but had affected adjacent sheets as well. He discovered that documents stored in contact with newsprint (ground wood) had been heavily discolored. Examples of low-grade papers causing such discoloration were observed in the case of file folders, interleaving sheets, end papers, book markers, cover boards, and similar materials. In a study reported in *Archivum*, Vol. III, 1953, he demonstrated that good paper in contact with acid paper is adversely affected by migration of the acid, with resulting loss in the physical strength of the affected document. From this it was a natural step to his recommendation that end papers, file folders, and all other materials used for storing valuable documents, or which might be in contact with such papers, should have a low acid content and should contain no ground wood fibers. Today, storage of manuscripts and documents in acid-free folders is accepted practice.

His investigations of the possibilities of reproducing documents by transferring the ink from a deteriorating page to new and stronger paper led to the development of successful procedures for such transfer. Although the technique was employed occasionally by the Library of Congress and others, it fell into disuse because of the slowness of the process and the competition of cheap methods of reproduction.

In 1961 the Council on Library Resources made its first grant directly to Barrow for the construction of a modern laboratory designed especially for paper testing and equipped with the most modern and precise instrumentation. With these new facilities he continued his studies of the characteristics of book papers and began a fresh series of experiments in paper preservation and related fields.

Among the first projects to be undertaken in the new laboratory, and one of particular interest to librarians, was a research program to develop performance standards for bookbinding conducted for the Library Technology Project of the American Library Association. Begun in 1960 and completed in 1965, Barrow and his staff developed standards for bookbindings based upon performance rather than upon materials and methods. The provisional standards developed by the laboratory defined the quality or performance of book bindings used in libraries as affected by three characteristics: openability, workmanship, and durability. This investigation resulted in the development by Robert E. Sayre, a member of the Barrow staff, of the "Universal Book Tester," a machine which made possible for the first time an evaluation of the actual durability of bookbindings by simulating conditions of normal use. A simple but effective device for testing the degree of openability of a book was also developed in the Barrow laboratory in connection with this same program.

An investigation of the permanence and durability of catalog cards was begun by Barrow about the same time, again at the instance of the Library Technology Project of ALA. The results of this study revealed wide variations in the durability and permanence of catalog cards then available. Some 100% rag cards were shown to possess less durability than some 50% rag cards. Strong chemical wood fiber card stocks with a pH of 8.0 or higher showed excellent durability and permanence. Catalog cards of 100% cotton stock with low acid content were shown to produce the most durable and most permanent cards. However, card stocks of 100% rag with short, weak fibers and high acid content, proved to be less durable than the strong chemical wood fiber stocks. This program resulted in tentative recommendations for standards for both heavily and moderately used catalog cards. An indirect result was the marketing of catalog cards produced from strong chemical wood fibers in general accordance with the specifications for permanent/durable paper previously developed by Barrow.

In his work on polyvinyl acetate adhesives, Barrow concluded that those which retained their adhesive qualities and flexibility longest, and therefore gave promise of suitability for bindings for the library market, were the internally plasticized copolymers. Two widely used hot-melt adhesives used in adhesive bindings proved to be unstable under heat aging, and were judged unsatisfactory for library bindings since they would not retain their essential characteristics longer than a few months. Mr. Barrow observed, however, in his report on these adhesives, that these results did not necessarily mean that relatively stable hot-melt PVA adhesives could not be made.

Despite the success and wide acceptance of his deacidification process for manuscripts and other unbound materials, it was uneconomical (because of the high labor costs involved in taking books apart, deacidifying the individual sheets, and rebinding) for treating bound materials. With this in mind, one of the early projects undertaken by Barrow after moving into the new laboratory in 1961, was to find a method for treating such materials quicker and at less cost.

When preliminary experiments using ammonia gas as a deacidifying agent proved unsatisfactory, he turned to spray deacidification as a possible solution to

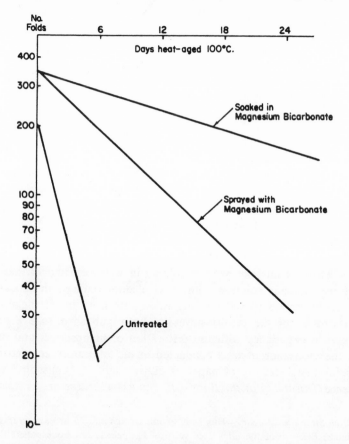

FIGURE 4. *The folding endurance regression lines formed from an average of the control and heat-aged data (average both directions) of untreated samples and those sprayed and soaked in a solution of magnesium bicarbonate. (Barrow, 1964)*

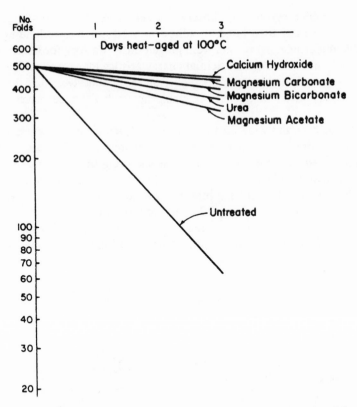

FIGURE 5. *The folding endurance regression lines, formed from control and heat-aged data, adjusted at the control to show the rate of deterioration of a modern book paper untreated and after spraying with the indicated solutions. (Barrow, 1964)*

the problem. He first tried an aqueous solution of magnesium bicarbonate. This method proved satisfactory as far as neutralizing the acid was concerned, but the cockling effect on paper, and the tendency for an aqueous solution to produce feathering when used on inks or dyes soluble in water created further problems. Dilution of the aqueous solution with ethyl alcohol reduced the cockling effect, but proved to be only a partial answer. Additional work in this field was undertaken by Barrow, but the results have not been published (see Figures 4–7).

Barrow's wide experience with the restoration of manuscripts and other documents and the thousands of tests conducted in his laboratory enabled him to develop a useful categorization of paper as either usable or unusable. As set forth in *Permanence/Durability of the Book—II*, pp. 41–42, these are as follows:

> "*High Strength Category*—Has 1000 or more folds and 75 or more grams tear resistance. Because of the filler used to provide opacity, few book papers fall in this category. Many bond and ledger papers composed of strong chemical wood or cotton fibers fall in this category and can be expected to withstand hard usage.
>
> *Moderate Strength Category*—Has 300–1000 folds with 60–75 grams tear.

Book papers of this strength have good potential use in the average library. The permanent/durable type book papers fall in either this category or above.

Low Strength Category—Has 10–300 folds with 25–60 grams tear or more. These papers have limited potential use and especially those in the 10–50 folds category (newsprint). Many scholarly publications occur in the range of 50–75 folds and will soon need restoration because of the fast rate of deterioration due to high acidity.

Weak Category—Has 2–10 folds with 13–23 grams tear. Such a paper is below newsprint strength and should not be subjected to hard use. It is suitable only for a rare book room where users are cautioned to handle it with care.

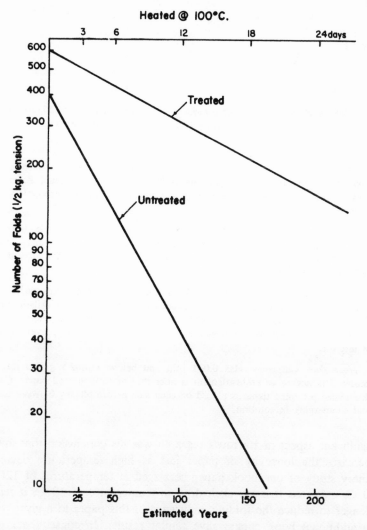

FIGURE 6. *The regression lines for folding endurance (MIT ½ kg tension—average both directions) of 7 book papers (text) before and after spraying with magnesium bicarbonate solution with 25% ethyl alcohol added. (Barrow, 1963)*

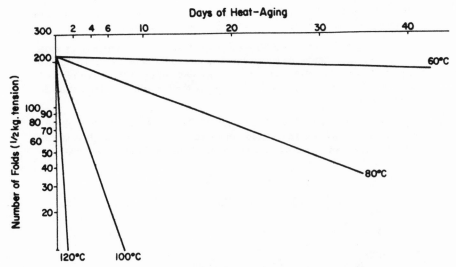

FIGURE 7. *The folding endurance of a modern book paper heated at 120, 100, 80, and 60°C to form regression lines, exhibiting a time factor of 7½ for each change of 20°C. (Barrow, 1963)*

Unusable Category—Has 1.0–0.1 fold with 8–12 grams tear. Such a sheet breaks when creased by the thumb and is difficult to sew if rebound. A leaf in a book of this strength should be turned with much care and is unsuitable for use unless restored.

Brittle Category—Has 0.1–0.01 fold with 4–8 grams tear. Crumbles into small and medium size pieces when crushed in the hand. Is unbindable and unusable under normal conditions. Will require a skillful operator to handle without damage during restoration.

Very Brittle Category—Has 0.01–0.001 fold with 2.5 to 4 grams tear. Can be reduced to very small particles when rubbed in palm of hand. A skilled restorer of documents should use extra care to prevent damage when applying restoration procedures. The restored sheet should be handled with care to prevent splitting of interior.

Near Dust Category—Has 0.001 fold and below with 2.5 grams tear and below. The degree of embrittlement is near that of well-charred paper. Can be deacidified provided tissue is placed on each side before placing between screens and submerging in solution."

A significant aspect of Barrow's research was his conclusion that low temperature increases the longevity of paper just as high temperature decreases it. A preliminary study of one book paper heat-aged at temperatures of 120, 100, 80, and 60°C, indicated that for each drop in temperature of 20°C, it required 7½ times longer to reduce the folding endurance of this paper to a given value. Tests on two additional book papers gave similar results. In consequence of this discovery, he built into his laboratory a series of refrigeration chambers capable of providing complete control of temperature and humidity (see Figure 7).

At the time of his death he was pursuing his investigation of the effect of humidity and temperature on the longevity of paper, in an attempt to identify optimum storage conditions for library collections, and was conducting further research on the effect of alum and alum rosin sizing on the deterioration of book paper.

In addition to the major investigations always underway in his laboratory, Barrow often tackled special problems. Thus, he put his talents to work in an investigation of the sizing to be used in restoring the thousands of volumes damaged in the Florence floods of November 1966. He made two trips to England to assist papermakers there in the production of permanent/durable paper for the *National Union Catalog*.

Barrow was a member of many professional organizations, including the International Council on Archives; the American Society for the Advancement of Science; American Institute of Chemists; Technical Association of the Pulp and Paper Industry; International Centre for the Study of the Preservation and Restoration of Cultural Property, Rome; and the Association for the Preservation of Virginia Antiquities. In 1966 he was awarded an honorary Doctor of Laws by Randolph-Macon College.

The reports he authored or which emanated from his laboratory are listed in the Bibliography.

BIBLIOGRAPHY

Barrow (W. J.) Research Laboratory, *Permanence/Durability of the Book:*
  I. *A Two-Year Research Program,* Richmond, Virginia, 1963.
  II. *Test Data of Naturally Aged Papers,* Richmond, Virginia, 1964.
  III. *Spray Deacidification,* Richmond, Virginia, 1964.
  IV. *Polyvinyl Acetate (PVA) Adhesives for Use in Library Bookbinding,* Richmond, Virginia, 1965.
  V. *Strength and Other Characteristics of Book Papers, 1800–1899,* Richmond, Virginia, 1967.
  VI. *Spot Testing for Permanence/Durability of Book Papers,* in press.

Barrow, W. J., "Hot vs. Cold Extraction Methods for Making a pH Determination," *Tappi,* **46,** 468 (1963).

Barrow, W. J., *Manuscripts and Documents: Their Deterioration and Restoration.* University of Virginia Press, Charlottesville, 1955.

Barrow, W. J., and R. C. Sproull, "Permanence in Book Papers," *Science* **129,** 1075 (April 24, 1959).

Virginia State Library, *Deterioration of Book Stock—Causes and Remedies; Two Studies on the Permanence of Book Paper,* conducted by W. J. Barrow, edited by Randolph W. Church, Richmond, 1959. (*Virginia State Library Publications,* No. 10.)

Virginia State Library, *The Manufacture and Testing of Durable Book Papers. Based on the Investigations of W. J. Barrow,* edited by Randolph W. Church, Richmond, 1960. (*Virginia State Library Publications,* No. 13.)

17: RESEARCH ON MASS TREATMENTS IN CONSERVATION*

John C. Williams**

George B. Kelly, Jr.***

Introduction

The investigations of Barrow and others have
established that acid paper has a short life. If, however, the pH
of the paper is brought to 7 or slightly above, and buffered at
that point, the paper will become much more permanent. Unfortunately, paper has been made on the acid side since the early
years of the 19th century when rosin/alum sizing was introduced.
Even today, the major portion of the paper produced is of this
type. The libraries, therefore, are filled with books in which
the paper is degrading, not too slowly, into dust. The Library
of Congress has an estimated 6,000,000 books which are already
in such a condition that they should not circulate and, with
minor exceptions, the whole collection should be neutralized and
buffered to halt the degradation. At a pound a book there are
thus 3,000 tons of books that require emergency treatment. We
have no figures for the United States total, but there must be
100 times this or 300,000 tons in the emergency class, and this
is just the start. The job is evidently beyond the power of the
individual conservators. There is an obvious pressing need for a
process as simple as ethylene oxide fumigation in which the books
are put into an autoclave and treated by some sort of gas or
vapor.

Granted that this can be done, the successful vapor
phase treatments must meet some rather stringent and difficult
requirements.

*Talk presented at the AIC Second Annual Meeting in Cooperstown,
New York, May 30-June 1, 1974.

**Research Officer, Research and Testing Office, Library of
Congress, Washington, D. C.

***Chemist, Research and Testing Office, Library of Congress,
Washington, D. C.

Reprinted from *Am. Inst. Conserv. Hist. Aristic Works Bull.* 14(2):69-77 (1974).

Requirements of Vapor Phase Neutralization and Buffering

(1)   The paper must be uniformly neutralized.

(2)   The paper should be buffered as close to
pH 7 as possible, on the alkaline side. Higher pH changes the
color or tint of inks and art work and yellows paper which
contains groundwood.

(3)   The paper should be given an alkaline reserve
equivalent to 3% calcium carbonate.

(4)   The treatment must penetrate books and masses
of books in a reasonable time.

(5)   The treatment, although applied as a gas,
must not come back out of the paper. This implies that a
reaction with cellulose takes place or that there is a polymerization of gaseous material in the cellulose or that two
gases react to make a non-volatile product in situ, etc.

(6)   The treatment should not impart an odor to
the paper.

(7)   The treated paper should be nontoxic to humans.

(8)   No new problems should be introduced by the
treatment such as darkening of the paper, damage to the leather,
etc.

(9)   The treatment should be reasonable in cost.
Binding a book costs roughly $5. The book paper may degrade so
as to be unuseable within 50 years. Treating the book so that it
will last 500 years should be worth at least another $5.
However, price schedules and what is "reasonable" have not been
established.

Volatile Alkaline Compounds

There are several volatile phosphorous compounds
which are alkaline. They are, however, so extremely toxic that
they can be dismissed from consideration. There are also many
volátile alkaline nitrogen compounds such as ammonia and the
related compounds, the amines. Work on vapor phase neutralization and buffering using amines has been carried out by
Langwell and also at the Barrow Laboratory. Langwell supplies

paper impregnated with cyclohexylamine carbonate which can be interleaved in a book to raise the pH. DuPuis, Kusterer and Sproull discussed the method in the Restaurator. The Barrow Laboratory has recently received U. S. P. 3,771,958 on vapor phase neutralization and buffering using morpholine.

Morpholine, as a volatile alkaline amine, will behave somewhat similarly to cyclohexylamine, showing some of the same advantages and disadvantages. Both processes more or less disregard item (5) of the requirements. These amines do come back out of the paper and give treated books an unpleasant odor for a time.

The necessity of holding the volatile amine in place in the paper guided our work on amines in the Preservation Office laboratory and led us to study ethyleneimine. This reactive chemical can be introduced as a gas and polymerized in place to make a non-volatile alkaline polymer. Ethyleneimine will also react directly with cellulose to give aminoethylated celluloses. A cooperative project was set up with Dow Chemical Company to investigate the reaction. Paper was successfully neutralized and buffered at a pH of 8.7. Additions of as much as 4.5% nitrogen to the cellulose were achieved. There was no odor imparted to the treated paper. Unfortunately, however, there was no substantial improvement obtained in the aging character of the paper. Brightness was also seriously lowered by the treatment.

After various similar disappointments with amine treatments, we began to look for other classes of volatile neutralization and buffering compounds. Calcium and magnesium which have functioned so well as carbonates do not seem to give volatile organometallic compounds. Volatile organoaluminum compounds are known, however, as are volatile dialkyl zinc compounds. The boiling point of diethyl zinc at one atmosphere pressure is 123°C. Dimethyl zinc boils at 44°C and di-isobutyl zinc at 180°C. The aluminum compounds will be satisfactory neutralization agents while the dialkyl zinc compounds can be both neutralizing agents and buffers since they will deposit zinc oxide in the paper. In this and other work we have had the advice and assistance of two consultants to the Preservation Office, Dr. C. H. Fisher, formerly head of the U. S. D. A. Southern Regional Laboratory and now Adjunct Professor of Chemistry at Roanoke College, and Dr. H. Jonassen, Irby Professor of Chemistry at Tulane University.

The organoaluminum and organozinc compuounds are made in large quantities as catalysts for the polymerization of

olefins. They are dangerous and must be handled with proper
equipment and by trained people since they are pyrophoric and
burst into flame on contact with air and react explosively with
water. There is no problem, however, in using the materials in
books in an evacuated autoclave or in neutralizing the excess
reagent after the books have been treated. Since the zinc
alkyls readily react with the hydroxyl groups of cellulose, there
is also a mechanism for holding the zinc in the paper. The zinc
cellulose compound will then be hydrolyzed on the first contact
of the paper with the moisture of air to regenerate cellulose and
form zinc oxide. Zinc oxide is an innocuous paper-loading
material which is already widely used in copying papers. For
laboratory work, diethyl zinc is supplied as a 15% solution in
heptane, which is not pyrophoric under normal circumstances but
which is extremely flammable and requires great care in use.

The work with the dialkyl zinc and the organoaluminum compounds has been greatly advanced by assistance given
by Mr. Robert Brand of the Stauffer Chemical Company. In the
first experiment, Mr. Brand dipped a number of our test papers
into several concentrations of diethyl zinc and also into a
combination of an organoaluminum and organomagnesium compound.
This work was done under nitrogen. The papers were then given
accelerated aging in the dry and humid ovens and tested in the
L. C. laboratory.

The untreated papers all dropped in pH in the oven
aging, but this change was prevented by even the most dilute DEZ
dip. The buffering value of the zinc oxide is evidently adequate.

Some of the current neutralization and buffering
treatments raise the pH of the paper as high as ten. This causes
a loss of brightness, especially in groundwood-containing papers.
The DEZ treatment is notable in that the pH of the paper is
hardly raised above the neutral value.

Diethyl Zinc in Vapor Phase

The use of metal alkyls as a vapor phase deacidi-
fier requires relatively simple apparatus but great care and
rigid attention to detail for safe operation. In the work
reported here, 15% diethyl zinc in octane was employed. The
apparatus consisted of a heated vacuum chamber with a pump which
could be operated at about 0.05 mm of mercury absolute pressure.
Nitrogen or carbon dioxide was available for purging the
apparatus. The metal alkyl was transferred to the chamber

without contact with air or moisture by the use of a nitrogen-filled hypodermic syringe.

The material to be deacidified is placed in the chamber and the chamber evacuated until the pressure drops to less than 0.1 mm of mercury, absolute, and holds at this pressure when the pump is shut off for ten minutes. This is to make sure that the books are absolutely dry. Even traces of moisture inhibit the penetration of the alkyls, causing reaction to take place in the outer sheets and edges of the book leaving the center unchanged in acidity or inadequately treated. With dry material the penetration has been excellent in our experiments.

When the books are thoroughly dry, the metal alkyl solution (preferably diethyl zinc) is introduced into the reaction vessel which is heated to produce the metal alkyl gas.

Neutralization of the book or paper is extremely rapid and is accomplished in a few minutes, but exposures of 30 minutes to several hours are necessary to achieve a reasonable alkaline reserve in the paper. Temperatures of 40-60°C have been used in our experiments but this can be changed by varying the pressure within the vacuum chamber. Higher temperatures and pressures give a more rapid neutralization. The 60°C temperature and about 90 mm pressure represents a good compromise of rapid neutralization with moderate temperature exposure of the books. With rare or extremely valuable materials, longer exposure times and lower temperature would be employed to achieve the same results.

After treatment, the chamber is cooled, purged with dry nitrogen and the excess metal alkyl destroyed by addition of a small amount of alcohol. The chamber can then be opened and the books safely removed. The residue of diluent vapor left in the books diffuses away rapidly, particularly if the books are left in a current of air after being removed from the chamber. Alternatively, the diluent can be removed from the chamber by vacuum to the condenser traps protecting the pump.

With this method we have impregnated papers with zinc oxide at levels ranging from 0.5% to as much as 9.6%. Typical examples of impregnation obtained in a single treatment with nine different papers are shown in Table I. From the table it can be seen that the papers vary significantly in the amount of zinc oxide absorbed in a one hour treatment. These treatments were with the diluted diethyl zinc solution. However, the undiluted form should be much more efficient and rapid in its action. Studies with the undiluted material are in progress at this time.

The pure diethyl zinc vapor does not harm paper in our treatment. It can be seen from Table I that the diethyl zinc treatment has completely neutralized the acidity in the various papers and left a significant alkaline reserve in each case.

Several of these papers were subjected to accelerated aging tests in both the dry and humid ovens to demonstrate the effectiveness of the treatment in preserving the paper. Since these treatments are regarded as minimal treatment, the results are merely an indication that the treatment does prolong the life of the paper. We expect to substantially increase the amount of zinc oxide deposition as our work progresses and thereby to substantially increase the fold retention of the treated sheets and the brightness of the paper.

Table II shows the effect of the treatment on accelerated aging in the dry oven at $100^{\circ}C$. The newsprint apparently was not improved by the treatment when tested in the dry oven, but the Mead Bond and the offset paper show substantial gains in fold retention as a result of the treatment. The brightness was not affected by the treatment at this level of impregnation, but it has been recently demonstrated in our laboratory that higher levels of impregnation do result in improved brightness. Detailed data on the results are not available at this time.

The results for the humid oven aging are shown in Table III. Surprisingly the treatment shows up quite well on newsprint in the humid aging oven. The other two papers also show the significant retention of fold endurance in humid oven aging as they did with the dry oven aging.

We do not know exactly why the newsprint shows the difference in aging characteristics between the dry and humid aging oven. However, since the low humidity existing in the dry aging oven would not be experienced in normal aging except for a library in desert areas, it is believed that the treatment will be beneficial even for newsprint under all reasonable storage conditions. In the humid oven there appears to be some slight loss in brightness for the treated offset paper but the Mead bond is unaffected in brightness and the newsprint actually shows a significant improvement. All together, the diethyl zinc vapor phase treatment appears extremely interesting and promises a true mass vapor phase deacidification that will be effective for a mild bulk treatment of books, not only to neutralize acidity but also to produce a significant alkaline reserve in the books with little or no loss of brightness.

TABLE I

Impregnation of Papers with Diethyl Zinc
Vapor Phase--One Hour Treatment

Paper	pH		% Zinc Oxide in Paper After Treatment
	Before Treatment	After Treatment	
Newsprint	5.4	7.8	0.89
Offset Paper (LCIB)*	5.8	7.9	2.02
Made Rite Offset	5.6	8.2	1.48
Whatman Filter Paper, #1	6.6	8.1	0.94
100% Rag Ledger (GPO #773)	6.2	8.0	1.37
Old Book Paper (Rag) Published 1820	5.3	8.1	0.79
Berestoke Text (Handmade)	4.7	7.6	1.42
Crane's Distaff Linen, Antique Laid	5.2	7.7	0.54
Mead Bond	5.9	7.7	0.82

*Library of Congress Information Bulletin paper.

TABLE II

Diethyl Zinc Vapor Phase Treatment of Paper
Effect on Accelerated Aging Characteristics

Dry Oven Aging--100°C

		Characteristics			
	Equivalent	MIT Folding			
	Years	Endurance*		Brightness	
Paper	Aging	Control	Treated	Control	Treated
Newsprint	Zero--Start	118	135	54	53
	67 Years	2.3	3.2	--	--
	117 Years	1.5	1.7	40	41
Mead Bond	Zero--Start	465	476	84	83
	67 Years	64	274	77	77
	117 Years	25	92	75	76
Offset (LCIB)**	Zero--Start	604	652	76	75
	67 Years	207	432	71	71
	117 Years	20	252	70	7C

*1/2 Kg load.

**Library of Congress Information Bulletin paper.

TABLE III

Diethyl Zinc Vapor Phase Treatment of Paper
Effect on Accelerated Aging Characteristics

Humid Oven Aging--90°C, 50% R. H.

Paper	Equivalent Years Aging	Characteristics			
		MIT Folding Endurance*		Brightness	
		Control	Treated	Control	Treated
Newsprint	Zero--Start	118	135	54	53
	67 Years	3.5	60	41	45
	117 Years	0.6	36	36	41
Mead Bond	Zero--Start	465	476	84	83
	67 Years	92	134	77	78
	117 Years	54	122	75	74
Offset (LCIB)**	Zero--Start	604	652	76	75
	67 Years	240	441	72	69
	117 Years	145	315	70	68

*1/2 Kg load.

**Library of Congress Information Bulletin paper.

VI: BINDING

Papers 18 Through 21: Commentary

Philip Smith, a creative designer-bookbinder *par excellence,* has described what bookbinding is all about: "Binding methods consist in a variety of solutions to the problem of holding a number of leaves together and accessible to use and resistant to wear for a prolonged period. . . . No simple formula can be given on what to do in binding a book, because each book is so different. . . ."[1] Herein lies the heart of the problem in binding library materials: A library is an assemblage of single books, and each book is different.

Binding perforce occupies the central position in library preservation programs, yet there are probably few libraries today that can claim that each volume that is sent for binding receives the individually considered treatment it warrants. Probably the best that most libraries can achieve is to design a program that provides for binding materials promptly and at the lowest cost commensurate with the method and style of binding desired. Beyond this, libraries should assure that the binding program is well managed, preferably under the supervision of a professional librarian, and that it is adequately staffed and funded.

The four articles selected for this section deal with those aspects of binding that are most frequently encountered in the administration of library binding programs: binding procedures, selection of outside binding contractors, and standards.

Douglas Cockerell's small book, *Some Notes on Bookbinding,* was published in 1929 and has been described as "hard to find but well worth looking for."[2] It deals entirely with fine binding, a type of binding most suitable for volumes that are rare and that should be entrusted only to the care of skilled artisans whose training and experience qualifies them to work on materials of this nature. Cockerell's "How to Judge a Binding" is a brief description of the salient points to look for when judging the work of a hand bookbinder.

"Binding Procedures and Programs in Libraries" by Betty Jane Dillon is a comprehensive description of widely practiced library procedures involving the first-time binding of materials, a type of binding sometimes referred to in the specialized vocabulary of the industry as job binding. Although this selection does not dwell on preservation aspects in particular, it is of value to librarians who manage binding operations as part of their overall conservation responsibilities. Binding operations cannot be slowed down or stopped to allow time for the newly appointed librarian to study the system and become familiar with the formidable detail involved.

Matt T. Roberts, Binding Officer at the Library of Congress, has contributed several timely articles to the literature on binding for libraries. He has thought deeply on preservation aspects of library binding as evidenced by his articles on machine oversewing and the role of the librarian in the binding operation, both of which are required reading for the librarian with responsibility for binding programs. "The Library Binder" provides invaluable information that until now has been difficult to acquire except through on-the-job training and wide reading.

The Library Technology Project's "Provisional Standards" have been the subject of controversy since their publication in 1966. They have not been accepted or officially endorsed by the American Library Association or the Book Manufacturers' Institute, and only in part by the Library Binding Institute. Nonetheless, they were drafted by librarians from all types of libraries and by other experts.[3] Until these proposed standards are superseded by something better, preservation librarians should have a detailed acquaintance with them, particularly when appraising the quality of binding that they may purchase from bookbinding firms.[4]

NOTES AND REFERENCES

1. Smith, Philip, *New Directions in Bookbinding* (New York: Van Nostrand Reinhold, 1974), pp. 23–24.
2. Cunha, George M., "Bibliography," *Conservation of Library Materials,* 2nd ed. (Metuchen, N.J.: Scarecrow Press, 1971–72), p. 294.
3. For the role of the Barrow Laboratory in developing performance standards for bookbinding, see "William James Barrow" in Part V of this collection.
4. There is evidence of renewed interest in performance standards and the evaluation of binding methods and materials on the part of LBI. See "Upgrading Binding Quality: Report on the New RIT/LBI Book Testing Laboratory," by Werner Rebsamen, Assistant Professor, School of Printing, Rochester Institute of Technology, in *Library Scene* 5 (December 1976): 27–28.

ADDITIONAL READINGS

Alpers, Fred, "Library Binding," in Cunha, George M., and Tucker, Norman P., *Library and Archives Conservation* (Boston: Library of The Boston Atheneum, 1972), pp. 163–79.

Clough, Eric A., *Bookbinding for Librarians* (London: Association of Assistant Librarians, 1957), 204 pp.

Horton, Carolyn, *Cleaning and Preserving Bindings and Related Materials,* 2nd ed., rev. (Chicago: Library Technology Project, American Library Association, 1969), 87 pp. *LTP Publications* No. 16.

Lakhanpal, S. K., *Library Binding Manual,* rev. ed. (Saskatoon: University of Saskatchewan, Murry Memorial Library, Serials Dept., 1972), 47 pp.

Lehmann-Haupt, Hellmut, "On the Rebinding of Old Books," in *Bookbinding in America, Three Essays,* H. Lehmann-Haupt, ed. (New York: Bowker, 1967), pp. 189–283.

Roberts, Matt T., "Oversewing and the Problem of Book Preservation in the Research Library," *College and Research Libraries* 28 (January 1967): 17-24.

——, "The Role of the Librarian in the Binding Process," *Special Libraries* 62 (October 1971): 416-18.

Tauber, Maurice, ed., *Library Binding Manual; a Handbook of Useful Procedures for the Maintenance of Library Volumes* (Boston: Library Binding Institute, 1972), 185 pp.

18: HOW TO JUDGE A BINDING

Douglas Cockerell

Fine or 'Extra' Bindings

ALL bindings should protect the books they cover and should facilitate their use, but fine bindings aim at being something more than merely utilitarian covers: they should be minor works of art. In their making they demand fine craftsmanship working on fine materials, craftsmanship aiming at serviceable beauty rather than mechanical exactness, and it would be as reasonable to test the taste of a pudding by chemical analysis as it is to estimate the value of a work of art on the result of tests by square and compass. The proof of the pudding is in the eating, and the value of a thing of beauty lies in its appearance and fitness for its purpose. Sound construction and good workmanship there must be if a binding is to be satisfactory, for slovenly work is ugly and displeasing in its effect, but so also is the too hard machine-like finish that results from misapplied skill. A fine binding should in the first place be judged by its appearance and then can be examined in detail.

Sewing and Guarding

If a book opens reasonably well the sewing thread can be seen down the centre of each section and will show if the book has been sewn 'flexibly' round the cords or has been 'sawn in'. Care is needed in the first opening of a new binding, or the back may be broken. A few leaves should be opened at either end and gently pressed down, and then a few more until the centre is reached, thus easing the back. If the book is forced open in the centre without such easing, the back may

Reprinted by permission of the publisher from pages 78–85 of *Some Notes on Bookbinding,* London: Oxford University Press, 1929, 105pp.

crack, and a cracked back will not regain a good shape when the book is closed. When opening a book in this way, it can be seen if the pages have been neatly mended where necessary and if any plates and single leaves have been attached by guards. The connexion between the end-papers and the book should be examined to see that there is no tendency for them to break away. In estimating the quality of a free opening, the thickness and flexibility of the paper in relation to the size of the page must be taken into consideration. Some books by their nature cannot be made to open pleasantly.

Joints

The connexion between the book and its boards should be examined carefully, for it is here that many bindings fail in use. Some evidence there should be of the slips having been laced in if the book has been bound and not cased. The boards should fall shut freely of their own weight, and should not gape when the book is closed, which means that the leather, slips, and end-paper (or leather joint) should together be thin enough to be readily bent by the weight of the board. On a small book with light boards, leather and slips must be very thin, but this does not matter, as in such a book the strain on the joint is very slight, but for a heavy book the slips and leather must be proportionately thicker.

Some one started the theory that if a book is held up by the fore-edge, if the leaves and the boards are allowed to fall they should touch. This is a foolish test, for such extreme flexibility is incompatible with adequate strength. Generally, provided that the joint is reasonably free, neat, and square, some slight creasing of the outside leather on opening and some indication of the lacing in of the slips should not be objected to. and extreme flexibility may be looked upon with suspicion.

Freely opening joints that allow the board to open without affecting the adjoining pages of the book are of comparatively recent introduction. The old binders left leather and slips comparatively thick and their boards seldom opened freely and squarely, and generally a few leaves of the book were raised by the opening of the board.

End-papers

The paper for the ends should be of about the same colour and weight as that of the book. For books written or printed on vellum, vellum ends should be used, generally with a leather joint, as vellum pasted down in the joint is apt to be stiff. There is much to be said for the use of a coloured paste-down paper for fine bindings, because the turn in of the leather stains plain ends. Marble paper, that may in itself be interesting, is very suitable for the paste-down leaves, as having a mottled surface it shows stains less than any other paper. Silk ends are sometimes used on fine books, but they seldom look quite satisfactory. If the edges of the silk are turned in they make an unsightly lumpy edge, and if merely cut are apt to fray out. Any coloured ends have to be 'made' (pasted on) on to the adjoining white leaf, and consequently, if an over-thick leaf is to be avoided, the paste-down paper should be thin, but it should also be of good quality or it may split in the joint.

Sometimes the insides of the boards of fine books are lined with leather and decorated, and occasionally the opposite fly-leaf is also of thin leather.

Edges

Very few old books or modern books of value should have their edges cut with the plough. The fore-edge and tail of modern books printed on hand-made paper may quite reasonably be slightly trimmed if some uncut edges are left as 'proof' that the book has not been unduly cropped. These trimmed edges may be gilt in the rough before sewing. To get an edge that can be gilt 'solid' it must be cut down almost to the shortest leaves, and this in many cases would involve too great a reduction in size. It is fitting that the head should be gilt solid, as the head of a book, other than a true folio, consists of folds of paper which, if cut at all, will be solid.

There is little objection to cutting and gilding solid the edges of a modern book printed on machine-made paper, but if it is the first cutting the binder should endeavour to leave some 'proof'.

Squares

These are the projections of the boards beyond the edges of the leaves. They should be of even width and generally about as deep as the thickness of the leather-covered board. With an uncut book the squares cannot be controlled exactly, and generally, although evenness in the squares is a thing to be aimed at, its importance can easily be exaggerated.

Backing

The shape of the back of a book depends upon the backing and the amount of the swelling. A well-backed book should have an evenly convex back when closed, that will become flat or concave when opened. It is better for the back to be rather flat than too round, and anything approaching a half-circle either obstructs the opening or causes too great a movement in the back. A 'flexible' back should be flexible, and if it is lined up stiffly the special qualities of flexibility and toughness that make leather so admirable a covering for books is sacrificed. (See Fig. 29.) On the other hand, too great flexibility makes a floppy book that won't retain its shape or support the weight of the leaves.

FIG. 29

Generally fine bindings for normal books should have the leather attached directly to the backs of the sections, although for heavy books an underlining of leather is sometimes required. Sometimes, however, exceptional books are best bound with a hollow back without projecting bands and with a 'French joint'. It is difficult and sometimes impossible for the binder to get a well-shaped flexible back on a book that has irregular-sized sections, or that is printed on paper too thick and stiff for the size of the pages. The back of a book should be flexible enough to allow the leaves to open, yet firm enough to keep its shape and prevent the leaves from sagging.

Headbands

These should be worked with silk over vellum or gut and should be firm. They should be a little lower than the height of the squares.

Boards

The best millboard is very tough and hard, and the boards should be firm and stiff and should curve very slightly towards the book. Heavy boards on a small book look clumsy, and thin boards on a heavy book are not stiff enough to bear the weight.

The Covering

The leather on a well-bound book should look as if it had grown there; it should be free from unevenness caused by faulty paring, and the edges of the boards should be square and even in thickness and the head-caps should be well and symmetrically shaped. The 'turn-in' of the leather on the inner sides of the boards should be even and the corners should be neatly mitred. While it is well that the edges of the boards should be square, extreme sharpness is not desirable, as this can only be got by paring the leather 'paper thin'. A certain softness of the edges, indicating that there is a reasonable thickness of leather, should not be objected to.

The leather may or may not be crushed and polished, its colour and texture should be pleasant, and there should be no objection to slight unevenness in the dyeing. If there is a leather joint, this should be of the same thickness as the turn-in of the cover, and should join the turn-in a little way down from the head and tail, so that enough of the leather of the cover may be left in the joint to take the strain of opening the boards. The inner surface of the boards should be filled in level with the leather margin before the board-paper is pasted down.

A book should stand squarely and the bands should be evenly spaced and straight across the back. The space below the bottom band and the tail should be rather longer than the space between the bands and between the top band and the head. When there are two or more volumes in a set, the books should be of the same height and the bands 'range' evenly.

Finishing: Lettering

Lettering should be well spaced and the letters should be good in form and as large as the nature of the title and the size of the back panel will allow, and there should be no objection made to the use of obvious contractions or to the turning over of long words when this makes for greater clearness and pleasant arrangement. The arrangement of the lettering on the back of a book should be as carefully designed as any other part of the ornament and should be treated as a decorative feature of great value. It is desirable that letters should be in line and upright, but, provided that there is no glaring irregularity, exact evenness is of no very great importance.

Decoration

The gold-tooling of both lettering and ornament should be bright and clean and the glair should not show on the leather, but it is easy to exaggerate the importance of mere mechanical dexterity in finishing. Decoration aims at beauty; the degree of beauty achieved is the true measure of its value, and it is from this angle it should be judged.

The shape of the book, the colour and texture of the leather, headbands and end-papers, and the arrangement of the lettering, make with the purely ornamental features a single unit of design that should be judged as a whole. The binding as a whole will be pleasant or unpleasant to handle and to use, not because it has or has not reached some particular standard of mechanical exactness, but because it is or is not in some degree a work of art.

Bindings for Exceptional Books

Exceptional books call for special treatment, and their binding will often tax the ingenuity and skill of the binder. Sometimes books consisting of single leaves are best overcast, and sometimes it is necessary to guard every leaf. Some books will be wedge-shaped in spite of anything the binder can do. In judging such books the difficulties presented and the way these have been overcome have to be taken into consideration.

Less Expensive Bindings

While it is unreasonable to expect the same perfection of workmanship on bindings over which the binder has been hurried as on those with which he has had time to do his best, there is no reason why comparatively inexpensive bindings should not be sound in construction and pleasant in colour and in shape.

A book sewn on tapes, with the tape slips firmly secured to the boards, and with a tight leather back and a French joint can be thoroughly strong and flexible, and may be very pleasant to use. Leather can be saved by making the portion on the boards narrow and by omitting leather corners.

A book sewn on tapes with 'split' boards and a French joint can be covered with buckram or stout woven material and will be quite serviceable. Such a book will have a hollow back.

The ordinary binding of the trade with sawn-in bands and hollow back and thin leather has little strength, and in every considerable library many such bindings may be seen with their backs falling away.

19: BINDING PROCEDURES AND PROGRAMS IN LIBRARIES

Betty Jane Dillon

Binding procedures are the steps taken to ensure the preservation of written, printed, or near-print material through a process of attaching permanent covers to the gathered pages.

In libraries and in information services these procedures include such matters as the assignment of authority for materials preservation, the selection of a binder or binders, and the allocating of budget for current binding and of special funds for retrospective binding, as well as the establishing of those library routines necessary for the prebinding of new volumes, the binding of periodicals, and the rebinding of worn volumes.

It has been good practice to assign one person the responsibility for the binding program. He works with the administration on the allocation of binding funds, and the selection of a binder. He works with the acquisitions department on the determination of the binding of new acquisitions. He works with the public service departments on the rebinding or replacement of worn materials and the scheduling of binding. He sets up priorities and establishes the routines for a binding unit and selects and trains the personnel to carry them out. He may have had some instruction in library school related to this work, but much of it he will have to learn on the job and through the library literature. One of his best aids will be the bindery representative who will alert him to new materials, improved methods, safe price-saving corners to cut, and ways to handle difficult categories of materials. As a guest of the bindery he will acquaint himself with how a book is bound, the materials and skills used, the criteria for sturdy bindings, and the steps which can be taken within the library to facilitate the work of the binder, thus ensuring more prompt service.

Library budgets must be carefully planned to provide adequate funds for the maintenance as well as the acquisition and servicing of materials. In 1964 the Library Binding Institute conducted a survey which disclosed that public libraries and college and university libraries allocate about 10% of their total book and periodical budget for their binding. This percentage would have been higher except for the fact that book and periodical prices have gone up since 1948–1949 at about double the rate of binding prices. A basic estimate of binding cost such as $1 for every $8 spent on new books might serve for an initial budget estimate. This would be adjusted as soon as careful cost studies based on actual work done could be made. The budget must be revised from time to time to reflect changes in library acquisitions and changes in binding materials and standards. Current factors which might change these percentages are the increasing proportion of publications issued as paperbacks, the expansion of exchange programs between libraries, and the assumption of responsibility for acquiring materials in an area where many of the works are received unbound. These developments bring into the library a volume of material which, if it is to be retained any appreciable period of time, needs prebinding. Sound budgeting will also dictate that extraordinary acquisitions be accompanied with additional binding funds. Thus the acceptance of large gifts, the purchase of collections or private libraries, or the designation of the library as a depository for governmental publications or technical reports may necessitate special binding funds not available in the current budget.

It is not considered good practice to permit arrearages to accumulate. Proper budgeting and a periodic review of the collection can prevent them. Where they already exist they are a drain on the library's resources. Shabby, faded volumes, especially fiction and children's books, sit on the shelf unused, while other works are purchased to satisfy the reader demand. Rebound, they again become a vital part of the collection. With periodicals, deferred binding or rebinding can cause loss of valuable material, either irreplaceable or replaceable only at considerable expense. Attempts to work these arrearages into the regular binding schedule is usually unsuccessful unless priorities are established and can be maintained. The better plan is to make a complete survey and then fund it outside the regular binding budget.

Historically the purpose of binding has been for the preservation of the written word. Hence, prior to the book as we know it, we find small Assyrian clay tablets with their cuneiform inscriptions enveloped in outer shells also of clay, and early Egyptian papyrus rolls preserved in rectangular grooves cut out of wood, dyptychs protected with wooden or ivory covers hinged at the back with leather thongs, rolled-up scrolls of vellum, papyrus, or paper encased in cylinders of similar shape, and finally the orithon, fan-folded progenitor of the book, its pages guarded by boards and generally fastened along one side in the manner of a spine. With the illuminated manuscript in book form came the development of fine bindings, splendid work in leathers and metals ornamented with jewels, enamels, and carved ivory, the work of great craftsmen. The development of printing not only increased the availability of books, it also brought in the "publishers' binding," often of poor quality and workmanship. For those who wished their books, normally available only in sheets or these coarse paper covers, to be either long lasting or pleasing to the eye, there still existed a tradition of fine bindings of tooled leathers, velvets and satins, sometimes set with enamels or embroidered, and of fine binders, often family firms carrying the pride of their workmanship from father to son and grandson. These two classes of binders exist to this day (i.e., the publishers' binder and the fine or craft binder), but they have been joined with two other classes, the commercial binder, specializing in ledgers and similar binding, and the library binder, who, while concerned primarily with sturdy binding for libraries, is often also a family firm, substituting mechanical methods where possible for hand methods, but maintaining quality and service. Some of these voluntarily join trade groups (modern counterparts of the medieval guild) with rigid standards of performance. Such a trade group in the United States is the Library Binding Institute.

The selection of a binder must be made with care. The choice of whether to send material to a commercial binder or to maintain a bindery in the library is the first decision that must be made. As binderies become more and more mechanized the investment in machinery alone precludes considering one for most libraries, while spiraling labor costs, lack of trained help, and excessive labor turnover create constantly rising operational costs for those libraries already maintaining their own binderies. A home bindery is of greatest value in university libraries and some research libraries where the constant demand for the materials and the great value of some items make it advisable to keep them on the premises. Although these binderies may be able to compete on a price basis with the commercial bindery on such work as oversize books, sheet music, slip cases and portfolios, they seldom can compete on the general run of binding or satisfactorily handle extra heavy binding.

Local facilities and unusual circumstances naturally will affect the decision. A school teaching binding as a craft or an art may do some of its library binding. An institution with a supply of unpaid or low-paid workers available (such as institutions staffed by members of a religious order, or colleges where students are assigned to the library as part of a scholarship grant or work-study program) may utilize this help in binding-type operations such as reinforcing bindings, including paperbacks, and recasing books where the stitching has not been broken. These activities, however, should be limited to materials designated for eventual discard or replacement, and while they help to stretch the binding dollar they cannot take the place of a commercial binder. In those institutions having binderies such as a university press, relations should be the same as with an outside binder. If the librarian does not insist on this he may find library binding being pushed aside in favor of the press books, while standards may be reduced to those of publishers' bindings, and costs, rather than meeting competitive standards, may be so raised as to help subsidize the other work of the press.

Commercial binders are selected through competitive bidding or through free selection. Where it is required that bids be submitted for binding and the expectation is that the binding will be jobbed out to the lowest bidder (as in certain school districts, state institutions, and municipal libraries) some of the more established binders may decide not to submit bids, fearing that to make a sufficiently low bid to secure the work they would have to lower their standards or run the risk of losing money on the contract. This does not mean that the library must settle for inferior binding. If the librarian provides specific data regarding the size and condition of the volumes to be bound and requires workmanship and materials of a certain quality to be written into the specifications, the work should be satisfactory. It should go without saying that a bindery not meeting the requirements of its contract should forfeit the right to bid on future contracts.

Where free choice is permitted, the library should take into consideration the binder's reputation for good workmanship, his accessibility, the length of time he keeps materials and the care he gives them while in his charge, his ability to handle the quantity of work sent him, the financial responsibility he assumes, and the auxiliary services he offers, as well as his price schedule.

Although there is no required system of certification for binders, membership in a national trade association such as the Library Binding Institute does offer a guarantee that the binder is reputable in his dealings and maintains clearly defined standards. Binders, not members of such a certifying group may do quite adequate work based on the same specifications as those used by the certified binders. For reassurance on this point it is advisable to visit the bindery if possible and to consult with other libraries using their services. While it is not necessary for the binder to be in the same town, or even state, as the library it does offer clear advantages. Transportation expense is reflected in pricing, often showing up in special discounts rather than in the price schedule; pick-ups can be made on a more frequent basis, and "rush" items can be delivered by messenger rather than through the mails.

In the case of the public library use of a local tax-paying concern is good business, and in the case of a college or university library such use represents good public relations. The length of time a binder keeps material is the length of time the material is unavailable to the user. Proper scheduling assures prompt pick-ups and deliveries, and proper spacing of workloads so that the rush of school library books in the summer or other foreseeable demands do not backlog the books sent by other customers, nor do vacations disrupt regular binding schedules. It also demonstrates consideration on the part of the binder for its customer. In general a pick-up once a month is sufficient. Libraries requiring less frequent pick-ups usually notify the bindery when material will be ready.

Adequate care demands that loading and unloading should be carefully done, that the bindery should be fireproof, clean, dry, and with good air circulation. Should the amount of work to be bound be greater than the bindery can properly handle, it would be well to consider sending material to two binders. In this case they should be carefully selected to complement each other. It is not well to split up one type of binding, as this requires greater work in the binding unit of the library. All journals could be sent to one binder, while another does the monographic material. Since binders sometimes offer price inducements for quantity binding, this factor should be considered carefully before dividing the work. If possible, changing of binders should be avoided, for working out the problems encountered is more advantageous than choosing another binder. Often the services a new binder offers are already being offered or can be initiated by the current binder, and the lack is not in availability but in communication.

The binder should assume financial responsibility for the materials in his care. "Full coverage" listed by some binders is a misleading term and should be clarified. The Library Binding Institute is quite specific on this point. It provides "all-risk" coverage with the limit of responsibility for any volume being the sum equivalent to five times the selling price of the binding for such a volume, the maximum value of any single volume being limited to $25. For any volume on which the customer places a value in excess of this it will, upon notification in writing from the customer stating the value and the amount of coverage desired, obtain the coverage requested.

Other services the binder may reasonably be expected to offer are maintaining in stock such cloths and buckrams as the library has chosen, supplying the library with samples of cover materials upon which to base selections and securing picture covers for juvenile books when available. A good bindery follows a mutually agreeable list of general binding instructions prepared by the library, maintains a rubbing or pattern file for use in the uniform preparation of serial publications or sets, and supplies the library with instruction sheets for developing instructions for the first binding of these titles. The binder sends the library notifications of pick-up schedules and supplies boxes for convenient packing of materials, and shipping labels if needed. (If he pays the cost of shipment, he, quite properly, will usually stipulate the method of shipment.) Often the binder will provide assistance in evaluating the binding needs of the library, in working out a binding program, and in solving specific binding problems, and will alert the library to new materials, possible cost-savings, and shortcuts in the preparation routines, records, and similar matters.

Binding prices are competitive but slight variations do occur since there are variations in labor costs (about 40–45% of the total cost). If the price list of one binder is considerably under that of the others, the library should be sure that the guaranteed workmanship and quality are suitable, that errors are to be corrected, that there will not be an excessive return of books difficult to bind as books "not worth binding," that the lower prices quoted do not refer only to quantity shipments, and that extra cost is not above average for hand sewing, oversize volumes, and additional lines of lettering.

Billing procedures should be acceptable to the library, conforming to the requirements of its accounting department.

Having chosen the binder, the library must show its confidence in its choice by giving the binder certain freedom to make changes without prior permission if these do not seriously affect the quality of the materials or the work, nor substantially increase the price. It must also acknowledge its obligations by not making unreasonable demands, by recognizing the need to pay for extra demands, and by paying its bills promptly.

Bindings should be appropriate to the type of material and to the expected use to which they are to be put. Early binding for libraries stressed strength, appearance being only a secondary consideration. Books were usually bound in half-leather with cloth sides. Magazines and newspapers were generally bound with leather backs and corners and with cloth sides. Lettering was stamped in gold. Scarcity of leather during World War I led to the use of cloth for the entire cover. The early Karatols, Fabrikoids and starch-filled buckrams were unsatisfactory as none proved flexible enough to use as a tight back, and over-sewing by hand was necessary. An over-sewing machine was invented which proved very satisfactory, but not all early binding machines were adequate and library binding at this period varied from very good to very poor.

As a result the need for standards was recognized and the first specifications for library binding as a distinct kind of binding appeared. In 1935 the American Library Association issued its "Minimum Specifications for Class A Library Binding," followed in 1939 by its "Standards for Reinforced (Pre-Library Bound) New Books," issued with the Library Binding Institute. These standards have been combined and have been revised as needed to reflect new materials and new processes by the Library Binding Institute and are referred to by their certified binders as "LBI Standard for Library Binding." Other binders refer to this quality as "Class A binding, or Library binding."

Surveys made in 1954 and 1961 to determine the uses of volumes bound according to this standard showed an average of 104 circulations or uses, with some of the libraries reporting as high as 140 (in contrast, publishers' editions averaged about 27). Acceptability was shown since 75% of the libraries said that they used it for 100% of their binding. This specification provides for standards of materials and construction, and includes mending, collating, and maintenance of rubs or patterns for periodicals. Reinforced binding generally follows the specifications for Class A binding but with such variations (preferably with little additional weight) as will strengthen the binding.

Because not all library material needs quality binding the American Library Association has also approved minimum specifications for little-used materials. These are referred to as LUMSPECS. For these, Class A specifications are followed in relation to materials where applicable, but covers consist of hard-rolled binder's boards with buckram spines. Lettering can be added at extra cost. If lettering is needed the library may be wise to use Class A binding. Various types of bindings termed "Pamphlet" bindings are available. These eliminate mending and collating, offer little choice of color, and use only standard lettering. No patterns are kept but all volumes of a serial received in a single shipment can be bound alike. One form of pamphlet binding substitutes for lettering the mounting of paper covers on the front. This type is excellent for the prebinding of books and serials which will not have heavy usage.

The need·to find a less expensive process for binding paperbacks led to the development of the "perfect binding." This substitutes an adhesive for sewing. New materials have made these adhesive bindings as durable as oversewn bindings. They are not suitable for large or heavy volumes or coated papers. They are excellent for cheap and porous papers, for publications with narrow inner margins and where it is desirable for a book to open flat without undue strain on the spine. Binders are able to make up special variations on any of these bindings suitable to the individual needs of their customers. They are also equipped to make up cases for books too fragile to bind, portfolios for art works or for holding newspapers until microfilm copies are received, storage boxes, and binders for loose-leaf materials.

The same materials do not necessarily need the same type of bindings in all libraries. Estimates of their useful life in the collection and of the extent of use that will be made of them will help to determine the most economic form. Over-binding can be as wasteful as under-binding. Materials receiving the heaviest use should be bound according to Class A or similar standards; those receiving less use but which for historical or research purposes will be of value over a long period of time will also need this type of binding. Usually, large or heavy volumes and those which will receive extraordinary use should have reinforced bindings. Indexes, bibliographies, dictionaries, encyclopedias, book catalogs, and similar reference works are among those needing this special handling.

Permanent material which it may be inadvisable to bind are fragile, rare and expensive items, archives, and newspapers. For their protection they may be microfilmed for use and the binder can assist in protecting the originals. He can make slip covers or boxes for the fragile materials (rare materials may require laminating). He can make up file envelopes, and specially sized flat storage boxes for archives. For unique or beautiful works he may make up "Fine" bindings, especially if they are a part of a special collection, gifts, or vault or rare-book items. Newspapers can be bound in canvas covers or even in an economy form of binding, consisting of stout boards covered with a paperlike material with cloth or leather spines, providing care is taken that the volumes are not too heavy for an average assistant to handle. Some newspapers of small size (such as the weekly *Economist*) can be bound as periodicals. In this case it is often advisable to subscribe to the airmail or the edition on bindable paper. For the average newspaper substitution of a microfilm copy is advisable, with only special sections (as the *New York Times Magazine* and its *Book Review* supplement) being bound as periodicals.

Material which is not considered as permanent to the collection should be so treated if its initial use is heavy enough to warrant it. In some cases the library prefers to purchase multiple copies to satisfy heavy initial demand and bind only one copy for the occasional later request of which much current fiction, some reserve-room titles for infrequently given courses, and textbooks which are frequently revised would be examples. Class A quality binding should, of course, be specified for the copies retained.

Transitory material or materials having limited use can be bound according to the *Specifications for Lesser-Used Materials* or the binder can develop a type of suitable binding. A more durable binding is not needed except, perhaps, in school libraries.

Handling of problem materials should be worked out between the binder and the library. For music the library may request each sheet to be hinged, and pockets or envelopes made for loose parts. For technical reports some form of pamphlet or storage boxes may be needed. For specifications and other material subject to frequent revision some form of loose binder may be the answer.

Other choices relating to the binding are those of color and lettering. Monographs can well be left to the binder, saving the time of the binding librarian, but journals will need to have the color indicated on the initial instructions which accompany the first volume sent for binding. Medium and dark shades are preferable since these files are a part of the permanent collection and are often bound at varying times over a period of years. The darker shades show less soil, are more easily matched if the original fabric has been discontinued, and better set off the white lettering generally used. If two files with fairly similar titles are known to stand beside each other it is advisable to have them bound in contrasting colors to prevent misshelving.

Standard lettering is preferable since it is clear and easily read. White stands out best on medium and dark bindings, black on lighter colors if used. For books in literature and the arts the binder might be requested to use lighter colors, patterned covers, and occasionally colored lettering. Adults, like children, are attracted by the unusual and the varied. For children's books every effort should be made to entice the youthful reader. Bright colors, illustrations pasted on the covers, or covers with silk-screened illustrations on them should take the place of "dark covers that won't show fingerprints." The binder will be able to furnish the library with a list of illustrated covers available or he can be instructed to use them whenever it is possible to secure them or to have them made.

Having chosen a binder, an agreement on standards and materials for the different types of work and methods of invoicing and payment should be worked out. Certain general directions should be written up. Copies of these should be in the hands of both the binder and the library. The general directions may serve as a preparations manual for the binding unit. Once these instructions are in the hands of the binder no further instructions are necessary except to indicate changes or to give specific instructions for binding periodicals for the first time, or to indicate desired handling of materials or problems not covered by these instructions. A sample of such instructions (with suggested alternatives) follows.

INSTRUCTION TO .... BINDERY

LIBRARY: ....

EFFECTIVE DATE: ....

The binder should routinely notify the library of the date of the next pick-up by truck and the library will notify the binder by the return mail whether material is to be picked up at that time. (or: The binder will pick up material from the

FIGURE 1.

271

La
Emigración
de Braceros

—

Lazaro
Salinas

HD1525
L431

FIGURE 2.

library on the second Tuesday of each month. Notification will be sent the library in case this date is to be changed at any time.)

All material should be properly boxed and labeled and available at the stated time. Shipping lists will be included and the box containing the shipping list will be clearly marked. As far as quantity permits, material to receive similar treatment will be boxed together, and listed together on the shipping list.

Material will be returned to the library at the time of the next pick-up. Material designated RUSH will be returned prepaid to the library as soon as bound. Shipping or postage charges will be added as a separate item on the invoice.

Corrections will be returned with the next shipment unless requested RUSH. No correction or shipping charge will be made if the error is attributable to the bindery. In other cases a reasonable charge for the correction and the shipping charge will be added as separate items on the invoice.

Invoices will be mailed within one week of the return of the shipment and payment is to be made within sixty days of receipt of invoice.

Binding. Note: The library will attach special instructions to the volume, and so note on the shipping list, when these instructions are to be varied. Should the binder feel that a variation should be made to better the binding he may make it without consulting the library unless such a change would significantly affect the pricing of the binding or the uniformity of a set.

Monographs—Class A Binding. Collate. Return to library if more than six pages are missing. If less than six pages, bind with stubs. (Alternatives: Notify library of missing pages and hold volume; return volume.)

Covers. Choice of color is left to the binder.

Lettering. Black or white according to color of binding. Horizontal lettering on spine preferred. If lengthwise it should read from top to bottom (alternative: bottom to top). Where spine is too narrow for lettering, use front lettering (alternative: use front lettering enclosed in box).

No lines at top and bottom of spine. Title to be dropped ½ inch from top (it is indicated on title-page by one line under initial letter of first word and slash at end. It may be shortened if necessary). Author should be separated from title (it is indicated on title-page by two lines under initial letter of surname and slash at end). No first name or initials are to be used (Figures 1 and 2). Compound surnames must be given as marked on title-page. Corporate authors may be omitted if title is distinctive. Call numbers: Bottom row should be raised ½ inch from bottom of spine. If front lettering is used call number may be placed in lower left corner of front cover. Follow call number exactly as given for horizontal lettering. For vertical lettering, separate lines as given with dashes. The call number is written on the title-page (alternatives: verso of title-page; last page of text. Note: If on fly leaf it will be torn off as the covers are removed).

Monographs—Children's Books. Follow instructions for Class A binding. Use illustrated covers when available. In other cases use patterned covers and bright colors. Lettering may be colored when this is clearly legible.

Monographs—Pamphlet Binding. No lettering on spine or front cover except call number. Apply cover of publication to front.

Monographs—Reinforced Binding. Follow instructions for Class A binding with reinforcing. The binder will use his discretion on these volumes relative to amount of reinforcing needed.

Monographs—Paperbacks. Bind according to perfect binding specifications.

Periodicals—Class A Binding. Note: The library will send instructions with each new title, the bindery will keep these instructions on file for future volumes. When a title changes the library will send new instructions. The binder will keep the old instructions for use with volumes predating the change (Figure 3).

Bind in volumes as tied. If there are missing issues, return to library. (Alternatives: binder will secure missing issues; hold volume and notify library. Note: Binders generally prefer the library to hold the material and secure the missing issues since they have little room in their plants for dead material.)

Collate. Return to library if incomplete. (Alternatives: Notify library of missing pages and hold volume; return to library if more than 6 pages are missing, if less than 6 pages bind with stubs).

Covers. Library will choose color and fabric.

Lettering. Library will designate if other than white. Standard lettering, all capitals. Use arabic numbers *not* Roman. Use following forms (Figure 4):

VOL.   *not*   Vol., Vols., V., or VOLS.

NO.   *not*   No., Nos., N., or NOS.

PT.   *not*   Pt., Pts., PTS.

p. 1866–2051   *not*   pp. 1866–2051

col. 604–1208   *not*   cols. 604–1208

omit century in second half of date if same: 1898–1902 but 1903–10, *not* 1903–1910

sample: VOL. 1–2

   MAR.–APR.

   1965–66

Information for lettering will be marked on the title-page of the first volume

273

LETTERHEAD OF BINDER

PLEASE CHECK INFORMATION BELOW

NAME OF LIBRARY	HILLMAN (UNIV. OF PITTSBURGH)

Bindery Has Pattern . . . . ☐
1st Binding Make Pattern . . . . . ☑
Rub Sent . . . . ☐
Sample Sent . . . . ☐
Buckram Color No. 2293 . . . . ☐

Lettering Wanted on Spine

THE FOLLOWING NECES-
SARY FOR NEW TITLES
ONLY OR WHEN CHANG-
ING INSTRUCTIONS

Strip to Publishers Vol. . . . . . ☐
Bind Complete . . . . ☐
Bind As Is (Imperfect) . . . . ☐
Split If Too Thick . . . . ☑

JOURNAL
FOR THE
SCIENTIFIC
STUDY OF
RELIGION

Covers . . . . OUT ☑
. . . . IN ☐
Front Covers . . . . ONLY ☐
Ads . . . . OUT ☑
. . . . IN ☐
Editorials & Features . . OUT ☐
. . . . IN ☑
Index . . . . FRONT ☐
. . . . BACK ☑

VOL. 1-2

1961-63

Special Instructions:

Stub for index

FIGURE 3.

```
JOURNAL
FOR THE
SCIENTIFIC
STUDY OF
RELIGION




VOL. 1-2

1961-63
```

FIGURE 4.

being sent. If publication does not have volume title-page it will be indicated on first issue.

Library will send rub with binding instructions if old volumes are to be matched.

Make-up of Volume. Title-page placed at front of volume. Table of contents follows title-page. If table of contents is lacking and issues are to be bound intact, ignore. If table of contents is lacking and volume has index, ignore. If individual issues have contents, or contents on covers, bind these at front of volume in lieu of volume contents.

Covers are to be bound in when issues are paged separately. When paging is continuous covers are removed if they are not paged in. When there is significant text or information on covers, bind in even though they interrupt the paging or place together at end of volume. Index is bound at end unless it begins on verso of title-page or contents, in which case bind at front. (Alternative: bind at front, following Contents.) Advertisements: Remove if they are not paged in and contain no textual matter. (Alternatives: Bind in. Remove even though they contain such textual matter as book reviews and letters to the editor.) Maps, charts, and so forth are to be hinged and bound in place. (Alternative: Make pockets at end for loose maps, charts, and so forth.)

Supplements issued separately but designated as parts of an issue and paged continuously with that issue are bound in place but retain their covers. All supplements not paged in continuously even though designated as parts of an issue are bound at the end of the volume after a divider. These retain their covers also.

Proceedings and other special features, published in each issue but paged separately from the text of the issue and continuously with the same material in other issues, are bound at the end of the volume. They are separated from the volume index or from supplements with a divider. If they have their own index, this is paged with them, *not* with the index to the volume.

Periodicals—Reinforced Binding. Do not use unless designated on the pattern. If binder feels that such binding is warranted he should first consult the library. It may be decided to bind that title in small units instead.

SCHEDULING THE BINDING

Public libraries normally schedule the binding of their adult collection throughout the year. Since journals become bindable, i.e., completed, in large numbers in January and in July, normal loads may be scheduled by concentrating the rebinding of worn volumes in the lighter months. Heavy use of children's books during the summer months would suggest binding these during the school year. Children's books in school deposit collections can be bound during vacations but if the collections rotate it is desirable to have a surplus of volumes so that some newly bound volumes can be substituted for drab volumes at this rotation time. School libraries usually have their binding done during the summer vacation.

University libraries on a nine-month program, although they do have some binding done throughout the year, particularly periodicals, which might otherwise be lost, tend to concentrate their binding during the summer vacation. Those on an 11-month program spread the binding out during the year, trying to avoid heavy loads in the summer when the binderies are overloaded with children's books and school library work. An attempt is made not to have the most-used journals at the bindery during the term-paper period. Advance planning is also necessary to have needed materials bound before summer school, when there is usually an urgent need for educational materials for teachers fulfilling their certification requirements.

The scheduling of binding is the function of the public service departments which are well aware of these needs, but the binding unit can observe the flow of materials to the bindery and thus prevent all copies of a periodical volume or index going to the bindery at once when there are multiple subscriptions in the main library or in the main library and its branches or departmental libraries. It can also flag records for needed periodical titles so as to ensure that they will not be sent at critical times, or if sent they can be handled on a RUSH basis.

The Binding Unit and its Work

The binding unit is often also the unit of the library which cleans and mends books, especially children's books, and which prepares for the shelf materials not considered worth the expense of binding by inserting them in binders, or reinforcing the spines. In case of fire or flood the repository for damaged materials which must be properly handled to assure their continued worth. It is, of course, primarily the unit responsible for the binding preparation of library materials, and the watchdog for the library of binding standards. Binding records are kept here, as are the patterns which have been made up so that sets of books and runs of periodicals may be bound uniformly. Returns of shipments from the bindery are checked for quality and completeness, and invoices are checked and approved for payment. Often the budgeting of binding funds and the allocations to various departments are the responsibility of the binding librarian. Binders find this the place to sell their services, to introduce new binding methods, and, in times of emergency, to offer their advice and their immediate assistance. Although in a small library the librarian and a clerical worker must serve also as the binding unit, while in a large institution there may be special mending units, checking units, and accounting units, the responsibilities are the same: to ensure a collection of well-kept books and periodicals, available for public use.

BINDING ROUTINES

Routing Material to the Binding Unit. The binding unit does not initiate binding except as a part of a collection renovation program. New materials for prebinding are routed to it from the catalog department and from the serials department. Older materials are sent from the reference room, the circulation department, and the periodicals room via the serials department. Unless a branch library or a university departmental library handles its own binding, its materials also funnel through the binding unit. It is the responsibility of the initiating department or library to correctly mark the title-pages and to maintain their own records of the material sent to the binding unit with a record of date sent. The catalog department will note this on cards in its "control file," the reference and circulation departments on regular circulation charges, and the serials department on its check-in records. Periodical room records will simply show that the material has been sent to the serials department as for other material leaving that area.

When the book has been cataloged prior to sending to the bindery the call number and the proper form of the author's name can be stamped on the binding. This is a good way to handle material when books are cataloged upon receipt either from entries in the National Union Catalog and its predecessors, or with the use of Library of Congress proof sheets or "Title II" cards, or by original cataloging. Where books are held prior to cataloging for sets of Library of Congress cards, it may be preferable to send them to the bindery while waiting. In this case call numbers will have to be added by the library and the form of the author's name may be at variance with that used on the catalog entry (the situation which obtains when books are received bound with publishers' titles). When books are sent before cataloging, a title-page need only be marked if confusing, as in the case of compound names or names with prefixes, or if the cataloger knows that a change should be made, as in the case of a name which he recognizes as a pseudonym which the library does not use. Special instructions will be given if he feels that a cover should be bound in to retain a series note not found elsewhere, or to preserve an illustration, but such special instructions will be rare. A preliminary work card or a copy of the L.C. card order can accompany the book to the binding unit. It will be held there and returned to the catalog department with the bound book.

When books are sent after cataloging the title-page is marked according to the lettering desired, including the call number. Again, special instructions are given if necessary. The book card and pocket are made out and sent with the book to the binding unit. They will be held there and inserted in the book upon its return from the binder. The catalog department will send the work card to the typing unit for make-up of the shelf list card and cards for the card catalog. These will be sent to the binding unit upon completion. The binding unit will keep them with the book cards and pockets.

Books sent from the circulation department should have title-pages properly marked. If the call number is on a fly-leaf where it will be torn off, it should be copied onto the title-page. The binding unit will make slips for these, giving author, title, and call number.

Books sent from the reference department should have title-pages properly marked and should be accompanied by a sample volume if they are to match other books in a set. (If such set is bound in calf, or in buckram with colored labels, and it is anticipated that the entire set will eventually be rebound, it might be advisable to bind in a matching shade of buckram but not try otherwise to match the old volumes.) If a continuation or a serial (such as a bibliography or index) is being bound for the first time the title-page should be marked as the reference department wishes it bound, and any special instructions should be given on the accompanying slip. If a continuation or a serial has been bound previously, the reference department should mark the title-page, and insert a slip saying "Follow pattern."

Serials which are cataloged as monographs and classified separately are handled as other monographs through the catalog department. Serials which are analyzed even though classed together are also treated as monographs and handled through the catalog department. Serials which are not analyzed are treated as periodicals and bound according to pattern. These are routed to the binding unit through the serial department. The records in that department will show how the volume is to be compiled. Usually such material is small and may have a title-page, contents and index for binding several issues into one volume. If such are issued this information should be on the check-in records and the volumes should be bound accordingly. If there is no such binding pattern an arbitrary decision is made as to the number of issues to be bound together. If this number is five, those unbound numbers are pulled when the sixth is prepared for the stacks. A title-page and table of contents can be prepared or the front cover of the first number can be used as a title-page. Covers are, of course, bound in. The title-page or front cover is marked for author (if used), title, numbers, and call number. A slip accompanies this volume to the binding unit giving the same information and indicating whether the title is new for binding. The slip also indicates any special instructions, and, if new, any information which should be included on the binding record and the pattern sent to the binder.

If in gathering material for serial binding the serials department finds that one or more numbers were never received, or are now missing or badly mutilated, it is the responsibility of that department to secure or replace the issues before sending to the binding unit. If this is not feasible either the material should be boxed, or the binding unit should be instructed to have the material bound with stubs for the missing parts. (If it is possible to do so, volumes should be made up so that the missing number will fall between two volumes and can be bound separately if secured at a later date.)

The compilation of volumes of periodicals is handled in a similar manner. When the first issue of a new volume is received a slip is made up from the check-in record of the issues, supplements, title-page, contents, and index already received, and this information is sent to the periodical room with a request for that material to be returned to the serials department (often the title-pages, contents and indexes are kept in the serials department).

The periodicals room attendant gathers the material and sends it to the serials department indicating on the records that it is no longer in the room. If any issues are charged out, he holds the rest of the volume until the issues are returned. If any issues are missing he holds the slip for a week and rechecks. If still missing he sends the issues, supplements, and so forth on hand to the serials department with a notation on the slip of the missing issues. He also notes any issues obviously mutilated or with missing pages. He marks the record that the material has left the room and, if the missing issues appear later, he sends them to the serials department. Those periodicals which are shelved in the stacks are usually pulled by the serials staff rather than by desk attendants since this gives the department a chance to determine whether the format has changed or if any volumes need rebinding.

Serials department check-in records should show whether or not a title-page, contents, and index are issued, and if so whether they come with an issue or separately. They should also show if any supplement is issued regularly, how many issues in a completed volume, and if the index comes with the subscription or must be requested and/or paid for separately. Ulrich's *Periodical Guide,* including older editions for discontinued titles, and Faxon's *Librarians' Guide to Periodicals* are among the library and trade publications giving helpful information. While these show where the periodical is indexed, such indexing should not be used as an excuse not to put forth every effort to secure the indexes. It is unfortunate that some periodicals dropped their own indexing when the titles were picked up by *Readers' Guide, Education Index, PAIS, Chemical Abstracts,* and other indexing and abstracting services.

If there are missing or mutilated issues the serials department tries to replace them from the publisher or from a dealer. Dealers, although charging for their services, are often less expensive, since the personnel expense in handling many small orders from various providers can increase the overall cost more than their service charges. Library literature, the classified advertisements in the phone books (both local and metropolitan), and special lists which can be provided by the Library Binding Institute or certain binders give an idea of which dealer might specialize in the material needed. Exchange lists circulated by individual libraries and special library associations are also helpful.

If only a few pages are missing the usual procedure is to have them photocopied either from other copies in the same library or in outside libraries. A list of titles subscribed to by staff and faculty members and the length of time retained is maintained by some serials departments for requesting fairly current issues for replacement and for substitution for torn or missing pages. The material is usually returned to the stacks to await these replacements unless it is feared that further loss will occur. If it seems advisable to bind with missing pages or issues so that the material can be returned to normal use, the slip accompanying the material to the binding unit should so state and the binding unit will instruct the binder to stub.

PREPARING THE MATERIAL FOR THE BINDERY

The binding assistant divides the material for binding according to the type of binding it is to receive, based upon the instructions to the binder. If quantity is sufficient, or if material is needed RUSH, he notifies the bindery to stop on the next scheduled trip or prepares the material for shipping to the bindery immediately. If the library has requested the bindery to pick up regularly without prior notification, this step is omitted in the case of non-RUSH material. If there are items requiring special insurance, he notifies the bindery of this fact, stating coverage desired.

For material to be bound without a pattern, he checks the general instructions to the binder, then checks each volume to see that the title-page is properly marked, that the call number is legible, and, in case the call number has not been copied from a fly-leaf it is transcribed onto the title-page. In case there are any questions relative to either the book or the marking or the binding desirable for the book, he consults with the binding librarian. If there are special instructions for a volume he inserts a sheet giving these instructions between the front cover and the body of the book, tying the book, if necessary, in order that these instructions will not become dislodged. He notes these special instructions on the slip or book card which accompanied the volume to the binding unit. Handling only one type of binding at a time, he alphabetizes the slips and book cards and prepares a shipping list. For each title he lists the number of copies, the title and author, and indicates whether special instructions are in the book. If the work is in several volumes each is listed separately. The binding assistant then totals the number of volumes for each list, rechecks the number of volumes being sent to be sure it corresponds with the number on the shipping list, and then has the volumes boxed and labelled.

The binding unit staff pulls the binding records for material which must be bound according to a pattern where the bindery already has the pattern, setting aside volumes requiring reinforced binding for similar but separate handling. The volume as compiled is checked against the binding instructions to determine whether there are variations which would require special instructions. He checks to see if large volumes should be split up. (A good general rule for size is that the volume should be easily held in a woman's left hand.) Any doubt about treatment or size is decided by the binding librarian. If there are special

JOURNAL FOR THE SCIENTIFIC STUDY OF RELIGION		Saylbuck-Red 2293 covers out; ads out editorials and features in stub for index			
Vol.	Date	Sent	Returned	Inv.date	Est. price
1-2	1961-63	8/1/63	9/6/63	9/15/63	3.00

FIGURE 5.

instructions a sheet giving this information is inserted. If it is necessary to change a pattern a new binding record is made (Figure 5) and a new pattern sheet for the binder. Such sheets are placed between the cover and the first page of the first issue. If there is a title-page the assistant indicates on it the title (if not as given), volume, part, months, year, or years which are to be lettered on the spine. If the volume lacks a title-page he may type one or mark the cover of the first issue with this information. A binding record for each new title must be made with a pattern sheet for the binder, providing a rubbing if necessary. These will give the title arranged in lines exactly as it is to be stamped. They will give the form for the designation of the volume (volume or number, volume and number, year, or months and year, and so on) and the call number if one is to be used. No information already covered by the general instructions will be repeated. They will give the color of binding desired using the designation on the color sample provided by the binder, and the color of the lettering if different from that in the general instructions. They will give variations from the instructions, as in the case of antiquarian material where it may be necessary to bind with more than the allowable number of missing pages. Other important instructions useful in compiling the material, such as "bind 3 vols per year" or "duplicate index from center fold of last issue if text is on verso of these pages" are put on the bindery record. The assistant now marks the volumes as were the ones with patterns at the bindery, and ties the material in volumes as it is to be bound. When this is done he alphabetizes the slips for both sets of these volumes and makes up a shipping list giving number of volumes (as bound), entry as given on the pattern, volumes as they are to be lettered (each listed separately), and number of copies of each volume. Any volumes with special instructions, any patterns to be changed, and new patterns to be made are noted. The number of volumes to be bound are totaled and the number being sent is rechecked to be sure that it corresponds with the number on the shipping list, and then the volumes are boxed and labeled. This process is repeated for the volumes requiring reinforced binding.

Finally, any material being returned to the bindery for correction is listed and there is placed in each volume, a sheet showing the correction to be made. A notation is made on the bindery record indicating that it has been returned and the date.

If multiple forms have not been used for the shipping lists, duplicates must be made for the binding unit file, a copy for the use of the binding librarian for committing funds, as many copies as required by the financial office for clearing the invoice, and copies for departments or departmental libraries requesting them. The binding librarian signs and dates the original and inserts it in one of the boxes of binding, clearly marking that box so that it may be opened first, seals the boxes and has them sent to the shipping department to be held for pick-up by the binder. The duplicate lists are distributed as indicated, holding the ones for the financial office to submit with the invoice after shipment has been returned. Sample volumes which were sent for making rubs are returned to the departments. The attendant now alphabetizes all slips and book cards into one alphabetical file and refiles the binding records. As sets of cards and book cards and pockets which have been typed for new monographic material are sent from the typing unit they are filed with the slips which accompanied the unbound books.

It goes without saying that funds must be committed for all binding sent to the binder. Whether the binding librarian is responsible for budgeting the binding funds or whether he submits his estimates to another department in the library, he must be aware at all times of the funds remaining in the total binding budget and in the various allotments so that he can schedule future binding. His estimates must be made according to current prices and therefore his "rule of thumb" for estimating the costs per volume on each shipping list must be constantly revised. An example of how this estimated cost, based on 1967 advertised prices, can be arrived at follows. When prices for Class A binding range according to size from $1.60 to $4.50 with an average of 30¢ for the addition of call numbers, a public library might estimate $3.00 and a university library with many of the larger volumes might estimate $4.00 per volume. Periodical prices similarly varying from $3.84 to $7.00 with an average of 30¢ for the addition of call numbers might cause the public library to estimate $5.00 per volume while the university library with its files of scientific journals might estimate $6.00 or even $6.50 per volume. The binding librarian will take his copy of the shipping list and make his estimate by the simple process of multiplying the total number of volumes by the price per volume estimated for that type of binding.

CHECKING IN MATERIAL FROM BINDERY

When material is returned, it is checked against the shipping lists for completeness. Any item not received is so noted on the shipping list, also any returned unbound. The volumes are then examined for faulty workmanship or failure to bind according to specifications. This consists of two parts: examination of the book, and checking of the book against instructions. Books can be examined in accordance with the checklist proffered by the Library Binding Institute in its Library Binding Handbook. This check-list is for work bound by its LBI Standard. It is suitable also for other Class A-type binding, but must be modified for other types of binding, especially less expensive types. If a volume does not come up to proper standards it should either be returned to the binder for correction with the next shipment or it should be considered whether the library chose the binding most suited to the material. Each volume will hardly be examined this minutely; spot-checking usually is sufficient for a shipment with particular attention to the clarity of the lettering and the flexibility of the volume.

The second step is to check all items marked on the shipping list as requiring special treatment: Have instructions been followed (the slip in the binding file shows what these special instructions were)? If not, the material must be accepted as is or returned to the binder for correction.

Material returned bound but with missing pages should have a slip made for pages missing. This slip should be sent with the binding slip to the serials department so that it can try to have the pages photocopied and tipped in. Slips, book cards and pockets, and shelf-list and catalog cards are now pulled from the binding file and matched with the volumes. Pockets and book cards are inserted for new volumes, pockets only for rebound material. Marks of library possession (bookplates, embossing, and perforating) are applied. Call numbers are placed on the spines if not put on by the binder, and the volumes are sent to the stacks, reference department, or other indicated location unless they are rebinds with charges in the circulation records. In the latter case they are sent to the circulation or reference departments to have book cards inserted or charges cleared. These departments then have the books shelved. The slips from the binding file are returned to the catalog department to clear their "control file" and to the serials department to update their records. Shelflist cards and catalog cards are sent to the filing unit. The slips made for books from reference and circulation for the binding file can be returned with the books or discarded according to the wishes of those departments. In those libraries where the material is bound prior to cataloging, the procedure is changed since those books as well as the binding slips must be returned to the catalog department where it will then follow the procedures for books received bound from publisher or dealer.

CLEARING THE INVOICE FOR PAYMENT

When the invoice for a shipment is received from the binder it is checked against the shipping list. If all items have been received and the number of items corresponds with those on the shipping list, it can be cleared for payment. If some items were returned unbound and the invoice corresponds with the shipping list after those items have been canceled, it can be cleared for payment. (In this case the estimate for the items returned should be decommitted.)

If certain items are omitted from the shipment to be returned later the invoice can be held until these items are returned. If certain items are omitted from the shipment without explanation the binder should be contacted for clarification and the invoice held up. When the invoice is cleared it should have the required number of copies of the shipping list attached to it, be marked "cleared

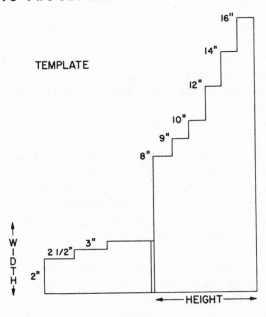

TEMPLATE

FIGURE 6.

for payment," and be initialed or signed by the binding librarian and sent to the financial office for further handling. The date sent should be added to the copy in the binding unit. Since the shipping list gives volumes and titles under each type of binding but does not give size, and since the invoice from the binder usually lists prices as determined by size, the binding unit may be requested to check an occasional shipment with the invoice. In this case a template can be used, made according to the sizes listed on the binder's price list (Figure 6). It can be made of press or heavy cardboard and the volumes easily sized by it according to the binder's scheduled list of prices. Extra charges made for extra lines of lettering, gold foil, lines at top and bottom of the spine, and so forth, are easily checked against the volumes, and any charges for extra sewing, and so forth, can be assumed to be correct if the binder is a reputable one.

Acceptable economies fall into two categories, those in the overall cost of book materials including binding and those in the binding costs themselves.

Overall savings include the purchase of materials so bound that there is no expectation of future binding costs, and the purchase of the binding with the book. Often a book is available in several different forms: publisher's edition (trade edition as sold in retail stores), publisher's library edition (with binding that the publisher feels is adequate for library use, not according to any set standard), library binding (according to LBI Standard for Library Binding Class A specifications), and paperback (issued in paper covers, generally with glued rather than sewed pages). Paperbacks may be purchased also in adhesive bindings with either the original cover attached to a heavy binder's board base and laminated for durability or with grade C cloth glued to hard binder's boards, with title and author imprinted on the spine.

Publishers' editions vary in price and in durability as do their library editions, but the following comparisons will indicate the comparative costs of the three types*:

Publisher's edition cost 2.06 est. 20 circulations 10¢ per circ.
Publisher's library edition cost 3.09 est. 35 circulations 8¾¢ per circ.
Library binding cost 3.25 est. 100 circulations 3¼¢ per circ.

When cost of library time needed to have publisher's edition rebound as well as the binding cost is considered it is obvious that the library binding purchased with the book in the form of a prebound book is a decided saving if the title is one that will be given considerable use. Since these prebounds are children's books and juveniles, especially the classics, a considerable saving can be made by their purchase. A similar situation exists with paperbacks. An increasing number of titles suitable to the school and public library are readily available in the new adhesive bindings which are guaranteed for 50 circulations or 2 years' wear (whichever comes first). Many other titles are available in paperbacks which are suitable for the college and university library, and many titles are being reprinted in this form which have been out of print. In some cases no publisher's edition is available. These paperbacks can be purchased bound for the library thus including the binding cost in the purchase price. The prices for these Permabound and cloth-bound adhesive bindings range from the list price of the paperback plus $1.05 for binding in lots of 10 to 20% off list price plus 84¢ for binding in lots of 500 (various titles). R. R. Bowker's *Paperbound Books in Print* currently lists 30,000 paperbacks available to the binders offering this service.

A similar saving in overall cost is made when books purchased abroad are bound abroad, the purchase price including the binding. While some of these bindings are merely adequate, others are excellent. Not only is the binding cost lower because of low labor costs, but such purchasing eliminates, as in the case of the prebound book and paperback, separate handling for the binding of the book after receipt in the library. For books with non-Roman alphabets it is an advantage to purchase this way as all binders are not equipped to handle these.

Savings in binding costs can be divided into savings in the actual binding bills and savings in the use of personnel within the library. The easiest saving is the elimination of frills. These consist of head and tail lines and panels, the library imprint, labels, and the use of gold foil lettering, all items for which an extra charge is made and which do not result in greater strength or durability of the volume or appreciably improve its appearance. More debatable is the elimination of collating by the binder, and the binding of journals intact (without removing covers or advertising). Justification can be made for the elimination of collating by the binder if the library has an abundance of help to which this can

* Dudley A. Weiss, "Statement Presented to the United States Senate Committee on the Judiciary (Subcommittee on Antitrust and Monopoly)," *The Library Binder*, 14(1), (May 1966).

be assigned. It can also be justified, except in the case of rare books, as the taking of a calculated risk since missing pages will be discovered as the book is used and present methods of photocopying will permit the pages to be reproduced and inserted at that time with no more loss of time than if discovered when the bindery collated the material, and at considerable saving in the overall cost to the binding budget.

Some binders have advocated the binding of journals intact since this preserves the advertisements, letters to the editor, and similar matter which may have a historical interest. The chief objection has been the increased size of the volume, because of binding pricing of journals by width as well as by height, the extra shelfroom required, and the lesser ease in handling. With labor costs such a great part of the bindery expenditure, some binders are offering considerable saving on volumes of three inches or less in width which are bound this way. (Here, too, collating is omitted.)

Perhaps the greatest saving that can be made since it saves both in the binding cost and in the library personnel cost is the elimination of instructions to the binder for the binding of periodicals and the elimination of bindery patterns for individualized styling of periodical titles. This is accomplished by utilizing the standard magazine binding. This binding collates the volumes, compiles the volumes according to good library practice, and uses the specifications for Class A binding, but it establishes the title according to the *Readers' Guide,* the technical indexes, or, if not found in these, according to the Union List of Serials or the Library of Congress cards, and it assigns a specific color for that title. All lettering is white and standard in form and placement. Volumes, although varying with the issues, are kept as close to 2½ inches as possible.

Two economies which can be effected in the use of binding unit personnel are the simplifications˙ of the shipping list and the eliminating of checking returned journals against patterns. Since the binding unit has an exact list of what is sent with each shipment in its binding file, and each volume to be bound has the title and author indicated, the shipping list could give merely the number of volumes of each type of binding which is being sent for monographic materials (such as 50 Class A monographs) and the title and number of volumes only of each periodical being sent (as "5 vols.-*Library Journal*"). Upon return from the bindery the periodicals could be sent to the shelves without any further checking than with the title-page. It would be expected that the page shelving the newly bound volumes would return to the binding unit any that did not correspond with the other volumes already on the shelf.

As for future developments there seems little likelihood that the automation of library services will decrease the need for books and therefore lighten the load of binding. In fact, increased bibliographic services made possible by computerized holdings will tend to increase the demand. Other changes to increase the demand have already been mentioned: paperbacks, expansion of exchange programs, and cooperative assignment of areas of acquisition. Another change is the quantity of materials of a permanent nature being issued in unbound form, particularly works suitable to the college and university library such as reproductions in book form from microfilms and facsimile reproductions of works long out of print.

While the American Library Association considers the need for a greater variety of standards and materials, the binders are tending toward greater standardization within present specifications. There is indeed a need for more variety in the binding of *belles-lettres,* and for more attractive cover materials, but a move to have publishers issue a certain volume of their new titles in library bindings which adhere to approved specifications would probably be of greater value than to expect the binder to vary his specifications. Further acceptance of the standardized binding and magazines is hoped for.

Automation will probably be limited to the work of the serials department, where records can be punched so as to indicate the materials ready to be bound, when indexes are received, and so on, and to the preparation of shipping lists from the automated circulation records. Simplification seems a more probable development than automation.

BIBLIOGRAPHY

American Library Association, Library Technology Project. Development of performance standards for library binding, phase I. Report of the Survey Team, April 1961. ALA, Chicago, 1961.

Library Binding Institute, *Library Binding Handbook,* LBI, Boston, 1963.

Schultheiss, L. A., "Two Serial Control Card Files Developed at the University of Illinois, Chicago," *Library Resources and Technical Services,* 9(3), 271–287 (1965).

Weiss, Dudley, "Statement Presented to the United States Senate Committee on the Judiciary (Subcommittee on Antitrust and Monopoly)," *The Library Binder,* 14(1), 13 (1966).

20: THE LIBRARY BINDER

Matt T. Roberts

LIBRARY BINDING is the business of supplying specialized binding services to institutional, private, public, and other libraries.[1] The Library Binding Institute (which may be defined as a trade association of commercial library bookbinders in the United States and Canada, suppliers to the bookbinding industry, and institutional bookbinders[2]) further defines *certified* library binding as bookbinding meeting the minimum specifications necessary to produce a volume which will achieve two objectives: (1) to meet the requirements of libraries for an end product capable of withstanding the rigors of normal library circulation or use, and (2) to provide maximum reader usability. The Library Binding Institute (LBI) goes on to say that "only binding, including rebinding, prebinding and periodical binding, in accordance with the standard is LIBRARY BINDING, but nothing in this standard excludes other types of binding, whether superior or inferior to LIBRARY BINDING, for library use, as determined by a librarian and his Certified Library Binder for any specific purposes."[3]

The qualification offered by LBI gives its definition a degree of plausibility which it otherwise would not have, because the definition without that qualification would not serve the total library community. One would have to ask which library and what user is intended. Insofar as this writer is aware, no one has ever adequately defined "rigors of normal circulation or use," or "maximum reader usability." Unless qualified, the definition fails to take into consideration the obvious fact that there are many different libraries serving widely differing clienteles, and the binding which serves the needs of one library may well be completely unsatisfactory when applied to those of another. A children's librarian, for example, may require a bright, attractive binding that can withstand the efforts of a user to tear it

Matt T. Roberts is Binding Officer, Preservation Office, Library of Congress, Washington, D.C.

apart, whereas the reference librarian of a research library may require a plain, unadorned flexible binding, yet one sturdy enough to be photocopied without splitting the spine.

Perhaps it is not possible to provide only one definition of library binding that will adequately serve all types of libraries. It would be just as logical, for example, to define library binding as binding which will produce a product that will endure as long as the paper on which the book is printed, or as long as the library chooses to retain the book, whichever comes first.[4] If all libraries pursued the same acquisition and weeding policies, and if all books were printed on the same quality of paper, such a definition might serve. Obviously it cannot, except possibly to the extent that some of the very largest research libraries retain all of their books until they literally turn to dust.

However one chooses to define it, library binding, regardless of cost, should provide a book that will: (1) open easily and lie reasonably flat at any place in the text to which it is opened; (2) retain its solidity and shape after repeated openings, including the extreme opening required for photocopying; and (3) be bound in such a manner that, should rebinding become necessary, the basic structure of the first binding will not make rebinding unduly expensive or impossible.[5]

SERVICES OFFERED BY THE LIBRARY BINDER

The services offered by the library binder include: class "A" library binding, prebinding (also called prelibrary or reconstructed binding), textbook binding, edition binding, storage binding (also called LUM-SPECS, and warehouse work), adhesive binding (also called perfect or unsewn binding), blank-book binding, pamphlet binding, binding of Bibles, fine binding (i.e., rare book binding, not artistic binding), binding of music materials, law book binding, theses binding, general repair work, and mounting of maps and works of art on paper.[6]

Class A binding is the very heart of library binding.[7] It is the library binder's bread and butter, and the foundation on which the LBI stands. By definition, it applies to the binding of serials and monographs; in practice, however, it applies principally to the binding of serial publications (the most expensive style of regular library binding, accounting for about 60 percent of the typical library binder's business).[8] Class A binding includes the binding of:

(a) Any ordinary-sized graphic material consisting of an appreciable number of leaves or folded sheets produced originally as a unit and submitted for binding, rebinding, prebinding, or sold pre-bound as such a unit, and not requiring special handling; (b) A series of multileaved, like-constituted, serially numbered graphic units submitted for binding or rebinding into a scheduled multi-unit volume and not requiring special handling; and (c) Any underdized, oversized or odd-sized volume, or any volume that requires special handling.[9]

Prebinding is the rebinding of edition, or publishers', bindings before they are received by the library (or before they are put into circulation), and is designed to provide a strong binding capable of withstanding the rigors of use made of books by the clientele of a circulating library. Prebinding may also include binding from gatherings or (rarely) sheets. The LBI also has a standard for this style of binding.[10]

Textbook binding is actually the rebinding of worn books for educational institutions. It is an economical style of binding, since the binder generally receives dozens (or even hundreds) of copies of the same title and is able to realize economies, such as precutting boards and cloth, that he cannot realize with most other styles. Textbook binding, for the most part, is also carried out during the summer months, when other binding activities are at a relatively low level.

Edition binding is the binding of numerous copies of a single title from sheets. Large edition binderies generally do not like to accept orders for a relatively small number of copies, because the equipment setup time is lengthy and therefore expensive; consequently, library binders having the necessary basic machinery (or access to that machinery)—notably folding machines, three-knife trimmers, etc.—will edition-bind small runs (e.g., 1,500 copies) of a title.

Storage binding is the binding of infrequently used materials according to the Specifications for Binding Lesser Used Materials, the so-called LUMSPECS.[11]

Adhesive binding is a form of library binding which does not utilize sewing. The leaves are secured by means of a hot-melt or cold (resinous) adhesive. Adhesive binding can be done by hand; however, it is better done by means of an adhesive-binding machine, such as the Sulby (hot-melt) or Ehlerman (resinous). This is a very economical style of binding.

Blank-book binding generally refers to the binding (or rebinding) of such materials as county or court record books, i.e., books meant to be written in, and which must, therefore, lie almost perfectly flat when open. This is a very specialized style of binding, calling for special sewing to webbings, and sometimes for split boards, a spring-back, round corners, and so on. Blank-book binding is undertaken by relatively few library binders and is expensive. This style of binding, insofar as library binders are concerned, does not include mass-pro-duction work, such as padding or checkbook binding, which is the work of the job binder.

Pamphlet binding is the binding of very thin monographs, i.e., those consisting of one signature or a relatively small number of leaves. The term *pamphlet binding,* which derives from the time when the writing of discourses on political, moral and social issues was popular, is unfortunate in that it is confused with the work of the pamphlet binder, whose activities include such diverse items as peri-odical issues and telephone books.

The binding of Bibles—which is almost invariably rebinding—is rather specialized work, but is nonetheless done by many library binders. It is specialized in that the Bibles are often bound in limp leather covers which have extending squares (Yapp style), sometimes with zippers, and have round corners. If the binder must trim in the course of rebinding, he may spray or otherwise color the edges.

Fine binding usually refers to the rebinding (or restoration) of valuable books, usually in leather, but it would also include the binding of keepsakes, presentation books, table books, diaries, signa-ture books, and the like. The term is something of a misnomer in that most, if not all, such binding is case work and not "in-board" binding.

The binding of music materials is accorded a separate category because it is often necessary to sew music materials through the folds so that the publications may, if necessary, stand open and flat on stands. Music books also frequently require pockets and compensa-tion guards.

Law-book binding is distinctive largely because law books are com-monly covered in so-called law (tan) buckram in imitation of the fawn-colored calfskin they once were bound in. They frequently have red and black (paper) labels in lieu of the title skivers used when they were bound in leather.

Newspaper binding is somewhat different because of the size of the publications, and because some require whip-stitching. The margins of newspapers are usually so narrow that they cannot be sidesewn or oversewn.

Thesis binding—a highly lucrative business for those library binders fortunate enough to get it—might actually be considered job binding, or even a form of edition binding, except that it is done almost exclusively by library binders.

The mounting of maps, works of art on paper, etc., is a very specialized type of work better left to those who are experts in the field. General repair work includes tipping-in of loose leaves, maps, charts, etc.; refolding maps; repair of hinges; and the like. Some library binders will even attempt to salvage smoke- and/or water-damaged books.

Few library binders undertake to offer all of the services outlined above. Indeed, it is the unusual library binder who does edition binding, fine binding, blank-book binding, and extensive repair and/or restoration work.

THE LIBRARY BINDER AND THE GRAPHIC ARTS INDUSTRY

The library binder, while representing only a tiny part of the graphic arts industry, is almost unique. Library binding differs from edition, pamphlet and paperback binding in one important respect: unlike those forms of binding, it relies heavily on handwork, supplemented by the use of specialized machinery such as nippers, smashing machines, rounding and backing machines, guillotines, and hydropresses—all of which are also to be found in the edition bindery, but usually in larger and more sophisticated forms. Since it does involve so much handwork, it is inherently a style of bookbinding which is more expensive than most other kinds of commercial binding. Library binding is not, and probably never will be, highly mechanized, mainly because the library binder does not bind large runs, e.g., 10,000, 50,000, or 200,000 identical copies of a single title. The library binder must treat each book as a separate item, although he can rough-sort by size.

The 200 or so library binders in the United States and Canada gross roughly $40 million per year, of which approximately $30 million is taken in by the fifty or so certified library binders.[12] The industry has expanded rapidly in the past twenty years, as evidenced by the fact that it grossed approximately $3 million in 1955.[13] All types of libraries utilize in some way the services of the library binder (see Table 1).

TABLE 1
DISTRIBUTION OF SERVICES

Type of library	Percent industry average of sales
Public Libraries	13.0
Schools (Elementary, junior and high)	15.0
Junior colleges	7.0
Colleges and universities	50.0
Federal government	4.0
Industrial	4.5
Hospital	4.5
Church	.5
Other	1.5
	100.0

Source: Tauber, Maurice F., ed. *Library Binding Manual; A Handbook of Useful Procedures for the Maintenance of Library Volumes.* Boston, Library Binding Institute, 1972, p. 31.

SELECTING A LIBRARY BINDER

The selection of a library binder can be a difficult and uncertain process, unless the only criterion is low price, in which case the official can simply accept the lowest bid or cheapest price list. On the other hand, if the librarian is interested in the highest quality regardless of cost (and surprisingly, there are libraries that can afford this luxury), the problem possibly becomes even more complicated because the highest bid or the binder with the highest price list may not offer the highest quality. Somewhere between these two extremes the librarian should be able to locate a binder who offers good quality at a fair price. The problem is finding him.

In order to be successful, a library binding program must be built on mutual understanding and cooperation between the librarian and the binder. Library binding does not represent the sale of a commodity, but of a service. In a sense, the library binder is actually an extension of the library. The really good library binder knows something about the library he binds for—the use to which the books will be put, the purpose of the library, the clientele it serves, and the like. He must know, in other words, which kind of binding the library needs. On the other side, the librarian should become informed about bookbinding in general, and good binding in particular, in order to be able to communicate his needs intelligently and accurately. If the binder does not know what the library expects in the way of binding, obviously he cannot supply it. Conversely, if the librarian does not know what the binder is capable of offering—the state of his technology, the experience of his staff, the quality of his materials, new materials he may have developed or identified, the degree of training and abilities of his supervisory personnel (an all important consideration because the quality of work produced by any library binder is directly related to the quality of his supervisory personnel)—he may demand too much of the binder or, what is worse, too little.

It is essential for the library to find a competent library binder and retain his services permanently, assuming he continues to do a good job. This is important because it takes several years for both parties to work out the many details involved in a successful binding program. It is very difficult to maintain a mutually satisfactory binding program if the library changes binders every year, or even every few years.

There are several possible approaches the library can pursue in its search for a competent library binder. The librarian may simply write to the LBI and ask for the names of several member binderies. Such an approach, however, excludes binders who may be highly qualified but are not members of the institute. As a second approach, the librarian can visit several binderies, inspect their facilities, look at their work, and judge for himself whether or not they are qualified to bind for his library. This method can be expensive and time-consuming, since there are not many library binders and the nearest one may be several hundred miles away. In addition, it can be difficult to assess the quality of binding unless one has time to inspect thoroughly the work he is shown. The third possibility, and one which several libraries (or groups of libraries) have found worthwhile, is to request interested binderies to submit samples of their work for inspection and evaluation.

The purpose of such samples is to eliminate from further consideration those binders who cannot produce binding meeting the library's needs or specifications. It is important, therefore, for the library to have some statement of specifications, even if they are purely eclectic in nature and draw heavily on the LBI's own minimum specifications, which cover class A binding reasonably well. The library's own specifications can cover binding other than class A binding, as well as fold-sewing, trimming, margins, procedures for handling special format materials, brittle paper, adhesives, chemicals, and even when not to bind.

Sets of samples should be as uniform as possible, so that all binderies work with the same problems. The samples should also consist of books representing the normal work the library expects to have done during the course of the contract. It is pointless, for example, for the library to ask for an example of binding a Braille book if the library does not acquire books in Braille. The same may be said for newspapers, portfolios, slipcases, etc.

THE SAMPLE

A typical set of samples might include:

1. *A periodical volume* made up of thick issues with relatively narrow margins or even center spreads. This will pose a special problem, since such a publication must be sewn through the folds. The thick issues will also make it difficult to round and back the book properly. It is a fair test, however, because the binder who can bind such a serial properly will also be able to bind ordinary serials equally well or better. It is an unfortunate fact that some library binders cannot (or will not) cope with unusual binding problems.

2. *A monograph* one and one-half to two inches thick, with an inner margin adequate for oversewing (at least three-fourths of an inch and preferably more). This type of sample will indicate whether the binder is capable of binding a book according to the LBI's minimum specifications.

3. *A monograph* one or more inches thick having an inner margin of less than three-fourths inch, which the binder has been instructed to tape-sew. This will indicate whether the binders have the personnel to sew a book by hand on tapes. (Some binders cannot or will not do this.)

4. *A monograph* approximately one-half inch thick, which is to be adhesive-bound using a hot-melt adhesive. The binder should be instructed not to round and back this book, and to cover it in a cloth lighter than buckram, such as "C" cloth. Some library binders do not have the equipment for this style of binding, and adhesive-binding can be expensive when done by hand.

5. *A very thin publication,* e.g., a single periodical issue, to be covered in a light cloth, as above, and without rounding and backing. Casing-in a thin book can be a troublesome operation, especially in obtaining a proper joint.

6. *A monograph* of any thickness more than one-half inch, containing fold-outs, maps, etc., as well as pocket material. This will indicate how well the binder can make both a pocket and a compensation

guard. It will also determine whether he checks for fold-outs, etc., before trimming the fore edge.

7. *A publisher's binding* with instructions to rebind. The original sewing should be weak in all samples, or strong in all, so that each binder will have to decide whether to resew or retain the original sewing.

Each prospective binder is sent a sample package, a copy of the library's specifications, a list of instructions, and a deadline beyond which the sample will not be accepted.

The logic of using a sample to determine which binders are qualified is simple. If a library binder cannot do a good job on a sample of seven volumes, especially when he knows he will not be considered for the contract if his sample fails, then he is certainly not going to be able to do even a satisfactory job on the library's yearly work, be it 700 or 70,000 volumes. A sample is an effective means of permitting a library binder to demonstrate that he is capable of meeting the standards the industry has established for itself, as well as satisfying the individual library's specifications. It can be of use in eliminating the incompetent binder, which in itself will be of benefit both to the industry and libraries.

Judging of the sample should be rigorous and the passing score should be high, i.e., 85-90 percent. The prospective binders should be informed of the passing score, and warned that no work may be subcontracted. They should also be informed that failure to follow instructions (a not uncommon shortcoming among library binders) or excessive trimming will result in loss of all points for that particular book.

EVALUATING THE SAMPLE

The most convenient manner in which to evaluate the sample is to prepare a chart listing the pertinent aspects of a binding. A 100-point score for each book is convenient; however, the pamphlet and adhesive binding should be scored below 100, because they are not rounded and backed. It should be noted that those persons judging the samples should not know the source of any sample, in order to eliminate any accusation of bias. An evaluation sheet should consist of the following elements.

1. Failure to follow instructions and/or excessive trimming—loss of all points for that book.

2. Followed instructions and did not overtrim:
  a. Sewing or adhesive structure (one of the following)
    Sewing through the folds
      good "openability"
      tapes properly spaced
      sewing thread of proper weight
      tapes extended onto boards
    Oversewing
      good "openability"
      minimum back margin taken by sanding and sewing
      sewing uniform and not ragged
      sewing does not extend all the way to head and tail
    Adhesive structure
      leaves firmly secured
      depth of penetration of adhesive onto leaves adequate
  b. Endpapers
    construction suitable to book
    width of tipping not too great
    absence of drag on first and last leaves
    correct weight of paper
    grain direction of paper parallel to spine
  c. Trimming
    square
    smooth
  d. Rounding and backing
    shape of round
    shoulders even along length of book
    depth of shoulders equal to thickness of boards
    signatures or leaves properly folded over to form round and
      backing
  e. Spine lining
    well attached
    proper material and of proper weight
    second (kraft paper) lining over first lining on books sewn
      through the folds or books more than two inches thick
    lining extended onto boards
  f. Case-making
    covering material well secured to boards
    properly pressed (absence of wrinkles or other defects in
      covering; no adhesive on covers)

turn-ins proper extent and adhering well
corners neatly done and adhering well
squares of proper extent (1/8″ maximum)
inlay
cord (covering material turned over cord at head and tail,
except for books with headbands)
g. Casing-in
proper adhesion in joint and of board papers to boards
French joint even and of adequate depth
spine solid and properly shaped
boards even at head and fore edge
h. Lettering
accurate
properly positioned
clean and legible

PRINCIPAL QUALITIES OF A WELL-BOUND BOOK

Several writers have described the principal qualities of a well-bound book, including Bailey, Clough, Cockerell, Coutts and Stephen, and the Library Binding Institute.[14] Basically, the qualities are:

1. The signatures or leaves are solidly secured, with no starts or unevenness at the fore edge and no splitting in the spine.
2. The book opens easily and lies reasonably flat at any place in the text.
3. The spine is thoroughly glued up and appropriately lined, so that repeated opening does not cause the book to lose its shape.
4. Tapes and/or spine lining extend well onto boards (one to one and one-half inches).
5. The endpapers do not pull at the first and last leaves, i.e., there should be no drag due to excessive width of tipping.
6. The spine is rounded to an arc of approximately one-third of a circle and the shoulders created by backing are of an extent equal to the thickness of the boards.
7. Trimming is minimal (no more than one-eighth inch) and is straight and smooth.
8. The boards and covering material are of a weight (thickness) appropriate to the size of the book.
9. The covering material and board papers adhere firmly in the joints and to the boards.

10. Squares are appropriate to the size of the book.
11. A reasonably thick book (one-half inch or more) stands vertically with no support.
12. When the book is lying flat the upper cover remains flat, and when the book stands by itself the covers remain closed.
13. The lettering is accurate, properly positioned, and legible.
14. The binding is clean, neat, and shows evidence of good work-manship.

TRENDS IN LIBRARY BINDING

Before 1900, binders who did work for libraries did so entirely by hand and as more or less a sideline, their principal source of income being work done for private collectors. There was no distinctive style of library binding as such, nor was there any library binding in-dustry.[15] Frank Barnard, one of the earliest library binders, was able to say as late as 1929 that "binderies devoted exclusively to rebinding [that is, library binding] are of quite recent origin; most of them are less than fifteen years old and few go back twenty-five years."[16] The library binding industry emerged as a separate sector of the book-binding industry "because of the increase in the circulation of books by public and semipublic libraries, and because of the general use of free text-books in the public schools."[17]

Prior to the rise of library binding as we know it today, library books were always sewn on tapes. The use of four tapes was traditional, but the number varied with the size of the book. The tapes were secured between split boards and the book was covered in full or half leather. This was the economy binding of that day. The increasing number of books in public and school libraries, however, called for an even more economical style of binding.

The concept of oversewing is not new. It was in common use at the end of the eighteenth and the beginning of the nineteenth century,[18] although not in its present form. Various forms of whip-stitching, overcasting, etc., went through periods of experimentation, enjoying varying degrees of success. It was not until 1904, when Sir Cedric Chivers patented his method of oversewing, that library binding as we know it had its start.[19] This early form of modern oversewing was, of course, done by hand, and it was not until the period 1916-22 that Elmo Reavis and his associates were able to design and put into operation a machine that oversewed. Machine oversewing began a relatively rapid growth in the early 1920s and became the dominant form of library sewing by the early 1930s.[20]

Oversewing is the principal method of securing the leaves of books in the library bindery, at least in the United States; however, in the opinion of this writer, it is currently being challenged, and will be challenged to an even greater extent in the immediate future by one or more of the methods of adhesive-binding in use today. There are two reasons why this will take place. One reason is that publishers are issuing more and more books that are adhesive-bound rather than sewn and, although this in itself does not preclude oversewing, the adhesive binding seems to go hand in hand with diminishing binding margins, which in turn frequently precludes oversewing. Other publications, notably periodicals, are also being published with narrower margins.

If the cost of paper continues to rise (and there is no indication that it will not), the margins will continue to diminish. While as recently as ten years ago the average journal issue had a binding margin of about three-fourths of an inch (which is about the minimum margin needed for oversewing that is to have any openability whatsoever), the average journal today has a binding margin closer to one-half inch.

The second reason relates to the economics of library binding. Just as oversewing is considerably less expensive than hand sewing, so is adhesive-binding considerably less expensive than class A binding. Adhesive binding is faster, and speed is the economy. In addition, more skill is required to operate an oversewing machine than to operate an adhesive-binding machine.

The rising costs of materials and labor, particularly the latter, will force library binders to seek more ways in which to reduce costs, and adhesive-binding is a most appealing way. A given library binder may not like adhesive binding, but if the alternative to adhesive binding is bankruptcy, he has little choice.

One can see other trends, also. Many, if not most, of the early American library bookbinders were craftsmen, and some were highly skilled in the craft of bookbinding. That day is coming to an end. Many of today's library bookbinders, and probably all of tomorrow's, are economy-motivated individuals who may well be competent businessmen, but they are not bookbinders. They will continue to seek (and undoubtedly find) faster and more economical ways to bind a library book. It can only be hoped that what they find will prove to be in the best interest of the library and its book collection.

There is also the trend, at least in college and university libraries, toward taking the responsibility for library binding away from the professional librarian (where it belongs) and giving it to the business manager of the institution.[21] All too often this individual is interested solely in obtaining the lowest-cost binding possible, regardless of quality. If this trend continues, it can only have a deleterious effect on library binding.

References

1. Strauss, Victor. *The Printing Industry*. Washington, D.C., Printing Industries of America, 1967, p. 618.

2. Weiss, Dudley A. (Executive Director, Library Binding Institute). Letter dated March 7, 1973.

3. Library Binding Institute. *Library Binding Institute Standard for Library Binding*. 4th ed. rev. Boston, Library Binding Institute, 1963, p. 1.

4. Clough, Eric A. *Bookbinding for Librarians*. London, Association of Assistant Librarians, 1957, pp. 80-81; and Bailey, Arthur L. *Library Bookbinding*. New York, H.W. Wilson, 1916, pp. 121-22.

5. Dana, John Cotton. *Notes on Bookbinding for Libraries*. Rev ed. Chicago, Library Bureau, 1910, p. 23; and Coutts, Henry T., and Stephen, George A. *Manual on Library Bookbinding; Practical and Historical*. London, Libraco Ltd., 1911, pp. 28-29.

6. Tauber, Maurice F., ed. *Library Binding Manual: A Handbook of Useful Procedures for the Maintenance of Library Volumes*. Boston, Library Binding Institute, 1972, p. 31.

7. Feipel, Louis N., and Browning, Earl W. *Library Binding Manual*. Chicago, ALA, 1951, pp. 46-54; and Library Binding Institute, *op. cit.*, pp. 1-6.

8. Tauber, *op. cit.*, p. 32.

9. Library Binding Institute, *op. cit.*, p. 1.

10. —————. *Library Binding Institute Standard for Pre-Library Bound New Books*. 3d ed. Boston, Library Binding Institute, 1960.

11. "Minimum Specifications for Binding Lesser Used Materials," *A.L.A. Bulletin* 52:51-53, Jan. 1958.

12. Weiss, Dudley A. Personal communication, Oct. 2, 1975.

13. Stratton, John B. "Libraries and Commercial Binderies," *Library Trends* 4:302, Jan. 1956.

14. Bailey, *op. cit.*, pp. 49-50; Clough, *op. cit.*, pp. 81-82; Cockerell, Douglas. *Bookbinding and the Care of Books: A Text-Book for Amateurs, Bookbinders & Librarians*. 5th ed. London, Sir Isaac Pitman, 1902, p. 174; Coutts and Stephen, *op. cit.*, pp. 28-29; and Library Binding Institute. *Library Binding Handbook*. Boston, Library Binding Institute, 1971, pp. 13-14.

15. Library Binding Institute, *Library Binding Handbook, op. cit.*, p. 46.

16. Hitchcock, Frederick H., ed. *The Building of a Book; A Series of Practical Articles Written by Experts in the Various Departments of Book Making and Distributing*. 2d ed. New York, Bowker, 1929, p. 235.

17. *Ibid.*, p. 235.

18. Middleton, Bernard C. *A History of English Craft Bookbinding Technique*. New York, Hafner Publishing Co., 1963, p. 24.

19. Coutts and Stephen, *op. cit.*, p. 30.

20. Weiss, Dudley A. Personal communication, Oct. 2, 1975.

21. *Ibid.*

21: PROVISIONAL STANDARDS

1. Scope

These standards define the performance of binding used in libraries as affected by three characteristics: openability, workmanship, and durability. For the purpose of these standards, binding used in libraries includes any finished work produced by any process which joins together leaves or sections of leaves into a single physical unit, i.e., book or volume. Volumes may be newly bound or rebound. These standards may be applied to special binding, i.e., any volume that, because of some atypical characteristic such as size or shape, requires special binding methods and materials. However, these standards do not include specifications for special binding.

The standards are presented in the order in which they should be applied in a test situation—a binding should first be tested for openability, then workmanship, and finally, durability. A binding must pass all three tests to qualify for use in libraries.

2. Sampling Procedure

For testing to determine compliance with these performance standards, samples shall be chosen at random from a given printing, prebinding, or rebinding run. The quantities required for testing are based on the degree of structural uniformity between volumes in a given run which in turn is dependent on the quality control measures exercised during manufacture. The binding groups and the number of samples required per group for test purposes are shown in Table 1.

TABLE 1

TEST SAMPLES REQUIRED PER BINDING GROUP

Binding Group*	Degree of Structural Uniformity	Number of Samples Required for Testing
A	High	5
B	Average	8
C	Low	10

*Examples for each group are: (A) Books bound according to ALA Class A or LBI Standard specifications; (B) textbooks and publisher's reinforced bindings; (C) publisher's trade edition bindings.

Copyright © 1966 by the American Library Association; reprinted from pages 5–15 of *Development of Performance Standards for Binding Use in Libraries, Phase II,* Library Technical Project, Chicago: American Library Association, 1966, 53pp.

3. Openability Standard

3.1 Scope. This standard defines performance of binding as affected by the ability of a bound volume to be opened easily and to lie open unaided. This performance characteristic relates directly to the ability of a volume to open relatively flat, especially along the gutter of the book. This standard does not measure the readability of the text.

3.2 Test Apparatus. The apparatus for this test shall be the Openability Test Plate (see Part I, Appendix A), a 1-kilogram weight, a strong, nondiffused light source, and a horizontal surface.

3.3 Test Method. The procedure used in making the test for openability on new (unused) bindings is as follows:

(1) The sample to be tested is opened gently at the center and placed on the horizontal surface directly beneath the light source

(2) The test plate is placed on the opened book with the center line of the plate directly above the gutter of the book (with proper direct light, the shadow of the line scored across the center of the plate will fall along the center of the gutter)

(3) A 1-kilogram seating load (additional to the ½-kilogram weight of the plate) is placed on the handle of the plate for 5 seconds, and is then removed

(4) The book is examined to determine which pairs of lines scored on the plate are in contact with the surfaces of the facing pages (these pairs of lines will not cast shadows) and which pairs of lines are not in contact with the surfaces of the facing pages (these pairs of lines will cast shadows)

(5) The test plate is then removed by sliding it off the book. Neither of the pages on which it rested shall rise to or pass a vertical position within 10 seconds after the removal of the test plate

3.4 Evaluation of Test Results. If shadows are cast on the surfaces of the facing pages by the pairs of lines scored 1½ inches, 1 inch, and ½ inch on either side of the center line of the test plate, the openability of the book is inadequate; the binding fails to pass the openability test and is given a "poor" rating. If shadows are cast on these surfaces only by the pairs of lines scored 1 inch and ½ inch from the center line of the plate, the openability of the book is acceptable, and the binding passes the openability test with a "fair" rating. If shadows are cast on these surfaces only by the pair of lines scored ½ inch from the center line of the plate, the openability of the book is above average, and the binding passes the openability test with a "superior" rating. In the event that only one line of any pair of lines casts a shadow, the binding fails to pass that particular level of the openability test.

TABLE 2

MEASUREMENTS AND RATINGS FOR OPENABILITY

Outmost Pair of Scored Lines Casting Shadows, in Inches from Center Line	Openability Rating
1½	Poor
1	Fair
½	Superior

4. Workmanship Standard

4.1 Scope. This standard defines performance of binding as affected by workmanship. Its purpose is to help secure good workmanship by providing guides to those characteristics which result in a more useful volume for libraries.

4.2 Test Method. Workmanship is evidenced by appearance; compliance of binding to this performance standard will be determined through inspection of the binding's appearance by a qualified person. This person shall rate the binding as poor, fair, or superior for each of the items listed here. To qualify for use in libraries, a binding must be rated either as fair or superior, for all applicable points cited in this standard.

4.3 Appearance – General. Volume shall be clean, without smudges, apparent residual adhesives, or other evidence of careless handling and/or workmanship.

4.4 Outer Appearance – General. Over-all workmanship shall be evidenced by the general appearance of the cover, the lettering thereon, and the edges of the leaves.

4.4.1 *Cover.* The cover shall be rectangular and of a size appropriate to the size of the book. It shall support the contents with minimum sagging. Front and back covers shall open easily. Top and bottom ends of the backbone shall be smoothly formed. If present, the ridge along the hinge line shall be straight.

4.4.2 *Lettering.* All lettering on the binding shall be neat, legible, and of a size suitable to the size of the book. The lines shall be straight and parallel to an edge of the cover unless otherwise specified. If the volume is too thin to be lettered horizontally on the backbone, lettering shall be vertical and read down.

4.4.3 *Boards.* Front and back boards shall match in size; the corners shall be cut squarely. Boards shall be free from warpage. Combined thickness of the two boards shall be suited to the thickness, size, and weight of the volume.

4.4.4 *Cover Materials.* When cover materials and boards are used together, the cover materials shall adhere smoothly to the boards at all points and shall be neatly folded around the corners and sides of the boards.

4.4.5 *Edges.* Where trimming is appropriate, edges of leaves shall be trimmed as slightly as possible and be clean and smooth.

4.5 Inner Appearance—General. Over-all workmanship shall be evidenced by the general appearance of the end leaves, margins, fastening of leaves or sections of leaves, stubs, collation, and mending and repairing.

4.5.1 *End Leaves.* When end leaves are used, the paste-down shall adhere squarely, firmly, and smoothly to the inner surface of the cover.

4.5.2 *Margins.* The method of locking the leaves or sections of leaves of a volume together shall be consistent with the width of the back margin; that is, the narrower this margin, the more conserving of it the binding method must be. Back margins must not be so narrow as to result in the obscuring of any part of the printed page.

4.5.3 *Fastening of Leaves or Sections of Leaves.* Leaves, or sections of leaves, shall be held uniformly and securely at the binding edge only.

4.5.4 *Stubs.* When necessary for readability or to keep the volume in shape, inserts and all double or folded leaves shall be set out with stubs of suitable weight. Extra thickness existing, or anticipated, shall be compensated for by stubs.

4.5.5 *Collation.* Contents shall be complete and in proper sequence.

4.5.6 *Mending and Repairing.* When present, all tears shall be mended, and, if necessary, all margins shall be pieced out.

5. Durability Standard

5.1 Scope. This standard defines performance of binding as affected by durability.

5.2 Test Apparatus. The apparatus for this test shall be the Universal Book Tester (sometimes here called UBT). See Part I, Appendix B.

5.3 Test Method. For testing to determine compliance with this standard, samples shall be conditioned for testing by exposure, standing upright in an open position (covers spread to an angle of at least 90°) for a minimum of 16 hours, to an atmosphere having a relative humidity of 50 ± 2 percent at a temperature of 73 ± 3.5 degrees F. These conditions are in accordance with the Standards of the Technical Association of the Pulp and Paper Industry (TAPPI).[1] After the binding samples have been properly conditioned, these will be placed in the Universal Book Tester with the backbone of the book perpendicular to the squared ends of the test chamber and with the front cover of the book facing toward the abrasive metal material lining the test chamber. The binding is then tested in the Universal Book Tester for a specified time. This time is translated into anticipated levels of use, as shown in Table 3.

TABLE 3

NUMBER OF CIRCULATIONS CORRELATED TO HOURS IN UBT,
EXPRESSED IN LEVELS OF USE

Estimated Number of Circulations*		Hours of Testing in UBT	Anticipated Levels of Use
Adult	Juvenile		
34	28	1	Light
68	56	2	Medium
102	84	3	Heavy

*The estimated number of circulations is for normal handling. In situations where the bindings are subjected to rougher handling, the estimated number of circulations should be decreased by approximately one-third. Where bindings are handled more carefully, the estimated number of circulations should be increased by approximately two-fifths.

[1] Technical Association of the Pulp and Paper Industry, TAPPI Standard T 402 m–49, "Conditioning Paper and Paperboard for Testing" (New York: The Association, 1949).

5.4 Evaluation of Test Results. After testing in the Universal Book Tester for the length of time specified in Table 3, any area/type of damage shown in Table 4 shall be determined and recorded. Where present, numerical quantities for each area/type of damage shall be averaged for each set of samples tested. If the average extent of damage to the samples does not exceed that prescribed for any one area/type of damage, the binding *does comply* with this performance standard. If the average extent of damage exceeds that prescribed for any one area/type of damage by 10 percent or more, the binding *does not comply* with this standard. If the average extent of damage exceeds that prescribed for any one area/type of damage by *less* than 10 percent, additional sampling and testing according to this standard shall be performed before a final decision is made.

TABLE 4

MAXIMUM ALLOWABLE DAMAGE AFTER TESTING IN UBT ·

	Type of Damage by Area	Maximum Allowable Damage
E X T E R N A L	Break in Cover Material along Ridge Exposed to Wear in UBT	1 Inch (Total)
	Wear along Top and Bottom Edges (Head and Tail) of Back	None Apparent
	Break in Cover Material along Edges of Covers, Front and Back	2 Inches (Total)
	Loosening of Hinge Structure	None Apparent
I N T E R N A L	Break in Material Covering Hinges, Front and Back	1 Hinge Length (Total)
	Break in Hinge Reinforcements	None Apparent
	Break between Leaves or Sections of Leaves along Binding Edge Observed in Any One Opening of the Book	1 Inch (Total)
	Break or Loosening of Sewing	None Apparent

307

Appendix A

Openability Test Plate

The Openability Test Plate is made of clear, rigid plastic, 8 by 12 by ¼ inches, with edges beveled. The bottom side of the plate is scored across the 8-inch width at the center, and three parallel lines are scored at ½-inch intervals on each side of this center line to a distance of 1½ inches. The center line is darkened to provide good contrast and the other lines may also be color-coded to make using them easier. A handle is fixed at the center of the upper side of the plate to ensure ease of operation. (See illustrations following.) Total weight of plate, including handle, is ½ kilogram (1.10 pounds).

Openability Test Plate in position
with weight added.

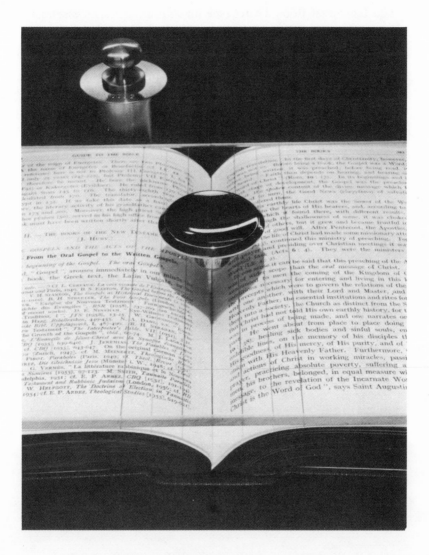

Openability Test Plate in position. One-kilogram
weight, used in conjunction with the test
plate, is shown in background.

Appendix B

Universal Book Tester

The Universal Book Tester (see illustration) consists essentially of a rectangular test chamber made of ¼-inch aluminum, lined with 50 by 50 mesh, No. 304 stainless steel wire .009 inches in diameter. The test chamber is supported and rotated by a steel drive shaft attached perpendicular to the center of its bottom. Viewed from the front of the UBT, the drive shaft is rotated, in a clockwise direction, at a speed of 20 rotations per minute and is inclined at an angle of 20° with the horizontal. The dimensions of the test chamber will vary, depending on the size of the volume undergoing testing, according to the following table.

TABLE B1

RELATION OF UBT TEST CHAMBER SIZE TO DIMENSIONS OF VOLUME
TO BE TESTED

Test Chamber Type	Internal Dimensions of Chamber in Inches*			Over-All Dimensions of Volume to be Tested in Inches	
	Width	Height	Depth	Width	Height
A	13	16	4	5 to 7	7 to 10
B	15	19	4	8 to 10	10 to 13
C	15	15	4	8 to 10	6 to 9
D	11½	13	4	4 to 7	5 to 8
E	18	23	4	11 to 13	14 to 17

*Each chamber is rounded to a 1½-inch radius along the sides of the bottom, to concentrate the abrasive stresses along the edges of the backbone of the book. The chamber was designed in this fashion to simulate observed patterns of wear.

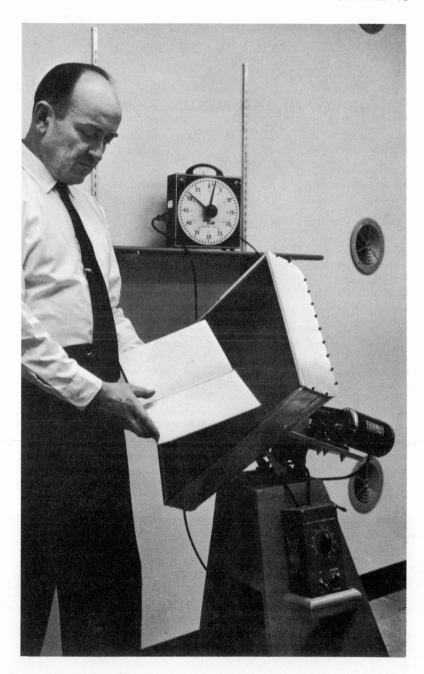

The Universal Book Tester shown with its
inventor, Robert E. Sayre.

VII: MANUSCRIPTS AND DOCUMENTS

Papers 22, 23, and 24: Commentary

Manuscript collecting, although often considered of peripheral interest in the past, is a legitimate function of libraries, regardless of type of institution.[1] Although administrative support is often inadequate, there are thousands of libraries today that include important manuscript collections among their holdings.[2] For this reason, it was decided to include a section on manuscripts in this book.

Librarians rarely receive library school training in the principles of archival management and the care of manuscripts, although they frequently find themselves coping with these matters in the institutions they are eventually selected to administer. This responsibility can be a daunting one, particularly for a librarian working in a smaller institution, where he or she may be the only professionally trained person on the staff and responsible for the general collections as well as for rare books and manuscripts.

Manuscripts are most vulnerable to damage under the following circumstances: when they are processed into the collections by members of the staff; when they are entrusted to the public for examination and study; when they are placed on exhibition or loaned to other institutions for exhibit purposes; when they are entrusted to specialists for repair; and when they are photographed or otherwise reproduced for educational, publicity, or republication purposes. The selections chosen for inclusion in this section deal with three of the more common "human" aspects of archival security.

Roger Ellis is a well-known British archivist and the first editor of the journal, *Archives.* His 1951 address to students enrolled in a course of document repair at the London School of Printing and Graphic Arts[3] was subsequently published as a pamphlet. The original, which is unavailable today in all but a handful of libraries, deserves wider acquaintance. With clarity and economy of word, Ellis describes the principles that should apply when the repair of documents is undertaken. Although his remarks are addressed to students training to become repair specialists, rather than to administrators and curators, those responsible for the management of manuscript collections must also be fully aware of the principles outlined by Ellis.

"Handling practices" is an excerpt from a longer article on archival preservation by Clark W. Nelson. His suggestions are basically prescriptive, but they are important in terms of principle, as well. Nelson, who is currently the Archivist of the Mayo Foundation Medical Library, describes simple operations that the librarian with a minimal staff and little specialized training in archival practice can perform to assure better preservation of materials over the long term.

Robert H. Land's "Defense of Archives Against Human Foes," while written from the viewpoint of a specialist in one of the largest manuscript repositories in the country, the Library of Congress, contains a number of important insights that are of value to all who have curatorial responsibility for manuscript collections. Human beings themselves constitute an important element to be considered in the security and preservation of manuscripts, and it is not always easy for the curator to distinguish friend from foe. Human enemies can be "either members of the staff or persons from outside." The comments by Lucille Kane and Richard D. Higgins, both curators of large and significant collections, provide further evidence of the need to be alert to human factors and to exercise continuous vigilance in protecting manuscripts.

Manuscript collections cannot be administered in the same manner as collections of printed books, but the preservation aspects are similar. Frazer Poole recently observed, "Because the materials of archives and library collections exhibit so many basic similarities and almost no differences, the preservation problems of the one are also the preservation problems of the other."[4]

NOTES AND REFERENCES

1. See Clark, Robert L., Jr., ed., *Archive-Library Relations* (New York: Bowker, 1976), p. 17.
2. See Brubaker, Robert L., "Manuscript Collections," *Library Trends* 13 (October 1964) for an analysis of institutions that include manuscripts in their holdings. See also his remarks on the administration of collections, as reported in "Manuscript Collections," *AB Bookman's Weekly* 60 (September 5, 1977): 1190-91.
3. The London School of Printing & Graphic Arts is now the London College of Printing.
4. Poole, Frazer G., "Preservation," in Clark, Robert L., Jr., ed., *Archive-Library Relations,* p. 142.

ADDITIONAL READINGS

In addition to the general works listed at the end of Part I of this volume and those referred to in the footnotes above, see the following.

Archives Procedural Manual (St. Louis, Mo.: Washington University, School of Medicine Library, 1974), 118 pp.
Minogue, Adelaide, E., "Physical Care, Repair, and Protection of Manuscripts," *Library Trends* 5 (January 1957): 344-51.
Protection of Records (Boston: Mass., National Fire Protection Association, 1970), 93 pp. NFPA No. 232.

"Marking Manuscripts," *Preservation Leaflet* No. 4 (Washington, D.C.: Library of Congress, Assistant Director for Preservation, Administrative Dept., 1977).

"Historical Society Records: Guidelines for a Protection Program," *History News* 27 (September 1972), 8 pp. *Technical Leaflet* 18.

"Protective Display Lighting of Historical Documents," in U.S. National Bureau of Standards, *NBS Circular* 538 (April 1, 1953), 8 pp.

Schellenberg, Theodore R., "Physical Arrangements," Chapter 13 in *The Management of Archives* (New York: Columbia University Press, 1965), pp. 199–218.

22: THE PRINCIPLES OF ARCHIVE REPAIR

Roger Ellis

THE PURPOSE of this course is instruction in the art or craft of archive or record repair, and the greater part of the course will be spent in practical work under supervision; but before we begin this practical work I want to talk to you for a short time upon the *principles* of archive repair. There is a great deal more in the repair of archives than the simple application of paper and paste; the whole process of repair may defeat its own object unless the true nature of the archive—and hence of the repair which it is to undergo—is fully understood. These principles and their corollaries underlie every act of record repair that you will carry out, and it is important to understand them before even the simplest repair is undertaken.

We have called them the principles of *archive* repair, not of manuscript repair simply. The distinction is purposely made. A number of processes will be taught here which are applicable to the repair of manuscripts of all kinds, and indeed of printed pages; other processes, which in some quarters are regarded as essential to manuscript repair, will not be taught; but we shall teach, and insist upon, certain processes and practices which would be out of place in the repair of manuscripts which were not of *archive character*.

It is this *archive* or *record* character of the manuscripts with which we shall deal that determines the nature of their treatment, and for this reason I make no apology for restating here a definition of this character, as given by Sir Hilary Jenkinson*: '*Archives are the documents accumulated by a natural process in the course of the conduct of affairs of any kind, public or private, at any date; and preserved thereafter for reference, in their own custody, by the persons responsible for the affairs in question or their successors. . . .* Archives are an actual part of the activities which gave them birth, material

---

* *The English Archivist: a New Profession*, London, H. K. Lewis and Co., 1948. The indebtedness of the present writer to Sir Hilary Jenkinson, on many points besides this, will be very apparent.

evidences surviving in the form of writing.' *Material evidences in the form of writing*; in other words, a manuscript or document of archive character, whatever other qualities it may possess, is first and foremost a vehicle of evidence, of impartial evidence; it is for this quality, in the first place, that it has been preserved, and it is this quality above all others that any process of repair must respect. The record may indeed possess other qualities; it may be monumentally large or microscopically small; it may be thousands of years old or merely a matter of days; it may be an object of great beauty or an offence to the eye; its contents—the written evidence which it conveys—may be trivial or revolutionary, scandalous, treasonable, pious, comic, or merely dull; but all these qualities are secondary to the prime fact that the document conveys, and is, a piece of evidence, and that it is on this account that the document has been, and must be, preserved.

But if the soul of archives resides in their evidential quality, they have also bodies which are hardly less important. The message of a document is of little avail if it exists only invisible and disembodied. 'I've often seen a cat without a grin,' thought Alice, 'but a grin without a cat! It's the most curious thing I ever saw in all my life.' Alice was lucky to be able to see it at all. The message must normally be conveyed through some visible and tangible medium, and in the course of successive civilizations this medium has displayed a protean variety. Aurignacian man painted upon the walls of a cave; Assyrians and Babylonians impressed cuneiform characters upon tablets of clay; the Egyptians fastened together the fibres of a water-plant and wrote upon them with reed pens; Romans made notes with a spike upon tablets of wax; Athenians scratched the name of Aristides upon potsherds; and Man Friday left his footprint upon the sandy beach. Almost every record office contains its freak document of abnormal materials; but by far the greater part of the documents which you will be required to handle will have been written, in ink, upon paper or parchment, and it is with these that our course here will deal. Upon each of these—ink, paper, and parchment —whole books have been written, and in this short introduction to your practical work we cannot discuss them at length. You must all, if you please, study the nature and behaviour of these materials, by reading and by observation, whenever opportunity offers; but as a starting-point for your studies may I offer these briefest of notes:

1. PARCHMENT is of *animal* origin. It is the skin of a sheep (sometimes of a goat or other animal) with the hair removed by the action of lime, all fat and fibre removed by washing and scraping, and the surface smoothed and refined with chalk and pumice. Its name, incidentally, derives through French and Latin from the Greek, the material having been produced in great quantities, in the second century before Christ, in the kingdom of Pergamum.

2. PAPER is of *vegetable* origin. Fibrous or cellulose material such as linen rags, cotton rags, straw, wood, grass, etc., is macerated into a pulp with water; the pulp is spread into thin layers and the water drained and pressed out; the resulting sheet is impregnated with a glutinous solution called *size,* and dried; and paper is the result.

3. INK is prepared in a number of ways, but there are two main kinds with which are written almost all the manuscripts that will pass through your hands. The first and less common consists of a black pigment, generally finely-divided soot, suspended in a solution of gum; this kind of ink rests upon the surface of the paper or parchment and is easily washed away. The second, and fortunately the more usual kind, is a solution of gallic acid and salts of iron, which darkens by oxidation upon exposure to air; generally some dye is added to make the ink visible before oxidation has taken place. This ink penetrates the pores of parchment and the fibres of paper, and is not readily washed off.

How, then, do these qualities of the archive, spiritual and corporeal, affect its repair? In this way: *first,* that no process of repair may be allowed to remove, diminish, falsify, or obscure, in any way, the document's value as evidence; and this must apply not only to the evidence obviously conveyed by the writing upon the document, but also to those overtones of evidence conveyed by it through other means, of which I shall have more to say presently. *Second,* that no process of repair may be used which could in any way damage or weaken the material of which the document is made. Since the processes of which we are speaking are designed to strengthen and preserve the document, this may seem something of an oxymoron; but an ill-conceived method of repair, or one insufficiently tried, may prove to be a cure worse than the disease. I have seen a parchment membrane reduced to a ferment by an attempt to damp and flatten it in the wrong way, and fine linen-rag paper made completely transparent by a plastic adhesive. There are also methods of repair, now being widely practised, which yield immediate results of a most satisfactory kind, but whose final effect, after the passage of many years, has yet to be determined. Reducing all this to simple practical rules, the repairer must endeavour to put nothing into his document which was not there when he received it, and to take from it nothing which was. And before starting on a repair, he may well ask himself, 'How *little* need I do to this document to make it fit for use again?'

The repairer will therefore begin his operations by examining his document to see what it has lost; and here he will find at once that (as we have already suggested) there are two parts of the document which can grow weak or disappear—the writing, and the material upon which it is written. Between the modes of treatment of these two he will draw a sharp line.

First, the writing. Where this has vanished, he will make no attempt to reinsert it. The reasons are, I think, too obvious to require emphasis. The most the archivist can permit himself here is a signed and dated note stating where, if anywhere, another version of the missing text can be found—in a printed calendar, or a transcript, or in some parallel class of record; though even this may fairly be regarded as the business not of the repairer but of the editor. Then where the writing is faded, the repairer will best not attempt to revive it by chemical reagents. It has yet to be shown that any one of these will not, after the passage of sufficient time, leave the document worse than it was. The effects of ox-gall, applied in the seventeenth and eighteenth centuries, are all too evident in the Public Records, where dark brown stains have in some places quite obliterated the writing that the gall was applied to restore. Ammonium sulphide, recommended by some authorities in recent years as a harmless if evil-smelling alternative, is not above suspicion; many years ago your present teacher painted a streak of ammonium sulphide solution upon a piece of rag paper and put it away in a box, and when he opened it in my presence not long ago the streaks, invisible at first, had turned yellow. How will they look in another twenty years? Fortunately such reagents have now been rendered un-necessary by developments in the use of infra-red and ultra-violet light, both with photographic apparatus and with the naked eye; and although these processes are outside the scope of this course, I recommend them to you in this context. The only case of this kind in which the repairer can safely inter-vene is when the writing, though neither lost nor obscured, is becoming *loose* through, for example, the decay of the pre-pared surface upon which it is written; here the repairer may and must refix it, by the use of materials and adhesives whose properties are known and whose behaviour is predictable—a mechanical, not a chemical, process.

The greater part of any repair process, however, will be directed towards fortifying, or replacing, the vehicle upon which the writing is borne; and here the repairer must observe three simple but fundamental rules:

1. As far as possible, to replace missing material with new material of the same kind;

2. To leave the nature and extent of his repair unmis-takably evident;

3. Never to do anything which cannot be undone without damage to the document.

From the first of these rules occasional departures are neces-sary. Although a repairer must try to avoid adding to a docu-ment anything which was not there when he received it, yet clearly he must do this when large parts of the original paper or parchment are missing, in order that the document as a whole may be given back its original strength; but though he cannot avoid adding what is *new,* he can and will avoid adding what is *foreign* to the material of the original. He will repair a paper document with paper and a parchment document with parchment; a broken seal with new wax; and where old size has perished from the paper he will add new. The result will be not a patchwork but a homogeneous document, having throughout its constituent parts, old or new, the same pro-perties as the original document, and responding in the same ways to temperature, humidity, handling, and the passage of time. From this rule he may allow himself two departures, in the use of (first) an *adhesive* for fixing the material of a repair, and (second) some *transparent* material, through which the writing can be read when the document must be strengthened all over its surface or upon both sides. And perhaps the experienced repairer may add a third: when the material he would prefer is not to hand, and the document will perish if not repaired, he will use an effective and harmless substitute— thus a large parchment membrane may on occasion be backed with linen.

The second rule has its origin equally in the archive character of the document. This allows it to be accepted without question as precedent or evidence since, having been always in official custody, it can never have been tampered with. Repair must never become tampering, and never can become so provided that it obscures nothing of the original, and is itself clearly distinguishable. The repairer, then, will never tint his paper or parchment to 'harmonize' with the original; indeed he will encourage a contrast, and will rely upon the excellence of his new materials, and the neatness of his work, to avoid offence to the eye when the document happens, by chance, to be a thing of beauty. He will also be at pains not to conceal by his operations any portion or feature of the document which is a part of, or could shed light upon, its evidential value; and this means not simply that he will never paste new paper over old writing (though it is easier than you might think to do this, when an endorsement is faint or the edge of a closely-written document is tattered), but also that he will observe, preserve, and on occasion reveal such other incidental features as original sewing-holes, dustings of pounce, marks of folding, traces of seals, watermarks, old end-papers, even on occasion stray blobs of wax or old stains—and a great many more. The applications of this apparently over-fussy rule will appear in the course of practical work, but it is worth while to emphasize now how essential it is to preserve *all* the features of a record—even those, as Sir Hilary Jenkinson has remarked, that you cannot see. Sewing-holes, for instances, when they are found in the document, must be carefully preserved; if the document has to be stitched again, the new stitches must pass through the old holes and no new ones must be made; and

321

these holes must not be covered or concealed. For these sewing-holes may be the only remaining evidence of a previous gathering or binding, and so of a previous or original order of the documents; while a correspondence of these modest holes may establish that two documents now widely separated were once joined. Every archivist in due course discovers his own favourite examples of the value of such incidentals.

Proportionately more must we value the original *make-up* of a record, when it survives. When dealing with a single document, or a number of documents whose order is of no significance, this question does not arise. When, however, the documents are attached together in order and by design, as a file, roll, volume, or whatever it may be, this original make-up must be treated with the utmost respect. The rule here must be: the archivist or repairer must never interfere with, still less destroy, the existing make-up of a record if he can possibly avoid doing so. Not only does this make-up hold the papers or membranes in an ordered relation, but it is itself part of the record—a form purposely given to it by its creators or custodians. Though venerable, however, it may not be perfect, and it is allowable for a repairer to alter a document's make-up for three reasons, viz., convenience of consultation; convenience of storage; and protection of the document itself.

The first reason is perhaps the most obvious. If the make-up prevents a document from being consulted, it defeats its purpose. The best example is perhaps that of a file of documents pierced through the centre and strung tightly on a cord; the top and bottom documents can be read on one side only, and the rest not at all. Convenience of storage is a consideration which will appeal to most local archivists, cramming more and more records into what seems like less and less space; a good example here is that of a small letter illustrated by, and attached to, a large drawing or map. Here the repairer may be allowed to separate map and letter, and store them upon different sizes of shelving; noting, of course, upon each of them what has been done. And lastly, a document may need more protection than its original form affords against dirt, light, or continual use—as when a rolled-up bundle of Chancery Proceedings, the outer membrane serving as a cover for the others, is flattened out and put into a dust-proof portfolio; or sometimes its original form may be positively harmful, as when loose papers have been too tightly overcast and bound, and are torn by the searcher's efforts to open the inner margin. A volume, equally, may be clumsily made up of uneven sections, or may be so heavy that it falls out of its binding; here the answer will usually be to remake it as two volumes or even three. And in this context I will mention to you the magic word *guarding and filing*; you will learn all about this later on, and will find it the key to many of your difficulties.

The third of our rules touches upon another basic quality of the archive, implied if not expressed in the definition which I have quoted—that it is *unique*. It is the only document, or set of documents, *produced by* the transaction (whatever that was); it is *the record*; it cannot be replaced. So to proceed hopefully upon a course of repair from which no retreat is possible may at the worst destroy this record, and will at best irrevocably alter it.

Finally, may I emphasize the importance of the quality of your materials. The task of the archivist is to preserve his records to eternity, and when choosing materials for repair he must be certain that they have at least the same expectation of life as the original material of the record, and that they have no destructive chemical reaction. For these reasons he will be wary of plastic foils and chemical adhesives whose behaviour has not been tested over long periods of time, and he will rely on parchment prepared by traditional methods, paper whose composition and manufacture he knows and approves (with hand-made linen rag paper he cannot go far wrong), natural silk, linen, or cotton fabrics whose life is known to run into many centuries, and—for adhesive—a simple paste of white flour. Where metal is used, e.g., for stapling, it must be non-corrosive. Fungicides and insecticides must be used with caution, since what is destructive to moulds or insects may not be harmless to the tissues of paper or parchment. Consult the chemist; sometimes a dangerous guide but always a valuable ally.

These methods of repair which you are about to study are not, of course, the only methods. New methods have recently been developed of which no doubt you have heard—not least the technique of lamination, invented in America and transplanted to France and Belgium, which uses a hot press or rollers, and acetate foil. All such new methods deserve the most careful study, and in some cases—for example, where huge quantities of modern documents require protective treatment—their value is evident. But the methods which are to be taught here are the result of careful experiment and observed success in more than one repair shop over many years; and although other methods may perhaps, in time to come take their place, these remain at present the methods which most faithfully embody the *principles of archive repair* of which I have spoken, and which must underlie every process of repair which fulfils its first purpose—that of transmitting to future generations, strengthened in body but unchanged in spirit, the impartial evidence of the Record.

23: ARCHIVAL PRESERVATION

Clark W. Nelson

[*Editors' Note:* In the original material precedes this excerpt.]

Handling Practices

One of the important aspects of archival preservation is the development of handling practices that will further the longevity of the collection. As mentioned earlier, cleanliness offers many benefits. This should be carried further by emphasizing to one's staff the care of their hands and their surroundings. Separate work tables in areas away from storage rooms will do much to keep the normally dirty task of cleaning and organizing records from contaminating those already boxed. If one can afford a cleaning table with an exhaust, so much the better. Many, though, utilize a conventional table with room for sorting and cleaning records.

Upon arrival in an archives, most records need not only arranging but cleaning. Their prior storage conditions usually are not conducive to cleanliness. Consequently, dust, dirt and even insect life will be found. Before adding such materials to the collection, they must be cleaned. Soft brushes made of sable, etc., can be used for this purpose. It does not take long to recognize that brittle, frayed documents lose pieces easily unless gently handled. Soft erasers can also be used to minimize dirt, etc. A most effective cleaner is that used for wallpaper. It is kneaded like dough and gently drawn over the surface of a paper document from its center out. The document is held firmly during the process to prevent damage. The cleaner will easily remove much grime. There is one caution. Care must be taken to keep the small flecks of cleaner from remaining on the document before it is boxed.

Vacuum cleaners can also be of assistance in the cleaning process, but they must be handled carefully. A nylon stocking placed over the suction tube will reduce the possibility of drawing weak pieces of paper into the canister. The lowest possible suction must be used, and the especially weak and brittle materials avoided. If a reverse (blowing) action is available, it can sometimes be more useful. With large quantities of materials in both boxes and stacks, one can then quickly remove great quantities of the looser dirt and dust. A compressed-air hose coupled with an exhaust provision on a hooded table is the ultimate. For those handling large numbers of materials, varied or otherwise, it is a blessing. Records, books, artifacts, etc., can all be quickly and easily dusted with such equipment.

After cleaning, the question of insect life and mildew should be considered. In humid climates, this will be routine consideration. No matter where one lives, however, the tendencies to store records in almost every cubbyhole, whether in institutions or dwellings, usually produces some evidence of insect interest or mildew involvement. Exposure to sunlight and a good airing can be beneficial. Obviously, with the possibilities of further fading, this approach is not the best. Rather, fumigation by the use of a simply constructed box containing thymol is one of the easiest and least expensive approaches for small quantities of materials. Though lacking in permanency, thymol can be an effective sterilizer. The items needing attention are placed in a cabinet where the chemical is melted in watch glasses by the heat of 25-watt bulbs. In the case of insect life, a saucer of paradichlorobenzene crystals (1.5 oz. per cubic foot of air space) is placed in the cabinet and the contents sealed shut for two weeks.

The length of time required, coupled with the difficulty of penetrating the centers of books and stacks of paper documents with the vapors, makes the above approach a poor processor for large quantities of materials. For these, the vacuum method is recognized as the most efficient and effective. Its equipment costs, until recently, have been near the $10,000 mark. Within the last few years, a small unit has been developed which sells for around $3,000. It will fumigate a small cart of books and papers within a matter of hours. Fumigation cabinets designed for furriers have also been used for large quantities of documents. Since they operate without the benefits of a vacuum, they are slower and less efficient.

After cleaning and fumigation comes the task of boxing the materials. Here one can use a number of handling techniques that will minimize wear and strain on the paper documents. All sheets should be unfolded and boxed flattened out. Folds which are particularly stubborn or sheets that are badly wrinkled can be flattened by first humidifying them and then gently ironing at a low heat setting. Care must be taken to avoid wetting the inks and causing them to bleed or transfer. A simple press can also help the flattening process.

When handling documents, avoid the use of pressure-sensitive tapes. The dark brown stains from the older tapes should provide ample warning. While it is true some of the newer products are superior, they still offer hazards that make them undesirable. If documents are torn or separated, either leave them that way or earmark them for the attention of a restoration expert. If tape is still your choice, always use it on the reverse side, not on the side of the writing. But think twice before resorting to such an expedient. Any future restoration of the document will be made more difficult, if not impossible, by such action.

Before boxing, remove rubber bands, clips and staples. If staples are used, those made of rust-free stainless steel are best. Keep aged, badly stained papers separated from the others by interleaving sheets of acid-free paper between them. Such deteriorating papers should, ideally, be separated and duplicates inserted in their place. If their value warrants, they should be scheduled for deacidification and restoration.

Currently there are a number of storage boxes available that are acid-free in construction. These are highly recommended. While it is true some repositories use boxes of a low-acid nature, this practice has its hazards. The so-called records center boxes usually fall into this category. One must remember that they are designed for relatively short-term storage, and while cheaper in cost, do encase documents in a less desirable environment.

The use of acid-free folders is also recommended. Here again, there are also low-acid types available. These should be avoided if possible. If the budget is low, however, the low-acid folder is preferable to the regular kind. The more acid-containing materials we bring together in storage, the more difficult our preservation task becomes. Whenever possible we should try to upgrade our storage containers and file folders to the acid-free type.

There are now available on the market alkaline papers that contain a buffering agent which reduces the chances of future acid development. Permalife is one of these. It is available in several forms, such as folders, boxes, etc. It is a highly recommended paper for long-life use. For those needing a long-life writing paper, it can be readily substituted. Permalife's longevity is projected in the centuries. It is one of the developments from research conducted since World War II in paper.

When boxing and shelving paper documents, the boxes should be full or their sheets blocked up so that they stay flat. Most boxes today are designed to store paper vertically. This method is usually satisfactory, provided the documents are not allowed to sag in their containers. A few archives store their papers horizontally. This does eliminate sagging and other strains on the paper. There are special boxes available for this purpose. Such boxes as the Hollinger can be laid horizontally on the shelf so their contents remain flat. Unless one has specially constructed boxes, they cannot normally be stacked in such a position. Despite the larger shelf space required, horizontal storage is still a desirable method and can be used even in a smaller facility for valuable items of a limited number.

Before committing documents to permanent storage, each archivist faces the major question of why he is doing so. It is well to note that at this point one should also examine all possible alternatives to storing the documents intact. If the items are fragile and difficult to use, it is possible that microfilm or xerographic copies would be a better choice. The originals can then be permanently stored and the copies made available to the searcher.

This same approach can be used as a collection ages. At any time, duplicate copies will help preserve originals. In certain cases, the copy can become the "original" if other factors have become so persuasive. Miniaturization is part of today's archival world. Many of our materials come to us that way. It is important to remember that we can use such a method to further preserve older, more valuable and fragile collections. While preservation is mainly concerned with an original document, we as custodians of the past must make every effort to preserve the information it contains for as long as it is physically possible, in whatever form offers the longest life.

[*Editors' Note:* Material has been omitted at this point.]

24: DEFENSE OF ARCHIVES AGAINST HUMAN FOES

Robert H. Land[1]

THREE years ago the Library of Congress issued a bibliography entitled *Safeguarding our Cultural Heritage . . . in Time of War*. This suggested, as an appropriate title for this paper, "Safeguarding our Cultural Heritage . . . in Time of Peace," because I was not asked to discourse on the harm done to records by human enemies when they are national enemies and when their havoc is incidental to military action. Neither is it concerned with the baleful influences of such natural or unnatural peacetime enemies as fires, floods, insects, mice, sunlight, dampness, dryness, heat, cold, dirt, dust, bacteria, acidic pollution in the air, and low grade paper. Its concern is with the direct destruction or abuse of documents (whether knowingly or innocently performed) by human beings. There have been far more papers intentionally sacrificed on the altar of Vulcan than have been accidentally burned, and many papers said to have been sacrificed on the altar of Mars were harmed by soldiers not acting in the line of duty.

I am using "archives" in the broadest sense of the word, as it is applied in reference to all of the historical papers in the Adams Manuscript Trust or in the Franklin D. Roosevelt Library. It has seemed apt in treating the enemies of archives to use the idea of warfare and to divide this paper into two parts and in allegorical manner to discuss, first, the enemies a document or body of documents might encounter before reaching the safety and protection of a citadel. This fortress, of course, would be a repository, whether one of the two great national repositories (the Library of Congress and the National Archives), some other public institution, a State or local archives (or historical society, library, or museum), a university or college library, or an independently endowed library, such as the Huntington. The staffs of such institutions would be the guards under orders to defend their holdings. The second

[1] This paper, in a shorter form, was read at the annual meeting of the Society of American Archivists at Nashville, Tennessee, on October 11, 1955. The author is assistant chief of the Manuscripts Division, Library of Congress. Comments of two members of the panel that discussed Mr. Land's paper follow this article.

part of the paper then would deal with the measures taken and stratagems devised for the defense of archives against the various types of sieges and assaults made upon them by their human foes. In considering their human foes, I was even inclined to attribute to documents characteristics of living beings. (Are they not said to "live" and to "speak" to us? Were they not called "living organisms" by Mr. Radoff in his presidential address?) I realized, however, that I was here straining to create an illusion and had to admit that a poor defenseless document could not tell a human friend from a human foe and that the survival of the "fittest" was surely a matter on the lap of callously fickle gods.

Having abandoned this idea, I still planned to handle the subject in two parts: documents in private though perhaps corporate hands and documents in repositories. It was with considerable reluctance that I came to discard this plan also. I regret this, too, for your sakes because the deleted portion of my paper was by far the most, if not the only, dramatic part. In preparation to write it, I began to absorb the lore of manuscript enemies from Biblical times to the present and I found numerous and harrowing illustrations of their methods and their devastations. I meant to regale you with these and only refrained from doing so when I realized, almost too late, that this was not the subject assigned me. I was asked to speak about defending archives, not to describe their human enemies. You must know their foes in order to protect them. Having fully dissected the enemies of papers privately held, however, what can you say about defending them, short of getting them into a repository? It seems futile to characterize the various types of enemies, if the only means to protect documents in private ownership appears, over and over again, to be to educate those who, by happenstance, may have them even momentarily in their keeping. The pedagogic requirements, to be effective, are hopelessly insuperable because of the wide disparity in the characteristics of these enemies ranging from religious zealots to unconscionable forgers, from brilliant scholars to ignorant housemaids, from collectors with delicate sensibilities to second-hand furniture dealers with indelicate sensibilities, from efficiency experts to inefficient file clerks, from royalty and the families of Presidents to butchers, bakers and candlestick makers, and from censors to grangerizers. In truth, the danger points are so numerous that there is no assurance that papers in private hands will be preserved, even for the owner or his heirs, unless they are placed in a repository equipped with proper facilities and staff. Even then, we know they may not be out of harm's way and the problems of their protection from that point on are enough to occupy us today. Indeed, even in this area, there are aspects of the subject on which I shall not discourse. It might be well to epitomize these to forestall a possible criticism that I have unintentionally overlooked them.

To return for a moment to the allegory of war, we know of the fifth columnists and of the feelings of jealousy and distrust frequently experienced among allies. Repositories then may be called allies and, if jealousy and distrust do not exist among them, competition and rivalry certainly do. This reminds me of an article published 18 years ago in a library journal that yet enrages many in the library profession. The very title of this provocative piece by the late Randolph G. Adams, director of the William L. Clements Library, suggests the high words he used in chastising his fellows: "Librarians as Enemies of Books." [2] Some of the barbs that Adams directed at librarians could be aimed with equal force at archivists and curators. I say this not to stir up controversy or to create bad blood. Without weighing the relative merits among varying custodial policies, procedures, and practices, but considering the friends of archives to be those who insure their physical safety and make them readily accessible to all qualified searchers, I wish briefly to suggest some areas in which curators might be enemies of archives:

1. Curators should give good counsel. When prospective donors of collections confer with repository officials it provides an occasion: to abstain from accepting material which should be directed to a more appropriate repository; to advise against the dispersal of a collection among repositories and to decline accepting part of a collection when it is known that the major portion already has been placed in another repository; to caution against the reckless weeding of the collection; to secure freedom of access for all serious investigators or to recommend only a reasonable period of restricted access with a definite terminal date for materials of a very personal nature or of possible embarrassment to living persons, and to urge that permissions of access be not then arbitrarily denied or not limited solely to a favored user; and to secure a dedication to the public of such literary rights as the donor possesses in the collection. If curators give bad counsel on these matters, should they not be called enemies of archives?

2. Curators should maintain proper safeguards. An erratic acquisition rate, which in many repositories cannot be controlled, may mean the accumulation of vast quantities of unorganized materials ripe for pilfering without risk of detection. If curators permit readers to use or staff members to have access to such materials without special precautions to safeguard them, are they not foes of archives?

[2] Randolph G. Adams, "Librarians as Enemies of Books," in *Library Quarterly*, 7:317-331 (July 1937).

3. Curators should not split up collections. Those who, without reference to provenance, heedlessly split up collections or create miscellany collections or add materials to wholly different collections can cause endless trouble for their successors in office and misunderstanding and misinterpretation for an unending line of investigators. One authority has expressed the view that the worst human enemies of archives are those who ignore the basic doctrine of *respect des fonds*.[3]

4. Curators should exercise great caution in weeding, pulping, and making collections difficult of access. There are some who would quibble at any new development, but many would proscribe as enemies of archives those who advocate that records be preserved by microfilming them and then destroying the bulky originals; or those who ruthlessly purge records, deciding in haste (but for all time and eternity), what is of value to the historian here and hereafter; or those who determine on the basis of service requests to rusticate or sequester classes of records.

5. Curators should appreciate the value, meaning, and use of collections. To use a phrase of Adams, repository administrators might be ascending "into the heaven of efficiency," having had all feeling and sentiment trained out of them. The size and complexity of repositories have meant that administration has become a full-time and all-demanding occupation. The inevitable result is that some in authority — especially those never having served an apprenticeship as investigators and not always understanding the consequences of what they are doing — are so largely concerned with budgets, enlarged staff and personnel matters, facilities for public service, air-conditioning, statistical analysis, or processing activities that love of, and enthusiasm for, manuscripts have been crowded out of their temperaments. Can those who still feel that enthusiasm — collectors and specialists, whose intimate knowledge and appreciation of the value of documents have been gained by their application to scholarly pursuits — be blamed for calling such officials enemies of manuscripts?

6. Curators must be impartial. Should we be surprised when a disappointed scholar, denied access to or full use of material, censures as an enemy of archives the curator who withholds it for exclusive exploitation by himself, by a colleague, or by some favorite?

These questions suggest the areas in which the relative merits of repositories or curators might be debated. Another similar matter of concern is whether greater benefit will be derived from the concentration of important collections in Washington or from their decentralization throughout the United States. In this connection it seems ironic that the principal promoter of the establishment of the National Archives, John Franklin Jameson, stood firmly for concentration. In regard to the Harding papers, he commented in 1929:

[3] Francis L. Berkeley, Jr., to Robert H. Land, Sept. 9, 1955, in correspondence file, Manuscripts Division, Library of Congress.

There is no doubt something attractive about the notion of placing the statesman's papers in a building especially erected to commemorate him, but as a matter of fact experience shows that papers thus placed are used only sparingly. It is thought that they can be conveniently used for his biography, but even for that purpose their location is less advantageous, for the biographer of a president needs constant use of the papers of other public men, his contemporaries and of a great collection of books.[4]

About the Hoover papers, in 1933, he wrote from the Library of Congress:

As things are now, the serious student is almost obliged to come to Washington, and to the millions of manuscripts for American history in this repository, and this will still more be the case when the new National Archive Building is completed and its contents are available to their use. To have the papers of a president stored elsewhere is to cause them to be little used by the future writers of history, in comparison with their use if they are preserved here, along with the papers of other presidents and other contemporaries in public life.[5]

It is, however, even more ironic that a document of greatest prestige at the National Archives, the Declaration of Independence, indicts George III for having "called together legislative bodies at places unusual, uncomfortable, and distant from the depository of their Records, for the sole purpose of fatiguing them into compliance with his measures."

Since I am not attempting to draw distinctions among repositories, you may think that I have now worked myself completely out of giving a paper, that there is little left to speak of. Yet there remain matters for an impartial treatment of the defense of papers already in a repository, papers which it has decided to retain, which it has repaired, which it has organized for use, and for which it has compiled finding aids. Who are the enemies of such records; how does the repository protect them? Unlike the document itself, the archivist, who may not be able to distinguish friend from foe, is still not without defenses. The human enemies are either members of the staff or persons from outside. The size and complexity of the staff and the clientele served are determining factors in establishing safeguards. For endowed institutions that have a staff made up of especially trained authorities and a small clerical and maintenance force and that limit service to a select number of well qualified scholars of known identity, it is possible to enforce only a few formal rules and yet observe strict security measures. Their holdings are exactly cataloged so as to provide ready identification and quick

---

[4] Correspondence file, Manuscripts Division, Library of Congress.
[5] *Ibid.*

means of discovering losses or abuse. It is easy for them to take frequent inventories and to serve material singly or in small units. For many public repositories, however, the situation is quite different. Their staffs include a variety of grades, with much of the work of accessioning, arranging, boxing, and shelving of records in the hands of nonprofessional employees and with many clerical and maintenance assistants. Their holdings are maintained in large groups difficult to inventory and are served to readers in boxes or folders so that it is hard to detect missing or damaged items. The clientele of public repositories is more numerous, and it includes persons who arrive unannounced, with no experience in handling original records but with legitimate reasons to consult them. The manner and degree of protecting these large collections and of supervising their users can vary greatly.

There is a striking characteristic common to both staff members and outside investigators. Persons impressed with the importance of the work on which they are at the time engaged and hurriedly bent upon achieving the best possible results in the shortest space of time and with the greatest saving of energy are frequently careless in their handling of manuscripts. If a document is of immediate use to them, whether it be for an exhibit, a photocopy, or a quotation, they apparently think it can serve no more noble purpose and are oblivious to any concern over its subsequent fate. This is the only way of accounting for the inexplicable handling of manuscripts by persons of whom you would expect sympathetic compliance with all regulations for preserving them.

As indicated, those on the staff who appear to be most susceptible to such an inimical trait are photocopyists and arrangers of exhibits. Special safeguards are necessary to protect material in their hands, and a careful collation should be made of material returned after their use. (I mention this hesitantly because it may be taken to reflect on staff members at my own institution, whom instead I can compliment for meticulous adherence to our standards. Again, as in all of this section, I speak without personal reflection.) There are also staff members or board members who are, or who consider themselves to be, privileged characters and demand that favors be granted in behalf of themselves or those whom they wish to impress. They are incapable of realizing that rules and regulations were meant to apply to them or to their friends. You must parry their requests, limit materials placed in their hands, and insist that the official in highest authority assume responsibility for making exceptions for these people of self-appointed importance. There is a difference between them and the official who knows when it is in order to request or to make an exception to a rule and when exigencies demand prompt decisions.

Repositories may also have in their employ those too rapid workers, careless of detail, inaccurate, and tending to an attitude towards papers wherein familiarity breeds contempt. Some seem never to have made the record note required or returned a document as or when or where they should. Others mean well but lack judgment or may have blind spots or rank prejudices. It is requisite to hold these employees to a high standard of performance, always to correct and call attention to their errors, and to exercise close supervision and review of their work. You do not have to encourage the incompetent to remain on your staff and you can permit them to resign to accept more promising offers or more congenial positions. People do change, or at least they begin to exhibit traits not discernible at the time when they made application for archival work and showed bright promise and a real affection for manuscripts. Or do they, in handling inanimate objects, seek release from their anger with animate objects? Some have been known to move speedily from an institution guarding records into an institution guarding persons, but with them it will require the advice of a psychiatrist to stipulate preventive measures.

Lastly, the staff member most inexcusably an enemy of archives is the one who came meaning to steal or the one with a weak character for whom temptation proved too great. I shall cite a sad case at the Library of Congress that made the headlines in 1897. Early the year before, Louis McKenzie Turner, a music clerk in charge of the Music Division, and Philip McElhone, a copyright clerk, began breaking into the private office of the Librarian of Congress, then in the Capitol, after hours and on Sundays to steal manuscripts. The lock on the door was a very poor affair, easily manipulated with any old key when applying a little pressure. The Librarian on first discovering the thefts, largely from the Peter Force collection, did not know whom to suspect among his 42 employees, any one of whom could have got to the papers. The two thieves over a period of several months went repeatedly to the office and abstracted hundreds of valuable documents of the colonial and revolutionary periods — mainly Washingtoniana, including his orderly book of the Braddock expedition and his diary for 1787, a number of Benedict Arnold and John Hancock letters, and letters of Thomas Paine, Nathaniel Shaw, Benjamin Franklin, Ethan Allan, Thomas Jefferson, John Jay, John Adams, Lafayette, Robert Morris, Israel

Putnam, and others. These they sold to dealers and collectors in New York, Philadelphia, Baltimore, and Washington. The Secret Service recovered all of the stolen documents through the aid of Turner, who turned state's evidence, and the cooperation of the purchasers. McElhone was brought to trial and convicted in May 1897. The statement made by Turner described a brazen collaboration in thievery and his habits of betting and gambling.[6] This experience taught us to doubt our fellow man, particularly if he shows evidence of playing the races or living beyond his means. It indicates also that "all out" efforts must be made promptly to recover misplaced materials, to discover the cause of error in replacing or damaging documents, and to make each such instance a lesson for future guidance. It is bad to be suspicious of an employee's honesty in handling documents; it is far worse not to have your doubts resolved.

We have noted that the same tendencies in staff members and in our clientele make persons enemies of archives. If by the nicest definition, a scholar could not be an enemy of archives, then our reading rooms receive those who come in the guise of scholars, but who must be something less than true. Have not all of us been shocked by the shameful manner in which authors of repute have marked documents, folded them, disarranged them, and treated fragile material as insensitively as you would wrapping paper? Have not absent-minded professors made you doubt they ever had a present mind? Would not some actually have filched documents, but for the fact they could not then serve their purposes of documentation? I personally seem to have given mortal offense to a professor not long ago, when I told him I hoped that he would in future be more lenient with his students who failed to follow his directions. Having dutifully agreed to preserve the existing order of the papers he was using, he was, in working with a box with folders of loose papers in perfect order, placing at the end of each folder the documents he selected to serve his purpose. When he finished reading the entire contents of a folder, he would stop and at one time take all his notes from this residue cache. Upon completing his note taking, he promptly closed the folder, leaving its contents in the disorder he had created. He had not realized that this practice, so convenient to him, would be considered an infringement of our rule against altering the existing order of papers or that it rendered a disservice to other searchers and to our staff.

If a scholar, by hook or by crook, becomes so privileged a person

[6] Library of Congress archives, Manuscripts Division, Library of Congress.

as to secure the right of sole access to a collection until he has published a certain book or has completed his use of the collection, he will invariably delay until the last possible moment permitting its use by others; but it never occurs to him that he is a foe of archives.

Some repositories must serve documents to innocent, inexperienced, and dull-witted persons. While they mean no harm, their lack of research ability and appreciation for manuscripts can be dangerous. Then there are the crackpots, zealots, and perverts, who may be grouped together because their harm to documents is of a similar pattern. With plausibility they establish a need to consult manuscripts. Then, all the while sustained by a sense of justice, satisfaction, or righteous indignation, they craftily proceed to remove and secrete for themselves documents that support their cause, mission, or conviction or that delight their disordered minds; or they proceed to damage or destroy that which offends them. Such people, however, are more often caught in the act of stealing or damaging material than another more cunning enemy of archives — the thief who comes with criminal intent. The defenses against both are the same: close supervision over readers, early detection of losses or mutilations, and intelligent detective work; but for the latter enemy there is required cooperation from dealers and collectors. The thief may also be one and the same with yet another type of archival enemy — the forger; and he, with book thieves, represents "the aristocracy of the literary underworld," the brainiest of all criminal types, who combines adroit craftsmanship with astute erudition.[7]

Thieves have operated, not always with immunity, against some of the most carefully guarded repositories in the world. From these they have stolen rare manuscripts no matter how exactly the documents were foliated or how conscientiously and immediately collated they were both before and after use. Thieves have presented themselves equipped with aliases and false credentials and with accessories and accomplices. What are our defenses against them? An incidental, even fortuitous one, is that our rarest treasures are so thoroughly known and identified that no thief could sell them. They would be worth something to him only if he sold them for what they actually are and as such they are too easily recognized to be marketable. There was an instance, apparently, when a valuable manuscript was boldly carried off for ransom. In 1932, Sir Walter Scott's manuscript of "Guy Mannering" was lent to Co-

[7] John Cobler, "Trailing the Book Crooks," in *Saturday Evening Post*, 215:101 (Mar. 13, 1943).

lumbia University for exhibit by its owner, J. P. Morgan. There were a few visitors in the room where it was displayed and two supervisors were in attendance when, in a moment, it was removed by forcing the lock of the glass case that held it. Before the mystery was solved, the owner recovered it, but by what means he never explained.[8] Exhibits attract thieves because cases often are easy to open and if they are indifferently guarded a thief can spirit away a valuable document without exposing his features to anyone's close scrutiny. Although the Walt Whitman commonplace book stolen in March of 1955 from an exhibit in the Detroit Public Library has been returned, we do not know what motivated the theft.

Pieces less well-known can be protected from thieves and reclaimed, if found, by having indelible indicia of ownership stamped upon them so that their removal would destroy the commercial value of the documents. Documents are further protected by doubts that a thief may entertain about the speed with which the losses will be discovered and about what information the repository has at hand or can assemble on the missing pieces. Can it describe its losses accurately? Can readers identify them as the property of the repository? Are there photocopies of them to prove their ownership?

Funds permitting, steps that might be taken by repositories to protect their holdings are:

1. Organizing and indexing collections to reduce the wear and tear on documents. Scholars then could call for only the items they need to examine.

2. Providing service photocopies of rare and fragile documents and those involved in controversies. A photocopy will serve as a perfect inventory, identification, and insurance that information will be protected if the original manuscript is lost.

3. Warning readers of the penalties for theft or damage to public property; supervising all use of archives by investigators, enforcing the observance of reasonable rules for safeguarding them, and developing procedures for handling persons apprehended in breaking these rules.

4. Admitting losses — even to the embarrassment of the repository with the public, prospective donors, or board members or other governing bodies — taking steps to recover documents by notifying police authorities and dealers if robbery is suspected. An illustration of this is the 1954 publication of a descriptive brochure of pieces missing from the Walt Whitman collection at the Library of Congress.[9]

5. Examining carefully material of questionable provenance and exercising care in labeling forgeries.

[8] *Ibid.*
[9] Library of Congress, *Ten Notebooks and a Cardboard Butterfly Missing From the Walt Whitman Papers* (Washington, 1954).

6. Prosecuting thieves, thus describing them and their methods for the benefit of other repositories.

7. Maintaining records of all investigators and all materials served to each of them.

Some repositories have been reluctant to take obvious steps to supervise readers, to ask them to submit their parcels for examination before departing, and to correct them (particularly if they are well-known persons) in their mishandling of documents. Declining to subject distinguished investigators to possible discomfiture, they are forced to excuse others. It has long been the practice at the Library of Congress to supervise all searchers in its Manuscripts Division reading room and to inspect all cases and parcels taken by anyone from the Library buildings. A staff member also has interviewed each reader before permitting him to use manuscripts and has asked him to read and sign an agreement to abide by the rules and regulations governing their use. In the fall of 1953, a person using an alias and a fictitious identification credential came with a plausible request to consult materials and this was granted. A dealer, who had purchased a stolen item from him, began to investigate it only to learn that it was credited to the Library's collection. When this dealer got in touch with us we learned for the first time of our loss of a dozen documents from the Andrew Ellicott papers. All of these were recovered by the FBI, but thus far the thief has escaped detection.

Although the Division had earlier requested the assignment of a guard, one was not provided until after this unfortunate episode. Now an armed guard from the Library's guard force is stationed on a raised dais in our reading room whenever it is open to the public. We have revised our rules to include his inspection of materials taken from the room. He initials each reader's card in the presence of the reader. Except for keeping a daily record of the time present and the designated table space occupied by each investigator, this guard is under instructions to devote his entire attention to supervising readers, the entrance door to the Division, and the door to the stacks, where no one but staff members may go without an escort. He has definite instructions as to what to do when he observes an infraction of our rules.

We have felt no need to apologize for the guard or for our rules; most of our previous investigators have accepted both in good grace (though with some chiding); and new readers seem to consider them natural. Our rules are based upon the 7 rules recommended in the report of the Ad Hoc Committee on Manuscripts set up in 1948 by the American Historical Association and approved by the Association of Research Libraries in 1951.[10] All but one of these rules is included in 5 of our 12 rules. We included no prohibition on readers' smoking because no smoking is permitted in the part of the building where manuscripts are served, but we adopted the following rules from the committee's recommendations:

1. Use no ink except in fountain pens and exercise caution in the use of fountain pens.
2. Refrain from marking manuscripts and writing notes on top of manuscripts.
3. Preserve the existing order of manuscripts in their volumes or containers' and report to reading room attendant manuscripts apparently misplaced.
4. Exercise care in preventing damage to manuscripts and extreme care in handling fragile material.
5. Obtain, before publication of, or from, manuscripts in the Library of Congress knowledge of the libel law and of literary property rights at common law.

The seven rules that we ourselves devised are:

1. Sign the register daily.
2. Handle manuscripts only at the assigned table space.
3. Open only one volume or container of manuscripts at a time except with special permission.
4. Submit to the guard for inspection any briefcase, typewriter case, or any other parcel, book, or notebook before taking it from the room.
5. Bring into the room only the minimum number of such items mentioned in 4 above as are necessary for the effective use of manuscripts.
6. Return all manuscripts to the issue desk before leaving the room for the day or for an extended period, and request the reservation of material to be used again soon. (Note: A reader who plans to leave the room and return within an hour may, under certain conditions, leave manuscripts at his table).
7. Comply scrupulously with conditions on access to restricted materials.

Of course these rules will not preclude damage, disarrangement, and losses, but they will minimize their likelihood. Every reader is seen for identification purposes by at least three members of the Library staff: the person who interviews him and checks his reader's card to determine his identity and his qualifications and need for consulting original sources, the guard, and the issue desk assistant. Each reader signs his name on at least three permanent

[10] "Report of the Ad Hoc Committee on Manuscripts Set Up by the American Historical Association in December 1948," in *American Archivist*, 14: 229-240 (July 1951); "Report of the Committee on the Use of Manuscripts by Visiting Scholars Set Up by the Association of Research Libraries," in *College and Research Libraries*, 13: 58-60 (Jan. 1952).

records: the reader's card, the register, and the call slip for materials. On the reader's card and the register, he is required to give us considerable information about himself.

If investigators have resented our guard, though only two have actively so expressed themselves, donors have not. His presence has assured them that a gift to us will be protected. It has given us a greater feeling of security than we enjoyed at the time of our last known theft.

Maybe at this point you, like me, will feel that we have wallowed long enough in the seamy side of archival matters. My having talked so long of their foes may make you wonder if there are left any friends of archives. Of course there are, but I was asked to talk only about the enemies. Doing so has not distorted my outlook on life. I know, and I am glad to reassure any who need reassurance, that there are more friends than enemies and that most of the latter are speedily converted when they come to realize the ill effect of their malpractices. It is a propitious sign that the number of those employed in repositories as staff members and as investigators is increasing. These we can reach and these we can educate. There is hope for the future.

Comments by Lucile Kane

No curator of manuscripts could listen to the words of Mr. Land without a sharpened realization of the dangers that hover whenever a collection is opened to public use. When we place manuscripts before a scholar, who through them will add new dimensions to the understanding we all seek in history, we are fulfilling one of the highest obligations of our profession. The documents are for the moment entrusted to him and, fortunately for us, most scholars respond generously to the privilege. The experienced scholar knows that behind the simple statement, "Here are the manuscripts you requested," is a series of circumstances — the confidence of the family which gave them, the skill of those who processed them, and the support of those who pay the bills for maintaining the collections.

In a measure it is a sad subject that we discuss today, for its very presence on the program is public admission that not all scholars feel a responsibility for the materials they are privileged to use, that some of them sin through ignorance, and that some of these have no desire to have their ignorance dispelled — and that not all people who come to us are scholars. In considering his duties to the scholar and to the materials, there can be no doubt in deciding to which the curator owes the greater responsibility. It is, of course, to the materials entrusted to his care.

We are all in harmony, I believe, about the principles of security controls. Thus I turn quickly from theory to the practices of the Minnesota Historical Society. At the society, the major deterrents to less than perfect security are budgetary limitations that deny us the luxury of a guard and a physical arrangement of the department that would put the burden of reading-room supervision on one person. Many of our practices, however, do work for security. Here they are in brief.

Every person who uses our manuscripts signs a register daily, a record that includes his name, his home address, and the titles of the papers he plans to consult. In the list of rules that is handed him, he reads that he may not use ink, that he may not take a brief case or other container into the reading room, and that he must return manuscripts to the reading-room attendant when he is through with them. Students new to us are asked if they have used manuscripts before. If this is their first research experience, we caution them about removing documents from folders, marking passages for copying, and using paper clips to hold pages back. When the searcher opens the file box, he sees before him a printed warning of fine and imprisonment, under Minnesota law, for mistreating documents.

On rare occasions a scholar who plans to work in the collection for a year or so is granted the privilege of using one of the studies next to the reading room, out of the immediate view of the reading-room attendant. Such a scholar must be recommended to us in such terms that doubt is reduced to a minimum. One can never be completely easy, however, in granting this privilege. Recently I discussed this subject with a well-known archivist, whose institution grants stack and after-hours privileges to people who come armed with recommendations. He was disturbed about the ease with which historians have written letters to him, recommending that the bearer, often a student on his first research expedition, be granted the full freedom that would be accorded the most trusted scholar. He felt strongly enough about the lack of discrimination evident in such letters to speak plainly on the matter before an historical association. In this, as in many other areas, there must be the closest cooperation between the historical and archival professions.

After manuscripts are returned to the reading-room attendant, we try to refile them the same day. If little time is allowed to elapse between the time of return and the filing, losses can be more easily detected and the possibility of filing error is reduced. Since we have an inventory of all the volumes in each group of manuscripts, a missing volume can be detected immediately. Not so the loose, uncalendared material in the file boxes. Our only safeguard in preventing the loss of these loose papers is the surveillance by the reading-room attendant.

A few months ago, I was reminded that certain kinds of manuscripts try the will power even of honest men. An avid private collector of early Minnesota autographs came to look at our Henry Hastings Sibley manuscripts. When I opened the folder displaying letters of Minnesota fur traders — signatures that were missing in his own collection — his eyes took on an acquisitive glitter. He picked up a letter with a show of reverence and said, "Please don't turn your back on me."

Because we do have many manuscripts that are particular temptations, we have formed a "reserve collection." In this group are papers of numerous literary and political figures, papers of Washington, Lincoln, Franklin, and others. Some of these items came to us as individual pieces; others are taken from our larger collections. When a letter is removed from a collection, a cross-reference sheet bearing its number in the reserve collection is put in its place. A calendar card is made for each item in the reserve collection. All reserve materials are stored in a special vault. Staff members and searchers alike treat with considerable respect manuscripts precious enough to be promoted to the reserve class.

We long ago abandoned the practice of allowing a stack attendant to help us either in bringing manuscripts from the stack area or in refiling them. The physical labor for the professional staff is arduous, particularly in handling business records. But we have found it less strenuous in the long run than repairing bindings or spending days of hunting for a volume lost in a complex filing system by a stack attendant who thought that at last he had mastered all those catalog numbers.

One of our most annoying and disturbing problems is that for years we have not had a complete reinventory of the collection. Periodically we have inventoried the smaller classifications, correcting misfiling, recording missing items, and noting physical condition. In January of 1956 we shall at last begin the overall inventory. When it is completed, we shall know just how good the society's security controls have been in the past decades. The inventory will reveal, too, documents that need restoration and those that must be removed from general use until they can be repaired. We have already had microfilm, photostatic, and typewritten copies made of some collections that are too fragile to be used by the general public.

I like the optimistic note on which Mr. Land ends his paper. I, too, want to end on such a note. When we have executed our responsibilities to manuscripts to the best of our ability and to the limits of our physical resources, we need, I believe, to unknit our brows and to think often and long about the privileges of working with manuscripts. Last summer, after supervising the packing of some hundred cartons of historical materials in an old house in western Minnesota, I sat on the steps, warm, slightly soiled, and tired, but elated, waiting for the truck that would carry the boxes to St. Paul.

When the truck driver arrived, he looked at me curiously and asked, "You work for the State?"

"Yes," I answered.

"Well," he said, "I suppose that jobs are hard to get."

I agreed with him, but personally I add another meaning to his comment. Jobs such as ours, jobs that — in spite of worries about mutilated or pilfered manuscripts — offer a maximum of continuing pleasure, are indeed hard to get.

COMMENTS BY RICHARD DUNSTAN HIGGINS

The problem of providing defenses against human foes has been quite thoroughly covered by Mr. Land's paper and all that remains, it would appear, is the recitation of specific cases involving theft and damage or threat of damage by human beings.

Questions have been directed to me from time to time — with such frequency that I am no longer embarrassed — concerning the theft of certain documents and papers from their vaults in the Archives of Massachusetts. Unhappily, I am not able to answer such questions. The thefts took place some time ago, before my appointment as chief of the Archives Division. Furthermore, the vast collection of material in the Archives of the Commonwealth has never been cataloged; and it is thus impossible to determine the extent of our losses.

With respect to the problem of having the archives cataloged, the present secretary of state, Edward J. Cronin, whose responsibility includes the Archives Division, has made repeated appeals to the legislature to provide at least five persons to be assigned to such work. Secretary Cronin, who has always demonstrated an intense interest in our particular problems, has made herculean efforts to improve the situation.

I can say this, that some documents and papers are still missing and that others turn up at irregular intervals. I must also inform you that the person responsible for the recent thefts from the Library of Congress, mentioned by Mr. Land, caused much consternation in our institution.

Two other episodes come readily to my mind, involving two different problems faced by archivists and librarians in whose custody important records are kept.

Last year, for the first time in history, we removed the constitution of the Commonwealth from its vault in the Archives and placed it on public display in a State House hall near the Hall of Flags. This was done at the urging of the Massachusetts Law Association, which sponsored Massachusetts Heritage Month, a laudable program that did much to awaken interest in our constitutional processes among our school children, lawyers, and many other citizens. In Massachusetts, I might add, we are inordinately proud of our constitution. It is the oldest in the Nation, older than the Federal Constitution. It was placed under glass and vigilantly guarded by a Capitol police officer.

I was later informed that on one occasion during its exhibition an individual with a peculiar sense of humor approached the display case and attempted to lift the glass that covered the preamble and declaration of rights.

Said the police officer, "What are you trying to do?"

The man replied, "I just want to sign the Constitution!"

Whereupon the police officer retorted, "Well, my friend, I am afraid that your are 174 years too late!"

This true story illustrates, I think, the extreme care that must be exercised whenever the original of a priceless document has been put on public display.

The second incident, entirely devoid of humor, involved a number of important personages and a piece of paper that under ordinary circumstances would have been of no consequence. It was an "expense return," temporarily in our care until the date of its destruction under the law. This paper was removed by a person who signed our register with a false name and an illegible address. The person in question had asked for and received a number of such political expense returns made by several parties and candidates in a State election 5 years ago. On his departure from the room, he surreptitiously removed one of the papers. This proved to be the expense return of one of three individuals under investigation by the Supreme Judicial Court — a controversy long drawn out that evoked massive newspaper publicity.

Needless to say, the paper did not reappear, nor was the culprit responsible for its theft ever discovered. The unfortunate disappearance of this paper was another incident in a case that terminated calamitously for all concerned.

We have since been pledged to even greater vigilance with respect to our signature roster. Persons visiting our office and seeking to examine material are now required to provide legitimate identification, unless they are known to us.

As has been so eloquently illustrated by Mr. Land, there are really only two different types of human foes — those we know, such as persons who work for or near us, and total strangers. We archivists have had unfortunate experiences with both types of human foes and it is understandable that the more fatal foe is the Enemy Unknown. Taking into consideration, however, the inadequate physical facilities with which many of us have to cope and the lack of proper protective devices in most areas, I am immodest enough to think that on the whole we do a rather good job of protecting what is in our care.

VIII: PRESERVATION MICRORECORDING AND OTHER COPYING METHODS

Papers 25 Through 29: Commentary

The intent of this section is to heighten librarians' awareness of the potential offered by microform technology in preserving their fast-crumbling collections. Although microrecording is the only practical means at the present time of assuring large-scale preservation of intellectual resources, there is increasing doubt that this approach, given present estimates of the paper deterioration problem, will be equal to the task without vastly increased expenditures and a nationally coordinated effort.

Pamela W. Darling's "Developing a Preservation Microfilming Program" is based on the practical day-to-day experience she gained as Head of the Conservation Division's Preservation Programs Office in the Research Libraries of the New York Public Library. The unit is responsible for planning and coordinating programs for preserving the intellectual content of library materials through preservation microrecording and through the loan of original copies in the collections to reprint and microform publishers. At present, Mrs. Darling is Head of the Preservation Department at Columbia University Libraries; she also represents the American Library Association on the ad hoc Advisory Committee for a national preservation program, based at the Library of Congress.

Don M. Avedon is one of the most knowledgeable experts in the field of microform technology in the United States. Although "Selecting a Service Bureau" is addressed primarily to commercial businesses that may be contemplating a microfilming program, the article contains much that is useful to the librarian as well. So far as is known, it is the only article in the literature that deals specifically with what to look for and what to consider when selecting a service agency.

Vertical files constitute a particularly vexing problem to the librarian when their permanent preservation must be considered; yet there is scarcely anything in library literature that serves as a practical guide in this troublesome area. For this reason, Otillia M. Pearson's article on preserving the Schomburg Center's vertical file via microfiche is a particularly welcome case study. The single most compelling drawback to this method of preserving vertical file material is its high cost, but if funding can be obtained, it is a worthwhile investment provided that the files contain information of permanent reference value and that the microfiche are arranged and indexed for easy access.

Thomas E. Jeffrey describes another unusual application of microfiche technology in his article, "The Papers of Benjamin Henry Latrobe." Although this project was conceived as a means of publishing for the first time an important corpus of historical source material, there are additional advantages pertaining to conservation that are also realized. Upon completion of filming, access to the originals need be granted only to qualified researchers on a selective basis, thereby significantly reducing the necessity of handling the original documents. Furthermore, microfilming collections of manuscripts provides insurance copies should the originals be irreparably damaged, stolen, or lost.[1]

Microfilming and other reprographic processes do not provide a persuasive panacea for the preservation of all types of library materials. William R. Hawken has observed that there are problems connected with designing a suitable microfilming system that stem from the endless array of physical formats encountered in large collections.[2] Particularly in the case of scarce and rare books, materials must not be subjected to copying methods that will result in any possibility of harm to structures and paper that have been rendered weak and fragile by the passage of time. The thoughtful article by John Alden, formerly Keeper of Rare Books at the Boston Public Library, points up some of the problems that microfilming and other reprographic processes have created for rare book librarians. Due in part to improved bibliographic access and burgeoning commercial republication projects, the problems are greater today than they were a decade ago when Alden's article was first published.

NOTES AND REFERENCES

1. For a review by Mark R. Yerburgh of the published Latrobe Collection on microfiche, see *Micoform Review* 6 (May 1977): 169-71.
2. Hawken, William R., "Systems instead of Standards," *Library Journal* 98 (September 15, 1973): 2515-25.

ADDITIONAL READINGS

Diaz, Albert J., ed., *Microforms in Libraries: A Reader* (Weston, Conn.: Microform Review, 1975), 428 pp.

A Guide for Microfilm Documentary Publication Projects (Washington, D.C.: National Archives and Records Service, 1964), 17 pp.

Hawken, William R., *Copying Methods Manual* (Chicago: Library Technology Program, American Library Association, 1966), 375 pp. *LTP Publications* No. 11.

International Microfilm Source Book (Wykagyl Station, New Rochelle, N.Y.: Microfilm Publishing). Issued annually.

Lahood, Charles G., and Sullivan, Robert C., *Reprographic Services in Libraries; Organization and Administration* (Chicago: Library Technology Program, American Library Association, 1975), 74 pp. *LTP Publications* No. 19.

Microform Review (Saugatuck Station, Westport, Conn.), vols. 1– (1972–). Issued quarterly.

25: DEVELOPING A PRESERVATION MICROFILMING PROGRAM

Pamela W. Darling

WHEN a recent series of METRO seminars on the conservation of library materials was first proposed, there were some who wondered why microforms were being given a prominent place in the topics included. Most of the literature about conservation, as well as syllabi for courses in conservation, mention microforms only in terms of "what is the best way to store, preserve and repair them." Such a limited view of microforms is a pity, because several significant voices have been saying for some time that microforms, while they have certain preservation requirements of their own, can perform significant preservation functions appropriate to a broad range of library materials. The voices are growing louder—many had to be turned away from that seminar session—and there is growing recognition of the importance of microforms in a library's conservation activities. But a brief examination of the cause for this delayed recognition of the vital contribution of microforms to the solution of library preservation problems suggests a "first principle" upon which to base a preservation microfilming program.

The reluctance to apply microforms as a tool for preservation can be traced to the old stereotype that "libraries are places for books." Books have been the chief medium for storing and conveying information; and many books possess an intrinsic value-as-object due to their beauty, rarity, associational value, and so forth. But many books derive their value *only* from the information which they contain: it is the information, the intellectual content, which must be retained and made available, not always the physical book. If this distinction between books and the information they contain is not clearly made, the approach to dealing with deteriorating books tends to be "repair, rebind, restore the physical volume." But even if there developed an unlimited pool of skilled repairers, rebinders, and restorers, the costs for physical treatment (still a painstaking handcraft) are so high that it must be reserved for rare and special materials. It would be madness to spend a dollar a page to de-acidify, laminate, and rebind a dog-earred government pamphlet on poultry-raising or a crumbling city directory. We cannot hope to save our collections by physical restoration alone. We can save most of the information in our collections by transferring it to a medium more stable than paper, a medium which precludes the mutilating and tearing out of pages, takes up 90 percent less space to store, can be duplicated easily without damage to the original, and is less likely to be stolen—at least until the hardware people have their way and install microform readers next

Pamela W. Darling is Head, Preservation Programs Office, Conservation Division, New York Public Library

350

to the TV in every living room. Our "first principle," then, is that information is different than books. Microfilming must be recognized as a vital conservation technique, not because it preserves books (indeed it may hasten their destruction), but because it preserves the information for which those books were originally acquired.

Costs of microforms

Microfilm doesn't come cheap. To use it the library must invest in reading machines and reader-printers; train staff and patrons; and pay for continued maintenance and repair. Sturdy readers for library use run in the three to eight hundred dollar range; reader-printers cost several thousand dollars. One or two printers will suffice for most libraries, but half-a-dozen or more readers may be needed, especially if more than one format must be read—there are roll film readers and microfiche readers and micro-opaque readers, etc. This equipment requires a significant investment, but one which most libraries must undertake quite apart from a preservation program, as more and more materials are published in microform.

As for the costs of microforms themselves, there is no such thing as an "average." It depends, for instance, on whether film is bought from a commercial micropublisher, who can spread production costs among a number of customers, or whether it is made by the library itself. Cost depends on the format, and whether there are extensive bibliographic aids and indexes, internal and external. An example of the buy-it vs. do-it-yourself cost differential illustrates the range: for many years the New York Public Library regularly filmed a certain newspaper, at a cost of between $200-$350 per year for the master negative and one service copy. A commercial micropublisher acquired the micropublishing rights to this particular newspaper, and NYPL now buys a service copy for about $40 a year. (Binding would have cost between $30 and $75 per year, depending on the type; and the paper itself would be well on the way to the dustbin.)

A 400-page book can be bound for $4 to $12, depending on the type of binding needed and assuming that the paper does not require extensive reinforcement; Xerox University Microfilm's books-on-demand project might supply the same book in Xerox hardcopy or microfilm for $20; NYPL could film it in-house for $30; it might be available, singly or as a part of a set from a micropublisher for $3 or $4; it could be deacidified, repaired, laminated, and rebound for several hundred dollars. Are you confused? Microfilm costs and cost-benefits are confusing; they vary considerably, as do prices for physical restoration. But it is generally true that: 1) commercially-produced film is cheaper than binding; 2) in-house filming costs are higher than binding but considerably cheaper than full restoration; and 3) film has a potential life-span stretching into future centuries while most bound materials will need additional treatment or rebinding every 20-40 years, *if they last that long*—a cost factor which should not be overlooked.

Organizing for microforms

Assume that a library has agreed in principle that a preservation microfilming program should be established, and that a reasonable sum of money is made available for this purpose. The next step must be to assign the responsibility for developing and coordinating this program to someone, somewhere within the administrative structure. In large libraries, able to support full-scale divisions devoted to all phases of the preservation of the collections, the preservation filming function is naturally located within the preservation or conservation division. In other libraries, it would make sense to locate it within the technical services department, possibly within an acquisitions or order unit, but preferably as a special office reporting to the head of technical services. "Preferably," because a comprehensive preservation microfilming program will affect acquisitions and cataloging activities, the physical processing of materials before they are added to the collections, and continuing maintenance long after materials have been turned over to the care of reading room supervisors, stack personnel, and other public service staff. The preservation microfilming officer, therefore, must have the organizational flexibility and authority to work with staff in all of these units, to develop cooperatively policies and procedures which will affect them all, with some hope that they will in fact be implemented.

Once the appropriate organizational unit has been established, someone must be found to run it. Ideally, this person should have an extensive background in microform technology, a broad acquaintance with micropublishing resources, an in-depth knowledge of the library's acquisitions and cataloging procedures, and administrative skills and experience. Since few librarians possess this range of qualifications, find a quick learner with creative organizational abilities, and lock him/her up for a couple of weeks with a good collection of microform literature. (The bibliography included in this ar-

Transformation: Inside the New York Public Library Photographic Service. . . .

ticle will provide a starting point.) The budding expert should also visit a photo lab or two, and several libraries with already-established programs; get on the mailing list (i.e., become a member) of the National Microfilm Association; and attend as many meetings of the Reproduction of Library Materials Section of ALA's Resources and Technical Services Division as possible.

The microform work

With the initial education process begun (it never finishes), attention can be turned to the actual work..The first step involves the identification of materials which might appropriately be retained on film rather than in original form. This requires adopting policies for various categories of materials, developing guidelines for distinguishing those categories, and implementing procedures for applying those guidelines. Policies might cover such materials as newspaper backfiles, long-run serials, documents and technical reports, and unbound pamphlets. Policies should also cover cataloging and recataloging; the location of film and reading machines; the types of microformats appropriate for different materials, given the library's particular needs; the disposal of originals once the film is available and the keeping of some materials in two formats (for example, maintaining current periodicals in hard copy, with back files in microform; or filming exceedingly rare materials, making the film available for general use and preserving the originals for the use of specialized scholars).

Guidelines based on such broad policies should both spell out in detail the categorical definitions and indicate the exceptions to the general policy which should be anticipated. These guidelines should take into account such things as: size, paper quality, bindability, importance of color or pictorial matter, likelihood of theft or mutilation, usability in microform (a library which circulates scores to music students might not be performing the

greatest service by converting them wholesale to microfilm, unless pianos have built-in film readers, or someone can afford to feed quarters into the reader-printer all day), and criteria for weighing an item's value-as-object against present or potential deterioration and restoration costs. Policies and guidelines should address themselves both to materials being added to the collections for the first time and to things which have been quietly self-destructing in the stacks for decades. The problem must be attacked at both ends; otherwise we will either lose the bulk of our retrospective holdings by concentrating on current acquisitions, or create a whole new backlog out of current items which turn into retrospective holdings while we concentrate on the older material.

Priorities must be implicit, sometimes even explicit, in the stated policies and the day-to-day procedures, priorities which must be shaped by the library's service goals, the nature of its collections, the value, uniqueness and condition of its materials, and the availability of funds. Taken together, libraries have enough material that should be filmed to keep all the cameras in the world grinding away from now till 2001, so we'd best order our priorities lest we lose the irreplaceable whilst tending to the dispensable.

The pesky details

After the plans, the policies and guidelines, have been established, the pesky details of day-to-day procedure must be worked out. Procedures for the identification of materials which should be kept in microform might appropriately be developed for several different units within the library. Acquisition and selection officers should be alert to the possibilities of acquiring appropriate items in microform to begin with; the receiving unit should spot new materials on poor quality paper which might be converted to film before being added to the collections; at the bindery preparation stage there should be

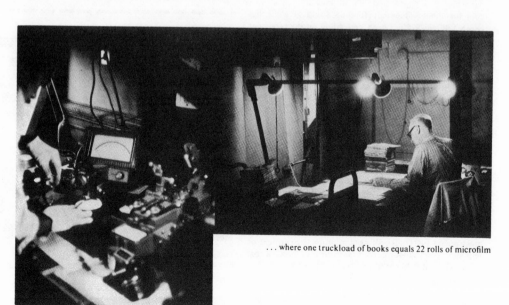

... where one truckload of books equals 22 rolls of microfilm

a system for determining whether things should be filmed instead; circulation staff should be trained to recognize potential microform candidates. When deteriorated titles must be replaced, the microform market should be searched along with the reprint and out-of-print markets. Shelf surveys, whether systematic or the more normal kind forced upon us by pressing space needs or the sight of crumbling pages littering the floor, should include a mechanism for identifying materials which should be converted to microform. The degree of formality which must be built into such procedures and systems will vary significantly with the size and nature of the library; but at the very least all staff should be made aware of the overall goals and of their role in meeting them.

Getting the microfilm

Along with establishing procedures for identifying materials to be kept in microform must go the simultaneous development of means for getting them in microform. There are three possibilities: buy microforms from a commercial micropublisher or another library; have your copy filmed for you by an outside filming agency; or film your copy yourself.

First, buying microforms: this is almost always preferable to getting something filmed yourself—it's much easier, and most of the time much less expensive because the production costs can be divided among a number of purchasers. You must know where to send the order, so you must search; and since bibliographic control of microforms still leaves much to be desired, this searching can be time-consuming, frustrating and inconclusive. A collection of microform bibliographies and catalogs should be set up, either in connection with the acquisition department's catalogs or in the preservation microfilming office, if there is one. The appendix lists the tools which form the core of the NYPL working collection of catalogs, and outlines the first steps in searching for various types of materials. Reasonable limits to the search should be established, both by ruling out catalogs irrelevant to the title in hand (don't search the 1969 National Register for an item published in 1972), and by limiting the time spent on each. For example, pamphlets of up to 85 or 90 pages could be put on microfiche by a microfilm service bureau for $5-$8; it wouldn't pay to spend many hours searching for such items. On the other hand, a 40-volume serial, or 25 years of a newspaper is worth a long search.

Ordering microforms

Once availability has been determined, place an order. (Depending on the library's policies, general acquisition money might be used, or special microform acquisition funds, book replacement or preservation funds, etc. If there is not a legitimate budget line to charge for such purchases, it should be fought for in the next budget.) The microfilm order should clearly specify the format and quality of film which the library will accept—that is, 35 or 16mm roll films, or microfiche or whatever, indicating maximum reduction ratios acceptable (if your reader magnifies only 20 times and you get film reduced 40 times you're in trouble), your choice of negative or positive polarity, whether you insist on silver halide film or will accept diazo or vesicular film, and a general statement to the effect that the film should conform to all appropriate national standards for archival quality and bibliographic integrity. A careful study of published standards and specifications will simplify the task of developing an order statement. Although many outside sources of film can be trusted to conform to standards without being told, there are others for whom such instructions may not be superfluous. In addition, because publisher's catalogs often give very few technical facts about the film they are offering, the instructions relating to format, reduction, and so on may be crucial.

Once the film arrives, check it carefully. Make sure that what's on the reel agrees with the box label and that both agree with the order; be sure the film is of the type specified. Study Allen Veaner's booklet, *The Evaluation of Micropublications* and do as much of the technical inspection he describes as the library has the staff and equipment for, particularly if this is the first film received from a company. Frame by frame inspection is a luxury few can afford; but examination before the invoice is paid can save a lot of trouble later on if the sixth fiche card out of 20 turns out to be missing, or if volume 5 turns up on the reel between volumes eight and nine.

Outside filming .

If the material wanted is not already available in microform, consider getting your copy filmed. If there is no in-house filming laboratory, search out a microfilm service agency. The *Microfilm Source Book* and the NMA's *Buyer's Guide* list many of these firms with indications of the type of filming they can do. After locating an agency, DO NOT pack up everything and send it off to be filmed. Sit down with the company's technical director—not the sales representative—and go over in great detail the technical and bibliographic specifications for the product to be delivered. If the library has not developed such specifications tailored to its own needs, the Library of Congress specifications will cover most of the ground. When you feel confident that they understand your needs and you understand their capabilities, and if the two seem compatible, select a representative batch for a pilot project. When this comes back, examine it *rigorously*—if the library does not have all the necessary equipment for testing density, resolution, residual hypo, etc., find another lab, preferably in a library, that can do these tests. (There will probably be a fee, but it's worth it.) If the results are satisfactory, establish a schedule for sending out work and spot-testing the returns; determine an acceptable percentage of error and agree in advance on who shall pay for necessary remakes. Maintain close personal contact with the people doing the work. If the first test results are not satisfactory, sit down with the technical director again and go over the problems thoroughly. Repeat the pilot batch and again examine the results. It may take months to get the quality product needed; it may be necessary to give up on one service agency and start over with another. Many microfilm service agencies were set up to film bank checks, computer print-outs, office records—fairly uniform materials which do not present anything like the range of filming problems which library materials present, and which usually do not require the bibliographic apparatus essential for good library service. Some can learn, and learn fast, particularly if the library can muster enough technical knowledge to clearly identify the problems and explain the requirements. But be aware of the pitfalls, and plan on a significant start-up time. Whatever you do, don't sign a contract until you know the firm can produce what you want.

Do it yourself

The third alternative for getting things on film is to do it yourself. This is not an alternative available to everyone; the latest *Directory of Library Reprographic Services* lists only 242 libraries, some of which do little more than make Xerox copies. The investment in costly equipment and skilled personnel is significant and can probably be justified only if a steady volume of filming can be guaranteed for years to come. This is not the place to describe in detail the essential ingredients of a good lab; but if the library has, or can set up, an in-house laboratory, be as rigorous about inspection and quality control with yourself as you would be with an outside service

LOCATING MATERIALS IN MICROFORM

The tools described below, while by no means all the available catalogs, make up a core collection for searching out titles available in microform. A suggested beginning sequence for different forms is indicated here, but should not be thought a comprehensive searching strategy. Most micropublishers issue periodic catalogs, some general and some in specific subject areas, which should be assembled and searched as appropriate.

A final report is to compare the holders of the desired title listed in the *National Union Catalog* with the *Directory of Library Reprographic Services*. Many large libraries can microfilm materials from their own collections on order, with the customer usually absorbing the full costs of the filming.

Initial Searching Sequence

Monographs

1) *National Register of Microform Masters*, 1970 to date
2) *Guide to Microforms in Print*
3) *Books on Demand*

Serials

1) *National Register of Microform Masters*, 1969 to date
2) *Guide to Microforms in Print*
3) *Serials in Microform*

Newspapers

1) *Newspapers in Microform*
2) *Newspapers on Microfilm and Special Collections*
3) *Guide to Microforms in Print*
4) *Serials in Microform*

Major Microform Bibliographies and Catalogs

Books on Demand: a Catalog of OP Titles. The 1971 edition plus supplement includes roughly 60,000 out-of-print titles, primarily monographs, which are available either on 35mm film or as bound photocopies. Write for catalogs from: Xerox University Microfilms, 300 North Zeeb Rd., Ann Arbor, Mich. 48106.

Guide to Microforms in Print. A *Books-In-Print*-type listing of monographs, serials and newspapers in microform being actively marketed in the United States, primarily by commercial publishers but also by some libraries. The 1973 edition contained about 25,000 titles, arranged by main entry for monographs and serials, by state and city for newspapers. The current edition lists at $6 and may be ordered separately or on a standing order basis from: Microcard Editions Books, 901 26th St., Washington, D.C. 20037.

National Register of Microform Masters. Published by the Library of Congress, it includes reports of master microforms of monographs and serials

held by various libraries and commercial firms, from which copies can be made. The publishing history of the Register is complex: the issues from 1966-1968 are arranged primarily by LC card number, which is *not* convenient for searching. The 1969 issue is arranged by main entry, includes only serials, and cumulates the serial entries from 1966-1968. There is no cumulation of the 1966-1968 monograph entries. The 1970, 1971, and 1972 annuals include serials and monographs, arranged by main entry, as will the 1973 annual which was scheduled for publication during the winter of 1974. Prices: 1969, $5; 1970, $12.50; 1971, $25; 1972, $25 (when published); *Free* to subscribers of the *National Union Catalog*. Available from: Card Division, Library of Congress, Building 159, Navy Yard Annex, Washington, D.C. 20541.

Newspapers in Microform. Supersedes the old *Newspapers on Microfilm* published by the Library of Congress. The United States section includes 34,000 reports, from 1948-1972, plus an extensive index. The foreign countries section

contains almost 9000 reports, also from 1948-1972. There will be supplements. Price: *Newspapers in Microform: United States, 1948-1972*, $30; *Newspapers in Microform: Foreign Countries, 1948-1972*, $10. Available from: Card Division, Library of Congress, Building 159, Navy Yard Annex, Washington, D.C. 20541.

Newspapers on Microfilm and Special Collections. An annual catalog listing over 5000 newspapers, primarily from the United States, a few serials, and a number of "special collections." Available from: MicroPhoto Division, Bell and Howell, Old Mansfield Rd., Wooster, Ohio 44691.

Serials in Microform. An extensive list (600 pages of title entries, plus an 80-page subject index) of serials available on microfilm. The current cumulation has a list price of $4.95, which includes periodic supplements. Available from: Xerox University Microfilms, 300 North Zeeb Rd., Ann Arbor, Mich. 48106.

agency. There are several advantages to having this in-house capability: there is less risk of damage or loss of valuable materials, much closer control can be exercised over all phases of the film process, and the laboratory staff can develop a high degree of expertise specifically tailored to the peculiarities of filming library materials. Since in-house costs tend to be higher than commercial costs, it may be well to divide the work, sending routine items outside and reserving the in-house lab for fragile, difficult-to-film materials. It will also be important to establish a balance between preservation microfilming and other kinds of photoduplication services which may be offered to readers, to the library administration, or to the world at large.

Preparing materials for film

Time and effort must go into preparing materials for filming, whether in-house or by a service agency. Every reasonable effort should be made to film a complete copy. This means a page-by-page collation to be sure that sections are in the proper order and to identify missing pages or issues. Wherever possible, such gaps should be filled before filming—by borrowing copies from other libraries, dunning publishers for missing volumes, etc. Gaps which cannot be filled must be clearly indicated on the film, through the use of contents targets, missing or mutilated page statements and other explanatory notes. The Library of Congress specifications provide excellent guidance. Unless the original is to be retained after filming, it is often better to remove the binding so that the pages can lie completely flat on the camera board. This can be done by guillotining or, if the paper is too brittle for such treatment, by carefully taking the volume apart by hand. In some cases, this will be unnecessary: newspapers, unbound single-signature pamphlets or magazines such as *Time*, or bound materials with very wide gutter margins may lie perfectly flat without cutting. In other cases the book may be so badly deteriorated that handling should be kept to a bare minimum—just get it gingerly onto the camera board or book cradle and hope that the pages will stay in one piece long enough to be photographed. Process records should be kept, like bindery process files, to facilitate the location of materials and permit follow-up on delinquents mislaid in someone's lab; and such records could be built into the next stage of cataloging procedures. Such preparation and record-keeping take time and require trained staff. The initial planning should be done at the professional level, but most of the daily routine can be carried out by library technical assistants or other nonprofessional staff.

Cooperative efforts

There is actually a fourth alternative for getting materials on film, and that is to cooperate with micropublishers who plan to market microform copies. In most such cases, the library will receive free film in return for the loan of the original material; reprint fees or royalty payments on sales are sometimes involved. Such arrangements can be of great benefit to the library, *if* they are entered into cautiously and carefully, without giving a single firm exclusive access to the library's collections and provided that such cooperation does not interfere unduly with the library's own priorities.

In most instances, once materials to be kept in microform have been identified, and in one way or another the microforms have been obtained, the original materials may then be disposed of (unless they are so valuable they should be restored and kept for restricted use in a rare book or special collection). Materials being added to the collections for the first time can be cataloged straight off as microforms. Previously cataloged materials which have now changed format may be completely recataloged, or the original records may be annotated to indicate the change. All cataloging decisions, including classification schemes or location number systems should be determined in advance, particularly if the library is having its own materials filmed rather than purchasing from outside. It may be, for instance, that the microform call number is to be included in the eye-legible header of the microfiche, or on the title target of the roll film—if so, it's much easier to build that into the initial preparation of materials for filming than to set up a labeling system for adding the number to the completed film.

If the library has filmed its own material, and therefore owns master negatives in addition to service copies, they should be reported to the *National Register of Microform Masters* so that others will be spared the unnecessary expense of duplicate filming. It is a simple procedure (instructions appear in the introductory pages of the Register) but is too often ignored or done in a haphazard way. In the face of the gigantic tasks before us we cannot afford not to support and expand this important tool—nothing is more discouraging than to spend $1000 filming a large back file only to discover that another library filmed it years ago and could have sold a print for $100. Libraries actively seeking to sell copies of their microforms should also list them in the *Guide to Microforms in Print*, being sure there are no copyright limitations first. It is not essential to have an in-house laboratory in order to provide copies for others. Most microfilm service agencies will store masters for their customers, reproducing them on request, and duplication costs are only a fraction of the original filming costs.

Microforms can play a tremendous role in preserving the information, the intellectual contents, of a great proportion of library materials, both current and retrospective. If properly stored and handled, microforms will last as long as acid-free 100 percent rag paper—several hundred years—which is six to ten times longer than most book papers used since the mid-19th Century. If the master negative is kept under archival conditions, the material will never again be "out of print."

But a word of caution: don't be fooled into thinking that a secondhand camera and an automatic processor installed in the coat closet equal an instant preservation microfilming program. This is approximately equivalent to renting a computer terminal and calling it an automated cataloging system. The same sort of careful analysis and program development that is essential for automation is needed to establish a feasible preservation microfilming program. The technology is not as complex, of course; but it demands respect and attention to detail, both technical and bibliographic. If we plunge in thoughtlessly we may end up with miles of film which is self-destructing due to improper processing, or whose contents are inaccessible because of inadequate internal and external bibliographic control. But if we take the time to learn what it's all about and to make the technology work to meet our needs, we may yet save the millions of volumes which will otherwise crumble to dust on our shelves before this century is over.

BIBLIOGRAPHY

This list, an expansion and updating of the bibliography issued in June 1973, by the ALA/RTSD Micropublishing Projects Committee, provides an introduction to the proliferating literature on microforms and microform equipment. Many items cited here contain bibliographies leading the reader to more extensive treatments of particular topics. (Items listed in the boxed material within the article are not repeated here.)

General

Hawken, William R. *Copying Methods Manual*. Chicago: Library Technology Program, American Library Assn. 1966. Covers reproduction processes in general and gives considerable space to microforms with a description of each format. May provide more than the beginner wants to know, but illustrations and evaluations of different formats are useful. Glossary.

Microfilm Source Book. Microfilm Pub., 1971-. An annual volume containing indexes to products, trade names, associations, micropublishers, service bureaus, consultants, storage centers, distributors, publications, and free literature. Available: Microfilm Publishing, Inc., P.O. Box 313 Wykagyl Sta., New Rochelle, N.Y. 10804.

National Microfilm Association. *Glossary of Micrographics*. 1973. An industry standard, containing over 1000 terms, including trademarks and trade names. $4 to NMA members; $5 to others.

_____. *Introduction to Micrographics*. Silver Spring, Md., 1973. Describes the common formats and equipment used to make and reproduce microforms. Well illustrated, with glossary. $1.

_____. *A Microform Handbook*. Silver Spring, Md., 1974. 128 pages on selection, acquisition, and use of both software and hardware, written by Dale Gaddy of the American Association of Junior and Community Colleges, under a contract from the Office of Education. Includes several other NMA publications in appendix. $5.

Nitecki, Joseph Z., ed. *Directory of Library Reprographic Services*. 5th ed. Weston, Conn: Microform Review, 1973. Sponsored by the Reproduction of Library Materials Section of RTSD/ALA; a listing of 242 libraries offering various microform and full-size copying services; charts indicate types of services available, approximate costs, full addresses (including NUC and TWX codes), and a handy glossary of common terms. Available: Microform Review, Inc., Rogues Ridge, Weston, Conn. 06880.

Rice, E. Stevens. *Fiche and Reel*. Rev. ed. Ann Arbor, Michigan: Xerox University Microfilms, 1972. This free booklet is well illustrated and designed to answer questions on scholarly micropublishing frequently asked by librarians, educators, scholars, and others.

Spigai, Frances G. *The Invisible Medium: the State of the Art of Microform and a Guide to the Literature*. ERIC, in cooperation with the ASIS Special Interest Group on Reprographic Technology, 1973. In three sections; the first covers aspects of micropublishing, the second provides an overview of equipment, the third contains a select guide to micrographic literature. Available: American Society for Information Science, Suite 804, 1140 Connecticut Ave., N.W., Washington, D.C. 20036. $3.50.

U.S. Library of Congress. *Specifications for Microfilming of Newspapers in the Library of Congress*. 1972. Prepared by LC's Photoduplication Service as a procedural guide and to establish criteria "to evaluate microfilms under consideration as additions to the Library's permanent collections." Available: Superintendent of Documents, GPO, Washington, D.C. 20402. Stock Number: 3000-0055; 30¢.

_____. *Specifications for the Microfilming of Books and Pamphlets in the Library of Congress*. 1973. A companion volume to the specifications for newspapers. GPO Stock Number: 3000-00068; 40¢.

Veaner, Allen. *The Evaluation of Micropublications*. Chicago: Library Technology Program, American Library Assn., 1971. Written specifically for librarians and others responsible for acquiring and/or evaluating micropublications. Covers technical and bibliographic aspects of micropublishing, microreproduction, and methods of inspecting microreproductions.

Veaner, Allen B. & Alan M. Meckler. *International Microforms in Print, 1974-75*. Weston, Conn., Microform Review Inc., 1974. A listing of over 6000 titles available in microform from non-US micropublishers.

_____. *Microform Market Place, 1974-75*. Weston, Conn., Microform Review, Inc. 1974. A first attempt at an "international directory of micropublishing," this includes listings of micropublishers and libraries providing photographic service, a subject index, bibliography, directory of organizations, and a names and numbers section to facilitate direct personal contact. While much of the information is available in other published sources, it is gathered together here in a single volume; the subject index might prove particularly useful in tracking down those who produce, or might be interested in producing, microforms in specialized areas.

Equipment

American Library Association. Library Technology Program. *Library Technology Reports*. 1965- . A full section is dedicated to ongoing evaluation of microform readers and reader-printers. Compilations of equipment features in tabular form are helpful in making comparisons. Illustrated evaluations are extensive and cover such areas as operator-machine relationships and hazards as well as technical details.

National Microfilm Association. *Buyer's Guide to Microfilm Equipment, Products and Services*. 1971- . Annual listing of Sustaining Members of NMA by product and service; designed as a concise introduction and continuing reference for present and potential users of microform equipment, products and services. Free.

_____. *Guide to Microreproduction Equipment*. 1st ed.; 1959- . Under the editorship of Hubbard Ballou, an essential reference for information on specifications and capabilities of cameras, readers, reader-printers, processors, contact printers, enlargers, accessories (e.g. film splicers, storage equipment), computer output microfilm, and specialized microform retrieval systems. Arranged by equipment categories and manufacturer; information is descriptive, not evaluative. The 5th ed., 1971, is supplemented by *The 1972 Supplement to the Guide . . .*; previous editions are still useful for information on older models still in use. 1971 edition, $17.50 to NMA members, $21 to nonmembers; 1972 supplement, $6.50 to NMA members, $8 to nonmembers; package price for both, $21 to NMA members, $26 to nonmembers.

_____. *How to Select a Reader or Reader-Printer*. Silver Spring, Maryland, 1974. Twenty-page illustrated consumer guide; provides description of various features available. $2.

Journals

Foreign Newspaper and Gazette Report. An occasional newsletter issued by the Coordinator of LC's Foreign Newspaper and Gazette Microfilming Project; includes progress reports from the ARL Foreign Newspaper Microfilming Project, information on new publications. Available: Central Services Division, Library of Congress, Washington, D.C. 20540. Free.

Journal of Micrographics (formerly *NMA Bulletin*), Vol. 1- ; Fall 1967- . Professional journal containing technical articles, systems and case studies, scientific communications, standards, book reviews and other material of interest to the field. Originally a quarterly; bimonthly since 1971. Library subscriptions: $20; NMA membership includes subscription.

Library Resources and Technical Services. For some years the Spring issue has carried a review of micrographic events, products, and literature of the past year.

Microform Review. Vol. 1- ; January 1972- . Articles, comments, news items, numerous reviews of micropublications, cumulative author-title index to microform reviews, materials in simultaneous publications; clearinghouse section listing recently completed microform projects. Available: Microform Review, Inc., Weston, Conn. 06880. $20 a year for printed or microfiche format; $30 for both.

Note: All NMA publications available from: National Microfilm Assn., Publications Sales, 8728 Colesville Rd., Silver Spring, Md. 20910.

26: SELECTING A SERVICE BUREAU

Don M. Avedon

Don M. Avedon is technical director of the National Micrographics Association where he is responsible for all technical activities, including the development of standards, publications, educational programs, and the NMA Resource Center. He is also the editor of the *Journal of Micrographics*. He was previously project engineer at Bell Telephone Laboratories, Mr. Avedon is a Fellow of NMA and a former member of the NMA Board of Directors. He is the chairman of the NMA Standards Board, and the current secretary of the ANSI PH5 Committee on Micrographic Reproduction. He is the author of the book, *Computer Output Microfilm*, and the editor of the *Glossary of Micrographics*. Mr. Avedon has presented over 60 papers in the areas of micrographics, standards, and COM.

ABSTRACT

The purpose of this article is to discuss the many factors that should be considered in selecting a service bureau, not to recommend either using a service bureau or establishing an in-house micrographic operation. It is assumed that two decisions have already been made: (1) a micrographic system is required and (2) a service bureau will be employed in lieu of, or in addition to, an in-house production operation.

Before selecting a service bureau, a preliminary investigation of both micrographics and the potential system requirements is imperative. A recommended strategy is to first research and become familiar with the terminology and fundamentals of micrographics. An effective initiation to micrographics may be accomplished by obtaining publications from the National Micrographics Association and/or from other organizations and by attending micrographic seminars, which offer direct exposure to professionals in the field who will be able to answer specific questions.

Next, a basic analysis of the organization's priorities, goals, and objectives should be made, considering the following factors.

Special Microfilming Needs. Will the microfilm have to pass archival quality tests? Is there a specific national or industry standard with which the microfilm format will have to comply? Is there a specific resolution or reduction that is needed? How many copies will be distributed? How many readers, reader/printers, and accessories will be needed?

Security Regulations. If the potential application is for a government or military installation, are there security clearance regulations that service company facilities and personnel might have to pass? Are there any rules regarding the removal of documents from the premises? If the application is for a private company, what security policies will affect the micrographic system?

Turnaround Time (The Time It Takes to Complete the Job). Will turnaround time be a critical factor? How quickly must the service be completed?

The potential service bureau user should decide in advance what requirements a micrographic system for his organization *must* meet in order to be effective, then a service company may be selected with those needs in mind.

After analyzing the company's needs, the user has several options: designing an in-house micrographic system using existing staff (various training programs are available through NMA and other educational institutions), hiring experienced micrographic personnel, engaging an independent consulting firm,[1] or locating a service bureau that offers system consulting in addition to its other services. All options have advantages and disadvantages. In using consultants it is wise to select those who are not connected with equipment sales and thus can be objective in recommending systems and hardware.

Once it becomes obvious that a service bureau is needed, bids should be obtained from a number of service companies. Companies may be located by looking in the yellow pages of the telephone directory or by using the NMA *Buyer's Guide,*[2] which lists not only names and addresses of service companies in the United States but also each company's specialties and abilities, including whether they offer consulting services.

After obtaining bids from various companies, the user should conduct the following investigation:

- Tour the service bureau's facilities.
- Investigate the company's reputation and financial strength.
- Determine its reliability in meeting schedules and in preserving the integrity, privacy, and fire protection of its clients' records.
- Determine the expertise of personnel and quality of work.
- Contact other users in the area for recommendations on their experience with the service bureau.
- Investigate its services and specialties.
- Consider costs and physical location of the service bureau.

TOURING THE SERVICE BUREAU'S FACILITIES

The tour of the service company's facilities should reveal whether the company is run as a production operation and whether it has all the equipment it claims. The facilities should be clean and orderly, although not necessarily elegant. Many small companies do not have the capital to invest in an expensive building, but during the tour it should be easy to observe whether the service bureau personnel are working in an environment that is conducive to efficiency and quality output, whether the operation is chaotic and unorganized,

and whether clients' jobs are handled with the care they deserve and for which they pay. The user should also be prepared to ask if the company makes use of the latest national or industry standards.

If the service company maintains that it has certain equipment, all of the equipment should be seen during the tour. Many service companies subcontract work to other companies that have special equipment or capabilities that they do not have, and, while subcontracting may not necessarily be disadvantageous, it may be more economical to go directly to a service bureau that has the needed capabilities.

REPUTATION AND FINANCIAL STRENGTH

The service bureau should supply a list of references, preferably five or more of its past and, particularly, its present clients. It is important to contact these references; however, the company will naturally give only the names of satisfied customers, so the user should try to locate some customers whose names were not supplied.

If possible, a Dunn & Bradstreet rating for the company should be obtained, but the user should keep in mind that if the service bureau is small its cash flow may be somewhat erratic, since payment for a job presently being completed may not be received for several months. When estimating financial strength, the user should also consider how long the company has been in business.

RELIABILITY

Turnaround Time and Backup Facilities

A service company's reliability in meeting deadlines may be determined by conducting a pilot test, which can be simply accomplished by sending a representative mix of good and poor quality documents to each service bureau in consideration. Three additional factors to examine at this stage are: (1) how quickly the company can handle corrections, (2) whether the service bureau has backup facilities in case of equipment breakdowns, and (3) whether the service bureau provides adequate and reliable pickup and delivery service. If turnaround time is critical, then these three factors assume major roles in the ultimate choice.

Many large service bureaus run continuously and will be operating during the time the user needs service. Usually, the service bureau will have peak load periods. If the user requires a job to be completed during these periods, the service bureau may have trouble meeting the deadline. Different service bureaus have different peak periods, and not all service bureaus operate continuously. So the user should check both their load schedules and their operating schedules. Another point the user should consider is whether the company can handle increased volumes as the user's system grows.

Privacy and Integrity of Data

The privacy of the user's documents, or privacy of information, involves a variety of aspects. The user should inquire how many people will be handling the material and he may want to investigate the company's previous history in security-type situations. There are two methods of obtaining this information: (1) by asking other customers and (2) by noting whether the company's personnel supply too much information about its other clients and their records. Most service companies, however, are acutely aware of each client's need for privacy and take the necessary precautions to insure discretion is rigidly practiced and enforced.

Protective storage of documents should also be provided in the service bureau's facilities. The user's records must be protected from loss or damage, and, after they are filmed, the service company should have some means of adequately disposing of the documents if they are not to be returned to the customer. Unacceptable film should also be destroyed. It is advisable to ask what the service bureau's destruction methods are. If company records are sensitive, paper shredders or comparable methods of obliterating material should be available so that discarded record fragments are not readable. The service company should have a security and fire alarm system and should also be bonded or insured against loss of data by theft, fire, etc.

EXPERTISE OF PERSONNEL

A service bureau should employ micrographic specialists who have had several years of experience. It should have trained operators and qualified supervisors and employees for all microfilming and/or COM processes it offers. Its staff should be knowledgeable enough to provide assistance with most problems, and, if it offers consulting services, its consultants should be experienced in systems design. It is desirable for a COM service bureau to employ programmers and EDP systems analysts, and, for source document service bureaus, film

experts and records management systems designers are helpful.

QUALITY

Guaranteed Quality

One of the most important factors to ascertain about a service bureau is whether it guarantees the quality of its work. The contract with the company should state specifically that the microfilm (no matter what format) must be able to pass specific tests for archival quality, unless the application does not require archival-quality film (such as in a COM application where the film is only kept for 1 or 2 weeks). (It is not unusual to send a trial run batch of film processed by one service company to another agency to assure the archival quality of the film.[3])

Quality cannot be sufficiently stressed. If, for example, the application uses microfiche and automated retrieval equipment, one warped fiche may cause equipment malfunctioning. Poor resolution of images will limit readability, and low contrast may hinder reproduction of the microform at a later date. (However, one must realize that contrast is a function of the contrast of the input documents.)

Archival Standards/Inspection and Quality Control Facilities

Quality should be a major factor in choosing a service bureau. The bureau's inspection and quality control department should be well equipped with both trained personnel and with equipment to perform the following tests and inspection of processed film:

- Visual checks of film for any obvious defects, using a lightbox and/or a reader with rewind capabilities (the reader must not scratch the film);
- Measurement of film density with a properly calibrated densitometer;
- Inspection for reduction consistency and accuracy;
- Microscopic inspection for image resolution;
- Residual thiosulfate testing (to insure all processing chemicals are properly washed out after development) using one of two methods—methylene-blue or silver densitometric—per American National Standard PH4.8-1971.[4] (The Ross-Crabtree test is no longer considered an acceptable method of conducting this test.)

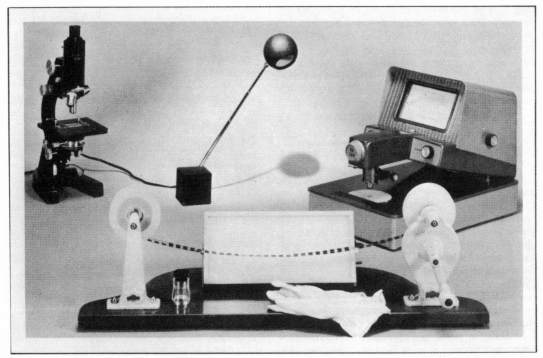

Figure 1.   Typical microfilm inspection equipment.

Minimal equipment needs for inspection and quality control would include a densitometer, microscope, and lightbox or rewind (Figure 1). In addition, the film should be handled with lint-free gloves. During the tour of the facilities, the user should notice whether all of these essentials are present.[5]

Industry Standards

The service bureau should also be a member of the National Micrographics Association since with such membership service bureau personnel should be knowledgeable about progress and advancements in the field and should be up to date about industry standards. If there are specific standards that will affect the proposed micrographic system, then it is necessary to ascertain whether the service bureau personnel is familiar with them.

Admissibility of Microfilm as Evidence

In order to meet legal requirements for film to be admissible as evidence, the service bureau should record a certificate of authenticity stating that all of the documents filmed on that particular microform are "accurate and complete reproductions of the records of (company and department) as delivered in the regular course of business for photographing."[6] The certificate also includes the date, location, signature of the camera operator, and indicates first and last documents recorded. Since admissibility of microfilm as evidence varies from state to state, it is recommended that legal counsel be consulted for any additional local requirements.

SERVICES/SPECIALTY

A service bureau may specialize in one type of microfilming and in one or several types of clientele. It may offer consulting services, and it may act as an equipment distributor.

Consulting

As mentioned earlier, if the user decides to use the consulting staff of a service bureau, he should be aware that he may not obtain objective advice if the company sells one vendor's equipment or has one area of microfilming in which it specializes. However, there are companies that do not sell equipment or that sell several vendors' equipment and will be anxious to assist the user in designing a system that will benefit his organization. One specific advantage of using the service bureau's consultants is that they may have had experience in designing a variety of micrographic systems.

Specialty/Clientele

Many service bureaus tend to concentrate on one or two microfilm areas and, consequently, they usually appeal to a particular type of clientele. For example, a service company with only roll-film capabilities might normally service banks, libraries, and legal firms. COM service bureaus generally have alphanumeric capabilities, but not very many have graphic equipment. Many service companies claim to be able to handle all microfilm formats—roll film, microfiche, aperture cards, etc. The service bureau selected should have experience with the microform that best meets the user's system needs.

Most service bureaus only provide one type of duplicate film—silver, diazo, or vesicular. It is recommended that this capability be matched to the system's needs.

Also, the type of clientele with whom the service company normally deals may affect a final decision. If the company is experienced in the user's particular field, then the service bureau staff will be familiar with the kinds of problems that may arise, and they will already have tried-and-true solutions. Again, NMA's *Buyer's Guide* or the yellow pages will indicate specialties.

Pilot Tests

If the user has any doubts about a service company or wishes to preview the new system, he should run a pilot test. Many service companies perform pilot tests for free; other service companies may charge a minimal fee.

The film from the pilot test should be examined to check whether (1) the characters are crisp, clean, and easily legible, (2) there is sufficient contrast to make viewing easy, and (3) the forms slide is properly aligned (for COM applications). The user should insist on seeing both the master and the copy (if a copy is utilized).

Equipment

Service companies often sell and repair equipment. Some companies sell used equipment that

has been repaired and reinstated to a good working condition, and usually this equipment sells for considerably less than brand-new equipment. It may prove invaluable if the service bureau selected can repair readers, reader/printers, and other micrographic equipment.

COM is generated through computers and, therefore, imposes software requirements. Depending on the application, retrieval specifications, and the sophistication of the computer system, the proposed system may need only minimum software or it may necessitate complex software. The service bureau should be surveyed carefully to determine what software it offers, what kind of support it can provide, and what its capabilities are.

1. Can the service bureau handle all tapes and formats needed for the system? Some service bureaus may not be able to handle 7 track or special tape densities, character sets, or tape formats.
2. Can the service bureau provide software for the computer and assistance in using it, and can it provide all the functions required? Some service bureaus may not be capable of providing full systems support, forcing the user to use a less efficient system.
3. If the service bureau uses a minicomputer, does it charge extra for this service, and can the mini handle the user's needs and formats?

The user's requirements will grow, and, if the service bureau cannot provide support software, growth may be hampered or the user may not be able to utilize full micrographic capabilities.

Education/Training

Personnel in a new micrographic application will need some type of orientation and training. Many service companies provide personalized seminars for its clients, so the user should inquire whether the service bureau can adequately conduct training sessions. Employee reactions and attitudes toward the new system very often affect the workability of the system.

COST AND LOCATION

The user should beware of companies that offer very low prices for their services. These companies may be financially unstable and are attempting to secure more business by not providing adequate value. The company should not, of course, charge exhorbitant rates, and, naturally, one of the main determinants will be whether the costs fit into the user's budget. The cost of corrections (errors made by the service bureau) should be absorbed by the service bureau; and, if the user engages the company's consultants, he should know in advance whether their fees will be extra or included with the package bill. All charges should be stated so that there will be no surprises on the final bill. An escape clause should be written into the contract to allow the user to go to another company if the first proves unsatisfactory.

Some service bureaus, especially in the COM area, run or will run a second shift on a "time available" basis to support already existing systems of large companies. If this is the case, the user must determine the actual priorities of his micro-filming job before he can take advantage of the reduced rates that are usually offered.

The service bureau should be located within a reasonable distance so that transportation costs (if they are not included with the entire bill) are not excessive and so that turnaround time will not be adversely affected by travel time. If the service bureau does include delivery costs in its overall bill and if turnaround time is not critical, then the user may wish to consider a company that is not located immediately within the specified radius, especially if the company specializes in a particular require-ment of the system.

CONCLUSION

To summarize, the proper selection of a micro-film service bureau requires some knowledge about micrographics itself and industry practices. The user who is specific about his needs and prepared for observation and inquiry will be able to select the most appropriate service bureau capable of handling his needs adequately and economically. **◑**

ACKNOWLEDGMENTS

Appreciation is due to the following people for their assistance in reviewing and contributing to this article: Truett E. Airhart, Zytron Corporation; Richard W. Batchelder, consultant; Franklin I. Bolnick, Microfilm Sciences Corporation; Alex Brunner, Mark Larwood, Inc.; Robert A. Glotfelty, The Computer Company; George Harmon, Micord Corporation; Susan L. Hiser, Mantra, Inc.; Loretta J. Kiersky, Air Reduction Company; Dean Putnam, Mag-nagard, Inc,; A. Harold Rack, Southern Microfilm Corporation; and David R. Wolf, A. B. Dick/Scott.

FOOTNOTES

[1]For advice on how to select a consultant, refer to Susan M. Law, "Consultants—How to Use Them and Get the Most for Your Money," *Journal of Micrographics*, no. 6 (1975):289–92.

[2]The *Buyer's Guide to Micrographic Equipment, Products, and Services* is available free from the National Micrographics Associ-ation, 8728 Colesville Road, Silver Spring, MD 20910, (301/587–8444).

[3]See *Residual Thiosulphate Testing Laboratories*, RR7-1975 (Silver Spring, MD: National Micrographics Association, 1975).

[4]*Methylene Blue Method for Measuring Thiosulphate, and Silver Densitometric Method for Measuring Residual Chemicals in Films, Plates, and Papers*, ANSI PH4.8-1971 (New York: American National Standards Insitute, 1971).

[5]For more information, see *Recommended Practice for Inspec-tion and Quality Control of First Generation Silver Halide Micro-film*, MS104-1972 (Silver Spring, MD: National Micrographics Association, 1972).

[6]For futher information, see Nixon, Hargrave, Devans, & Doyle, *Admissibility in Evidence of Microfilm Records*, RS9-1971 (Rochester, NY: Eastman Kodak Company, 1971) (distributed by the National Micrographics Association) and see *Operational Practices Manual*, MS110-1974 (Silver Spring, MD: National Micro-graphics Association, 1974). In regard to the certificate of authen-ticity, however, some attention should be paid to the proposed NMA Recommended Practice MS19, *Identification of Microforms*, which states that the use of the certificate "is no longer viable or acceptable" since the "practice precludes or unreasonably adds to the cost of the use of microfiche and other microforms and micro-graphic techniques, such as COM. It also generally involves the use of forms in which both the official with custody of the original records and the camera operator are required to certify to certain facts of which they have no direct knowledge. Finally, the mere placement of certificates at the beginning and end of a roll of film do not and cannot guarantee the integrity of the serial order, the completeness of the files, or the accuracy of the contents of individual documents."

However, the proposed Recommended Practice continues: "Nevertheless, until current statutes are revised, particularly at the state level, there will continue to be a requirement in some jurisdictions for roll film with certificates at the beginning and end of each roll."

SUGGESTED READINGS

Avedon, Don M., ed. *Glossary of Micrographics*. MS100-1971. Silver Spring, MD: National Micrographics Association, 1973.

Blue, Roger E. "Why a COM Service Bureau?" In *NMA 1975 Annual Conference Proceedings*, edited by Ellen T. Meyer. Silver Spring, MD: National Micrographics Association, 1975.

Costigan, Daniel M. *Micrographic Systems*. Silver Spring, MD: National Micrographics Association, 1975.

Exelbert, Rodd S. "Microfilm Service Firms—A Blessing to the New User." *Microfilm Techniques* 5(1975):10–11.

Harmon, George H. "A Service Bureau—How to Select One." *Journal of Micrographics* 3(1975):135–37.

Kober, S. Arnold. "What to Look for in a COM Service Bureau." *Journal of Micrographics* 4(1976):187–90.

National Micrographics Association. *Fundamentals of Computer Output Microfilm*. Silver Spring, MD: National Micrographics Association, 1974.

National Micrographics Association. *Introduction to Micrographics*. Silver Spring, MD: National Micrographics Association, 1973.

Putnam, Dean H. "The Do-or-Buy Decision: In-House Versus Contractual Microfilm Service," *Journal of Micrographics* 3(1970):103–105.

Williams, Robert. "Implementing a Microfilm System." In *NMA 1975 Annual Conference Proceedings*, edited by Ellen T. Meyer. Silver Spring, MD: National Micrographics Association, 1975.

27: THE PAPERS OF BENJAMIN HENRY LATROBE: Problems and Possibilities of Editing Historical Documents on Microfiche

Thomas E. Jeffrey

Thomas E. Jeffrey is microfiche editor of The Papers of Benjamin Henry Latrobe, a ten-year editorial project located at the Maryland Historical Society and supported, in part, by matching grants from the National Endowment for the Humanities and the National Historical Publications and Records Commission. Dr. Jeffrey is a graduate of The Catholic University of America, where he received his M.S.L.S. and Ph.D. degrees. He is currently writing a political history of antebellum North Carolina.

ABSTRACT

As the costs of letterpress publication steadily rise, editors of historical documents are turning increasingly to microform as a substitute or supplement to traditional methods of publication. This account of microfiche edition of The Papers of Benjamin Henry Latrobe is written for the benefit of editors who—like ourselves—may have had little previous experience with microforms. Should roll film or fiche be used? What are some of the problems encountered when historical sources are filmed on microfiche? How can the possibilities of committing costly filming errors be minimized? How can the microfiche format enable an editor to prepare a comprehensive index with a minimum of difficulty? The answers provided to these questions will, we hope, impel editors to give greater consideration to the unique advantages of microfiche publication.

Although the microfiche format has long ago proved its usefulness for the micropublication of business records, scientific and technical reports, serials, and rare and out-of-print books, its potential in the publication of primary historical sources has never been thoroughly explored. Admittedly, certain types of historical records are now readily available on microfiche. For example, scholars may acquire microfiche editions of the *North American Review* and *Southern Quarterly Review*; the state records of Connecticut, Georgia, and North Carolina; and the journals of the Continental and Confederate Congresses. These editions, however, are merely micrographic reprints of previously published records. The problems of filming and indexing such records are no different from those encountered for other rare and out-of-print books.

The corpus of historical research in this country lies not in these published records but rather in the numerous collections of unpublished personal papers, institutional records, and other manuscript sources scattered in historical societies, universities, state archives, and other repositories throughout the United States. As the costs of letterpress publication steadily increase, editors of such collections have been turning to micropublication as an alternative or supplement to traditional inkprint publication. In recent years, the scholarly community has benefited from micropublication of the collected papers of James Buchanan, Albert Gallatin, Washington Gladden, Robert LaFollette, Henry Laurens, Henry Demarest Lloyd, Henry A. Wallace, Daniel Webster and other prominent Americans. To date, however, such collections have appeared exclusively on microfilm, and the potential of microfiche publication has been overlooked. The Papers of Benjamin Henry Latrobe is the first editorial project to undertake the task of publishing a large and complex collection of personal papers on microfiche.

Benjamin Henry Latrobe (1764-1820) is best remembered in connection with his work on the U.S. Capitol, but America's first professional architect and engineer also distinguished himself as an amateur artist, literary critic, philosopher, botanist, geologist, and social commentator. Latrobe's correspondence with such notable figures as Thomas Jefferson, James Madison, Robert Fulton, Albert Gallatin, Robert Goodloe Harper, and Charles Willson Peale provides invaluable documentation of the leaders of the post-Revolutionary generation and offers illuminating insights into the society, politics, and culture of the new nation. His sketches and drawings present the finest existing pictorial representation of early American towns, landscapes, and everyday life. Latrobe's papers thus offer scholars of various interests many approaches into the world of early America.

The core Latrobe collection at the Maryland Historical Society in Baltimore contains a variegated assortment of documents ranging from correspondence, journals, and bound letterbooks to watercolor sketches and large architectural and engineering drawings — about 6,400 items in all. This collection has been supplemented by the acquisition of correspondence, legal papers, reports, essays, and drawings from the National Archives, the Library of Congress, and all other repositories known to contain Latrobe documents. We acquired these "outside documents" in the form of photocopies, photographs, photostats, or copyflo. The quality of these reproductions varies considerably depending on the condition of the original document and the quality of the copying devices employed by each repository. Few collections of personal papers contain a wider variety of materials or a greater range of potential filming problems than the Latrobe collection. For this reason, the microfiche edition of The Papers of Benjamin Henry Latrobe stands as a serviceable model for similar editions of other significant collections. It is hoped that an account of our efforts and accomplishments will induce future editors to consider the unique advantages of microfiche publication.

FICHE OR ROLL FILM?

Two major considerations impelled us to depart from the example of sister projects such as the Daniel Webster Papers and choose fiche rather than roll film as our publishing medium. One important consideration was the ease of access which the microfiche format can allow the scholar. Anyone who has never experienced the frustration of cranking through yards of microfilm, starting and stopping to check position, in order to find a single reference, must have said to himself: "there has to be a better way!" With its eye-legible headings and its convenient 98-frame row-column format, microfiche allows the reader to locate the desired image quickly and directly and avoids the necessity of prolonged searching.

Scholars can derive full benefit from microform publication only if the documents contained therein are adequately indexed. This is true whether fiche or roll film is used. A serviceable index must, of course, allow the reader to turn immediately to the appropriate roll or fiche, but it should also give him quick access to the *exact location* of the desired document on that particular roll or fiche. The sequential page numbers contained in previously published material, or in typescript prepared specifically for microform, minimize the difficulties of indexing. With a large collection of unpublished manuscripts, however, the task of indexing and numbering becomes a major editorial consideration.

The problem of indexing historical documents on microfilm has never been satisfactorily resolved. The editors of some important microfilm collections, such as the Henry Laurens Papers, have considered the task too formidable and have published their collection without a printed index. Most editorial projects do not have the financial resources to emulate the method used by the editors of the Daniel Webster Papers, who produced xerographic printouts of each document, stamped each page with a sequential number, and then refilmed the entire sequence of numbered pages! This method would be doubly impracticable for the Latrobe collection, which contains numerous sketchbooks, large drawings, and other material which do not lend themselves easily to photocopying. On the other hand, we discovered that the microfiche format could allow us to prepare a comprehensive index without the necessity of numbering each frame individually. A detailed discussion of the index to the microfiche edition of The Papers of Benjamin Henry Latrobe follows.

The microfiche format is not equally suited for every editorial project. Besides having certain advantages over microfilm, microfiche also presents some disadvantages which must be given full consideration. One such factor involves the size limitations of the microfiche format. The standard 98-frame fiche, with a 24X reduction, can accommodate a document no larger than 8-1/2" x 11". A double-frame fiche camera, producing 49 frames at 24X, can handle documents no larger than 11" x 14". As we shall see, a collection containing a limited percentage of "oversize" documents (larger than 11" x 14") can readily be adapted to meet the demands of microfiche publication. However, a collection with a high percentage of oversize documents — for example, a collection consisting primarily or entirely of newspapers, oversize letterbooks, or large drawings – can still best be accommodated by the traditional roll-film format.

Another factor which every editor must consider is the increased possibility of filming error when microfiche is used instead of microfilm. With a microfilm format, the cameraman's main concern is that he has not exceeded the 100 feet of film in his camera. If he misses a document, forgets to film the inside of a folded letter, or if an image is blurred or overly light, the appropriate frames can be refilmed and butt-welded onto the master negative with a minimum of difficulty. With microfiche, on the other hand, the cameraman must continually be conscious of his position on the fourteen-frame row. If he accidentally films fifteen frames on a particular row, or if he fails to film a page of a document, the error cannot easily be rectified. Moreover, the microfiche format necessitates the refilming of an entire row, even if only one of the frames on that row appears illegible. This should not be a deterrent to microfiche publication, however. The possibility of committing costly filming errors can be minimized – or even eliminated – by conducting extensive voltage tests before filming and by using an automatic fiche programmer and program sheets during filming.

PRE-FILMING VOLTAGE TESTS

Whether fiche or roll film is chosen as a publishing medium, the editor of historical records must deal with filming problems not ordinarily encountered in other micropublishing projects. Only rarely does the editor enjoy the luxury of working with "clean copy" – i.e., high-contrast black ink on white paper. Often the documents which he must film are hundreds of years old and in various stages of deterioration. Individual collections pose specific filming problems. For example, the 5,700 items of correspondence in Latrobe's letterbooks were written with a polygraph – a primitive copying device which the architect acquired from his friend, Charles Willson Peale. Very seldom does the quality of a polygraph copy equal that of an original. The Latrobe letterbooks presented numerous problems of faded ink with little contrast between ink and paper and, conversely, "bleedthrough" where the writing on the back of a letter was clearly visible. Moreover, a substantial number of the "outside documents" in our collection were poor-quality photocopies, often with a grayish or sepia background.

Because of the diverse nature of the documents in our collection, the automatic exposure meter, which is usually used to determine the correct voltage for a given item, sometimes provided the cameraman with false information. With many of the off-white photocopies, for example, the meter discerned the dark background and indicated that the voltage should be increased. In the process, the fine lines of ink were overexposed and thus appeared too light to read. After the initial filming, we discovered to our chagrin that many of these photocopies were illegible. Many of Latrobe's faint pencil sketches and numerous letterbook pages with faded ink also appeared too light to discern.

Before refilming, we grouped the unacceptable images into as many categories as possible – e.g., sepia photocopies, grayish photocopies, photostats, faded ink, bleedthrough, light pencil sketches, watercolor sketches, photographs consisting primarily of line drawings, photographs with a great deal of dark background, etc. Sample documents from each category were tested at various voltages and the optimum voltage was noted for each. Sometimes we found that no single voltage adequately brought out all the salient characteristics of a document. For example, we discovered that a high voltage brought out the darker shades of Latrobe's watercolor sketches admirably, but lost much light background color (water, clouds, sky, etc.). A lower voltage emphasized the light watercolors and pencil inscriptions but did not clearly distinguish the darker shades. (Figure 1 illustrates a typical sketchbook fiche.) Despite such technological limitations, the voltage tests offered us sufficient guidance to strike a balance, in most cases, between overly-light and overly-dark exposures.

Although we did make a few random and haphazard voltage tests before the initial filming, it is clear – in retrospect – that we should have taken the time to conduct a more detailed and systematic series of tests at the very beginning of the filming process. Had we done so, much of the refilming would have been avoided and the additional time spent in testing would have been considerably less than the time consumed in refilming.

TWO INVALUABLE FILMING AIDS

The Papers of Benjamin Henry Latrobe could not have been filmed on microfiche without the aid of program sheets and an automatic fiche programmer. The automatic programmer, which can be easily attached to a standard planetary camera, is designed to indicate exactly which row and column is about to be filmed. It has to be reset at the end of fourteen frames (seven frames, if a double-frame camera is used), thus making it impossible to accidentally film too many images on a row. We used the automatic programmer in conjunction with previously prepared program sheets, such as the one illustrated in Figure 2. Each 8-1/2" x 11" program sheet contains a grid pattern corresponding to the row-column arrangement of a microfiche card. Before each fiche was filmed, all documents to be contained on that particular card were marked on a program sheet. In the case of journals, letterbooks, and sketchbooks, the appropriate page or sketch number was noted for each frame. The unbound manuscripts were coded with sequential numbers, M1, M2, M3 . . . M1700 (one number per document). Unbound architectural and engineering drawings were designated A1, A2, A3 etc. (one number per project).

At short intervals, spot checks were made to ensure that the document under camera agreed with the document indicated on the program sheet. Thus, if a page was accidentally filmed twice, or not filmed at all, or if the proper spaces were not taken between documents, this fact became immediately known to us and the appropriate correction was made. It is worth noting that subsequent proofreading revealed not a single instance of a frame being out of its proper sequence — a rather remarkable achievement considering that there are

approximately 12,700 frames on the microfiche edition of The Papers of Benjamin Henry Latrobe, and, consequently, 12,700 opportunities to have made a mistake!

OVERSIZE DOCUMENTS

Although a majority of documents in our collection fit well within the 11" x 14" capacity of a double-frame microfiche camera, a substantial number of documents — approximately thirty manuscripts; fifty original architectural/engineering drawings, such as the one illustrated in Figure 3; and about fifty photostatic copies of architectural/engineering drawings — were "oversize." An additional 400 oversize drawings from outside collections had been reduced to 8" x 10" photographs, and we decided that these, too, would not adequately reproduce with the standard 24X reduction.

The oversize manuscripts were filmed in two successive frames, but we decided that the oversize drawings would have to be scanned as a single unbroken unit. We therefore filmed the drawings on

Figure 1.   This fiche is one of sixteen from the sketchbook series. A comprehensive catalog appears in the upper left corner. Reproduced by permission of The Papers of Benjamin Henry Latrobe, Maryland Historical Society.

366

standard 35-mm microfilm at a 15X reduction. (A higher reduction was used whenever a 15X reduction could not accommodate the entire drawing.) The processed film was not cut down to standard 12-1/2–mm microfiche specifications, but was stripped directly onto microfiche cards. Thus only two rows of oversize documents appear on each fiche card.

The photographs were also filmed on 35-mm microfilm at a 15X reduction. We discovered that small inscriptions, numbers, and details on these photographs appeared more legible on the fiche reader than on the actual photograph, since the blowback image was substantially larger than 8" x 10". It should again be emphasized, however, that this method is feasible only if the total number of oversize documents is within manageable proportions. To cite an extreme example, it would be impossible to film the New York *Times* on microfiche, since no more than fourteen pages of each issue could be accommodated on a single fiche card!

INDEXING THE MICROFICHE EDITION

"Information without indexing," as James B. Adler of the Congressional Information Service has recently noted, "is hardly information at all. . . . You can microfilm all the data you want . . . but a

Figure 2. Program sheets, such as this one for fiche 165, were used to mark the location of each document before filming. Reproduced by permission of The Papers of Benjamin Henry Latrobe, Maryland Historical Society.

Figure 3. This watercolor rendering of the Bank of Pennsylvania, the first monument of the Greek Revival in this country, is one of about fifty original oversize drawings in the Latrobe collection. Reproduced by permission of The Papers of Benjamin Henry Latrobe, Maryland Historical Society.

huge file on microfilm without a good retrieval system is virtually worthless." It was this consideration – the need to provide our readers with a means of quickly and easily locating each document in our collection – which provided the greatest incentive for us to choose fiche rather than roll film as our publishing medium.

The raw materials used as the basis for our index were the 4" x 6" control slips which were typed for each document in our collection. Although these slips were originally prepared for internal control purposes, we subsequently realized that they contained most of the information necessary for indexing – i.e., the date of the document; the name of the correspondent or other descriptor; and, wherever appropriate, a project reference (U.S. Capitol, St. John's Church, Stephen Decatur House, etc.). After the collection had been filmed, we devised an alphanumeric location number for each document and added it to the control slip. For example, the number 176/A13 on a control slip indicated that the document could be located on fiche 176, row A, column 13. (The entire set of fiche was numbered sequentially from 1 to 315.) It was not necessary to wait until a positive fiche set had been generated before adding these location numbers, since the necessary information was already contained on our program sheets. Thus the initial steps of indexing proceeded concurrently with the generation of positive fiche for proofreading.

After the appropriate location number had been added to each control slip, the entire series was filmed with a rotary microfilm camera. We then produced two sets of copyflo on heavy-duty card stock and cut the cards to the original 4" x 6" size of the control slips. We arranged the first set in alphabetical order by correspondent. Essays, reports, and other items of non-correspondence were grouped together under the entry, "Latrobe, Benjamin Henry." Within each alphabetical sequence, the cards were sub-arranged in chronological order. All information on the cards which was not necessary for the index was crossed out, and – in order to ensure that the cards remained in proper order – a running number was added to the bottom of each card. We arranged the second set of cards alphabetically by project. Within each project, the cards were sub-arranged in chronological order. (Cards in the second set which contained no project reference were thrown away.) The two sets were then interfiled into a single alphabetical sequence. Our use of this microfilming/copyflo process saved us the time and expense of typing, proofing, and correcting a manuscript index for the printer.

Wickham, John, House 171

Watkins, John		Wallack, William		Whan, Mr.	
28 May 1814	117/D8	13 Jul 1812	100/G13	18 Jan 1811	83/A1
9 Jun 1814	118/B5	Waln, Jacob.		Whann, William	
Watson, Ch[arle]s		28 Apr 1805	39/E5	19 Dec 1817	235/A7
7 Nov 1803	27/B8	Waln, William		Wharton, Franklin	
13 Apr 1805	39/C2	26 Mar 1805	38/B14	28 Mar 1805	38/F6
7 Nov 1805	45/G2	1 Apr 1805	39/A6	26 Jun 1805	40/G6
23 Jul 1807	58/B2	6 May 1805	39/F14	30 Dec 1805	46/F1
31 Oct 1809	71/C12	25 Jan 1806	47/B14	4 Apr 1807	56/C9
2 Nov 1809	71/D5	28 Dec 1806	53/C12	Wharton, James	
31 Aug 1810	77/G3	22 Jan 1807	54/F14	19 Feb 1811	83/G8
10 Aug 1811	89/B10	3 Mar 1807	55/E13	Wheaton, Mr.	
9 Apr 1812	97/A9	15 Apr 1807	56/B7	19 Jul 1806	50/B14
15 Sep 1813	112/G4	10 Jan 1808	62/C10	Wheaton, Mrs.	
Watson, I. F.		5 Jul 1808	65/E7	13 Jun 1806	49/E9
24 Jan 1812	94/F9	Jul 1808	65/E13	Wheeler, John	
Watson, William		21 Aug 1808	65/F8	25 Feb 1808	63/A13
26 Apr 1804	31/E8	25 Aug 1808	66/A6	Wheeler, Luke	
Watson, Mr.		30 May 1811	85/E12	16 Dec 1803	28/A4
1 Apr 1807	56/C2	Waln, William, House, Phila-			171/A3
Weightman, Roger C.		delphia, Pa.		Wheeler & Peacock *see* Peacock	
17 Mar 1812	96/A13	WILCOCKS, JAMES S.		& Wheeler	
2 Apr 1812	96/E1	12 Mar 1805	38/A6	Whetcroft, Henry	
11 Jul 1812	100/F5	GILPIN, JOSHUA		12 Sep 1816	133/B9
17 Sep 1812	103/C1	23 Mar 1805	38/D9	Whipple, Oliver	
18 Jan 1815	123/G14	WILCOCKS, JAMES S.		12 Apr 1810	74/C1
Wells, Bazileel		23 Mar 1805	38/D8	White, Thomas	
22 Apr 1814	116/D8	GILPIN, JOSHUA		17 Mar 1807	55/G7
6 Aug 1814	119/A12	26 Mar 1805	38/B12	White, William	
12 Aug 1814	119/B10	WALN, WILLIAM		27 Dec 1807	61/C4
15 Oct 1814	120/C12	26 Mar 1805	38/B14	21 Dec 1810	80/F14
7 Nov 1814	120/G7	WALN, WILLIAM		30 Dec 1810	81/A8
22 Nov 1814	121/C8	1 Apr 1805	39/A6	Whiting & Bosquet	
1 Dec 1814	121/E4	GILPIN, JOSHUA		20 Nov 1814	121/B5
8 Dec 1814	121/F7	7 Apr 1805	39/B6	[22 Nov 1814]	121/C6
29 Dec 1814	123/B8	WALN, WILLIAM		Whitlaw, Thomas: [Bill for	
5 Jan 1815	123/D11	6 May 1805	39/F14	work done. Signed by BHL]	
28 May 1816	131/A12	25 Jan 1806	47/B14	22 Oct 1798	160/C11
Welsh, John		28 Dec 1806	53/C12	Wickersham, Mr.	
9 Sep 1807	59/D6	22 Jan 1807	54/F14	25 Aug 1814	119/E2
Wendell, John		3 Mar 1807	55/E13	Wickham, John	
23 Aug 1814	119/D10	15 Apr 1807	56/E7	16 Mar 1811	84/E14
1 Jan 1815	123/C4	MILLS, ROBERT		26 Apr 1811	85/C11
22 Oct 1817	138/F6	28 Jul 1807	58/B9	21 Jan 1812	94/E2
Wendell, Mathew		20 Sep 1807	59/G2	8 Nov 1812	104/A2
16 Oct 1817	138/E11	23 Sep 1807	59/G7	2 Dec 1812	104/E6
Wetherill, Samuel		WALN, WILLIAM		Wickham, John, House, Rich-	
20 May 1808	64/F13	10 Jan 1808	62/C10	mond, Va.	
4 Aug 1811	88/F8	TRAQUAIR, ADAM		WICKHAM, JOHN	
7 Nov 1811	92/B7	11 Jan 1808	62/D2	26 Apr 1811	85/C11
27 Sep 1813	112/G6	MILLS, ROBERT			
		12 Apr 1808	63/C5		

Figure 4.   A mock-up of a page from the index to the microfiche edition. Reproduced by permission of The Papers of Benjamin Henry Latrobe, Maryland Historical Society.

Our experience with scholars who have viewed our microfiche edition at the Maryland Historical Society indicates that, once the user has grasped the fundamentals of the indexing system, he is able to locate any document in the Latrobe collection in a matter of seconds. A scholar wishing to view a specific document or series of documents (for example, all correspondence between Latrobe and President Thomas Jefferson) can look up the appropriate references under the alphabetical sequence of Latrobe correspondents. On the other hand, an architectural historian wishing to research a specific Latrobe project can conveniently locate the desired references under the appropriate project entry. (See Figure 4.) To facilitate use of this part of the index, we have included a list of project headings at the beginning of the index. Thus a scholar wishing to investigate all the private residences designed by Latrobe (but who might not know all these residences by name) would turn first to the list of project headings before attempting to locate the specific frame references in the index itself. Although the project index was created to fit the specific demands of the Latrobe collection, the same principle can be used by other editors to prepare a subject index, whenever such an index is deemed feasible or necessary.

THE FUTURE OF MICROFICHE IN SCHOLARLY MICROPUBLISHING

Even as this account is being written, other editors are beginning to explore the feasibility of microfiche for their collections. For example, the editor of the Peale Family Papers has decided recently to film this important collection on microfiche. The editors of the Papers of the Marquis de Lafayette are also using fiche to supplement parts of their letterpress edition. Perhaps the greatest difficulty which we encountered during the filming of The Papers of Benjamin Henry Latrobe was the lack of a suitable model. Most of the problems which arose before, during, and after filming had to be solved by the process of trial and error. Each collection, of course, poses unique filming problems, and our own experience cannot provide answers to every question which may arise during the filming process. We hope, however, that this account will suggest to other editors some of the possibilities, as well as the problems, of microfiche publication.

The Papers of Benjamin Henry Latrobe: Vital Statistics

Editor in Chief: Edward C. Carter II
Microfiche Editor: Thomas E. Jeffrey

Filmed at the Maryland Historical Society between October 1, 1974 and October 13, 1974 by Princeton Datafilm Incorporated, Princeton, New Jersey

Published for the Maryland Historical Society by James T. White & Company, Clifton, New Jersey

The documents in the Latrobe collection were filmed in five series:

Series I: *Journals.* 23 journals in the possession of the Maryland Historical Society (25 fiche)

Series II: *Letterbooks.* 19 bound volumes of correspondence in the possession of the Maryland Historical Society (114 fiche)

Series III: *Manuscript Documents and Published Works.* Approximately 115 documents in the collections of the Maryland Historical Society, and approximately 1,245 documents from outside collections (104 fiche)

Series IV: *Sketchbooks.* 14 sketchbooks, in the possession of the Maryland Historical Society, containing approximately 350 sketches and 150 pages of notes (16 fiche)

Series V: *Architectural and Engineering Drawings.* 54 drawings from the collections of the Maryland Historical Society, and 432 drawings from other collections (56 fiche)

Number of Documents Filmed: Approximately 8,000

Number of Frames: Approximately 12,700

Camera: Recordak Model MRD-2

Fiche Head (double frame):   Recordak MOdel MRD-1A-10

35-mm Head (for Series V):   Recordak Model MRD-2-friction drive

Negative Film: Fuji 35 mm perforated (Series I – Series IV)
                               Fuji 35 mm (Series V)

Duplicates: Recordak Print Film (Estar thick base) SO-215

28: PLANNING FOR PRESERVING THE SCHOMBURG CENTER VERTICAL FILE VIA MICROFICHE

Otillia M. Pearson

Background

The Schomburg Center for Research in Black Culture maintains a vertical file organized under some 10,000 subject headings. Included are clippings from non-black periodicals (those that are not kept on the shelves of The Schomburg Center), newspaper clippings, broadsides, programs, playbills, leaflets, pamphlets, newsletters, book reviews, typescripts, post cards, menus, and other types of ephemera. The vertical file has been maintained from the beginning of the collection in 1925 up to the present.

The ever-increasing size of the vertical file, the difficulty in preserving it adequately in file folders, the excessive amount of staff time required to clip and add to this file, and heavy reader use have all contributed to an urgent need to seek improved methods of preservation and easier access to this unique archive without further deterioration of the fragile materials.

At first, piece-meal efforts were made to preserve individual subject categories that were heavily used and badly deteriorating by photocopying entire folders and/or placing particularly fragile materials from this collection on roll microfilm. The undesirability of having such a file in varying formats is obvious. Also it is clear that such techniques could not keep pace with the long-range

Otillia M. Pearson is Project Director, National Endowment for the Humanities Project, Schomburg Center for Research in Black Culture.

needs for a more permanent form of preservation for the entire file.

Step 1

Two occurrences in 1972 set in motion the steps which will culminate early in 1975 with the beginning of a project to convert The Schomburg Center Vertical File to microfiche. The first action that proved significant was the administrative transfer of The Schomburg Center from The Branch Libraries to The Research Libraries of The New York Public Library. The second action was a grant to The Schomburg Center by The National Endowment for the Humanities.[1] The administrative change to The Research Libraries provided conservation consultants to The Center through the staff of the Conservation Division, and the grant from the National Endowment provided funding for a technical staff who could be trained in the preparation of materials for the camera.

Step 2

In 1973 another major event helped move this project along although at the time no one could have foreseen the direct relationship. In its 1973/74 legislative session the state of New York provided $250,000 in state aid to The Schomburg Center[2] as the result of legislation introduced by former State Senator Sidney von Luther. Another grant was received for 1974/75.[3] Included in this appropriation were funds for the maintenance and expansion of services, acquisition, preservation and restoration of materials and collections held at The Schomburg Center. Using funds provided for expansion of services, The Center was able to employ more professional staff. With additional librarians plus technical staff already at work there now existed sufficient personnel who could work as a team to sort and prepare the vertical file materials for lay-out prior to filming. This group working at The Center plus experienced conservation librarians who could assist in planning and working through the technical and bibliographic details brought the project a step closer to reality.

Step 3

Within The Research Libraries the usual procedure is to forward material for filming to the in-house Photographic Service, located in the main building in midtown Manhattan, some 90 block south of The Schomburg Center. However, the quantity of material in The Schomburg Center Vertical File was so great that Center personnel began to think about other ways of handling this project, using available staff.

Late in 1973, following an exploratory visit, the NCR Corporation developed a proposal to convert the vertical file to microfiche. Using materials from the Center's collection, the NCR Corporation provided a sample to demonstrate the quality of microfiche produced using an NCR Model 457 Step and Repeat Camera. The sample microfiche, produced from the *Kurt Fisher Collection*, was of excellent quality.[4] The Fisher Collection represents many 200 year old documents in extremely poor condition and in urgent need of preservation.

However, many factors still had to be considered and worked through. Where would the funds come from to pay for a contract with the NCR Corporation? With no previous training in preparing materials for filming, could the technical staff be expected to meet production quotas that would form the basis for pricing in a contract? Who would be responsible for packing and shipping materials from The Center to the NCR filming laboratory in Beltsville, Maryland? How much turnaround time would be required? What assurances could the NCR Corporation provide that would allay the anxieties of The Chief of The Schomburg Center and her staff regarding

potential loss or damage to materials in transit? While there were no immediate answers to all of these questions, efforts continued to resolve each of them.

Step 4

During the six month period, from late 1973 until mid 1974, librarians at The Center continued to develop techniques for weeding the vertical file. Precise guidelines were established indicating what items were to be retained for filming and what items were to be removed from the file for cataloging as monographs, referred to the Archives, the Print and Poster collections, or discarded. Meantime, the National Endowment for the Humanities awarded a new two-year matching grant (July, 1974 - June 30, 1976)[5] to The Schomburg Center which assured continued funding for the technical staff. A proposal was drafted and forwarded to the Ford Foundation in which funding for the filming of the Vertical File was solicited.

Finally, the NCR Corporation submitted a new proposal which eliminated many of the serious objections to the project that existed in the original proposal. It appeared that the pieces, each one of unique importance if the project were to succeed, had at last fallen into place.

Step 5

The second NCR proposal contained two key features that eliminated the major objections of the first plan. One, an offer to install, on a rental basis, a Step and Repeat Camera on the premises of The Center and two, to recruit and train a Camera Operator who would work at The Center although he would be an employee of the NCR Corporation. It was understood that these features could be incorporated into a contract.

On August 15, 1974, The New York Public Library signed a contract with the NCR Corporation to produce (over a two-year period) 17,500 microfiche masters conforming to NMA standards. Training sessions began in earnest with all staff involved and the actual lay-out of materials started under the guidance of NCR technical staff. In October, NCR recruited a member of The National Endowment staff for the Camera Operator position. In November, the recruit went to the NCR Capitol Data Processing Center in Beltsville, Maryland for training in the operation of the Step and Repeat Camera. In December, word came that the Ford Foundation had acted favorably on our proposal and in January, 1975 the camera was installed, inspected, tested and ready for use.

Technical Data

1. Staff Involved

    4 Librarians .... part-time (this excludes Conservation librarians who act as consultants)

    4 Library Technical Assistants

    1 Master Typist

    1 Clerk-Typist

2. Bibliographic Control (see figures 1 and 2 for samples)

    The Schomburg Center Vertical File, in its original form, is arranged alphabetically by subject and has a card index with cross references. The file is organized for filming as follows:

2.1 There is a single main entry for the entire collection. The entry is "Schomburg Center Clipping File, 1925-1974" with an internal title breakdown by subject.

2.2 The entire file has a single fixed-order classmark (call number).

2.3 There is an internal subject number (to allow for the addition of supplements in later years) and (for file integrity and location) an individual fiche number. The FSN series for The Schomburg Center is preceded by the prefix SC, starting with SC - 001, to be used for the NCR Project only.

2.4 The hard copy index is in process of revision and will be issued on microfiche at the conclusion of the project.

3. Vertical File Weeding Process

    Newspaper and magazine clippings form the bulk of the file. All duplicate articles will be discarded, and the librarians responsible for the sorting will make the final decisions as to what will be included and excluded.

4. Physical Arrangement of Materials Within Each Subject (see Figures 4-8 for samples)

    Everything that can be dated will be arranged in chronological order, with undated materials grouped together at the end of each subject. All dates and sources will be clearly indicated on the face of each item. If the date or source is impossible to decipher but the item is in good condition, it will be placed with undated materials which have been organized by size and type.

    Materials are laid-out on black matte paper in chronological order. Both sides of the layout board are used and kept in numbered sequence. Pamphlets are not cut up or pasted to a layout board, but each page is numbered and all numbers for layout boards or individual pamphlets are recorded on the layout sheet as filming sequence instructions for the camera operator.

5. Categories of Material to be Filmed

    Broadsides

    Playbills and Programs

    Pamphlets - up to 50 pages

    Invitations

    Book Jackets

    Menus

    Small Maps

    Commemorative postage stamps

6. Materials to be Excluded from the Microfiche

    Picture postcards

    Letters and Manuscripts

    Large Maps

    Posters

    Calendars

    Photographs

    Annual Reports

Figure 1. Sample — Headers in Sequence

Schomburg Center Clipping File, 1925-1974
  AFRICA--ETHNIC GROUPS
NYPL (NCR)   Sc Micro F-1   FSN Sc 000,078-1

Schomburg Center Clipping File, 1925-1974
  AFRICA--FINANCE
NYPL (NCR)   Sc Micro F-1   FSN Sc 000,079-1

Schomburg Center Clipping File, 1925-1974
  AFRICA--FINANCE
NYPL (NCR)   Sc Micro F-1   FSN Sc 000,079-2

Schomburg Center Clipping File, 1925-1974
  AFRICA--FOOD SUPPLY
NYPL (NCR)   Sc Micro F-1   FSN Sc 000,080-1

Schomburg Center Clipping File, 1925-1974
  AFRICA--FOOD SUPPLY
NYPL (NCR)   Sc Micro F-1   FSN Sc 000,080-2

Schomburg Center Clipping File, 1925-1974
  AFRICA--FOOD SUPPLY
NYPL (NCR)   Sc Micro F-1   FSN Sc 000,080-3

Schomburg Center Clipping File, 1925-1974
  AFRICA--FOREIGN RELATIONS
NYPL (NCR)   Sc Micro F-1   FSN Sc 000,081-1

Schomburg Center Clipping File, 1925-1974
  AFRICA--FOREIGN RELATIONS
NYPL (NCR)   Sc Micro F-1   FSN Sc 000,081-2

Figure 2. Sample — Bibliographic Organization

Schomburg Center Clipping File, 1925-1974   main entry for
                                        entire collection
   ALI, MUHAMMAD: chronology, 1962-1965.
NYPL (NCR)   Sc Micro F-1   FSN Sc 000,223-1

Schomburg Center Clipping File, 1925-1974   subject with chronology
   ALI, MUHAMMAD: chronology, 1965-1966.
NYPL (NCR)   Sc Micro F-1   FSN Sc 000,223-2

Schomburg Center Clipping File, 1925-1974   fixed-order classmark
   ALI, MUHAMMAD: chronology, 1966-1967.   for entire file
NYPL (NCR)   Sc Micro F-1   FSN Sc 000,223-3

Schomburg Center Clipping File, 1925-1974
   ALI, MUHAMMAD: chronology, 1967-1969.   individual
NYPL (NCR)   Sc Micro F-1   FSN Sc 000,223-4   subject number

Schomburg Center Clipping File, 1925-1974
   ALI, MUHAMMAD: chronology, 1969-1971.   individual
NYPL (NCR)   Sc Micro F-1   FSN Sc 000,223-5   fiche number

Schomburg Center Clipping File, 1925-1974
   ALI,MUHAMMAD: chronology, 1971-1975; miscellaneous.
NYPL (NCR)   Sc Micro F-1   FSN Sc 000,223-6

Schomburg Center Clipping File, 1925-1974
   ALI, MUHAMMAD: chronology, miscellaneous.
NYPL (NCR)   Sc Micro F-1   FSN Sc 000,223-7

Figure 3. Photograph of vertical file folder showing deteriorated
condition of material before layout.

Figure 4. Photograph of layout sheet.

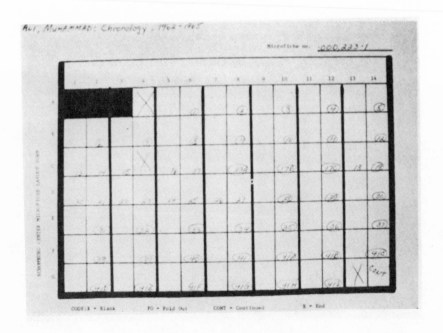

Figures 5 and 6 (see explanation next page)

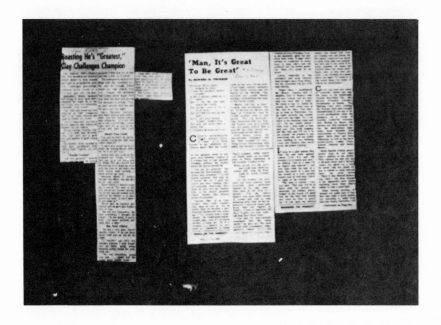

Figures 5, 6, 7 and 8.

Photograph of layout board. Note the assignment of a number in the lower right hand corner. As each individual item is mounted on the layout board, it is given a frame number, corresponding to a location on the layout sheet instructing the camera operator on the exact sequence of filming. In this way, the final arrangement of items on each microfiche is planned in advance, insuring maximal use of each fiche without splitting up multipage documents between two fiche.

Single Issues of Newspapers

Diplomas and Awards

Sheet Music

7. Materials Required

Microfiche headers are typed on Hammermill Index Stock - 110 lb. weight, 8½"x 11" white.

Master Typist uses an IBM Selectric typewriter with Letter Gothic type font - lower case for the main entry and upper case for the subject heading.

Layout Sheets are pre-printed and supplied by the NCR Corporation. (see Figure 4 for sample)

Materials are laid out on Black Matte Finish Cover Stock. The paper comes in size 20"x 26" and is cut to required size for layout which is 11½"x 18".

Scotch Brand Magic Transparent Tape - used for pasting materials to matte board is 1/2"x 2592" in 72 yard spools. Tape No. 810.

Required paper supplies are expensive and are being ordered in large quantities to secure the best price.

Desk Organizer - 11½"x 12" anodized aluminum enclosure with 25 aluminum dividers. This equipment is essential for arranging large subject folders in chronological order.

8. Equipment Used

A high quality Photocopy Machine will be available near the work area, since many clippings, in poor condition, require reproduction prior to layout for filming. The Schomburg Center chose a Royal Bond Copier primarily because it reproduces excellent half-tones.

Camera - NCR Model 457 Step and Repeat Microfiche Camera

Film - Camera uses a 100' roll of standard 105mm film. After the roll is processed it is either kept intact to reproduce additional master negatives or microfiche duplicates—or cut to individual fiche for filing in sequence and printing individual fiche copies.

Microfiche Readers - NCR 456 "A" Series, Model 456 D - 2 with 24X lens.

Microfiche Reader Printer - 3M Model 275 AGM Series "500" Microfiche Reader Printer with 20.78 magnification to blow back 24X reduction fiche at 87% of original size. This equipment is bi-modal and will reproduce negative or positive fiche.

Conclusion

It was estimated that The Schomburg Center would need at least 1000 layouts prepared before filming commenced. This quantity of material is estimated to provide the camera operator with at least two months of filming work and give librarians and technical staff lead time to complete an additional two months filming work. If such a schedule can be maintained, there should be little down time, and maximum use of the camera and the operator's time to provide the best product for The Research Libraries - Schomburg Center.

References

1. National Endowment for the Humanities Grant RO-6272-72-182.
2. State of New York Bill 1878-B, 1973/74.
3. State of New York Bill S9929, 1974/75.
4. The Kurt Fisher collection is a collection of documents and manuscripts collected by Kurt A. Fisher, an Austrian who settled in Haiti in 1935. This collection covers more than two centuries (1745-1957) of Haitian history.
5. National Endowment for the Humanities Grant RC-21349-74-565.

29: REPRODUCTION VS. PRESERVATION

J. Alden

T HE EXTRAORDINARY INCREASE since 1946 in the photoreproduction of books, especially by microphotography, has perforce a place in the preservation of books and manuscripts themselves. As a means of conserving verbal texts of materials which, because of advanced deterioration, cannot feasibly be saved, there is little doubt that putting them on film is a worthwhile if last resort. This presupposes that deacidification and strengthening by tissue or silk, or by lamination, is impossible or disproportionately costly. The saving in space which the microfilming of sulphite pulp newspapers makes possible gives further support to its use for them. And for making available out-of-print texts of interest so limited as not to justify reprinting by type composition or photolithography, the various photoduplication processes currently employed for this purpose can but be applauded.

Having said all this, one may also look at aspects of the larger picture frequently ignored by the microreproduction industry and by librarians themselves. For, to the misgivings expressed, mildly and urbanely, by the late William A. Jackson in "Some Limitations of Microfilm" concerning the inability of the camera to convey, with required bibliographical exactitude, an original text, further doubts have been added. These range from the effect of such widespread copying on the publishing industry and the antiquarian book trade, through the ethical morality of copyright violation, on to the uncertain permanence of reproductions and the damage done to original materials which cannot be viewed as expendable. It is with these two last factors that we are here concerned.

Not the less negligible of these is the uncertain character of microfilm. At its best, microfilm is no more lasting than good paper and is subject to comparable ills and damage. If it is to endure, similar conditions for storage must be provided in terms of temperature, humidity, and atmosphere, as set forth in *American Standard Practice for Storage of Microfilm*. It may be noted, in passing, that for the librarian, one means of meeting these standards of obtaining proper accommodations for master films is the use of vaults provided by commercial firms for this purpose.)

And at the present time we can neither

count infallibly on the stability of the film itself or of the photographic image. Speaking not only as a bookman for whom the reproduction lacks the appeal of the original but also as a scholar, Edwin Wolf, 2nd, has described, in his "Thoughts on Books and Libraries," how unique records have been filmed — to save space — and the originals destroyed, only to have the film itself become illegible. Though investigations have been undertaken of blemishes and of the aging of film, we do not yet know precisely where we stand. The continuing and time-consuming program of vigilance as outlined in the National Bureau of Standards' *Inspection of Processed Photographic Record Films for Aging Blemishes* is a desideratum rarely possible for institutions maintaining master films of archival value.

In our uncertainty regarding the permanence of microfilm, one thing does seem likely — that librarians are themselves in part responsible for the deterioration of films in their care. Forgetting the elementary fact that the photographic image is a silver emulsion, they have on occasion put rubber bands around spools of film. The effect of the sulphur in rubber upon silver seems too well known to require comment. Failure to maintain microfilm reading machines properly also contributes to the destruction of film.

Similar reservations may be expressed regarding many of the other processes for the copying of printed matter, described in William R. Hawken's *Photocopying from Bound Volumes*. All have their limitations. But the increasing reliance upon electrophotography, and more especially on the Xerox process, makes comment on the full range of techniques superfluous; we are concerned solely with those methods where permanence is an objective, and few, if any, of other existing methods make claims to meeting this aim, howsoever useful they may be for other purposes.

The merits of the Xerox process are numerous, both in its 914 Copier, which makes direct black on white copies from an original, and in the continuous Copyflo machine which provides prints from microfilm. The steps involved in Xerox machines are described fully by Hawken; suffice it to say that a special powder is concentrated by electrostatic attraction on a sheet of paper, and is then fused to the paper by heat. (The element of heat creates

its dangers, aging as it does the paper used. And a fire extinguisher is part of Xerox equipment!) One of the great merits of the Xerox process is that the paper employed can be archival standard, and University Microfilms commendably utilizes papers meeting Barrow standards in its reproductions of out-of-print books.

That Xerox prints vary in permanence has long been apparent to users of them, principally in the fading of the image.

In contrast to the Xerox print and microfilm, the Microcard combines both compactness and a surer prospect of permanence, but to be economically feasible, a substantial number of sets must be issued.

It is, however, the physical effect upon the original books and manuscripts of the act of microreproduction that disturbs many of us — not simply as bibliophiles but also as scholars aware that the original may yet offer research evidence of which even we are unaware, and that it should be kept intact. The fact has become manifest that it is virtually impossible to photostat, microfilm, or Xerox an item without some physical harm, especially if it is a bound volume. A human being can adapt himself to the tensions and weaknesses of binding materials. But, though we may yet hope for methods overcoming this defect, for the camera a flat surface is at present required, and all too often providing this does violence to the binding. Spine and hinges may crack, while, if the gatherings have been inadvisably oversewn or side-stitched, the linen thread will tear the leaves. From time to time the paper will simply crack at the inner margin. It does not take a great deal of experience to be able to recognize the ravages of reproduction.

In this context, the indifference of operators to the materials they are handling cannot be ignored. It is bad enough that original bindings of early books have been broken at their hinges, but when the operator re-affixes them with Scotch tape — as has been done in one of America's leading microreproduction laboratories — there is occasion for apoplexy.

In all this the lavish generosity of American librarians in making materials freely available if not by interlibrary loan then by photoreproduction has its disadvantages. Laudable as is this dedication to a concept of service, the American scholar has been led to expect to be able to obtain photoreproductions as an absolute right, not as a privilege extended by grace when the purpose of his undertaking and the nature of the materials justifies this. Admittedly it is usually cheaper and easier to dictate a letter requesting a reproduction than to obtain a copy of the original, or even to travel, say, the two or three miles from Roxbury to Boston, but it is also true that reproductions are sometimes requested when a clearly phrased question would make photoreproduction unnecessary. Librarians frequently do understand the needs and purposes of the scholar and can grasp his problems!

In his anxiety to please, whatever the cost to his collections, the American librarian has, in permitting and even encouraging reproductions, too often abrogated his responsibility to the future in maintaining the materials in his care. For one cannot fail to question the wisdom of certain large-scale microfilm or Microcard programs undertaken by commercial firms in our day or by individual college or university libraries, spurred on frequently by an aggressive faculty member whose interest or tenure may not endure. It is possible, moreover, that, beguiled by being able to point to vast resources otherwise unavailable, librarians are fostering projects for which use will never justify the often great expense. Often, it appears, the knowledge, by means of enumerative bibliographies, of what materials exist and where would probably suffice, to be consulted or reproduced when actual need arises. It remains to be seen, by an objective observer, to what extent the existence on Microcard or film of infrequently needed texts actually stimulates or promotes sound scholarship.

For reasons such as these, many a custodian of rare books and manuscripts is having second thoughts on the advisability of cooperating in extensive and comprehensive undertakings. It is difficult not to concur with the eminent librarian of a major research collection who will participate only where actual cerebral activity is exercised, as in the case of the Readex microprint series of *Early American Imprints*. For this, Dr. Clifford K. Shipton, director of the American Antiquarian Society, has undertaken a substantial amount of historical and bibliographical research, correcting and annotating Charles Evans' *American Bibliography*. But too

John Alden is Keeper of Rare Books at the Boston Public Library. This article is from a chapter of "The Care and Preservation of Books," a completely revised 5th edition of "The Care and Repair of Books" by John Alden and William Spawn, to be published by R. R. Bowker

often the selection and assembling of material is an uncritical and purely clerical task, sometimes based upon unsound guides, and thus perpetuating error.

Howsoever much one respects the initiative, imagination, and responsibility of private industry, one suspects that the future will see the need for closer correlation between commerical firms and librarians as suppliers and purchasers of materials. Before embarking on advertising or on ordering film, firms will explore the availability of material for this purpose, and not, as at present, take for granted that it will be accessible. Royalties will be paid for such use, consistently and commeasurably, compensating the institution for the extra burdens such requests place upon it. (Though this adds to the cost to subscribing libraries, this can scarcely be considered an injustice.) In turn, sounder scholarly advice will be sought on the need and wisdom of the patterns and scope of projects envisaged, establishing at the same time higher standards of editorial responsibility.

The individual scholar, on the other hand, seeking reproductions for actual and specific purposes evokes greater sympathy. But here again excesses occur. Requests are not unknown in terms such as "Please Xerox for me everything you have written by or to so-and-so," without appreciation of the magnitude of the task.

In meeting all such requests, it is perhaps wisest to take the stand that they will be individually considered in terms of the material in question, and passed on by a person of competence. Is the character of the material such that it should not be reproduced at all because of the degree and nature of the risk of damage? Or is the material expendable?

To these questions there can be no cut-and-dried answers. For materials that must be preserved a compromise can be reached — a policy adopted for an increasing number of rare book collections. That is, to microfilm the item, retaining the negative, from which Copyflo or other enlargement prints or positive microfilm is supplied. Wisdom perhaps dictates that this original film should be maintained as an archival master, and not be used for reading purposes. (As a corollary, in such cases, direct copies using a Xerox 914 Copier or the like will not be provided.) In this fashion, damage may be kept at a minimum. It is curious, in such cases, how often requests are received by a library for a reproduction of the same item, so much so that retaining a negative microfilm is not unrealistic. Such repetition of requests may be due to the outstanding quality of the original, in part because there are fads in scholarship which focus upon a particular work, or because a scholar has suddenly discovered a hitherto ignored source in one's collection.

While filming a work once and for all and retaining the negative, from which complete or partial reproductions can in turn be made, solves many problems, frequently the scholar will wish only a few pages or passages reproduced. More often than not this is to escape the labor of transcription. One can, in this instance, sympathize with the harassed doctoral candidate, short of funds, making the most of limited time in visits to libraries, and for whom the assemblage of "documentation" is the paramount concern. The facility, the ease, the economy, the accuracy, of mechanical copying weigh heavily in favor

of the process. Yet something is lost. The monk engaged in transcribing a medieval manuscript was not merely attempting to do something the printer does better; in his labors he had an opportunity, unknown to the typist, of savoring and absorbing the text he was copying. The commonplace book of our ancestors served not only as a storehouse of quotations but as a device for imprinting ideas upon the memory. But now, at its lowest common denominator, "research" has moved on from the reshuffling of 3 x 5 index cards to that of Xerox sheets.

Confronted with constant requests for reproductions of scattered passages of text, and bits and snatches of isolated volumes, it is sometimes tempting to adopt a policy — at least for fragile or early materials — of reproducing only entire works. Such a stand might often be unduly harsh and unreasonable. But if a fragment is worth reproducing, so probably the entire work will be in the long run. Perhaps one can do little more than attempt to keep such partial reproductions at a minimum, and, as elsewhere, consider such requests in terms of the individual item.

It is, of course, for irreplaceable originals, where preservation is a major consideration, that limits should be placed on photoreproduction, but in practice many a librarian of a reference collection occasionally wishes he had adopted the policy of retaining a master film for materials not usually designated as nonexpendable. Had one librarian foreseen the number of times she would be asked to Xerox Fleming's announcement of his discoveries regarding penicillin, she would have retained a negative. But now, innumerable requests later, the volume of the periodical containing the article is but a battered vestige.

This is indeed but one more of the many questions inherent in modern photoreproductive techniques. Perhaps the problem lies, not in the processes themselves, but in the uses to which the inconsiderate, the unreasonable, and the irresponsible sometimes put them, asking of them more than they are designed to do or are capable of accomplishing. If in this discussion the shortcomings and dangers may seem over-stressed and exaggerated, this is, we believe, a necessary reminder that reproduction at the expense of the original is rarely justified, in view of the limitations of existing methods.

IX: DISASTER AND SALVAGE

Papers 30, 31, and 32: Commentary

Incidents involving damage to small quantities of books and other materials are a fairly frequent occurrence in most libraries. Major disasters, though far less frequent, are nevertheless an ever-present possibility.

The authors of the selections chosen for inclusion in this section have all played major roles in supervising salvage operations following catastrophes of fire and flood. Their graphic descriptions provide first-hand information on such topics as how salvage teams actually perform when caught up in the pressing reality of an emergency situation; the questions that must be raised and answered promptly; the immediate actions that must be taken; and the very difficult, longer-range decisions that must follow in order to restore public service, while rehabilitating collections as quickly and fully as possible.

From these and scores of other articles that have appeared in the literature, particularly in the decade following the twin disasters of 1966 in New York and Florence, one clear principle emerges: A plan for safeguarding collections should be a key element of every library's conservation program. Nowhere is the principle of preventive conservation—action taken *in advance* to prevent or minimize damage— more important than in the area of emergency planning.

John H. Martin has outlined[1] the basic ingredients that he believes should be included in a disaster plan. In a version that has been slightly expanded, they are as follows: (1) an allocation of manpower, with a designated chain of command; (2) a listing of persons, and their telephone numbers, who can be counted upon to help in an emergency; (3) an identification of priority items to be saved and a chart of their locations; (4) a listing of needed supplies, materials, and tools, and their locations; (5) information on procurement of vehicles; (6) a listing of electrical switches; (7) a designated place for relocation of collections, if needed; (8) a set of procedures to be followed in securing the collections or moving them to safety; and (9) cameras and film to record damage.

A number of the recommendations listed above are elaborated upon in Willman Spawn's "After the Water Comes." Originally published in 1973 in an issue of *PLA (Pennsylvania Library Association) Bulletin* that was devoted in its entirety to preservation of library materials, Spawn's article is worthy of greater attention and wider dissemination than it has thus far received.

REFERENCE

1. Martin, John H., ed., *The Corning Flood: Museum Under Water* (Corning, N.Y.: The Corning Museum of Glass, 1977), p. 55.

ADDITIONAL READINGS

Goetz, Arthur H., "Books in Peril—A History of Horrid Catastrophes," *Wilson Library Bulletin* 47 (January 1973): 428–39.

Horton, Carolyn, "Saving the Libraries of Florence," *Wilson Library Bulletin* 41 (June 1967): 1035–43.

Morris, John, *Managing the Library Fire Risk* (Berkeley: Office of Fire and Risk Management, University of California, 1975), 101 pp.

Protecting the Library and its Resources; a Guide to Physical Protection and Insurance (Chicago: Library Technology Project, American Library Association, 1963), 322 pp. *LTP Publication* No. 7.

Protection of Library Collections (Boston: National Fire Protection Association, 1970), 28 pp. NFPA No. 910.

Waters, Peter, *Procedures for Salvage of Water-Damaged Library Materials* (Washington, D.C.: Library of Congress, 1974), 30 pp. *LC Publications on Conservation of Library Materials.*

30: FIRE AND WATER: Book Salvage in New York and Florence

Menahem Schmelzer

Since earliest times, fire and water have been enemies of the written and printed book. In *Protecting the Library and Its Resources*,[1] issued a few years ago by the Library Technology Program of ALA, there is a dramatic and tragic appendix: A 15 page list of library fires from ancient times to 1962. In the United States alone 360 fires were reported by libraries in the last 50 years. Since April 1966 the author witnessed a fire in the Library of the Jewish Theological Seminary, and saw the destruction of books caused by the disastrous flood in Florence. His impressions on the destruction and salvage efforts are summarized in this paper. Problems of re-establishing library services are also included.

THE BRITTLE AND FRAIL PAPER OF EGYPT and even the tougher skins of Pergamon seem fragile media indeed on which to confide the precious knowledge and wisdom of the ages. Ready victim of the accidents of nature, fire, water and the other elemental forces . . . the book would appear to have small chance of survival." These words introduce E. A. Parsons' account of the burning of the Alexandrian library, a fire which occurred some two thousand years ago.[2]

Librarians, the custodians of the wisdom of the ages, have long devoted much thought and effort to the protection of books against destructive elemental forces. There are now available scores of studies and reports about fire protection and prevention and also many papers advising the librarian about book salvage procedures.

Although we all know that it could happen to us too, and we even think we know what to do about it, when it does strike, one is shocked and found unprepared. This is especially true when destruction and damage spread on a large scale affecting rare and sometimes irreplaceable volumes.

Since April 1966 I have had, unfortunately, a great deal of first-hand experience

in this matter. I witnessed the fire in the Jewish Theological Seminary Library in New York City, and in November 1966 after the disastrous flood in Florence I saw the destruction of thousands of books and the heroic efforts made to salvage tens of thousands of them. I would like to share with you some of the impressions which these two events left with me.

Standing on Broadway on that April day, watching flames and smoke emerge from the windows of our ten-story stacks, not knowing yet about the extent of the damage, we were prepared for the worst. We were thinking of the irony and cruelty of fate. Thousands of books which escaped the barbaric destruction in Europe in the 1930's and 1940's and which found a haven in the Seminary Library in this free country were now being destroyed by nature. Almost a quarter of a million books relating to Jews and Judaism were enclosed in the walls where the fire raged. Works dealing with the history, religion and literature of the Jewish people from Biblical times until our own days in dozens of languages from ever so many countries had been collected during the past 80 years. Although the library's unique collection of Hebrew manuscripts and 15th and 16th century books were housed in a different wing of the building and therefore deemed to be safe, we knew that among the books in the general stacks there were many of utmost rarity. We knew that if this library were destroyed, it would be impossible to reassemble all the books and to achieve the completeness that we had had before.

Next morning when we were allowed to inspect the damage for the first time, we found that indeed the destruction was tremendous but also that there remained many books which could eventually be salvaged. Seventy thousand books were burned practically to ashes by the intense fire or were completely destroyed by the collapsing metal shelves which literally melted in the heat. Because of the open multitier stack structure in the library, water used for extinguishing the fire freely poured down seven floors and damaged the remaining 150,000 books.

Fire Damaged Stacks.
One Day after the Fire.

Among the 70,000 burnt books we found only one small section of some 200 rare books which were not completely consumed. They were badly charred on the edges, some of them with a great deal of loss of text, but since they were part of a very rare collection we saved them. They were immediately prepared for microfilming and lamination. The rest were abandoned and a few months later buried on the grounds of the Seminary in accordance with the Jewish custom, which prefers this kind of respectful disposal of unusable Hebrew texts of religious character.

Then we started hectically consulting with librarians and looking for prescribed remedies trying to save what could still be saved. We knew that the 150,000 wet volumes, some of them like well-soaked sponges, should be evacuated and dried immediately. The whole stack area became one large humidity chamber and that was no place for the books to remain.

It was not very encouraging to read in one of the most up-to-date studies that "there appears to be no really satisfactory rapid method of treating wet volumes on a large scale . . . if papers or books are allowed to remain in wet messes for any prolonged period, they not only stick together but may mildew."[3]

This was bad enough in New York, but how much more so in Florence, where there were at least ten times as many books flooded. Even according to modest estimates the Arno River innundated at least one and a half million volumes belonging to the National Library and 46 other institutions. And there in Italy it was not *clean* water doing the damage, but water carrying a mixture of mud, sewage and fuel oil.

The nature of the material affected in Florence was also different. In addition to regular printed books there were at the Florence State Archives alone tens of thousands of water-soaked manuscript volumes, among them many on parchment. The Jewish Community Library had 600 manuscripts of great value in the flooded area. Wet illuminated codices found in churches and libraries required a much more elaborate salvage technique than ordinary books. A unique collection of books on Etruscan art printed on coated paper had to be abandoned when experts found that nothing could be done to save them. Important original leather or vellum bindings had to be removed and preserved for restoration. In Florence I had to revise my opinion that I had seen the worst in New York. Florence was infinitely more depressing and hopeless, and still even in Florence miracles of salvage were performed.

Water Damaged Books
Standing on Edges for Drying.
One Day after the Fire.

Urgency Outruns Theory

If I had to name the most important and decisive factors which made a remarkably successful salvage effort possible in both cases, I would say without hesitation that it was human help, devotion and resourcefulness.

In New York hundreds—and in Florence thousands—volunteered to help. They came from all walks of life: students, children, housewives, scientists. Institutions and commercial establishments offered their help. Facilities, supplies and space were liberally made available.

Where so many people and so many books are involved, where untrained and unskilled volunteers act, many things seem to go against the instructions of scientific reports and papers. Procedures are unorthodox, the handling of the books is not as gentle as one would desire. We found that in an emergency practice is sometimes different from theory, but also that improvisation by helpful and devoted although untrained people in the long run can achieve miracles. The sooner the librarian realizes that he must act as an equal member of the salvage crew rather than as a professional librarian, the better. One should allow himself to be carried away, within reason, by the enthusiastic efforts of the volunteers. At the Seminary we

planned at first the evacuation of the 150,-000 books from the stacks according to priorities of rarity and importance. We decided to save certain subjects areas first. Even within each subject area we wanted to make selections as to the importance of the individual volumes. We asked the professional library staff and faculty members to make the selection. But we soon discovered that this process was discouraging the students and volunteers, slowing down the process, interrupting the human chain of hands which they had quickly established, and of course we got involved in controversy and in value judgements about the relative importance of various books.

It was much simpler to give free reign to the volunteers; to interfere as little as possible, and join their ranks, don boots and get one's hands dirty. Professor Cassamassima, director of the National Library in Florence, worked in overalls along with the others. I know that he became a legend and inspired the thousands of helpers. As I mentioned before, at times the youthful energy of the students did not allow them to pay enough gentle attention to the books. Many books swelled on the shelves and had to be rather forcefully removed. Of course, books became separated into parts, and pages became loose. There is no doubt that a certain percentage of the books was further damaged

Interleaving Books
with Water Damage.
One Week after the Fire.

during the salvage. But the choice is simple: either to let a large part of the books be completely ruined by being too particular and discouraging the helpers, or to take the risk of some additional damage while the major portion of the collection is saved. Both in New York and in Florence the latter course was chosen. The weighing of long-term advantages plays a decisive role in these emergencies.

The outpouring of help did not know geographic boundaries. To Florence supplies and experts were sent from East and West, from the United States, the Western European countries and from the Soviet Union. In New York we received offers of help and advice from all over the United States.

It seems that there was no single possible method of drying, demolding and disinfecting left unexplored. Fans, dehumidifiers, chemicals, paper towels, mimeosheets and blotting paper were used for drying and interleaving. The books were spread in every available space in the Seminary—in classrooms, offices, the gymnasium and in bathrooms. In Florence the books were sent to tobacco and brick drying factories, to the heating plant at the railroad station, to other cities in Italy, and abroad. Temporary wooden shelving was quickly constructed, clotheslines were hung for the drying of pamphlets and leaves, layers of nets were installed in large

rooms. In the Synagogue of Florence planks were spread on the pews to create more space for the drying. At the Seminary on a sunny May afternoon we spread hundreds of volumes on the lawn, and indeed the sun and the gentle breeze did a good drying job. At least until the breeze became too "helpful" and sent some loose leaves flying around in the air. We then decided to discontinue the sunbath project. Tents of heavy plastic were erected in Florence for demolding by thymol. I heard that equipment for gamma ray radiation was supposed to be brought from Belgium to Florence for the disinfection of the books. Whether it was indeed done, I do not know. Some of the methods failed, others worked but were too time consuming. Some international controversy developed between American, British and German restorers about the effects of certain chemicals. But whatever the merits of an individual method or chemical were, they all testified to the inventiveness and resourcefulness of people who cared and wanted to do their utmost to save a cultural heritage.[4]

Rebirth Out of the Ashes

Now I should like to turn to another aspect of library salvage. What happens after the thousands of volumes are dry and free of mold? How do you put a library back in working order after its services have been completely disrupted? As far as I know only very little has been written on this aspect of salvage. In contrast to the physical salvage, the library reconstruction phase can be done only under the close and direct supervision of professional librarians. This phase is extremely long and complicated.

In our case, at the Seminary, it might take a decade. I remember having read last year that the Turin Library, which burned in 1904, is still in the process of reconstructing its holdings and replacing its losses. I do not know what is being done in Florence at present in this respect, but I am sure that the complete reconstruction of the libraries there will take many decades.

What are some of the problems and tasks after the emergency is over? If, as in our case the stacks were to a great extent ruined, one must look for new facilities. Of course, the ideal solution is a permanent new library building. Until such a building can be planned and constructed, the rental of space and/or the construction of a temporary prefabricated structure is suggested. We indeed have rented shelf space at the Medical Library Center of New York and in addition we erected a prefabricated building in the courtyard of the Seminary. That building provides both shelf and working space. If a library serves a school, as ours does, one of the most pressing needs is to put at the disposal of the students a collection of those basic books and periodicals which they need for the curriculum. Books for this basic collection should be the first to be selected and processed for binding or, if they are unbindable, they should be replaced by new copies or by photocopies from other libraries.

After these immediate needs are met, one should get ready for a normal routine in an abnormal situation. Traditional attitudes of regular schedules should be discarded. The staff should get used to the idea that in addition to the regular work there is now the

Menahem Schmelzer, *the librarian of the Library of the Jewish Theological Seminary, New York, was born in 1934 in Hungary. Dr. Schmelzer has been in the United States since 1961.*

added task of forming a new library out of a disorganized, scattered mess of unbound, sometimes fragmentary books.

In a library whose history dates back eighty years, there is always a lot of talk about the need for recataloging and reclassification. If I would have to name a single positive aspect of our tragedy, it is without a doubt that it created the perfect excuse for a total recataloging and reclassification project. First of all we realized that every book would, in any case, have to be handled before it could be returned to the shelf. Then we saw that in many instances shelfmarks and title pages were missing or obliterated, and finally that many books were destroyed beyond repair and that the catalog would have to be adjusted to the new situation. One additional major problem was created by the scattering of the holdings of periodicals, serials and multivolume works. During the emergency evacuation and salvage it was impossible to maintain order, with sets of books and volumes of the same periodical surviving in different states of damage, and receiving different treatments at different times and sometimes in different locations. To bring these volumes together again involved a great deal of work with the catalog. Therefore, out of necessity, the long planned recataloging project turned into a reality. Our Acquisitions Department also underwent drastic changes. The acquisitions staff, in addition to regular duties, had to engage in the complicated task of replacing the missing or damaged books. New criteria were established and new contacts with dealers were made.

Thousands of old books, pamphlets and periodical volumes are not available any more, or at least no systematic effort can be made for their acquisition. Many of these volumes were, however, donated by generous individuals and institutions. Private collectors, libraries and publishers offered their help and through them many scarce volumes came to the library to replace the old copies. As an added benefit there were—among the gifts—rare books which we never had before. But even after the gifts and occasional purchases there remain many, many books which cannot be preserved and replaced but must be microfilmed. The search goes on constantly in bibliographies and library catalogs for copies of our lost books, and we order microfilms from many libraries here and abroad. I referred previously to the fragmentary books; their identification frequently calls for the talents of a skilled detective. There is also the major problem of paper preservation, restoration and binding. In the aftermath of the fire the librarians must spend a considerable amount of time on insurance claims, on setting up new insurance policies, on improved methods of fire protection and prevention, on the enlarging of the staff and, of course, inevitably, on giving reports to the administration and board, and finally on briefing curious news reporters.

The Road Back

We are still at the beginning of the road towards complete reconstruction. The dramatic story of destruction and rebuilding in New York and in Florence has not ended yet. According to the old Rabbinic dictum: *The day is short, the task is great, it is not our duty to complete it, but we are not free to evade it.*

References

1. AMERICAN LIBRARY ASSOCIATION. Library Technology Project. *Protecting the Library and Its Resources; A Guide to Physical Protection and Insurance.* A report on a study conducted by Gage-Babcock and Associates, Inc., Chicago, 1963. Appendix B, p.216-30.
2. PARSONS, E. A. *The Alexandrian Library; Glory of the Hellenic World, Its Rise, Antiquities and Destructions.* Amsterdam, London, N. Y., Elsevier, 1952. p.273.
3. p.256 of Ref. (1).
4. For a general survey on the Florence situation see: HORTON, C. Saving the Libraries of Florence. *Wilson Library Bulletin,* p.1035-43 (June 1967).

31: APRÈS LE DÉLUGE...
RESUSCITATING
A WATER-LOGGED LIBRARY

John H. Martin

In June of 1972 the Corning Museum of Glass and its library were suddenly faced with catastrophe; without warning most of the priceless collection was submerged by flood waters, the aftereffects of a hurricane.

During the first part of that month, Hurricane Agnes had swept up the eastern seaboard, but it seemed scarcely a threat to a museum 275 miles from the Atlantic. At the beginning of the third week in June, Agnes (now designated a tropical storm) suddenly swerved inland and then stalled for three days of continuous rainfall along the New York–Pennsylvania line in the western part of these states. One statistically minded observer estimated that the amount of water that fell would have filled a container 25 miles long, one mile high, and one mile wide —more water than had ever fallen before in this inland area.

Torrent tears through town

In the Painted Post–Corning area of western New York, three rivers join to form the Chemung, which bisects the city of Corning. On June 22, 1972 the river, a normally placid one- to two-foot deep stream, stood about 15 feet deep, well contained within its 23½-foot dikes. Worried citizens who remained awake that night heard assurances on the radio by local officials at midnight that there was no danger.

At 5:00 a.m. on June 23rd the river suddenly crested at 27 to 28 feet, topped the dikes, and poured into town. The action of the current as it coursed over the dikes ate into the rear of the embankments. Before long the dikes were badly breached in five places. The torrent which raged through the north side of town tore houses from their foundations, sweeping some downstream and scattering others in the valley. Water up to 20 feet deep raced over areas of the town. Without warning the city was split in half. When flood waters also cut the approaches to town, Corning was effectively isolated from the rest of the world.

The isolation was complete—suddenly the community was without electricity, natural gas, telephones, gasoline, drinking water, sewage disposal, or main highway access. On transistor radios townspeople could hear about the flood in Elmira, 18 miles downstream, but it was impossible to learn of anything occurring in an area only a few blocks away.

The next morning, miraculously, the river was back in its banks, but it was almost three weeks before all utilities were restored. Unfortunately for the Corning collections, the museum was situated in the middle of the disaster area; water surged 15 to 20 feet deep in the Glass Center and to a height of more than five feet on the museum's main floor. It was obvious that extraordinary problems confronted the staff.

One of the world's finest

A brief description of the museum would be useful at this point. The famous collection of glass is the reason for the museum's existence, but as a research and scholarly oriented institution, its library is of great importance. Although 528 of the 13,000 objects in the glass collection sustained damage, this article is only concerned with the devastation wreaked on the library's holdings.

Over the past quarter of a century the museum has been developing one of the finest library collections in the world on the art, archeology, and history of glass. Today the collection is the library-of-record for printed works in this field. It buys every book and periodical issued about glass and purchases in allied areas as well. It collects in all languages from countries around the world. The library obtains manuscripts, trade catalogs, archives, documents, pamphlets, prints, photographs, slides, movie films, and printed ephemera—anything concerning glass. It has medieval manuscripts, incunabula, rare books, first editions. The museum exchanges materials with countries around the world, and it publishes its own books and catalogs.

Once books, now debris: a discouraging scene in the library as the long clean-up began.

These listings are not meant as boasts; they are merely intended to show the breadth and depth of an exceedingly rich collection—thereby indicating the range of the restoration problems which were faced after the flood.

Incunabula beneath the mud

As fate would have it, at the time of the disaster the entire full-time professional staff of the museum—the director and curators—were attending the annual conference of the American Association of Museums in Mexico City. And the museum scientist had left the morning before the flood for Afghanistan to work on a research project.

Fortunately the staff members remaining rose to the occasion. The president of the board of trustees headed the salvage program until the professional staff returned. Library workers dug (actually) into the task of saving the book collection—half of which had been inundated. Staff who had lost their homes and their belongings, and who were temporarily living in public school buildings, pitched into the full-time effort. Volunteers appeared not only from the community, but from outside the area, from other states, and even from Canada.

What was the condition of the library on the morning of June 24, 1972?

Muddy water had swirled through the offices and library to a depth of more than five feet on the upper floor. Sodden books had expanded and bent the sides of the stacks, so that they bulged in a V shape. In their expanded state, books were so wedged into the stacks that crowbars had to be used to dislodge them. Other shelves, suddenly sprung free from the sides of the misshapen stacks, had dumped their volumes into the mud and water. The rare book and manuscript collection, shelved in separate stacks, had collapsed into the slime, burying incunabula and rare books in the mud. We literally walked on books in the first attempts to begin salvage.

Books on ice

Where does one start? How does one save a thoroughly ruined, irreplaceable collection of inestimable value? Fortunately our librarians remembered reading an article by Carolyn Horton containing George Cunha's advice on the subject. Miraculously the article was found, and we decided to follow its suggestion to freeze the books.

Easier said than done. Without electricity there were no freezers. Without gasoline stations, no transportation. With all the stores in Corning damaged, there were no boxes, no paper towels, no running water for cleaning mud from books. Somehow though, the impossible was achieved through the assistance of the local government and the Corning Glass Works, and emergency radio transmitters were brought in so we could reach beyond our area to find the needed supplies.

Under the direction of our librarians, the staff and volunteers of all ages—some of them children—began the difficult job of salvage. The rare books were gathered from the debris on the floor, some of them, unhappily, open face-down in the mud, some without covers. Minimal cleaning was all that could be done since there was no running water. It was cool and still raining. We knew that if we didn't work fast, mold would develop within five days.

The books were in such sorry condition that they had to be wrapped in paper towels to hold them together, to absorb moisture, and to separate volumes from one another. Herein was our first error, although it was a minor one. Had the books been wrapped in plastic, it would have been easier to separate the individual volumes later—and plastic would have kept the books in a state of damp equilibrium. Mud had been unevenly distributed; some books had been only partially wet from the flood. Subsequent sublimation in freezers was to dry some books unevenly, and in the case of coated papers, pages would solidify before the books could be worked on. But this was not known these first days, nor was there plastic available in the devastated valley.

Using what boxes could be scrounged, we trucked the books to home freezers and commercial freezing lockers 20 to 25 miles away—anyplace where they could be frozen to retard mold growth. It took five days to pack the damaged collection of approximately 6,500 books, plus pamphlets, files, catalogs, and other materials. Some 30 boxes of office files were packed and frozen as well. Those items beyond repair or those we knew we could not salvage before they became irreparably damaged were consigned to an ever-growing mountain of debris outside the museum. We decided to abandon part of the periodical collection, believing that it could be replaced without too much difficulty.

In time we would rue this decision, since many journals proved almost impossible to find.

Whereas the initial packing had been done in an orderly fashion as books were removed shelf-by-shelf from the stacks, the urgency to get materials frozen before mold developed led to packing in any order to complete this first phase of the job. All order disappeared, but things *did* get packed, which was the goal. By the time the last volumes were placed in boxes and on route to the freezers, colorful mold had begun to appear. We had finished just in time.

Mechanized scoops remove the mess

Efforts were now directed to other salvage work in the museum. When the staff reached two storehouses elsewhere in town, they found materials so badly damaged that it was necessary to use mechanized scoops to remove the odiferous mess. There was, however, one unsolvable major problem: The flood had ruined the card catalog, and it had to be discarded. Additional records had been either lost or damaged or were in deep freeze 25 miles away. One tool remained: the shelf list. Unfortunately it too had been damaged; but it was soon dried out, photocopied, and available both for restoration and the filing of insurance claims.

With the books now ensconced in freezers throughout three counties, the staff turned its attention to nonbook holdings. Corning Community College, located on a hill three miles away, cleared out the main reading room and other rooms of its library to provide space for storing the museum library's undamaged books (6,500 volumes had been above the waterline) on cement block and board shelves. This was a place to work, a place to begin the restoration process.

Photos in the swimming pool

Paper was placed on the floor, and the shelf list, art print collection, and various other paper collections were spread out to dry. The slide and photographic collection (over 72,000 items) were next approached. Half the photographic collection was frozen; the other half (about 11,000 prints) was dumped into a swimming pool to keep the photos wet and free from mold, to remove the mud, and to permit them to be cleaned and dried as weather and staff time allowed. A break in the eternal rain finally permitted them to be dried on the lawn.

On the basis of professional advice, the color slide collection (50,500 items) was stored in tubs of water in the college library, where they were —one at a time—removed from their aluminum-and-glass mounts, washed, and hung up to dry on clotheslines, with paper clips serving as hooks on the line. (The clip went through the sprocket holes on the side of the film.) The mounts were dried also, since they contained the cataloging information needed.

Ultimately the photographs and slides that had been immersed in water by us had to be abandoned. The color slides had suffered too much damage to be restored to usable condition. The dried black-and-white photographs were not of sufficient quality to be worth further restoration. We decided to give up this portion of the collections and rephotograph the glass objects later. That rephotographing schedule

Volumes knocked from their shelves by the racing floodwaters lie opened and soaked on the floor.

is now in the second year of what will be a ten-year project to return the collections to 1972 status.

Of the approximately 11,000 photographs frozen almost immediately after the flood, about 6,500 were eventually thawed, cleaned, dried, and hardened successfully. (An additional 4,000 photographs that were not frozen until the fourth day after the flood suffered too much mold damage to be restored.) A large selection of frozen 4″ x 5″ and 8″ x 10″ color transparencies and negatives were also successfully restored.

On Aug. 1, 1972, 39 days after the disaster, the museum was reopened to the public. Although reopening so quickly seemed an impossible goal in June, the decision was an act of faith in the future of the museum and of the community. So on that day a thoroughly restored (if one did not glance into the offices and workrooms) museum was open to the public once more.

In late August the college needed its library for student use, so the museum library returned to the valley and moved into a former supermarket. That autumn was spent in setting up shop once more so that restoration could begin in earnest. Files had to be reconstructed and plans made for the future. The time-consuming task of preparing an insurance claim to cover replacement and restoration costs was begun, a task which became an 18-month project. Loss of the card catalog made preparation of the claim more difficult.

The collections scattered throughout the neighboring counties had to be brought back from the various freezing plants. A freezer truck was rented and parked next to the library-restoration building. Our frozen assets were home again.

Overcoming a Catch-22

It was not until February 1st, seven months after the flood, that work could truly begin on book restoration. Actual restoration would not start for still another month, but a number of interconnected problems had to be faced first. Without an insurance settlement it would be necessary to borrow against the regular operating budget to support the restoration project. Clearly this could endanger the regular operations of the museum. Until the restoration project began, however, it would not be possible to estimate either the time such a restoration would take or what its cost would be. Without such figures there could be no settlement with the insurance company in order to obtain the money needed to undertake restoration.

stored. He was also commissioned to try new or unorthodox techniques to help reduce restoration time.

It soon became obvious that a freezer truck crammed with boxes of frozen books presented a monumental logistical problem. The truck was so crowded that there was no room to sort the boxes for assembling books of like nature. If books could not be grouped together by type,

Some photos float languidly while others, already plucked from the pool, dry out in the sun.

We had to get moving. So we set up a restoration assembly line. Money was borrowed, and book restoration proceeded concurrently with learning how to estimate the cost of restoration for the insurance claim.

The program began with moves in two directions. First, 200 of the most valuable books were sent to Carolyn Horton in their frozen state to be restored under her meticulous care. The remaining rare books would be handled in-house. Next an experienced paper conservator was hired, assisted by housewives and students working part-time. Also, a chemist was employed to supervise our work so that we would not unknowingly damage the paper being re-

an assembly line could not be set up. To accept books haphazardly from boxes would mean a program of almost individualized treatment. As a final blow, the truck frequently refused to work at night or on weekends! One such failure of the truck's freezing unit brought the interior temperature from zero to 30 degrees before we realized that something was amiss. The books could have been lost to mold after all.

Our solution was to order two walk-in freezers, each one 20' x 12' in size, and erect them within the restoration building. The boxes were removed from the truck, thawed slightly for identification of the books, and then repacked in smaller boxes after sorting by type of paper.

Each sheet on the floor can hold about 150 slides—or less than ⅓ of 1 percent of the number ruined.

Home free by Christmas?

To treat every book and record in the files would have meant individual handling, a task of five years or more. But there was not time or money or staff for a job of such magnitude. Moreover the temporary library was scheduled for demolition under an urban renewal plan. There was no other place to move, though, since all other suitable buildings had been destroyed.

A basic decision was reached: The restoration job would be completed by Christmas 1975, and all planning and efforts would be bent toward this goal. It was agreed, first of all,

that all volumes from the regular collection that could be purchased for less than $50 per volume (and less than $300 per volume from the antiquarian collection) would automatically be discarded. The insurance companies agreed to this program. Our reasoning, which the underwriters understood, was that it would cost at least as much—and probably more—to restore the individual volumes.

We also decided to discard our periodical collection. Either we would replace it through purchase (second hand) or we would buy it in microform. (The Kraus company was most generous in helping us in this area, and they deserve credit for their assistance.) If we couldn't rebuy the journals, we would in time try to obtain permission to microfilm journals either *in situ* or through loan.

We began soliciting book dealers throughout the world for their catalogs so we could order out-of-print volumes as they appeared. We sent our staff to New York City to buy in the second-hand market. We also commissioned foreign language book dealers to assist us in our search —since much of our collection is in languages other than English.

Because our library holdings date from the thirteenth century, it soon became obvious that no more than 15 to 20 percent of our collection could be repurchased in the market. Up to 85 percent would have to be restored.

Tradition, or innovation?

In our sorting and preparation to move books into the walk-in freezers, we had handled every volume and recorded its condition on a work-sheet in multiple copies. One sheet remained with the book, one went to the librarian, and one went to the conservator. As a book came out of the freezer, the conservator noted on its attached sheet the librarian's considered judg-ment on whether to restore fully by traditional methods, restore fully by new methods, or hold for future consideration. Volumes in the last category were those we hoped to find on the open market. If they were not found before the restoration process was nearing its end, these would be restored as well.

The two types of restoration—by traditional methods and by innovative methods—repre-sented a major policy choice in order to com-plete the task within the time allotted. As a re-sult we divided the collection in two, with the rarer books being cared for in accordance with established procedures and other volumes— those of more informational than intrinsic value —receiving innovative handling.

It's all in the proper technique

A National Museums Act grant from the Smith-sonian Institution let us hire a research chemist for technical advice. With his and our paper

conservator's assistance, we settled on three approaches:

1. *Traditional Techniques.* Volumes of intrinsic value in their original condition (i.e., because of their age, publisher, previous ownership, or association) we thawed, removed from their bindings, separated into signatures and then pages, and washed in water with brushes to re-move mud and staining. We then de-acidified and dried the pages, either by laying them out on long trestle tables covered with clean news-print or by hanging them on nylon fishline dry-ing racks we had constructed. (Valuable bind-ings were also dried and saved, at least for the time being.)

Pages were collated, sterilized, and wrapped for storage until they could be microfilmed. Each packet had its identification sheet with the complete history of its restoration attached to the paper wrapping. Its LC number or another identifying mark was placed on the spine of the packet.

2. *Dielectric Drying.* Through the assistance of friends in the Corning Glass Works, we ob-tained a dielectric CP 30 dryer. This device is about as large as a refrigerator, and it has a door that opens into a chamber about 8" high by 20" wide. Inside are two electrode plates between which a frozen volume is placed. When the door is closed, a burst of electrical energy is shot through the frozen book to dry it. We soon discovered that the covers would have to be removed from all books being treated, since they contained much water, making the task of drying the inner leaves more difficult. Not only were covers removed from books, but any staples, paper clips (in the case of files), or other metal also had to be removed. Otherwise an arc-ing occurred between the electrodes and charring or burning resulted.

By trial and error we worked out the duration and the number of electrical bursts necessary to dry the various kinds and sizes of books. Once we had established norms for procedures, we tried to group like items to simplify our task.

Since we did not know if we were doing per-manent damage to the paper with the electrical charge (e.g., prematurely aging it), we segre-gated the collection further so that books which

In a sea of paper, a solitary figure checks on the condition of materials waiting to be saved.

were valuable but did not quite fit into the category for traditional handling were thawed, but not dried, by the dielectric method. They were then washed, if necessary, before being deacidified, and dried leaf by leaf. In addition all dried papers were sterilized in a vacuum fumigation chamber in order to prevent further spore growth.

3. *Freeze-vacuum drying.* We gave much thought to freeze-vacuum drying, but decided that the technique was not then practical in our situation. To begin with, there were no such units near us. Second, most units were too small to handle materials in the amount we had. Third, would books with coated paper "block" into a solid mass in the drying process? Since museum book collections have many books with plates, there can be a great loss because the coated paper on which plates are printed tends to become solid after wetting and exposure to air.

Last, and of most concern to us, was the consideration that freeze-vacuum drying would not remove the mud or stain on the papers. We would then have to rewash all such dried volumes, and we might not be able to eradicate all the flood stains. We did, however, send some medieval parchment manuscripts to the Library of Congress for freeze-drying.

We also tried microwave drying, but did not find it satisfactory. Currently we are carrying out further experiments in the use of ultrasonic cleaning and drying (a technique successfully used in cleaning pieces of glass in the collection). We are also experimenting with drying by solvent extraction.

Success in the "space chamber"

By the end of the first year (using the above techniques), we had dried and cleaned 3,000 books and the boxes of files, and had them ready for microfilming. By this time our scientist had worked out the chemistry of coated paper, discovering how and why it tends to turn into a solid mass after wetting and then drying. Based on his experiments, we took the remaining frozen volumes (primarily of coated paper) by refrigerator truck to Valley Forge, Pa., to the General Electric "space chamber" to have them thawed and vacuum dried within the parameters he had determined.

After the nine-day process, 100 books were still damp and 25 were wet, but 95 percent of the coated stock was saved, the first time, to our knowledge, that such success has been achieved. The five-percent loss probably occurred because some books had become too dry through sublimation in the freezer; the paper had solidified *before* being placed in the vacuum chamber.

The dried but still dirty books were brought back to our restoration building, where the staff spent the next eight months removing the dirt with architectural dry-cleaning pads. In December 1974 the book restoration department closed, 12 months ahead of schedule. All 6,500 books were dry and clean, and all 30 cartons of files were also dry. Innumerable prints, photographs, and audio tapes were restored as well.

Fiche phase

The last phase of restoration is now in process. We have begun to microfilm our entire collection, and we shall turn duplicate microfilm copies into fiche. We do this for a number of reasons:

1. To preserve the information in the books we have restored—books that may disintegrate at a more rapid rate than is normal, due to the damage they have sustained.

2. To duplicate our collection as insurance against another catastrophe. We will therefore make two microfilm copies of the collection: one master copy for storage in safe vaults outside our valley and one for use in microfiche form within the library.

3. To not only make handling by our curators and by visiting scholars easier, but to help out-of-area researchers as well. We are more than happy to have scholars make use of our collections. We are, however, reluctant to mail one-of-a-kind volumes on interlibrary loan. With our own fiche duplicating equipment, we can produce copies of fiche for mailing to researchers at home or overseas. At the same time we can protect our irreplaceable items.

4. To one day be able to make portions of our library available to specific libraries in the United States and abroad in exchange for the privilege of microfilming items in their collections which we do not have.

Through microfilm we will protect a valuable collection against future loss and make the materials more readily available out of house, in all cases with due regard to copyright laws.

In passing I must remark that the rebuilding of the card catalog is being undertaken in conjunction with the Ohio College Library Center, a service that has already proved of inestimable value to our librarians. We trust that our entries in the system (which in time will hold all our listings) will aid the scholarly world, since our tracings will be more exact than the heading of "Glass," under which all of our collection now falls.

To enlighten others

The past three-and-a-half year period has been a difficult one for the library, which has continued to offer reference services to the world, to build its collections, and at the same time to be involved in a salvage and restoration undertaking which few libraries in the Western hemisphere have faced. In their spare time staff members have even taught conservation seminars so that others might profit from our misfortunes. And the museum is now in the process of compiling information that will be published; thus our experiences may enlighten others who find themselves suddenly overwhelmed by disaster. 🔲

John H. Martin *is the Administrative Officer of the Corning Museum of Glass.*

32: AFTER THE WATER COMES

Willman Spawn

From the beginning of libraries, fire and water have been the enemies of books, each in its own way. Fire is more spectacular and alarming, with its associations with book burning and vandalism, but water is equally harmful, as such recent events as the floods in Florence and Hurricane Agnes here in the eastern United States have demonstrated beyond question. In point of fact, water has always caused problems, as witness this testimonial published in the *Pennsylvania Gazette* for February 25, 1729, that John Hyndshaw, a bookbinder recently arrived from Great Britain, ". . . takes salt water out of books and papers so as the damage both have got thereby cannot be much perceived."

The danger from fire has lessened a great deal thanks to our fire-proof buildings and professional fire fighters. The major disasters that occur in libraries today are more often the result of misplaced water: plumbing leaks, roof leaks, breaks in steam lines, air conditioning breakdowns, floods, or water used to quench a fire. Each sort of water damage is, in turn, affected by the volume of water, from drip to deluge, by the cleanliness of that water, and by the time elapsed from the initial soaking to its discovery. In this article I will try to outline the general principles involved in the salvage of water-damaged materials, and then illustrate them with a hypothetical example drawn from my experience with wet books and papers.

Planning for Salvage

As a conservator of rare books and manuscripts for more than thirty years, I have often been called in as consultant in cases of water damage. In the past two years, I acted as consultant to a number of libraries damaged by Hurricane Agnes, and I was actively involved in the salvage operation that followed the Temple University Law Library fire. In almost every case, these questions have to be answered before a salvage operation can be planned: 1) How many books are affected? — if possible given in linear feet of shelving 2) What types of books are affected and have *all* items of value been accounted for? 3) Is there a contingency plan known to the staff to be followed in case of emergency? 4) Does the insurance, if any, cover water damage, and is the coverage up-to-date in terms of today's replacement costs?

In addition to these vital questions, the librarian must also quickly

Mr. Spawn is Conservator, American Philosophical Society.

learn the answers to a whole range of other queries: 1) First, the source of the water is important. A flood usually brings mud and oil with it, complicating the job of salvage; the flood in Florence is a typical example. On the other hand, the water from plumbing and roof leaks is usually clean, but the damage can go unnoticed for days if the seepage is gradual; this allows the growth of mold, especially in hot weather. Worst of all, the water used on a fire becomes mixed with ash and debris, mixing two sorts of damage and creating a really complex problem for the salvage team.

2) The next factor for consideration is the extent of the damage. The salvage operation undertaken will depend in part on whether two books are damaged, or five hundred, or ten thousand. It also depends on the type and value of the collection — reference books, circulating collections, serials, rare books, manuscripts, or some combination of these. The librarian will then have to decide, and quickly, whether the books can be replaced or must be salvaged. In any collection some parts are more valuable than others, and if the damage is really extensive, the librarian must be able to pick these out for priority attention. If rare items are shelved separately the problem will be very simple, but in any case a schedule of priorities will need to be established. The assessment will be hampered if the damaged area includes uncataloged material. Additionally, from my own experience I can point out that uncataloged material is seldom covered by insurance, and it is difficult to keep such material under control during a salvage operation.

3) A final consideration: the librarian must decide quickly whether it is necessary to keep the library open and carry on the salvage operation behind the scenes so to speak, or to suspend business and turn the full resources of the library to the salvage operation. Sometimes the question is already answered because of the extent of the damage, making it impossible to carry on business as usual. At other times, the decision may rest on the availability of the staff, the needs of the users, and the circumstances of the emergency. If the damage is due to the negligence of a staff member, is it wise to make it known to the public? On the other hand, if the damage is due to a widespread flood, the library may as well shut down, and in fact salvage may well have to wait upon the solution of other pressing needs such as shelter and food.

**Freezing
Wet Books**

The damage done to books and papers by water is two-fold; wet paper is extremely fragile and may tear at a touch, and moist paper combined with warmth provides an ideal situation for the growth of mold. While a book is immersed in water it cannot mold, for mold spores are carried in the air. Even if the spores are already in the book they will not grow without the presence of air. However, once the book is removed from the water and thus exposed to air, the combination of a high relative humidity and temperature provides perfect conditions for the growth of mold. To prevent this growth it is necessary to reduce either the humidity or the temperature, or both. As the inside of a wet book is at a relative humidity of 100% where mold will grow even at a temperature of 40° F., it is essential to reduce the temperature to freezing or below to inhibit the mold growth. The alternative to freezing is complete and rapid drying, involving disbinding the book and separating it into signatures which are then dried by circulating air currents. This is a long and expensive process if more than a few books are so treated. Freezing is thus the treatment of choice at the present time. Once the flooded area has been returned to normal, the frozen material can be thawed, any remaining moisture evaporated by forced air circulation, the necessary repairs and rebinding done, and the material returned to the shelves. Even books on coated stock, normally a total loss if exposed to water, can be salvaged successfully if frozen before any drying has taken place.

I will not here go further into the details of a salvage operation, for it is very well described in a manual prepared in 1972 by the Preservation Office of the Library of Congress, and is readily available from that source. The manual, entitled *Emergency Procedures for Salvaging Flood or Water-damaged Library Materials,* by Restoration Officer Peter Waters, was prepared primarily in response to questions raised by Hurricane Agnes. In twenty pages, it is the single most informative publication on its subject. It covers all sorts of materials, printed books, art on paper, photographs and microfilms, manuscripts, in careful and concise detail, outlining the procedures to be followed *and* the reasons for them. It warns against likely mistakes, especially those committed in a time of confusion and pressure, and ends with three appendices: a list of "Dos and Don'ts," a list of suppliers, and a directory of conservators with experience in dealing with water damage. The manual is not intended to teach the restoration of water-damaged objects (although a text on this subject is in preparation), but it is tremendously useful to anyone responsible for coping with such a crisis. As such, it needs to be acquired by every library in the country. Fortunately, it is not only free but LC allows duplication of it without restriction.

Speaking from my own experience, in those cases where a proper salvage operation was begun immediately upon the discovery of water damage, nearly everything can be saved. This was often at considerable expense, but certainly in the case of rare or irreplaceable items this expense was justified — and in the case of other kinds of material, some expense is equally unavoidable. In instances where salvage was delayed for three or more days (as in a library where the leak occurred during a weekend and was only discovered the following Monday), the delay resulted in a number of types of damage. Partially wet books began to dry out, leaving water stains or "tide lines" as the moisture receded. Books and serials on coated stock began to dry and

**Prompt Action
Essential**

Mold growth on wet book seven days after initial soaking.

then congealed into solid blocks of paper fibre, impossible to separate or restore. Worst of all, disfiguring mold began to grow, first on the backs of books, then moving inward as the exterior dried but the interior remained damp. This growth of mold spores can be delayed by treatment with thymol, the treatment varying with the number of books involved. If water damage is confined to twenty or thirty items, the pages can be interleaved with sheets impregnated with thymol (see *LC Manual,* page 7). If the damage is extensive, involving hundreds of books, the librarian should consider "fogging" the area with thymol, to kill the spores already present and prevent the growth of new ones. Fogging is done by a professional fumigator — it is not a home remedy — and adds another expense, but it buys time while damaged books are being removed.

In point of fact, if freezing must be delayed as long as five days after the wetting and mold is not yet visible, it is still possible that the mold is present on the wet material. Therefore, when these books are thawed, if they have not been thoroughly dried by the freezing process or by subsequent air drying, then the mold continues to develop and very soon bursts into bloom (i.e., the disfiguring spots). The freezing merely inhibits mold growth; it does not kill it as thymol would. It seems sensible, then, to prescribe thymol fogging for any water-damaged material, the freezing of which has to be delayed more than a day or two. This would have little effect on an old book which had previously been wet and dried and suffered internal mold growth.

Moving any quantity of books involves great amounts of effort and time, as well as the danger mentioned above if the books are wet. If I were now faced with a situation similar to that at the Temple Law Library, where some hundred thousand volumes, wet, damp, and dry, were housed in a basement with limited access, I believe I would do my best to avoid moving all the dry books. If the area could be sealed off from the outside, I would first fog the area with thymol, and then install freezing units of large capacity which would force freezing air through the stack area. By thus reducing the temperature considerably, the amount of moisture in the air (and the danger of mold growth) would be reduced also. The staff could then take the time to inventory the books completely and remove only the wet ones to be frozen.

The principles of a proper salvage operation are not always easily appreciated or understood without actual experience of the problems involved. I have therefore constructed a hypothetical case of water damage to illustrate the factors involved, their best solution, and the alternatives that can present themselves.

Let us suppose that the library in question is located in a small city of 75,000-100,000 population, within a few hours' reach of a large Eastern metropolitan area. The library has the customary staff and collections, a local history collection, a file of bound newspapers for the region, some dating from the eighteenth century, microfilm, and a little-used reader. The library building is nearly one hundred years old, in good structural condition, but crowded enough to warrant using the basement for the storage of the bound newspapers, duplicates, local history, uncataloged material, and the microfilms. The basement also contains the heating unit, the electrical connections, a walk-in vault used for storing valuable items, framed pieces, and books of restricted circulation, and three Globe-Wernecke glass-fronted bookcases containing the local history collection. The time is early July.

Hypothetical Case

Now let us suppose that the librarian arrives for work on a Wednesday morning to find eighteen inches of water covering the basement floor and the lower part of the stacks. It is apparent at once that the water came from a water main break in the street outside, as city crews are at work repairing the pipes. It can be assumed first that the water is clean, that the flood is confined to the library basement, that the city is responsible for the leak and will make amends by sending the fire department to pump out the water. These are certainly plus factors in the picture, for if the flood were regional, or the water oily or contaminated, or the leak the result of staff negligence, the situation would be much more difficult to handle; for example, if mud and silt were brought in with the water, the wet books would all need to be dipped in a large tub of clean running water to remove as much dirt as possible before freezing. Although the water has shorted out the electricity and flooded the boiler, the double loss is of little consequence for a short time. The librarian has worked in the system for ten years, and has been in charge for the last five; he knows his collections and also the resources of his community.

Given all these factors, or indeed in almost any other case of water damage, the librarian's first step should be to estimate roughly the number and types of books involved, and then call for professional advice from a conservator with experience in water damage. The librarian may know of such a person in the area, or be directed to one by the State Librarian, or choose one from the list in the Library of Congress manual. If the conservator can come at once, the fortunate librarian probably will want to await his arrival before undertaking any salvage steps; if he cannot come immediately, as is very likely, the librarian's quick survey of the damage will give him a basis on which to recommend some preliminary steps for the library staff to take. If *no* conservator is available, I would advise following the directions in the Library of Congress manual and consulting with LC

Conservator sectioning a wet book in preparation for air drying.

Racks constructed for air drying of damp signatures or pamphlets, using 40-pound nylon fishline.

for further help as needed. In every instance, it is essential to think before acting, and thus avoid confusion, error, and duplication of effort.

The second step will be an inventory to learn just how many books have been wet. As the fire department has by now completed the pumping out, the staff can make a reasonably accurate count of the water-soaked material on the bottom shelves, the only ones affected; there are nearly 600 printed books, mostly late 19th and early 20th century imprints and all cataloged, 200 bound volumes of newspapers of varying periods, 300 volumes of duplicates including a set of the *Pennsylvania Archives* which the librarian had planned to sell, and reels of microfilm. The Globe-Wernecke bookcases have tipped forward, spilling their contents into the water as they fell; the damage will be considerable but cannot be estimated with real accuracy until salvage actually begins. Finally, water also flooded the vault, wetting the lower edges of all the framed items stored within, and soaking the bottoms of some cardboard cartons containing material bequeathed to the library but not as yet examined thoroughly.

Immediate Steps

The conservator who hears this report, whether on the spot or over the telephone, directs the following action: place the microfilms in a secure container of clean water at once, and send them off to Eastman-Kodak for reprocessing, for if they dry out while rolled on reels they cannot be salvaged; reduce the relative humidity in the basement, to prevent mold growth, by installing an electricity source to run a number of twenty-inch fans and dehumidifiers, or place portable

405

air conditioners at the windows. In winter, the opposite would be proper, to open the windows and doors to bring down the temperature and reduce the humidity.

For ease of description, let us suppose that the conservator is now on the scene, and a further examination of the basement is made in preparation for a conference of the salvage team. He makes sure that the water did not splash above the bottom shelf, partially wetting more books than are apparently damaged. This is fortunate, for partially wet books are more susceptible to mold growth than ones that have been completely soaked. The framed items in the vault look all right, now that the water has drained away, but examination reveals that each one has a water stain or "tide line" across it. There are some framed photographs that must be removed from their frames at once, or they will stick irretrievably to the glass once they dry. A roll of architect's drawings of the building, standing in a corner, are wet part way up, and two oil paintings are similarly wet. An attempt to bring out the cartons stored in the vault fails when they disintegrate; they are found to contain personal letters and papers of a 19th century resident of the city, plus two items of great value — a Pennsylvania-German imprint dated 1739, and an Ephrata manuscript hymnal with Fraktur decoration.

Alternatives and Cost

The librarian, the conservator, and the insurance agent now hold a conference in order to plan a proper salvage operation. The conference is also attended by the treasurer of the Board of Trustees, representing the chairman who is out of town until Monday, and by a trustee who is very interested in the newspaper collection, and anxious to see it saved. The conference makes a number of important decisions, in something like this order:

1) Begin salvage now or wait until chairman of trustees returns? The decision is to begin at once before mold can get a start and because certain actions (microfilm, rare items in vault) must be taken at once.

2) The building is in good shape but will be without power for a couple of days; considering this, and the slower summertime pace, the decision is to close the library until Monday, and turn the staff's efforts toward salvage. It is also decided to proceed without asking for volunteer help at this time. If the damage were more extensive, or the library very busy and open to readers, volunteers would be welcome even though they would need close supervision and direction.

3) The insurance agent outlines the library's coverage so that all present understand the position. The insurance covers only the building and equipment, as coverage on the collection was given up as an economy measure some years ago. This calls forth a long discussion. The treasurer is adamant that the library cannot afford the conservator's services for very long. The trustee is willing to

contribute up to $2,000 for the salvage of the newspapers, as long as it is done right. Obviously the salvage cost will have to come from operating expenses, adjusting the budget to cover this emergency outlay. It is also obvious that the conservator must be kept on as long as possible in order to qualify for the trustee's offer. The conservator is willing to stay for another day in order to get the staff started in the right direction. In our hypothetical situation, the collection is uninsured. An alternative instance would be insurance coverage geared to the ALA replacement costs; occasionally the insurance company must be convinced that it is more important or less costly to salvage the material than to declare it a total loss and replace it. If convinced, the insurer may be willing to advance a sum towards the salvage costs; the insurer may even agree to pay the cost of the conservator, in order to make certain that the salvage is carried out efficiently and skillfully, and thus as inexpensively as possible. Remember that the insurance picture would change drastically if the water damage were the result of library negligence.

4) The conservator now decides what should be done for each category of material in the flooded area. Thanks to the librarian's quick action, the microfilms are already packed in water and on their way to Eastman-Kodak. The two rare books from the vault are turned over to the conservator for professional restoration. All wet books and bound newspapers, including the local history books which need especially careful handling, are to be frozen at once to prevent mold growth and stabilize any damage already sustained. All framed items are to be unframed and laid between blotters to dry. The same treatment can be used on the letters and documents found in the vault. The oil paintings are to be taken to a dry part of the building and left until a painting conservator can be reached for advice. The architectural drawings are to be flattened between blotters unless they are too brittle to be unrolled, in which case they should be frozen.

5) The librarian has been making notes steadily, and now has a checklist of jobs which reads something like this:

—Find donor to pay for restoration of two items from vault.

—Check that microfilms have been received by Eastman-Kodak.

—Obtain (borrow if possible) fans and dehumidifiers, set in place and operate around clock; make sure that no one turns them off.

—Ask for portable generator(s) from city to supply power.

—Rent freezer truck with forced air circulation capable of maintaining constant temperature of —15° F. (This is preferable to commercial food locker, as books would need to be transported there, and truck can be parked outside library and loaded easily.)

—Ask milk company for loan of plastic milk boxes to use in loading freezer truck; they are open-sided for better ventilation, easy to carry, and do not get soggy with moisture. If they are unavailable, beer cartons are best substitute, especially if waxed.

—Cover floor at one end of truck with brown paper, to lay bound newspapers on.

—Begin inventory of damage area at once so that shelf list can be marked with what goes into the truck.

—Begin to pack wet books into boxes as soon as inventory is under way. Don't pack boxes too full. Lay sheets of freezer paper between layers so that contents do not freeze into solid mass.

—Mark outside of boxes with identification of contents, in pencil only — no ballpoint or felt tip markers.

—Begin to load truck as soon as possible, leaving aisles for air circulation and ease of access. Have truck only moderately chilly for comfort and safety, then reduce temperature to lowest point as soon as loading is complete. Make sure truck is kept in operation as long as any books are inside.

—Call nearby art museum for advice on oil paintings.

—Alert fumigator to possible need for thymol treatment if mold appears.

—Finally, order supply of white blotters for drying prints, freezer paper, soft pencils for marking.

The conference is now over. Enough decisions have been reached to allow the salvage team to operate in an efficient, effective way, and to give it a sense of its own ability in coping with the crisis. The end is not yet, however, for once the basement is back to normal the frozen books will have to be brought out of the truck, gradually, box by box; what moisture remains evaporated by forced air circulation; necessary repairs and/or rebinding done; and the materials returned to their places. This procedure will call for a large, open work space, the constant use of fans and dehumidifiers, and workers aware of the need to proceed with caution.

In June 1972, Hurricane Agnes caused much damage from Virginia to New York State, with some libraries suffering great loss. Others are still working over their frozen collections, and it will be at least another year before their salvage operations are completed. The experience has taught conservators and librarians a good deal about water damage, and opened up new areas of research. The freezing of water-damaged books as part of their salvage has been a known technique for some years, but the amount of time it takes has made it expensive. Research into a faster method, by freeze-drying the books in a vacuum chamber, is now being carried on. A full evaluation of the method and its results is yet to be made, but it is expected that the per unit cost of salvage can be reduced to a few dollars a book rather than the old estimate of perhaps $50 to $100 per book for total restoration. Hopefully, such a technological advance will be perfected before another hurricane or similar disaster.

X: NATIONAL PLANNING

Papers 33 and 34: Commentary

In the first selection in Part I of this volume, "Deterioration of Library Collections Today," Edwin E. Williams briefly outlines the evolution of a national program for the preservation of research library materials.

A landmark document in the development of national planning was the (Gordon) Williams Report, issued in 1965 by the Association of Research Libraries under the title, *The Preservation of Deteriorating Books: An Examination of the Problem with Recommendations for a Solution.* Since this report was so extensively quoted in the article that constitutes Part I, it is not included in this section where it seemingly belongs. The central proposal of the Williams Report is that a federally supported central agency should be established that will represent research libraries, with responsibility for assuring "the physical preservation for as long as possible of at least one example of every deteriorating record, and that will make copies of these records available to any library when required."

The first selection in this group of readings, *Preparation of Detailed Specifications for a National System for the Preservation of Library Materials* by Warren J. Haas, is both an extension and a modification of the earlier Williams Report. In Haas's "Detailed Specifications" the idea of setting aside the best copy of endangered titles remains, but the goal would be achieved by "the creation of a coordinated system of collections in a national plan, each with distinctive and specific research orientation or, in certain cases, format orientation." This modification is based on the view that libraries are loath to give up their treasures, and that "institutional altruism," as envisaged in the earlier ARL proposal, is "overly optimistic." Haas, who is now President of the Council on Library Resources, Incorporated, was Director of Columbia University Libraries and Chairman of ARL's Preservation Committee when his report was issued in 1972. Prepared with the assistance of a grant from the U.S. Office of Education, the document belongs to the mainstream of the literature on conservation, but it has escaped the attention of many librarians.

Little conscious effort was made to advance a national preservation program in the years immediately following publication of the Haas Report. It was not until October of 1976 that the Library of Congress announced it was convening a two-day Planning Conference for a National Preservation Program. LC's background paper, prepared by the Office of the Assistant Director for Preservation and sent

409

in advance to the twenty-six participants from outside the Library who were invited to attend, is the second and final selection.[1] At the conclusion of the Washington conference, it was announced that a National Preservation Program for Libraries is now an established fact.[2] To assure that the established fact will be translated into meaningful reality, an ad hoc Advisory Committee consisting of seven persons was established subsequent to the conference to advise on further development and implementation.[3]

Despite seeming lack of progress in establishing a national program, there have been several developments in recent years that seem to hold promise for the future. Some of these are briefly mentioned below to help round out the picture with respect to current conservation activity in the United States.

In 1970, Richard D. Smith completed work on his dissertation, "The Non-Acqueous Deacidification of Paper and Books," at the Graduate Library School of the University of Chicago. Smith's work was the first of three major contributions in applied research leading to the development of a low-cost process for treating large numbers of books at one time, neutralizing the acidity in paper, while protecting it against future degradation.[4]

In 1973, the Council on Library Resources made a two-year matching grant to the New England Interstate Library Compact to assist the six-state consortium in establishing the New England Document Conservation Center in North Andover, Massachusetts.

In the same year, the National Conservation Advisory Council was established to serve as a national forum for cooperation and planning among institutions and programs concerned with the conservation of cultural property in museums, historic properties, libraries, archives, and related collections in the United States. NCAC includes among its standing committees a Committee on Libraries and Archives. The organization's Regional Centers Study Committee issued a report[5] in 1976 dealing with the advantages offered by regional centers in providing conservation services. In addition, the report included guidelines for planning and organizing such centers.

In 1975, The Research Libraries Group, a consortium consisting of the libraries of Harvard, Yale, and Columbia Universities and the Research Libraries of the New York Public Library, was incorporated. Included among its standing committees is a Preservation Committee made up of the Preservation Coordinators of the four member libraries. The committee was given the charge of recommending procedures and methods to assure, so far as possible, the systematic preservation of their collections. RLG would seem to offer a promising framework for the establishment on a shared-cost basis of a facility for emergency treatment, consultation, and restoration, as well as the development of cooperative programs in such areas as preservation microrecording.

During the five-year period from 1972 through 1977, funding, staffing, equipping, and program development in the Preservation Office at the Library of Congress were expanded significantly, thus providing a national base for training and research as well as a major facility for the treatment of the Library's own collections.

Although conservation has yet to take its rightful place in the curricula of library schools, interest in the field is evinced by a growing number of institutions including the library schools of the University of Chicago and Columbia. At Chicago, a course on the conservation of research library materials has been taught in alternate summers since 1971, and Columbia University's School of Library Service has announced a six-week institute in the summer of 1978 for the purpose of preparing professional librarians for careers in the administration of library conservation programs.

However promising collective action and national planning may appear, they are not enough. When Edmond L. Applebaum asked, "What can the librarian do right now to help in the development of national preservation programs?" he answered his own question with advice that is as relevant today as it was more than a decade ago: "First, he can turn his attention to establishing sound policies and practices for the preservation of deteriorating materials in his library's collections."[6]

NOTES AND REFERENCES

1. The document included in this collection is a slightly modified version of the original and is reprinted in this form at the request of the author, Frazer G. Poole, Assistant Director for Preservation, Library of Congress.
2. For a summary of the conference proceedings, see "A Report on a Planning Conference for a National Preservation Program," *Library of Congress Information Bulletin* 36 (February 18, 1977): 129-31, Appendix I. An offset edition of the Conference Proceedings has been distributed on a limited basis to invited participants.
3. The names of those appointed to serve on the ad hoc Advisory Committee are given in the *Library of Congress Information Bulletin* 36 (June 10, 1977): 399.
4. Smith's process was granted a U.S. Patent in July 1972 (U.S. Pat. No. 3,676,055) and was followed by that of Kusterer at the Barrow Research Laboratory (U.S. Pat. No. 3,703,353) issued in November 1972, and Williams and Kelly at the Library of Congress (U.S. Pat. No. 3,969,549) issued in July 1976. All three processes are undergoing further testing and evaluation in the field.
5. *Report from the Regional Centers Study Committee to the National Conservation Advisory Council* (Washington, D.C.: The Council, 1976), 25 pp.
6. Applebaum, Edmond L., "Implications of *The National Register of Microform Masters* as Part of a National Preservation Program," *Library Resources and Technical Services* 9 (Fall 1965): 489-94.

ADDITIONAL READINGS

Banks, Paul N., "Cooperative Approaches to Conservation," *Library Journal* 101 (November 15, 1976): 2348-51.

Conservation of Cultural Property in the United States (Washington, D.C.: National Conservation Advisory Council, 1976), 42 pp.

Miller, Edward A., *Determination of the Administrative and Functional Character-*

istics of a National Microform Agency* (Washington, D.C., Association of Research Libraries, 1972), 29 leaves.

Shaffer, Norman J., "Library of Congress Pilot Preservation Project," *College and Research Libraries* 30 (January 1969): 5-11.

Williams, Edwin E., "Magnitude of the Paper-Deterioration Problem as Measured by a National Union Catalog Sample," *College and Research Libraries* 23 (November 1962): 499-543.

Williams, Gordon, "The Preservation of Deteriorating Books, Part I: An Examination of the Problem; Part II: Recommendations for a Solution." *Library Journal* 91 (January 1 and January 15, 1966): 51-67, 189-94.

33: PREPARATION OF DETAILED SPECIFICATIONS FOR A NATIONAL SYSTEM FOR THE PRESERVATION OF LIBRARY MATERIALS

Warren J. Haas

AUTHOR'S ABSTRACT

        This report seeks to identify specific steps that might be taken by organizations, individual libraries, and libraries acting collectively to work towards resolution of the many problems that, taken together, create the difficult and complex situation facing research libraries that has been brought on by the physical dete- rioration of books and journals. The report, which takes the rec- ommendations made in earlier studies sponsored by the Association of Research Libraries as a point of departure, seeks to clarify the nature of the preservation problem and to assess progress made in recent years. Reflecting a synthesis of viewpoints from several sources, the report makes a number of specific recommendations for action.

        In the area of research into the causes of paper deterioration and remedial techniques, a method of generating broader participation is suggested. An analytical investigation of the merits of alternate methods of text preservation is also proposed. Additional needs in the area of education and training are identified, and the importance of specific preservation activity by individual libraries is under- scored. The fundamental requirement that preservation of library materials be seen as an inseparable part of the broader objective of extending access to recorded information is affirmed. Approaches to developing a capability for collective action are advanced, and specific steps to be taken in such areas as storage standards, iden- tification and recording of preservation copies, and preservation priorities are suggested.

Reprinted from *Preparation of Detailed Specifications for a National System for the Preserva- tion of Library Materials,* Final Report Proj. No. 0–8004, Contract No. OEG-3-70-0021 (506), Washington, D.C.: U.S. Dept. Health, Educ., Welfare, Off. Educ., Bur. Libr. Educ. Tech., 1976, 31 pp.

PREFACE

The Association of Research Libraries, primarily through its Committee on Preservation of Research Library Materials, has sought to direct attention to and promote action on the complex of problems related to the deterioration of books and manuscripts in the research collections and archives of the country. The Committee has promoted specific fact-finding projects; it has sponsored studies to assess the magnitude and significance of collection deterioration; and it has sought to formulate plans for a national effort directed towards a solution.

This statement is another step in this continuing activity designed to move towards an acceptable resolution of what is, in its essence, a most complex and difficult matter. The preparation of this paper has been accomplished under a grant made to the ARL in the spring of 1970 by the Office of Education, Department of Health, Education, and Welfare. Some initial work was done by Murray L. Howder, until late 1970 a member of the ARL staff, and the project was brought to completion by the undersigned. The members of the ARL Preservation Committee, as well as a number of others, participated in discussions that helped cast the nature of the suggestions made here, and many of these same individuals commented on and contributed directly to the substance of the report.

Warren J. Haas
Chairman
ARL Committee on Preservation
 of Research Library Materials

December, 1971

TABLE OF CONTENTS

1.   INTRODUCTION

1.1 Purpose
1.2 Scope and Method

1.1   Purpose

Late in 1962, the Council on Library Resources, Inc., granted funds to the Association of Research Libraries for a study to plan a program for the dissemination and preservation of research library materials. The study was undertaken by Gordon R. Williams, with the participation of the ARL Committee on the Preservation of Research Library Materials. The final report, The Preservation of Deteriorating Books: An Examination of the Problem with Recommendations for a Solution, was completed late in 1964 and its recommendations endorsed in principle by the ARL early in 1965. The report is published in the Minutes of the Sixty-Fifth Meeting of the ARL and in Library Journal, 91 January 1 and January 15, 1966:   51-56, 189-194.

After establishing the reasons for and the dimensions of the problem of the deterioration of paper and the impact of that deterioration on collections of books and manuscripts, the Williams report concluded that "The most effective and efficient way to insure the continued availability of this information to all scholars is to establish a central agency that will insure the physical preservation of at least one example of every deteriorating book and that will make photocopies of these preserved originals readily available to all libraries."

More specifically, the report asserted

... that the most practicable solution is a federally supported central agency that will assure the physical preservation for as long as possible of at least one example of every deteriorating record, and that will make copies of these records readily available to any library when required. Such an agency would (1) undertake the centralized preservation of deteriorating records deposited by libraries; (2) coordinate its own preservation program with local programs of individual libraries to assure that all significant records are preserved while avoiding unwitting duplication; (3) assure the ready availability of microform or full-size photocopies of deteriorating materials to all libraries; and (4) itself preserve, in the interest of textual preservation, economy, and the ready availability of copies, all microform masters made at its expense or deposited by others, and coordinate the preservation of microform masters made by other agencies.

The general objectives incorporated in the report and endorsed by ARL are still valid, but the proposals for action, now six years old, have not been transformed in any important way into actual operations. Meanwhile, the "preservation problem" is still with us and is, if anything, even more evident.

The reasoning prompting this study was based on the assumption that the general plan incorporated in the 1964 report needed only the addition of operational details and funding for implementation. During the process of preparing this paper, this initial view has been substantially modified and, as a result, the nature of the report itself has been affected. The objective, however, of suggesting specific steps that seem necessary to help move the research library community towards the preservation goals it has set for itself remains unchanged.

1.2   Scope and Method

This paper was not written to evaluate the scientific and technical work that has been undertaken to explain the causes of or to prescribe the cure for paper deterioration. Rather, it was written from the viewpoint of a library administrator who is aware of the preservation problem and its implications, and who is concerned that the right kinds of action be taken to work towards a solution. There is a conviction that, while there is no final solution to the preservation problem, certain actions can be taken now and in the future to reduce the dimensions of the problem to acceptable limits. There is recognition of the complexity of the topic and its relationship to other library concerns, of the economic implications of any program of action, of the social implications of the failure to act, and of the professional obligations to assume responsibility for the preservation of what man has recorded. This is not a research report but, rather, one of synthesis designed to help us use what we have and what we know instead of equivocating because of what we do not know.

The method employed involved reading, discussion, visiting selected libraries, reflection, and finally writing followed by more discussion, more reflection and final writing. A small number of individuals, most of them long concerned with preservation efforts, were consulted at various stages of this project.

2.   THE NATURE OF THE PROBLEM

The process of growing bald and the deterioration of library
collections have much in common. It is easy to ignore the loss of one
strand of hair at a time, so long as there is overall growth. So it
is with book collections. Individual volumes, by virtue of the fragility of the paper on which they are printed and in some cases by the
manner in which they are stored, deteriorate and become useless. Their
loss is regretted, but feelings of concern are muted by the security
generated by annual collection growth figures. However, a time comes
when even long hair can't conceal a shining pate, any more than current
acquisitions can mask the physical shabbiness and the prominent gaps
caused by the disappearance of thousands of volumes made useless by
paper deterioration. And, somehow, neither wigs nor reprints are fully
adequate substitutes for the original.

Even though the process that generates the preservation problem
is subtle and undramatic, the problem itself is both real and a source
of frustration to librarians and scholars alike. The frustration stems
in large part from the fact that this is not one problem but many, each
affecting scholars and librarians in different ways and to widely varying degrees. Because the problem is one of great complexity, neither a
simple definition nor a single all-encompassing solution seems possible.

Any consideration of the nature of the problem must start with
the established fact that a substantial portion of the books now on the
shelves of research libraries, notably those published during the past
100 years, are deteriorating and becoming useless by virtue of shortcomings in the paper on which they are printed and by the conditions under
which many of them are or have been housed. It would seem on the face of
these facts that this is a technical problem most likely to be solved by
technical means, but this is only partly the case, for the problem has
financial, organizational, and important social aspects as well.

The financial character of the problem, whether the implications
of information loss or the cost of remedial action is considered, is
difficult to assess because the extent of the potential information loss
is unknown and the value of information is seldom fixed. The financial
dimension of the problem will, in the end, be established by the amount
of money spent for preservation. For now, it should suffice to say that
the amount already spent is substantial and the amount that will ultimately be spent promises to be in the millions of dollars.

The organizational complications inherent in a comprehensive
national preservation program are as certain as the financial picture is
uncertain. To begin, the concern is for millions of items, physically

dispersed among hundreds (and possibly thousands of locations. Some items are duplicated many times over while others are unique or inherently distinctive. A study by the Library of Congress indicates that a wide range of physical conditions for individual copies of the same title can be anticipated. The history of past use for any specific item is largely unknown, as is the potential extent of its future use.

Although born of technical elements, assessed in significant though uncertain financial terms, and compounded by an inherent organizational maze, the preservation problem is in the end a social problem, for at stake are segments of our most important asset--the information that has been assembled, the experiences that have been recorded, and the wisdom that has evolved throughout human history.

To date, there is no evidence that the problem of preserving the human record will somehow be solved in the natural course of events. To the contrary, it seems that a conscious effort is required, not unlike that which has been devoted to saving historic landmarks after many were lost or that now being directed to our national resources after centuries of misuse and waste. The preservation effort requires some of the same elements common to these other efforts if it is to succeed: a dedicated group of individuals convinced of the merit of their cause and willing to work hard for it; presentation of sound programs of action in a way that generates confidence and respect on the part of those whose financial support is needed; and results that are readily evident to and respected by a significant and far larger group of individuals than the initial body of prime movers.

This prescription is a difficult one to fill. The membership of the group assuming developmental responsibility must be drawn from a relatively small number of individuals: librarians responsible for the oldest and largest research libraries of the country, especially those housed in urban areas where the ravages of their environment have compounded those of time; the few specialists in preservation processes; and certain interested scholars, especially those working in historical and humanistic fields where the endangered record is of immediate as well as of philosophical concern. Any program of proposed action must be realistic in both its aspirations and its financial requirements, goals that seem almost visionary given the dimensions of the problem. The final requirement for demonstrated results, readily visible and by their nature capable of generating expanded support, is perhaps the most difficult to meet, especially since the preservation of already existing collections is basically an unattractive topic and the temptation is to find a solution that would promote invisibility rather than prominence.

There are other limiting factors as well. Action is required now, but our knowledge of the chemical reasons for the deterioration of book paper is still imperfect; the ideal storage conditions for books and archives are not known with certainty; the techniques for stopping the process of paper deterioration on an economically acceptable basis are only in the early stages of development; and the methods for restoring large collections are limited to certain kinds of repair and treatment that focus more on the page than the volume. Meaningful action under such conditions is difficult.

The shortage of funds for current library development further handicaps preservation programs. In the best of times, preservation efforts have had a low priority. In recent years, for example, many libraries have spent substantially more developing computer-based operating systems than they have spent to preserve their basic research collections. Given the present and anticipated future financial picture where the competition for funds will become, if anything, more intense, and given the pressures to expand resources and services, widespread enthusiasm for spending large sums of money preserving and restoring what is already on the shelves at the expense of collection growth and service capabilities is unlikely.

Still another handicap is the fundamental conflict between local operating realities and preservation requirements. The growth aspirations of individual libraries and the understandable and powerful drive of library users, faculty and students alike, for uncomplicated and unrestricted access to library resources is at odds with preservation-oriented programs which would sequester and isolate books and drastically curtail direct access to items in the preserved collection. There is no evidence that libraries, especially those with distinctive and uncommon collections, are to be easily moved to withdraw copies of volumes in excellent condition for inclusion in a preservation collection, nor are the scholars who depend on such collections likely to support any such move.

Finally, the number of individuals who are trained and fully competent to work in one or another aspect of a preservation program whether within a library, a restoration shop, a research laboratory or a national preservation enterprise is limited, a fact that further constrains the growth of an appropriately extensive national effort.

3.   AN OVERVIEW OF CURRENT PRESERVATION ACTIVITIES

Because the present is the backdrop for the future, this chapter describes by example the range of current activities pertinent to book and archive preservation. While there is no intention to provide an exhaustive inventory of work being done, it is probably appropriate to note that there seems to be considerably more concern and actual effort devoted to collection preservation objectives now than at any time in the past and that the rate of increase in attention to certain facets of this work seems to have accelerated rapidly in just the past two or three years.

3.1   Research

Only research that is undertaken in the interest of libraries and archives (as distinct from that keyed to paper industry objectives and concerns) is pertinent to this report. This work might be seen as being of two types: (a) that focused on causes of paper deterioration and (b) that concerned with the development of preservation methods. One is obviously linked to the other, but after a decade and more of investigation into causes there is some indication that a growing portion of total research effort is now being directed to the development of preservation techniques. The total amount of such research is modest, because while there are several major paper research organizations in the country, only a few are concerned primarily with the interests of libraries and archives. The National Bureau of Standards has done some important work in the past and is continuing work in this area under the sponsorship of the Society of American Archivists and the National Archives and Records Service. A new and what promises to be an important laboratory has been recently established at the Library of Congress.

But by far the most important research organization, in terms of contributions and continuing effort, is the W. J. Barrow Research Laboratory of Richmond, Virginia. Established by Barrow and operated by him until his death in 1967, the Laboratory has an ongoing program of research investigating the causes of paper deterioration that has done much in the last decade to sharpen the understanding of librarians and archivists alike of the nature and the significance of paper deterioration.

The staff of the Barrow Laboratory, which has been funded by the Council on Library Resources, Inc., since 1957, has studied the characteristics of book papers, developed testing methods, established specifications for permanent/durable book papers and catalog cards, has investigated the effects of temperature and humidity on paper and in recent years has moved ahead with experiments on processes to strengthen weak paper and to deacidify paper by gaseous diffusion. In the process of conducting its work, the Laboratory has spent much effort developing new equipment and improving existing equipment and testing procedures. The reports published by the Laboratory, beginning with Deterioration of Book Stock, Causes and Remedies in 1959 and continuing to the present, have had substantial influence. They have made librarians and scholars more alert to the problems generated by paper deterioration and have helped encourage in at least a small way some manufacturers of book papers and some publishers to make and use permanent and durable (p/d) paper. The research program projected by the Laboratory for the next two years gives high priority to developing new processes for the deacidification of books by gaseous diffusion, but will also include such projects as updating p/d paper specifications, further experimentation on the effect of storage temperature on paper, and determination of maximum safe pH in paper.

While most basic research has been done by research organizations, several conservators and other individuals have made notable contributions. In recent years, Richard D. Smith, working at the University of Chicago as a doctoral candidate in the Graduate Library School, has been prominent because of his extensive research directed towards development of a nonaqueous process for paper deacidification that might be applied to whole books at a low unit cost. The results of his investigations have been published and his dissertation contains a wealth of information pertinent to our topic.

3.2   Training

In general, practitioners in the field of book and manuscript conservation in this country have learned their skills as apprentices working with individuals abroad or in one or another of the few American libraries or archives having substantial conservation programs. During the last two or three years, however, the training process has accelerated. There have been several major conferences, seminars, and even formal academic courses involving a number of practitioners and students. These have served to introduce more people to the general subject of collection preservation and to teach the fundamentals of certain phases of conservation work. Examples include: (a) the 1971 University of Illinois summer session course taught by Paul Banks of the Newberry Library; (b) the Seminar in the Application of Chemical and Physical Methods to the Conservation of Library and Archival Materials held during May, 1971, and sponsored by the Boston Athenaeum under the direction of George Cunha;

and (c) the University of Chicago conference of August, 1969, "The Deterioration and Preservation of Library Materials." National and some state library associations have also sponsored a number of workshops and program meetings.

3.3   Preservation Programs

In moving from research and training to the topic of actual operating programs in libraries, the complexity of the preservation problem becomes apparent. In a sense, it is as if there were two preservation problems, one reducible to specific items or specific categories of material in individual research collections; the other a seemingly unscalable mountain of the millions of volumes in the slowly crumbling collections of older research libraries of the country. In the first case, there is some action and perhaps even progress. Logic would suggest that such progress would naturally lead to improvement in the second case as well, but the change in scale from the first situation to the second seems somehow to undermine the possibility of even a fleeting sense of accomplishment.

Briefly stated, the situation is this. Certain individual libraries are taking action to safe guard and preserve some of the distinctive items in their collections. In a few cases, planned programs to preserve text by filming have been undertaken. But there has been no real progress in developing and implementing a program of collective action to safeguard the substance of the mass of deteriorating printed books that are at the core of the preservation problem.

In certain libraries, reasonably sophisticated restoration facilities have been installed, providing the capability to deacidify documents and printed sheets, to laminate, and to restore and repair bindings. The cost of equipment and of space with the special ventilation and air conditioning required, to say nothing of the skilled operating manpower, represents a sizable investment. Such installations exist at or are available to such institutions as the Newberry Library in Chicago, the New York Public Library, the Library of Congress, the Boston Athenaeum, and a few university libraries, archives, and historical societies. But by and large, the number of institutions that have developed this type of facility is small. A number of commercial restoration firms supplement institutional capabilities. Examples include the W. J. Barrow Restoration Shop, Inc., in Richmond; the Graphic Conservation Department of R. R. Donnelley and Sons Company in Chicago and the Archival Restoration Associates, Inc., of Philadelphia.

In only a few cases have major libraries actually moved to set priorities and formalize procedures for comprehensive conservation efforts. A recent example (May 1970) of such a plan is incorporated in the Memorandum on Conservation of the Collections by James W. Henderson of the Research Libraries of the New York Public Library. Observations made here on the status of institutional efforts are confirmed by Henderson, who notes (p. 16), "In spite of almost a quarter-century in which the need for administrative attention to conservation has been recognized, few libraries in the nation today have anything resembling a total conservation program or a conservation unit of significance."

There is not even this minimal level or activity when one moves from the case of the individual library working on its most obvious and, in a sense, most easily solved problems to the broader topic of collective action by research libraries to solve the massive problem of the deterioration of hundreds of thousands of books in each of their collections, most of them printed since the mid-nineteenth century on paper that bears the seeds of its own destruction. This is the problem on which the Williams report is focused, the problem that has stimulated the ARL effort during the past decade, the problem Barrow and his successors have defined so successfully, and the problem that still remains essentially unsolved.

By and large, with the exception of certain special projects, such as newspaper microfilming programs undertaken at the Center for Research Libraries under ARL auspices and a recently expanded program at the Library of Congress to film newspapers, little has been done. Concern about this failure is the stimulus for this report.

3.4   Reproduction

The obvious answer to a substantial portion of the preservation problem is text reproduction. By microphotography and other forms of republication, a tremendous amount of material housed not only in American libraries but in libraries elsewhere in the world has been reproduced by an essentially new branch of the publishing industry that has flourished during the past twenty years. An indication of the volume of reprinting can be had by noting that an analysis of the contents of the MARC file suggests that reprints currently constitute about 10 percent of all titles processed through the MARC system by the Library of Congress. The great bulk of this republication effort and the support given it by libraries has been generated by the unheralded expansion of educational and research activity in this country and elsewhere rather than by preservation objectives.

The primary purpose of this reprint activity has been to reproduce key publications in subject fields where a demand existed and the financial resources were available to build collections. Many of the oldest and largest research libraries provided access to their collections, often at little or no cost to the publishers, and in effect contributed substantially to this process of dissemination and collection development. However, recent years have seen a re-evaluation by libraries of their relationships with commercial pub-lishers, generated in part by the need to increase library income and in part by a growing conviction that a national republication program governed primarily by sales forecasts leaves unresolved the bulk of the preservation problem--that is, the many volumes for which demand is small but which, when taken together, represent an essential and critically important part of our intellectual heritage. This reapprais-al has .seen the development of better royalty arrangements, more formal contracts between publishers and libraries, and more interest in re-printing ventures by libraries themselves, all with the objective of turning back some of the profits from high demand items to the preser-vation of items of significant intellectual value but low economic potential.

One further concern of libraries is that much master negative microfilm made from volumes in research library collections, at times even at the sacrifice of the original volume, is now in commercial film vaults. Looking into the future as more volumes deteriorate, there is some real prospect of research libraries having to buy re-productions of material that was once in their own collections. More important, there is some concern that certain hazards to these re-sources or new constraints on libraries might develop in the future if ownership of these archives changes or access to them becomes more difficult.

3.5   Prevention

Any consideration of research collection deterioration would be incomplete without acknowledging the importance of prevention as a corollary to preservation.

While paper characteristics that enhance permanence and dura-bility have been known for some time, and while paper production methods that provide these characteristics are employed in some instances, the cause of p/d paper production and use is far less advanced than those concerned with collection preservation would have it be.

Some university presses and a few other publishers have made use of paper meeting long-life specifications; however, there is some evi-dence of backsliding on the one hand and possibly too much latitude in interpretation of specifications on the other. Further, permanence of the final produce is obviously not as important to the printer as it is to the librarian. The discussions on this aspect of the subject at the 1969 conference at the University of Chicago underscore the difficulty of establishing any sense of effective concern for paper longevity among printers and publishers, and even many paper manufacturers.

If manufacturers and printers are slow to respond to opportunities to end what might be termed unplanned obsolescence, many librarians themselves have not been as aggressive as they might properly have been in directing attention to this topic. On a different aspect of the same subject, that relating to storage conditions, too many distinguished research collections have been housed too long in overheated, poorly ventilated stacks, often exposed to all of the hazards of both gaseous and particulate air pollution.

Superimposed on these fundamental elements of paper characteristics and storage conditions are other factors such as types and quality of binding and rebinding and sheer misuse of books, a factor that becomes more pertinent as the books themselves become more fragile.

4.   SUGGESTIONS FOR ACTION

We have described the preservation problem and the status of efforts to solve it. From this review, it is fair to conclude that there has been substantial progress in clarifying our understanding of the process of paper deterioration; we know a great deal about the dimensions of the damage; it is evident that a few libraries have been taking specific steps to conserve and prevent deterioration in their own collections; there has been some recent effort to develop skills required for conservation work; some proposals have been made to help resolve the preservation problem; and perhaps most important there is substantially more general awareness of the issues involved today than at any previous time.

However, the complexity of the subject and the sheer quantity of the material with which we are concerned are such that, despite real progress in specific instances, the core of the problem--the deterioration of a huge number of volumes in general and research library collections--is untouched.

In the beginning of this paper, it was noted that there seems to be no prospect for a single and absolute solution. Rather, working in the context of our understanding of the problem and the status of present programs, efforts should be directed to identifying additional action that might best help control the effects of collection deterioration and keep the threat within acceptable bounds. This section of the report identifies several kinds of action that seem to offer promise and suggests methods of proceeding.

4.1   Research

More facts are needed to answer several fundamental questions concerning both the causes of paper deterioration and the methodology of preservation and restoration of books. Important work is going on in several places pertinent to these topics, but it is suggested that even more concentrated attention is needed on certain key issues, both

to stimulate research progress and to develop a sophisticated awareness of the issues in the minds of those responsible for research
collections. To promote these ends, it is suggested that the Library
of Congress sponsor a series of annual seminars to report and review
research activity on specific topics. The agenda of topics for the
next three or four years should be developed and publicized to bring
the chosen subjects to the attention of all individuals working in the
field. Examples of such topics are:

    (a)   Inexpensive methods for deacidification of whole books
    (b)   The optimum conditions for book storage
    (c)   The manufacture and use of permanent and durable paper.

It is anticipated that the combination of appropriate sponsorship and
the designation of specific topics as being of fundamental importance
would attract individuals working on or knowledgeable about the subject.
Such sessions might stimulate research activity and would help expedite
the evaluation of findings to the advantage of both researchers and the
library community at large.

    The methodology of text preservation is a second area requiring
further careful investigation. The process of preserving the textual
content of deteriorating printed materials involves one or another of
three approaches: republication, microphotographic reproduction, or
the conversion of printed text to the form required for a computer-based
storage and retrieval system. Because of the great magnitude of the
preservation problem, because of the complexity of the inter-relation-
ships of desirable concurrent objectives beyond simple preservation
(i.e., extension of access, economy of storage, improved transmission of
information, etc.) and finally, because of obvious economic constraints,
it seems essential that a systematic consideration of the methodology of
text preservation be undertaken. Drawing on the most sophisticated
techniques of operations research, this study should seek to establish
a long-term strategy for text preservation, including the formulation
of performance specifications for any technological elements required
to meet the economic parameters and service objectives judged essential
for a viable system. The results of such an investigation would add an
important and necessary dimension to the body of facts and practices now
at hand, and would help promote the adoption of those specific procedures and methods that would be consistent with long-term requirements
even while meeting immediate objectives. Research of this sort, which
might eventually become part of a larger study of the processes of information dissemination, would have to be undertaken by an operations
research team whose members would collectively provide the several specialized skills pertinent to the topic. The ARL Preservation Committee
should take the initiative to bring this topic to the attention of the
board of directors of the ARL and explore funding sources.

4.2   Education and Training

4.2.1   It is imperative, if substantial and appropriate support is to be developed for the full range of preservation activities, that the nature of the problem be brought to the attention of more librarians and, especially, more users of libraries. To accomplish this, it is proposed that several duplicate traveling exhibits be prepared to demonstrate the process of making paper, the effects of paper deterioration on collections and individual items, the causes of paper deterioration and methods being employed to curtail effects. Three or four such exhibits, modest in size but skillfully prepared and made available to libraries of all types for short periods of time, would help expand awareness among the general public of the preservation problem. The distinctive exhibition on paper-making mounted at the Library of Congress, coupled with the fact of expanded preservation activity and research there suggest the Library as a possible sponsor of this proposed program.

4.2.2   In order to keep those individuals who are administratively responsible for the preservation of large research collections fully informed, a more systematic and thorough method of disseminating information than those employed to date seems desirable. It is suggested that, perhaps on an annual basis, a report summarizing research activities and describing practical applications of new techniques and actual operating programs be prepared and distributed. While such a report might draw heavily on the occasional preservation notes in the Information Bulletin of the Library of Congress, preparation of this report should be a project of the Preservation Committee of the Association of Research Libraries.

4.2.3   Because the process of collection preservation has so many facets, ranging from such fundamental issues as the chemistry of paper deterioration on through the methodology of book and manuscript conservation, it is possible that a fundamental training program giving an overview of the subject might be developed for clerical and technical staff in libraries whose job is concerned with physical handling, preparation, and repair and maintenance of library materials. This would enable these staff members to see their work in the context of the broader issue of safeguarding library resources. If, in fact, the preparation of such a training tool is possible, it would prove of use in most libraries, especially where professional competence in the preservation area is limited. The program package might include a film as well as printed material.

4.2.4   An apprenticeship program to train technical staff
for archive and library conservation will be necessary if the
major libraries embark on substantial programs to safeguard
their resources. In larger urban areas, such programs might
best be promoted and sponsored by existing regional library
organizations (METRO in New York City, for example), possibly
contracting with a research library or a community college to
administer the training program.

4.3   Preservation and Conservation Efforts in Individual Libraries

The dangers of information loss and erosion of collection integrity will be overcome only by the efforts of libraries and librarians
acting individually and collectively. An upsurge of activity in a growing number of general and special research libraries to preserve their
resources is a cause for some optimism. It is of utmost importance that
this concern for the protection of distinctive resources be developed
much further and translated into effective action in every library that
sees within its own collections certain materials that might be regarded
as an indispensible component of the total human record. Among the
suggestions made to stimulate action by individual librarians and libraries are the following:

4.3.1   A carefully written and well designed booklet describing
the dangers of collection deterioration and encouraging a commitment to forestall those dangers should be prepared and distributed widely. Many librarians would find such a statement,
especially if it came from the ARL Preservation Committee,
useful in communications with trustees and institutional administrative officers.

4.3.2   Every research library should establish a specific program of action for the preservation of its own resources.
However modest such a program might be, goals should be carefully articulated and priorities for action set. The library
commitment must support continuing rather than sporadic effort,
and must not be allowed to ebb and flow with the interests of
migrating administrators and fluctuating budgets. The program
statement prepared by the New York Public Library is a useful
model.

4.3.3   In every collection there are volumes that are distinctive in themselves. They are often unique for reasons other
than their printed text, which might be duplicated in many
editions and be readily located. Examples include volumes
containing marginal notations of value, volumes that by virtue
of extra illustrations or possibly even errors add meaningfully

to the history of a publication, volumes that are distinc-
tively bound, or volumes reflecting prior ownership of
significance. When possible such volumes must be preserved
in their original form, because their distinctive characteristics are intellectually important and because a filmed
version of any other copy of the same title would not reproduce the very characteristics that lend distinction.
Volumes of this sort are found in every collection; each library has an obligation to identify such items and to guarantee their safety from misuse by individuals as well as
from deterioration brought on by inadequate storage conditions.

4.4   Collective Action

Specific action within individual libraries is essential to
overall progress, but the efforts of libraries acting alone cannot
in the long run fully meet the intellectual and social threats implicit in the face of massive collection deterioration. The 1964 ARL
report was in its essence a formal recognition of the need for collective action, and that recognition, as endorsed by ARL libraries, is
the appropriate foundation for any future action.

There are two basic requirements for effective collective
action, (a) organizational structure and (b) specific programs that
will contribute to a resolution of the preservation problem. These
topics are considered separately in this section.

4.4.1   Organization for Collective Action

The appropriate organizational structure to carry out
programs pertinent to preservation is difficult to establish for two principal reasons. First, the problem of massive collection deterioration is readily apparent in relatively few of the research libraries of the country. An in-
formal survey of libraries represented at the January 1971
ARL meeting reinforced the validity of earlier assumptions
that it is the oldest and the largest research libraries,
generally in urban locations, that view the preservation
problem most seriously. But the very fact that the resources of these libraries are those most endangered is
reason enough for wide concern because these libraries
collectively serve as ultimate national resources. Further,
the fate of these collections is a predictor of what will
happen in time to others. Thus, while perhaps fewer than
twenty general research libraries are concerned that massive
action on the preservation problem be taken quickly, many
more libraries and thousands of scholars will be directly
affected by such action.

431

The second element affecting organization for collective action stems from the fact that preservation activities tend to serve and are perhaps overshadowed by other functions. Because the products of much preservation work are reprints and microfilm, the process of preservation is one of information dissemination as well. The importance of this relationship, while always acknowledged, has not necessarily been fully understood.

The 1964 ARL report viewed dissemination as a by-product of preservation, a matter that has been given serious consideration by Edwin E. Williams, associate university librarian of Harvard University, in a paper read at the Thirty-Fourth Annual Conference of the Graduate Library School of the University of Chicago in 1969 and subsequently published in the Library Quarterly for January 1970. Williams' comments are especially important because he served as secretary of the ARL Preservation Committee for almost a decade and was central to many committee decisions and actions. In part Williams says, "Would we not do better, at least whenever nonlibrarians are listening, to speak of preservation as a by-product of accessibility and continued dissemination?" (p. 15). Williams continues, "As has been suggested, the ARL proposal could, without alteration, be given a better title. However, if it were rewritten to emphasize the objectives of dissemination and accessibility, it is possible that the reworking would suggest some modifications in the machinery that is recommended." (p. 16).

The case for advancing the cause of preservation in the course of improving the distribution of information and access to it has many points in its favor. Certainly the goal of dissemination and extended access is more attractive than that of preservation to the public at large, many library users, and even potential funding sources. In the end, however, the two must be seen as inseparable parts of the fundamental library obligation to create and maintain resources for research.

These two fundamental but essentially unrelated elements, i.e., (a) the small number of libraries vitally and immediately concerned and (b) the great importance of dissemination as the obverse of preservation, suggest both an initial and an ultimate organizational structure to support programs of collective action.

Because only a few libraries are most immediately concerned, it is suggested that ten to fifteen libraries join together for a period of no more than one or two years to carry out certain specific preservation projects of the type suggested in the following section of this report. Success in such projects would pave the way for next steps; failure would perhaps call for another approach or might even indicate that the time is not yet ripe for effective collective action towards preservation goals. A "preservation consortium," operating independently or under the auspices of the ARL or the Center for Research Libraries and investing a modest amount of time and money, would be the most direct way to test the validity of the proposition that collective action is essential to further progress, not only on the core of the preservation problem but on the broader but closely related matter of dissemination as well.

There is a fundamental question posed by this suggested demonstration, one that needs resolution before research libraries, taken together, are likely to be able to make any dramatic change in their service capabilities. Simply stated, the question is whether or not these libraries can act collectively towards specified ends through some appropriate new operating structure of which they are each a part. Whether the question at hand concerns a comprehensive national program for preservation, dissemination, or one of several other possible activities of like dimension, chances for success ultimately hinge on finding a permanent way for research libraries to take effective collective action.

Demonstrated progress by a "preservation consortium" towards the formulation of common preservation procedures and uniform performance standards is required before a continuing program of action can be installed. Such procedures might be suggested here, but they would be without the validity that would come if they were developed in discussions among equal partners. Given success at this basic level of effort, the way would be paved for what seems a major and necessary future step for the research libraries of the country--the creation of a national library corporation as a base for collective action in the full range of activities in the inter-related areas of preservation and resource development. The case for creation of such an organizational innovation might be presented as follows.

There are in the final analysis three fundamental activities central to all research library operations: (a) resource development, (b) item or information identification and location, and (c) service to individual users. The processes related to each of these are numerous and clearly inter-related, but the foundations on which they are based are quite different.

In the case of information identification and location, there is a clearly understood requirement for a comprehensive bibliographic record for recorded information in all forms.

To most people concerned with the problem it seems essential that the three national libraries acting in concert, but with the Library of Congress central, must assume responsibility for this activity, obviously with input from many sources.

Concerning service to individuals, the standards, operating style and quality of service for students and scholars must in the end be set by each library for its clientele. To be sure, many factors outside as well as within specific libraries affect performance, but in the end the responsible agency for service delivery is clearly the individual library itself.

As for the remaining activity, resource development (and its corollary, preservation), the appropriate underlying mechanism is less evident even though it seems that the rational development of research resources on a truly comprehensive scale and on a nationally and even internationally acceptable pattern that promotes access and equitable distribution on all counts (geographical, economic, etc.) is a responsibility that must be assumed and shared by all research libraries. The national libraries cannot by themselves be expected to take on this obligation. Rather, they should simply share in it, along with all other research libraries.

In the final analysis, however, the research libraries of the country lack a capacity for collective action that is suitable to the dimension of the job to be done. It is to fill this need that a national library corporation is proposed. Such an organization would both serve and be the responsibility of research libraries acting collectively and ideally would become an integral part of each individual research library. A single organization of the kind advocated here, rather than a multiplicity of agencies developed to solve individually what are really inter-related problems, would avoid duplicate organizing effort, unnecessary competition for the best administrative talent, and an excessive administrative cost to program cost ratio. Such a corporation would provide a useful backdrop against which regional and other cooperative ventures might be rationally and purposefully developed. Most important, a single, national, operating agency, focused exclusively on developing and maintaining the nation's research resource capabilities in a way that would expand their totality, preserve their integrity, and promote accessibility, would serve as a cohesive force for libraries whose stock in trade--recorded knowledge--is an indivisible asset of all of society.

Permanence, financial and operating stability, responsiveness to the needs of research libraries, and a capacity for formulating and undertaking major ventures effectively are only

a few of the many obvious qualities that the corporation
must have if it is to become an inseparable element of each
library, and this must be the case because significant
advances will not come in this area of collective action if
the "collective" element is viewed simply as an appendage
to existing individual operations.

The "preservation consortium" is seen as a logical
first step towards creation of the national corporation.
Additional "collectives" organized around other goals in the
same broad area of resource development and preservation
might also move towards the corporation concept, but in the
final analysis, only a structure as powerful as that envisaged can have the performance capacity and the durability
that seems to be required by the magnitude and the importance
of the job to be done.

4.4.2   Collective Action Programs

The preparation of this paper was undertaken initially
to identify and detail the steps required to implement the plan
advanced in general terms in the 1964 ARL report, i.e., to establish a responsible preservation agency and a national preservation collection. It has been suggested that formation of
a consortium of those libraries most immediately concerned with
preservation problems might be an appropriate preliminary step
towards creation of the larger national agency. In the para-
graphs that follow, it is suggested that these libraries work
together to establish specifications for several specific kinds
of action to be taken by each individual consortium member.
Participation in the process of establishing specifications for
individual action is seen as a useful and perhaps necessary
first step in the direction of the major collective action programs that seem essential if national preservation and dissemination goals are to be met.

Among the activities important to future progress are the
creation of prototype preservation collections at the local level,
the formulation of preservation priorities, and the preparation
of plans to establish, maintain, and finance a national collection
of negative microfilm.

4.4.2.1   For a number of reasons, it seems unrealistic
to assume that a new and separate national collection
devoted exclusively to preservation purposes will be
established in the near future. Many of the books for

such a collection would have to come from existing
libraries. This assumes an institutional altruism
that seems overly optimistic. Even given unexpected
generosity, the cost of such a new venture appears
beyond the means that are presently available. Further,
it has been noted that national efforts at preservation
seem, on reflection, to stand the best chance of success
when they also serve the equally important objective of
dissemination.

But given the difficulty of attaining this theoretical goal of a national preservation collection, the
principle of setting aside the best copies of "endangered
titles" under conditions that will slow the rate of deterioration and expedite access by reproduction or text
transmission is still eminently sensible. The only real
alternative to a central collection seems to be the
creation of a coordinated system of collections in a
national plan, each with a distinctive and specific research orientation or, in certain cases, a format orientation. Such collections would meet preservation purposes, but they would also serve the broader function of
a national research resource as well. As a way to test
the validity of the concept of a system of national collections, it is suggested that the consortium libraries
most immediately concerned with preservation constitute
themselves a test group to take certain preliminary
planning steps. Experience gained from this process
would be the best possible base for a further commitment
at the actual program operating level. Among these initial steps are formulation of standards governing storage, use, bibliographic control, and item identification.

Local preservation collections, whether established
as components of a decentralized national system or seen
as prototypes for an eventual national collection, must
necessarily be operated in line with commonly accepted
standards governing storage conditions and use. The
consortium, possibly with help from the Educational
Facilities Laboratory, should make it an early order of
business to formulate the required physical specifications.

While not all facts pertinent to book storage are
known, there is nonetheless a substantial body of knowledge concerning storage conditions on which realistic
specifications can be based, subject to refinement as
additional parts become known. Review of a number of
publications identified in the bibliographic notes at the

end of this report suggests that a brief publication
is needed to organize, assess, and synthesize the
information basic to preservation storage for the use
of librarians and architects. Additional information
in the building programs and architectural specifications prepared for several general research and rare
book libraries constructed in recent years might also
be drawn upon for the proposed statement.

Obviously, major structural changes cannot be
made in existing buildings to meet ideal, preservation
oriented specifications, but it is equally certain
that realistic standards established with preservation
goals in mind would be useful in planning new construction and modifying existing buildings. In the end, it
would seem that the parent institutions of libraries
professing to assume national responsibility for safeguarding significant research collections, whether
broad or narrow in scope, cannot properly avoid meeting
the obligation to house those collections in a way that
promotes rather than thwarts preservation objectives.

The specifications should include consideration
of structural topics such as load capacities, materials
used, and design characteristics important to preservation goals. Building systems for fire detection, fire
extinguishing, user control, emergency exit control, and
all environmental elements (heating and cooling, humidity control, air cleaning, lighting, etc.) also need to
be described in the light of preservation and protection
objectives.

Libraries participating in any national preservation program would be expected to meet specified minimum standards for physical storage. By the same token,
mutually established and accepted rules would govern the
use of items formally included in any preservation collection. At the minimum, it seems certain that books
would be noncirculating and would be used only under
controlled conditions. They would not be available on
interlibrary loan.

Given standards for storage and controls governing use, a method of item identification and a plan for
bibliographic control are also required elements for a
system of prototype preservation collections. While it
is important that the consortium members themselves work
out the details of these systems, preliminary investigation

suggests that reasonably efficient methods can be established by capitalizing on existing bibliographic tools and book identification systems. For example, a simple listing of the numbers already used (or assigned for eventual use) for each item in the published edition of the National Union Catalog could be annotated with the symbol of the library holding the "national copy." Continuation of the present NUC numbering system in the planned NUC supplement for pre-1956 titles not included in the basic catalog would open the way to locating national copies of these titles as well. It also seems possible to create a numbering system, using the Standard Book Number format, for purposes of supplying a number for any title not listed in the NUC. This approval should be considered especially if the SBN and its counterpart for serials (Standard Serial Number) become the standard for item identification in a national or international bibliographic system.

A second control element is a system for identification and reporting of national copies. An example of an approach that might be taken would involve use of a book label carrying specific wording such as "National Resource Copy" and the appropriate identification number. Periodic reporting to a central point of the identification numbers of items so designated would be required of participating libraries. The presence of the label in a book would commit the owning library to store the item under conditions agreed upon and to control use in accordance with the established plan. In a real sense, items so designated would become by definition a national asset as well as an institutional resource.

4.4.2.2 The 1964 report argued that on a cost basis alone selective preservation, as distinct from automatic inclusion of all materials found in any research library collection, could not be justified. Rising labor costs during the intervening years almost certainly reinforce that conclusion, but given the fact of minimal funding at best, it would seem important to consider the merits of purposeful inclusion over random selection, simply because the real objective is to preserve and extend access to the best and most useful material, not simply to the most material. Only if we assume that the great bulk of all published material will be protected within a reasonably short time is the random (or nonselective) approach valid. There seems little justification for this conclusion.

Individual libraries have been urged to identify and protect the "distinctive" volumes in their collections. It remains to consider categories and priorities for inclusion in any integrated system built around the mutual efforts of cooperating libraries. Those libraries themselves must ultimately set realistic goals, but several approaches seem open to consideration. First, there is considerable interest on a national scale in a journal lending library. Preservation as well as dissemination objectives should be given considerable importance in planning for such a unit. The assurance that volumes in such a collection (or collections) are in fact to be permanently retained and stored under appropriate conditions would reduce constraints on individual libraries, and open them to more reasonable approaches to resource retention. In another category, that of government documents, the depository system as it now operates provides an example of another approach whereby extension of presently stated responsibilities to include the elements central to preservation would help reduce the dimension of the total problem.

Even given the many opportunities to introduce preservation goals into such existing and projected projects, the dimension of the remaining task is still almost unsurmountable. Only by adding preservation goals to the prospect of national resource collections of the kind currently being considered in professional discussions does it seem possible to reduce a massive problem to manageable proportions. By not aspiring to preserve everything, and concentrating instead on discrete subject areas, some real progress becomes possible. For example, by identifying and establishing as preservation volumes acceptable copies of American imprints, 1870-1900, included in a collection designated a national resource collection for 19th century American literature, a first step would be taken towards a viable preservation program in a broad subject field. The designation of two or three libraries as resource collections for the same subject would extend coverage and would promote coordination of preservation efforts among those libraries having the largest and, in the sense of national interest, the most important collections.

In all probability, the consortium libraries should consider excluding certain categories of materials (e.g., textbooks, language grammars) from first priority efforts and should focus initially on certain subject areas (i.e., humanistic studies, all primary national sources, literary works, etc.). The extent of potential markets for films or reprints of items in proposed categories should weigh heavily in initial preservation program designations, both for the potential income and the high level of program visibility.

4.4.2.3   The objective of extending access to materials selected for preservation purposes and included in national resource collections calls for more sophistication in text copying and/or text transmission systems than most research libraries have been able to display. This general area of activity is one in which there is promise of considerable technological development. For example, computer-stored text might at some future time provide an economically sound alternative to microfilm and even certain printed material for at least some purposes. Further, there is already evidence that the forms in which information is recorded (microfilm, for example) must in the future meet the requirements of transmission equipment as well as of reading and copying machines. But regardless of the form technical advances take, it is essential that the research library community retain ownership and control of master copies made for the purpose of extending access to or preserving the content of physically deteriorating publications in research library collections.

It is suggested that the consortium libraries consider the concept of a planned program of microfilming, including collective ownership of master negatives produced as part of any text preservation project. This approach would standardize charges for film, would open the way for commercial publishers to obtain access on a royalty basis to consortium film, would expedite reporting of master negatives, would open the way to improved quality control, and would permit the consortium to contract with universities or with commercial firms for film production.

By way of example, a revolving fund might be used to pay for consortium negatives, with charges for positives set at total direct cost plus a uniform service fee of $3.00. A service fee, set at the $3.00 level, would in effect mean that the sale of two to three positives of any title would cover the cost of the original negative. Royalty income from commercial users

of negatives would likewise support additional negative
production. On the basis of cost studies made for this
report, creation of a $250,000 revolving fund would sup-
port master negative production at the rate of 2,000,000
pages anually for a minimum of three years. An experiment of at least this duration seems required to fully
develop the procedures and to test the market for positive copies in a reasonably wide range of subject fields.
A successful demonstration at this level might promote
the pooling of existing master negatives on some kind of
credit basis.

A second area of activity that might be considered by the consortium members is the involvement of one
or several university presses in a reprinting program
keyed to preservation objectives. Perhaps working on a
cost-plus basis, the production and manufacturing expertise of university presses might be put to use as part
of a total system of text preservation and distribution
designed for maximum results at minimum costs.

5.   FINANCES

Only after the merits of specific programs proposed are judged and decisions are actually made about how to proceed will realistic discussions about financing be possible. As we have seen, the preservation problem is complex, and it is probable that many kinds of action by individuals, organizations, libraries, and groups of libraries will be required.

Funding methods and funding sources are certain to be at least as difficult and as numerous as are the proposed programs for action. On the one hand, the case can be made that each individual library has a real obligation to use a portion of its operating resources for preservation, simply because this function is a kind of inseparable corollary to collection development. This point of view cannot be faulted, but one of the messages implied in what has gone before is that the investment of individual libraries in preservation related activities will produce more in the way of actual results through coordination and complementary efforts of many libraries than will independent action.

Certain other areas of activity seem completely appropriate for consideration of foundation support. Much of the present research effort is funded in this way, and extension of effort in this area would seem possible. Further, foundation support would seem worth exploration for development of the preservation consortium, especially if that organization could be viewed as a prototype for some form of permanent national corporation.

In the end, however, substantial additional funding will be required to preserve recorded information, to further develop national information resources, and to provide reasonable access to information for all who need it. We have argued that, in the end, these are inseparable goals. We would assert with equal force that these are goals of highest importance in terms of both social needs and national interest. Federal financial support of great magnitude is essential if the individual research libraries of the country are to become in fact as well as in theory a true national asset. It seems certain that the impact of federal funds would be amplified many times over if those funds are used to further develop already distinctive research resources, to promote a rational program of resource preservation, and to open the way to their most effective use.

BIBLIOGRAPHIC NOTES

I

The list of publications on one or another aspect of the preservation problem grows in length each year. Many of the most important items are identified in the extensive bibliographies or lists of references included with the following:

Smith, Richard D. "New Approaches to Preservation."
The Library Quarterly 40 (January 1970): 139-171.

Smith, Richard D. The Nonaqueous Deacidification of
Paper and Books. A dissertation submitted to the
Faculty of the Graduate Library School, University of
Chicago, Chicago, 1970.

Smith, Richard D. "Paper Impermanence as a Consequence
of pH and Storage Conditions." The Library Quarterly
39 (April 1969): 153-195.

Wessel, Carl J. "Environmental Factors Affecting the
Permanence of Library Materials." The Library Quarterly
40 (January 1970): 39-84.

Williams, Edwin E. "Deterioration of Library Collections
Today." The Library Quarterly 40 (January 1970): 3-17.

34: TOWARD A NATIONAL PRESERVATION PROGRAM: A Working Paper

Frazer G. Poole

I. INTRODUCTION

For practical purposes, major preservation problems in libraries may be generally classified as follows:

> ...the preservation of library materials published since about 1800, large numbers of which, especially printed books, are now reaching advanced stages of embrittlement and deterioration;
> ...the preservation of materials ranging from the earliest printed books and manuscripts in library collections to approximately the beginning of the nineteenth century;
> ...the preservation of library materials of the future.

Within each of the above categories there are numerous formats on paper, as well as an increasingly large number of items published in other forms and on other materials: microfilm, motion picture film, slides, videotapes, audio-tapes, phonograph discs, and others. Although a comprehensive National Preservation Program cannot ignore the newer forms in which knowledge is produced and disseminated, the present proposal is focused almost entirely on paper.

II. THE PROBLEMS

We can elaborate on the above as follows:

A. *Library materials published since about 1800* present the biggest preservation problem with which American libraries must contend. These materials, for the most part, are not rare enough or intrinsically valuable enough to justify restoration in their original form, but are of sufficient value to justify preservation of their intellectual content. In the Library of Congress alone, it is conservatively estimated that some six million volumes are so brittle they cannot be given to a user without significant risk of damage. In the New York Public Library, it is estimated that more than half of the collection has reached an advanced stage of embrittlement. While similar figures for other American libraries are not available, it appears certain that the numbers of deteriorating materials in research library collections are sufficiently high to pose major problems for the institutions concerned.

At the present time, there is no fully tested, feasible method for mass conservation treatment (deacidification and alkaline buffering) of such materials. Even if such a process did exist it would benefit no more than 65 percent of the brittle books in library collections, since deacidification does not restore strength to paper already embrittled. For all such brittle volumes there appear

Reprinted from *Toward a National Preservation Program: A Working Paper,* Washington, D.C.: Library of Congress, Off. Assist. Dir. Preserv., 1976, 11pp.

to be only two feasible preservation procedures: 1) low temperature storage, and 2) microfilming to preserve the intellectual content.

   B. *Materials in library collections printed before about 1800* are, for the most part, in better condition than the more recent materials described above, although there are many exceptions, especially among materials published toward the end of this period. In most cases, the paper in books dating from the 14th, 15th, 16th centuries is in good to excellent condition. In these instances, the problems are generally the result of wear and tear through the years, combined with vandalism, accidental damage, and insect or mold damage.
   The major approach to the conservation of these older materials must be that of providing suitable preservation, repair, or restoration treatment in all instances where the value of the item justifies the cost. Because every such artifact or document presents a wide range of different problems dependent upon many factors, including the age and value of the book, the type of binding, the condition and type of paper, the nature of the ink, and the vicissitudes to which the volume or other item has been subjected during its lifetime, only a trained conservator is capable of dealing with them.

   C. *Materials published today,* as well as those to be published in the foreseeable future, are being produced on paper which is no better than the book paper of the past century. In many cases, such paper is worse than that with which librarians contend today. Unless effective action is taken soon the preservation problems of the next hundred years will be more serious than those of the present century.

III. *A SUGGESTED NATIONAL PRESERVATION PROGRAM*

A. *Preserving the intellectual content of materials published since about 1800*

   Of the millions of embrittled and deteriorating volumes on the shelves of the nation's libraries, only a relatively small number have such intrinsic value as to justify the cost of repair or restoration. The intellectual content of the majority of such volumes is important, however.
   As indicated above, two methods are available for preserving the intellectual content of these books.
   1. ...storage at low temperature in warehouse-type structures or in underground caves where optimum temperature and humidity can be maintained. Without question, such storage offers the most economical and feasible method of preserving these materials for indefinite periods of time. It should be remembered, in this connection, that paper scientists generally agree that for every 10 degrees C. the storage temperature can be reduced, the life of the paper can be approximately doubled.
   2. ...microfilming to preserve the intellectual content at a significantly lower cost than the cost of restoration in the original format. At the Library of Congress, for example, it costs approximately 25 dollars to microfilm the average three-hundred page volume. To properly treat the same volume and restore it in its original format costs ten to fifteen times as much.
   At the same time, microfilming is more expensive than low

temperature storage. There is, moreover, the question of the life expectancy of microfilm. A properly processed silver-halide negative microfilm appears to have excellent prospects for archival permanence, but the fact remains that our experience with microfilm is limited to some fifty years or less, while our experience with paper goes back nearly 2,000 years.

Ideally, then, the solution to the problem of preserving brittle and deteriorating books would be to provide low temperature storage for all such materials. From the practical point of view, however, and in terms of preserving library collections nationwide, the assemblage of the brittle materials now stored in the nation's research libraries in one location (or in a limited number of locations) poses a major problem. In fact, the original proposal for a national program to preserve brittle and deteriorating books proved untenable, in part, because few libraries were willing to surrender enough of their materials to a national collection to make the concept feasible.

For this reason, the Library of Congress believes that a National Preservation Program, initially at least, should emphasize microfilming of the brittle materials published during the last century, with storage of the master microfilm negatives under ideal environmental conditions. However, L.C. also proposes that low temperature storage facilities be provided for books. In time, it is likely that a significant number of deteriorated materials would be assigned to a National Preservation Collection by the libraries holding them.

Although it is perhaps premature to discuss the location of a National Preservation Collection, it can be noted that physical security in the event of war should be given full consideration in the selection of a suitable site. Thus a surface structure near a major metropolitan area would have much less to recommend it than would an underground facility where stored materials could have both ideal environmental conditions and unexcelled physical security.

A national preservation project designed to preserve, by microfilming, the intellectual content of those deteriorating materials which do not warrant more expensive treatment should include the following elements:

1. ...the conduct of surveys of the major research libraries of the United States to determine those classes of materials most in need of preservation and the development of priorities for microfilming such materials.

2. ...the development of standards (both bibliographic and technical) for microfilming those materials to be included in a national preservation program.

3. ...the establishment of a national preservation microfilming center dedicated solely to microfilming deteriorating materials, equipped with special cameras designed for filming rare materials, and staffed with personnel trained in the techniques of handling fragile materials. In addition, this center should contain specially designed vaults for the archival storage of the master negatives of national preservation microfilms (or other microforms).

4. ...the establishment of effective, automated

bibliographic control procedures for microfilmed
materials through a national network.
5. ...the establishment of a procedure under which
participating research libraries would contribute
master microfilm negatives (i.e., those which meet
national microfilming standards) to the center.

B. *Preserving those materials in library collections which
justify preservation, repair, or restoration in the original
format*

1. *Training program for conservators*

Without question, the single most pressing and unsolved
problem in the conservation of library and archival materials is the
almost total lack of personnel capable of providing the expertise
needed for the conservation treatment of the hundreds of thousands
of items which justify preservation in their original form. If a
national preservation program did nothing other than to establish a
sound training program for conservators of library materials, it
would repay all the time, money, and effort expended.

The training program proposed here would utilize the academic program and degree granting facilities of a local university.
Students in the conservation program would receive special courses
in conservation chemistry, the history and technology of paper, book
structure, causes of deterioration, environmental aspects of deterioration, administration of conservation programs, and at-the-bench
training in the L.C. laboratory and workshops. Graduates holding
bachelor's degrees with majors in the conservation of library and
archival materials could enter the field or could go on to take a
master's degree in conservation.

2. *Regional centers for the conservation of library and archival
materials*

Each year the Preservation Office receives hundreds of
letters and phone calls asking for advice and assistance on conservation problems. Inevitably, the next question is, "where can I
have this work done." Unfortunately, there are a limited number of
private conservators capable of handling the wide ranging preservation problems typical of most large library collections. One of the
most effective and productive national conservation programs the
Library of Congress could undertake would be the establishment of
one or more regional conservation centers. In fact several university libraries have already requested that L.C. establish such
centers at their institutions.

Such a center (or centers) established on a regional basis
on university campuses, staffed by graduates of a cooperative training program in conservation, and supervised by the Library of
Congress, could probably become self-supporting in from two to four
years. The returns, in terms of improving library conservation
practices and conserving the nation's deteriorating collections,
would be enormous.

3. *National workshops in conservation*

It will require several years to establish a sound conservation training program and for the graduates of this program to

gain the experience needed for them to staff the proposed regional
centers. In the interim, the Library proposes a series of conservation workshops designed to educate librarians in the fundamental
principles of conservation. Such workshops should be conducted on a
regional basis.

4. *Training aids*

Despite a lack of professional training, librarians increasingly find themselves assigned duties related to conservation. In
such cases a series of carefully planned training films or videotapes, designed to present certain fundamental preservation concepts
and techniques, would prove invaluable. Such films would have equal
or greater value for workshops and seminars conducted by the Preservation Office.

5. *Emergency salvage teams*

Increasingly, the conservation staff of the Library of
Congress is called upon to provide its acknowledged expertise in the
salvage of materials damaged by fire and water. Within hours after
the Federal Records Center in St. Louis experienced a disastrous
fire in 1974, L.C. had been requested to provide the assistance of
its conservation staff. More recently at the request of the Geolog-
ical Survey, a member of the staff of the Preservation Research
Office went to Denver to assist in the salvage of the Survey's
library and aerial photograph collections which were badly damaged
in a weekend fire in the Federal Center. The Preservation Office
advises, usually by telephone, on several such catastrophes every
month. It would be a significant service to government agencies,
libraries, and archives if the Library could provide a specially
trained team of two or three persons who could be available to assist
in such emergencies anywhere in the United States.

C. *Preserving library materials of the future*

1. *A national preservation copy*

The preservation of future publications is as essential
for scholarship as is the preservation of retrospective materials.
One possible solution to this problem might be to amend the Copyright
Law to provide for the submission of three copies, the third copy to
become part of the national preservation collection. If this does
not prove feasible other solutions would need to be explored. In
any case, a new copy should be obtained for storage under the environmental conditions necessary to ensure the archival preservation
of these materials. Adequate bibliographic controls and facilities
for microfilming or otherwise reproducing these materials, when
copies held by libraries have become too deteriorated for use, would
also be required.

2. *Improvement of book paper*

Earlier in this paper it was proposed that one copy of all
copyrighted materials published in the future be stored under ideal
environmental conditions, thus creating a national preservation
collection of materials in original format. As a corollary to such
a project, a national program should make every effort to persuade
papermakers to produce better, stronger, long-lived paper.

D. *Funding*

A program of the magnitude proposed here could, in five to ten years time, make a significant and measurable impact on the preservation problems of American libraries, but it would require substantial funding and wide ranging authority to attack the problem simultaneously on several fronts. If, as has been suggested, there are foundations willing to fund a sound program to preserve national heritage in the nation's libraries, there is no better time to initiate such a program than the present.

INDEX

acquisition of replacements, 389–
    390, 393, 396–397
alternatives and costs, 406–408
cataloging aspects, 389, 399
discard decisions, 394, 396
emergency salvage teams, 448
estimating damage, 401, 405
general principles, 400–408
insurance aspects, 390, 394, 396,
    399, 400, 406, 407
prompt action essential, 386, 402–
    403

Water levels, in materials, 111–112
Waters, Peter, *Emergency Procedures
    for Salvaging Flood or Water-
    Damaged Materials,* 402
Williams Report, 102, 409
    excerpts from, and commentary, 12–
    15, 416–417
Wood fiber, in papermaking, 25, 198,
    234
Works of art. *See* Art objects